Reproduction
and the
Common Good:
Global Perspectives
from the
Catholic Tradition

Edited *by*

Simeiqi He
and
Emily Reimer-Barry

☙PICKWICK *Publications* · Eugene, Oregon

REPRODUCTION AND THE COMMON GOOD
Global Perspectives from the Catholic Tradition

Global Theological Ethics

Copyright © 2025. All rights reserved. Except for brief quotations in critical publications or reviews, no part of this book may be reproduced in any manner without prior written permission from the publisher. Write: Permissions, Wipf and Stock Publishers, 199 W. 8th Ave., Suite 3, Eugene, OR 97401.

Pickwick Publications
An Imprint of Wipf and Stock Publishers
199 W. 8th Ave., Suite 3
Eugene, OR 97401
www.wipfandstock.com

PAPERBACK ISBN: 979-8-3852-1426-6
HARDCOVER ISBN: 979-8-3852-1427-3
EBOOK ISBN: 979-8-3852-1428-0

Cataloguing-in-Publication data:
Names: He, Simeiqi, editor. | Reimer-Barry, Emily, editor.
Title: Reproduction and the common good : global perspectives from the catholic tradition /edited by Simeiqi He and Emily Reimer-Berry.
Description: Eugene, OR : Pickwick Publications, 2024 | Global Theological Ethics.
Identifiers: ISBN 979-8-3852-1426-6 (paperback) | ISBN 979-8-3852-1427-3 (hardcover) | ISBN 979-8-3852-1428-0 (ebook)
Subjects: LCSH: Catholic Church. | Catholic Church. Congregatio pro Doctrina Fidei. Donum vitae. | Catholic Church—Doctrines. | Human reproductive technology—Religious aspects—Catholic Church.
Classification: QP251 .R47 2024 (print) | QP251 .R47 (ebook)

Cover image: Tamara Adams, "Spirit of Midwifery," used with permission.

Dedication

To our teachers and mentors, who created brave spaces in the guild of Catholic theological ethics, with our deep gratitude.

Global Theological Ethics—Book Series

Series Editors
Jason King, St. Mary's University (TX)
M. Therese Lysaught, Loyola University Chicago

The Global Theological Ethics book series focuses on works that feature authors from around the world, draw on resources from the traditions of Catholic theological ethics, and attend to concrete issues facing the world today. It advances the *Journal of Moral Theology*'s mission of fostering scholarship deeply rooted in traditions of inquiry about the moral life, engaged with contemporary issues, and exploring the interface of Catholic moral theology philosophy, economics, political philosophy, psychology, and more.

This series is sponsored in conjunction with the Catholic Theological Ethics in the World Church. CTEWC recognizes the need to dialogue from and beyond local cultures and to interconnect within a world church. Its global network of scholars, practitioners, and activists fosters cross-cultural, interdisciplinary conversations—via conferences, symposia, and colloquia, both in-person and virtually—about critical issues in theological ethics, shaped by shared visions of hope.

Online versions of the volumes in the *Global Theological Ethics* series are available for free download as chapters at jmt.scholasticahq.com. Paper copies may be purchased from Wipf & Stock. This dual approach reflects the *Journal of Moral Theology*'s commitment to the common good as it seeks to make the scholarship of Catholic theological ethicists broadly available, especially across borders. Additionally, you can find the series listed on the CTEWC website at catholicethics.com/book-series/catholic-theological-ethics-series/.

Series Titles

Ethical Challenges in Global Public Health: Climate Change, Pollution, and the Health of the Poor, edited by Philip J. Landrigan and Andrea Vicini, SJ (2021)

The Rising Global Cancer Pandemic: Health, Ethics, and Social Justice, edited by Andrea Vicini, SJ, Philip J. Landrigan, and Kurt Straif (2022)

Doing Theology and Theological Ethics in the Face of the Abuse Crisis, edited by Daniel J. Fleming, James F. Keenan, SJ, and Hans Zollner, SJ (2023)

A Prophet to the Peoples: Paul Farmer's Witness and Theological Ethics, edited by Jennie Weiss Block, M. Therese Lysaught, and Alexandre A. Martins (2023)

Hacer teología y ética teológica frente a la crisis de los abusos. Editado por Daniel J. Fleming, James F. Keenan, SJ, y Hans Zollner, SJ. Traducción de Lourdes Calduch Benages (2024)

Reproduction and the Common Good: Global Perspectives from the Catholic Tradition, edited by Simeiqi He and Emily Reimer-Barry (2024)

Table of Contents

Acknowledgements vii

Part 1: Theoretical and Theological Reflections on Reproduction and Social Justice

1. Introduction
Emily Reimer-Barry and Simeiqi He 2

2. Structural Inequality and the Social Determinants of Unintended Pregnancy
Julie Clague 21

3. Never Just a Choice: Three Theoretical Approaches to Economic Constraints on Family Formation
Kate Ward 55

4. Reproductive Injustice as Social Sin: Mapping Sin Discourse into Debates about Fertility Decisions
Kathryn Lilla Cox 90

5. Fatherhood, Reproductive Justice, and Strategic Invisibility of Men
Hoon Choi 122

6. Thinking about Reproductive Justice in Contexts of Violence
Suzanne Mulligan 148

7. Reconceptualizing Human Reproduction beyond John Paul II
Simeiqi He 175

Part 2: Theo-Ethical Roundtable Discussions

8. On Threats to Women's Flourishing
Stephanie Ann Puen, Karen Peterson-Iyer, Mary M. Doyle Roche, Emily Reimer-Barry, and Mary Lilian Akhere Ehidiamhen 207

9. On the Role of the Catholic Church
Simeiqi He, Eric Marcelo O. Genilo, SJ, Kathryn Lilla Cox, Virginia Saldanha, and Julie Clague 225

Part 3: Seeking Reproductive Justice in a Broken World

10. Considerations for a Comprehensive Sex Education Grounded in Catholic Social Thought for Reproductive Justice in the Philippines
Stephanie Ann Puen 237

11. Reproductive Justice and Agricultural Labor Migrants
Karen Peterson-Iyer 257

12. Rachel is Weeping for Her Children: Theological Reflections on Intersectional Reproductive Justice and Maternal Health
Mary M. Doyle Roche 290

13. Reclaiming Women's Agency for Reproductive Justice in Nigeria Today: Flourishing for Mother and Child in Situations of Constraints
Mary Lilian Akhere Ehidiamhen 310

14. Risking Women's Lives, Denying Women's Experiences: CDF Statements on Sterilization in Catholic Hospitals
Eric Marcelo O. Genilo, SJ 334

15. Catholic Health Care and Reproductive Justice: Whose Conscience Has Priority When Conscience Claims Collide?
Emily Reimer-Barry 358

16. Religio-Cultural Underpinnings of Gender and Reproductive Injustice and Their Impact on Women's Agency in India
Virginia Saldanha 391

Epilogue
Emily Reimer-Barry 411

Acknowledgments

This collection results from years of conversations among the contributors. We thank all members, past and present, of the virtual table on reproductive justice and the common good. Our virtual table was supported by Catholic Theological Ethics in the World Church. We are grateful for the visionary leadership of James F. Keenan, SJ (USA), Soosai Arokiasamy (India), Bénézet Bujo (Congo), Margaret A. Farley (USA), Linda Hogan (Ireland), José Roque Junges (Brazil), José Rojas (Philippines), and Paul Schotsman (Belgium), who formed the international planning committee for the first Catholic Theological Ethics in the World Church conference, held in Padua, Italy, in 2006. The current planning committee members supported our conversations and deserve much praise for the work they do to build bridges among scholars of theological ethics around the world. Special thanks to Kristin Heyer (USA), Shaji George Kochuthara (India), Andrea Vicini, SJ (Italy/USA), James F. Keenan, SJ (USA), Pablo A. Blanco Gonzalez (Argentina), Teresa Kiragu (Kenya), Stanislaus Alla (India), Suzanne Mulligan (Ireland), and Antonio Autiero (Italy). We are deeply appreciative for the encouragement, patience, and attention to detail of Jason King, Editor Emeritus of *Journal of Moral Theology*, and of the wisdom and strategic planning skills of M. Therese Lysaught, Editor of *Journal of Moral Theology*.

Simeiqi He and Emily Reimer-Barry

Part 1

Theoretical *and* Theological Reflections *on* Reproduction *and* Social Justice

1. Introduction

Emily Reimer-Barry and Simeiqi He

Around the world, women experience disproportionate rates of violence, hunger, and illiteracy; carry an inordinate burden of care for children and the elderly; and suffer from inadequate health care that leads to what the late Dr. Paul Farmer described as "stupid deaths"—that is, deaths that result from tragic, unfair, and preventable causes.[1] In this collection of essays, scholars trained in the Catholic moral tradition seek to reflect on the suffering unique to women, with a special focus on human reproduction as a site of suffering, inequality, and violence. In this volume's introduction, we, Emily and Simeiqi, explain the origins of the contributors' collaboration, introduce two guiding frameworks (reproductive justice and Catholic social thought), and describe the book's organization.

Origins of and Development of the Virtual Table

In October 2019, a group of scholars met in Munich, Germany, to envision a way forward for the Catholic Theological Ethics in the World Church network that would facilitate international collaborations without necessitating expensive in-person conferences.[2] Those in attendance

---

[1] "Dying in childbirth because obstetric care cost too much was dying a stupid death; worldwide, there are five hundred thousand of these each year," Farmer wrote in "Landmine Boy and Stupid Deaths" (2008), in *Partner to the Poor: A Paul Farmer Reader*, ed. Haun Saussy (Oakland: University of California Press, 2010), 409–426. See also UN Women, "Facts and Figures," www.unwomen.org/en/news/in-focus/commission-on-the-status-of-women-2012/facts-and-figures.

[2] Founded by Jesuit moralist and teacher James F. Keenan, SJ, the Catholic Theological Ethics in the World Church network is an international community of ethicists that has become a catalyst for re-envisioning how we investigate ethics and how we report our findings better by

Introduction

shared a vision for bringing together scholars across continents to think together about the most pressing social issues facing the church and the world by creating 'virtual tables.' These spaces of ongoing debate and discussion were to be intentionally international and formative of younger scholars in the field. Emily attended the Munich conference and began planning a virtual table on reproductive justice and the common good soon after[3] and asked Simeiqi He to co-convene the virtual table.[4]

Our virtual table began to meet in July of 2020, in the pedagogical style of a round table. Unlike a rectangular table with a clear position of authority designated at the so-called 'head' of the table, when a group gathers in the round, each has the opportunity to see one another. No position has higher or lower status. Feminist scholars have for some time noted the value of "circle" discussions, or dialogues "in the round," which capture this framework of mutual listening and learning.[5] A round table

---

being better connected globally. Keenan has encouraged each of us to "talk about matters that others do not think should be discussed" and to support one another in our shared vocation. To read more about the virtual tables see the CTEWC website catholicethics.com/virtual-tables/. We thank the entire CTEWC leadership team for their support and encouragement as we sought to contribute to theological ethics in a world church. Special thanks to Linda Hogan, Andrea Vicini, SJ, Kristin Heyer, Shaji George Kochuthara, Suzanne Mulligan, Alexandre A. Martins, M. Therese Lysaught, and Jason King.

[3] Emily's travel was funded by an International Opportunity Grant (International Center, University of San Diego); her contributions to the volume were supported by a research sabbatical and the Steber Fellowship. Special thanks to the Dean's Office of the College of Arts and Sciences and the Provost Office, both of the University of San Diego.

[4] We had advertised the opportunity through the Catholic Theological Ethics in the World Church network and described it as an English-speaking closed group that would protect the identity of participants so that those present could speak freely about ongoing research questions related to reproduction, feminism, and social justice. While some members speak multiple languages, our group's dialogues proceeded in English. The conversations are inevitably shaped by this limitation. It was also shaped by practical considerations including the difficulty of scheduling synchronous meetings across different time zones.

[5] A notable example is the Circle of Concerned African Women Theologians (often simply called 'the Circle'), which is a Pan-African academic association of women researching, publishing, and interacting with communities on issues relating to religion and theology. Founded in 1989 under the vision of Mercy Amba Oduyoye, the Circle creates spaces for

communicates the idea that every voice matters.⁶ In our virtual table Zoom meetings, we sought to practice this kind of circle methodology, beginning with "check-ins" and enabling dialogue on the theme of the day. In our first meeting, we discussed our experiences of the Covid-19 pandemic and its impact on our work and family lives thus far, with special attention to issues of gender injustice. Emily described the challenges of online teaching in the spring of 2020 while her elementary-school aged children were also learning at home. Simeiqi shared the challenges of her experience giving birth and discussed the difficulties of finding diapers and wipes in the grocery stores after welcoming a newborn child.⁷ Personal sharing enabled us to create a space of mutual listening, solidarity and shared activism as together we reflected on what we were witnessing and experiencing from our various contexts around the world.

We decided that for the first year we would meet eight times for conversations around shared texts, working papers, and time for discussion and reflection.⁸ Our conversations were wide-ranging, covering

---

women from Africa to do communal theology. For more information, see Circle of Concerned African Women Theologians (2024): www.circlekenya.org/ and circle.org.za/.

⁶ For this reason, many found it significant that in the Synod on Synodality meetings in Rome, the seating arrangements were designed to be inclusive, with delegates seated at round tables. Nicole Winfield, "Vatican Document Highlights Need for Concrete Steps for Women, 'Radical Inclusion' of LGBTQ+," *AP News*, June 20, 2023, apnews.com/article/vatican-synod-women-lgbtq-pope-abuse-63b13399c4cd363a7a086c7b513e6283.

⁷ For a powerful reflection on spiritual lessons from a traumatic birth experience, see Simeiqi He, "Mother of One, Mother of All," *Mothering Spirit*, March 11, 2024, motheringspirit.com/2024/03/mother-of-one-mother-of-all/.

⁸ For example, some of the texts we read and discussed together include Francis, *Amoris Laetitia* (2016); United Nations Population Fund, "Covid-19: A Gender Lens," March 2020, www.unfpa.org/resources/covid-19-gender-lens; Margaret A. Farley, RSM, "Liberation, Abortion, and Responsibility," in *On Moral Medicine: Theological Perspectives in Medical Ethics*, 2nd ed., ed. Stephen E. Lammers and Allen Verhey (Grand Rapids: Eerdmans, 1998): 633–638; Farley's "Presidential Address to the Catholic Theological Society of America: The Church in the Public Forum: Scandal or Prophetic Witness?," *Proceedings of the Catholic Theological Society of America* 55 (2000): 89–101; Loretta J. Ross, "Conceptualizing Reproductive Justice Theory: A Manifesto for Activism," in *Radical Reproductive Justice: Foundations, Theory, Practice, Critique*, ed. Loretta J. Ross, Lynn Roberts, Erika Derkas,

such topics as gender norms in *Amoris Laetitia*, child care, ecofeminism, contraception, clericalism and seminary curricula, conscience formation, politics, racism, and population control. We did not initially have a book project in mind. Rather, we slowly came to understand, over a three-year conversation, that our conversations were unique, and could contribute fruitfully to global conversations in Catholic theological ethics. While some participants in the virtual table were not able to participate in the book project because of other writing commitments, their voices shaped the chapters that follow, and we remain grateful for each person who shared their stories, expertise, and hope for a better world throughout our multi-year collaboration. As we began to plan for a published collection, we reflected on how we might convey our dialogical method in published form. We decided to write single-authored chapters as well as roundtable discussions in which participants respond to the same prompt from their particular context. This approach can show how theologians from various positions around the table both share common concerns and propose variable solutions to complex problems.

Why Reproduction and the Common Good?

Reproductive health is a complex issue. To speak of human reproduction requires reflection on the body, on intimate relationships, on health and

---

Whitney Peoples, and Pamela Bridgewater Toure (New York: Feminist Press, 2017); Loretta J. Ross and Ricki Solinger, *Reproductive Justice: An Introduction* (Oakland: University of California Press, 2017); Rickie Solinger and Mie Nakachi, eds., *Reproductive States* (New York: Oxford University Press, 2016); Sisters in Islam and Asian-Pacific Resource and Research Centre for Women, *Child Marriage: Its Relationships with Religion, Culture, and Patriarchy* (2018): arrow.org.my/wp-content/uploads/2018/03/National-Report-Child-Marriage-Single-Page.pdf; Agnes M. Brazal, "Ethics of Care in *Laudato Si'*: A Postcolonial Ecofeminist Critique," *Feminist Theology* 29, no. 3 (2021): doi.org/10.1177/09667350211000614; United Nations Population Fund (UNFPA), *Seeing the Unseen: State of World Population Report 2022*, 38–41, www.unfpa.org/sites/default/files/pub-pdf/EN_SWP22%20report_0.pdf; and an earlier version of a chapter later published in Lorraine Cuddeback-Gedeon, *The Work of Inclusion: An Ethnography of Grace, Sin, and Intellectual Disabilities* (London: T&T Clark, 2023).

wellbeing, and on the nature of community and the care for future generations. To speak of reproduction and the common good is to ask about our obligations to one another in the human family. It requires inquiry into themes of social responsibility, social structures, welfare, interdependence, concern for the vulnerable, and justice. Human reproduction can be a site of immense joy, bonding, and life-affirming care, but it is not always so. Further, feminist discourse requires attention to power, agency, and the relationship between the personal and the political. As theologians who seek to better understand the signs of our times regarding human reproduction, we have come to see how—to adopt the language of *Gaudium et Spes*—the joys and the hopes, the griefs and the anxieties, especially those who are poor or in any way afflicted, are also the joys and hopes, the griefs and anxieties of the followers of Christ (no. 1). The work of human reproduction cannot be equitably shared and thus raises additional questions about which bodies—which persons—can or should be asked to carry communal burdens.[9] From the beginning, we sought to discuss these complex themes by holding together the concrete realities of human experiences and the wisdom of the Catholic intellectual and spiritual traditions. We also sought to hold together the importance of particularity—including recognition of our own positionality and context—while also approaching our conversations with a focus on dialogue in the midst of difference. While this volume brings together voices from around the globe, it cannot possibly capture the varied experiences of all Catholics around the world. Each of us speaks from a particular place, embedded within particular relationships and institutions

---

[9] See Cristina L. H. Traina, "Between a Rock and a Hard Place: Unwanted Pregnancy, Mercy, and Solidarity," *Journal of Religious Ethics* 46, no. 4 (2018): 658–681; Patricia Beattie Jung, "Abortion and Organ Donation: Christian Reflections on Bodily Life Support," in *Readings in Moral Theology, no. 9: Feminist Ethics and the Catholic Moral Tradition*, ed. Charles E. Curran, Margaret A. Farley, and Richard A. McCormick (New York: Paulist Press, 1996): 440–480; Lisa Sowle Cahill, "Abortion and Argument by Analogy," *Horizons* 9, no. 2 (1982): 217–287.

that shape us and our moral imaginations.¹⁰ We share explicitly feminist commitments, including defense of the dignity of women and a desire for women's voices and experiences to shape Catholic theological ethics now and in the future. Writing about reproductive justice together is an act of collective resistance to patriarchy.

Okay, but What is Reproductive Justice—Really?

We decided to build our conversations around reproductive justice because of the fruitful overlap between commitments of Catholic social teachings and the reproductive justice movement. Reproductive justice is a social movement that brings together diverse individuals and community organizations to foster holistic flourishing, especially for persons marginalized by race and class. The movement builds on the work of womanist and Black feminist scholars of the 1960's in the United States, who pointed out the multi-faceted and layered oppressions that women of color experienced in the US.¹¹ Loretta J. Ross and Toni Bond, early leaders of the reproductive justice movement, explain that when Black women came together to organize around their needs in the US in 1994, abortion was just one of a constellation of complex issues that they discussed.¹²

---

¹⁰ On positionality and intersectional methods in Catholic moral theology, see Meghan J. Clark, Anna Kasafi Perkins, and Emily Reimer-Barry, "Special Issue on Intersectional Methods and Moral Theology: Introduction," *Journal of Moral Theology* 12, Special Issue no. 1 (2023): 1–18, doi.org/10.55476/001c.75198.

¹¹ Frances M. Beal, "Double Jeopardy: To Be Black and Female" (1969), reprinted in *Sisterhood is Powerful: An Anthology of Writings from the Women's Liberation Movement*, ed. Robin Morgan (New York: Random House, 1970); Kimberlé Crenshaw, "Demarginalizing the Intersection of Race and Sex: A Black Feminist Critique of Antidiscrimination Doctrine, Feminist Theory, and Antiracist Politics," *University of Chicago Legal Forum* 1 (1989): scholarship.law.columbia.edu/faculty_scholarship/3007/; and Audre Lorde, *Sister Outsider: Essays and Speeches* (Berkeley, CA: Crossing Press, 1984).

¹² The main catalyst that brought scholar-activists together in the early 1990's was dissatisfaction with Democratic leadership on issues of Black women's holistic health and frustrations that the pro-choice community focused too narrowly on abortion rights instead of holistic flourishing in community. See Chicago Public Library, "Toni Bond: The Fight for

Introduction

Loretta J. Ross and Rickie Solinger explain that founders of the reproductive justice movement were inspired by the human rights movement and, especially, the international coalition of activists who prioritized gender equity in the Fourth World Conference on Women in Beijing, China, in 1995, which resulted in the Beijing Declaration and Platform for Action.[13] Further, they attend to the ways that neoliberal capitalism and white supremacy negatively impact persons marginalized by race and class. The movement seeks to center the stories of persons on the peripheries, including people who are vulnerable because of complex systems of oppression and domination.

Committed to achieving human rights for all, the leaders of the reproductive justice movement prioritized three rights in particular: the right to have a child; the right to not have a child; and the right to parent children in safe and healthy conditions.[14] Ross and Solinger explain that people who reproduce and become parents require a safe and dignified context for these most fundamental human experiences. Reproductive justice expands reflection to include a broad range of factors that impact women's decisions regarding reproduction, including health care access, housing, education, political structures, and the safety of one's environment.

Today, reproductive justice remains a holistic framework for seeking justice for vulnerable women and children. The threats to reproductive justice are experienced differently around the world. Migration, polluted environments, human trafficking, gender based violence, political violence and war, and many other social issues impact the decisions women make about their fertility. Reproductive justice advocates work to transform

---

Women's Reproductive Rights," June 24, 2022, www.chipublib.org/blogs/post/the-fight-for-womens-reproductive-rights/; Loretta Ross and Rickie Solinger, *Reproductive Justice: An Introduction*; and Zakiya T. Luna, *Reproductive Rights as Human Rights: Women of Color and the Fight for Reproductive Justice* (New York: New York University Press, 2020).

[13] United Nations, *Report of the Fourth World Conference on Women, 1995* (New York: United Nations, 1996), www.un.org/womenwatch/daw/beijing/pdf/Beijing%20full%20report%20E.pdf.

[14] Ross and Solinger, *Reproductive Justice*, 9.

Introduction

unjust social structures so that people flourish in healthy sexual relationships and parents have all they need to care for their children.

Okay, but What Does that Have to Do with Catholic Theology?

As Catholic theologians, we draw on the breadth of the Catholic moral tradition as we address different aspects of the reproductive justice debates going on around the world. We bring to this conversation a special concern for those most marginalized, most traumatized, most impoverished, and least able to join the conversation in their faith communities. Gender inequality structures women's lives and constrains women's choices. This too must be a factor in ecclesial discernment about how to foster reproductive justice in an unjust world. All-male episcopal conferences rarely attend adequately to women's lived experiences when addressing these complex issues in their own pastoral letters. Unfortunately, Vatican dicasteries don't always get it right either.[15] In our work, we seek out areas of common ground while also pointing to needed developments in church teachings.

Catholic social teaching refers to the authoritative documents of the Catholic Church dealing with social issues.[16] Four principles of Catholic

---

[15] M. Therese Lysaught, "Vatican's Own Gender Ideology Makes 'Dignitas Infinita' Incoherent," *National Catholic Reporter*, April 26, 2024, www.ncronline.org/opinion/guest-voices/vaticans-own-gender-ideology-makes-dignitas-infinita-incoherent. For theological analysis of papal teachings on gender and family life, see *Modern Catholic Family Teaching: Commentaries and Interpretations*, ed. Jacob M. Kohlhaas and Mary M. Doyle Roche (Washington, DC: Georgetown University Press, 2024).

[16] Since the promulgation of *Rerum Novarum* by Leo XIII in 1891, Catholic leaders have condemned social injustices and sought to inspire the faithful to address issues of inequality, exploitation of workers, consumerism, war, and environmental destruction. The method of Catholic social teaching is not legalistic and top-down. Thomas Massaro explains: "Catholic social teaching is not a set of preprogrammed answers that anticipate all of life's challenges but rather a remarkably flexible and open-ended set of tools." See Massaro, *Living Justice: Catholic Social Teaching in Action*, 2nd ed. (Lanham, MD: Rowman and Littlefield, 2012), 145.

social teaching shaped our collaborative conversations: the common good; human dignity; preferential option for the poor and vulnerable; and solidarity. In the rest of this section, we briefly explain each principle and name some of the ways it intersects with reproductive justice scholarship.

The principle of the common good is rooted in a theological anthropology that sees the human person as inherently social and interdependent.[17] The common good indicates "the sum total of social conditions which allow people, either as groups or as individuals, to reach their fulfilment more fully and more easily" (*Mater et Magistra*, no. 65). According to the *Compendium of the Social Doctrine of the Church*, "Everyone also has the right to enjoy the conditions of social life that are brought about by the quest for the common good" (no. 167). John Paul II explained that the common good seeks the "good of all and of each individual" (*Sollicitudo Rei Socialis*, nos. 38–39). Moreover, governments have important roles to play in securing the common good. "The government of each country has the specific duty to harmonize the different sectoral interests with the requirements of justice" (*Compendium*, no. 169). The principle of the common good intersects with reproductive justice in compelling ways because both are rooted in an understanding of the social nature of the human person and both see an important role for the government in safeguarding the welfare of all. This leads activists within both frameworks to advocate for policies such as the paid family leave, nondiscrimination policies, distributive justice through taxation, and a strong social safety net for the vulnerable.

A second shared principle between Catholic social teaching and reproductive justice is the defense of human rights. In Catholic teachings about labor justice, the principle of human dignity yields slogans such as "persons over profits!" and "work is for the person, not the person for work!" As the *Compendium of the Church's Social Doctrine* explains, "The whole of the Church's social doctrine, in fact, develops from the principle

---

[17] For example, *Gaudium et Spes* taught that human beings were created for life in community (no. 32).

that affirms the inviolable dignity of the human person" (no. 107). In Catholic teachings, the human person is created *imago Dei*—that is, in the image and likeness of God (Genesis 1:26). Recognition of basic human rights emerges from this recognition in the sacred dignity of the human person. In *Dignitatis Humanae*, the church affirms rights of religious freedom, family life, and freedom from unjust coercion (nos. 1, 2, 5, 9). John XXIII, in *Pacem in Terris*, defended a human rights framework that included the right to bodily integrity and "to the means necessary for the proper development of life, particularly food, clothing, shelter, medical care, rest, and, finally, the necessary social services" (no. 11). Reproductive justice scholarship intersects in important ways with this rights-based approach. Previously we noted that reproductive justice advocates for the right to control one's fertility and the right to safe and healthy conditions for family life. These conditions include the very same conditions laid out by John XXIII: food, clothing, shelter, medical care, and so forth.

A third key principle of Catholic social teaching that intersects with the scholarship of reproductive justice is the preferential option for the poor and vulnerable. This principle explains that we have a special duty to give priority to those most marginalized. In the words of the Latin American bishops at Puebla, "We affirm the need for conversion on the part of the whole Church to a preferential option for the poor, an option aimed at their integral liberation."[18] Christians through the centuries have asked what it means to see the face of Christ in the person who is hungry, thirsty, a stranger, sick, or imprisoned (Matthew 25: 40–45). In the papacy of Francis, this means care for those on the peripheries. Jesuit moralist Thomas Massaro explains that "advocating for social change by encouraging structural reforms that will benefit those on the periphery" has been a central focus of Francis throughout his ministry.[19] In addition, the papacy of Francis has focused on inclusion, accompaniment, and mercy, which

---

[18] Conference of Latin American and Caribbean Bishops (CELAM) Puebla (1979), 1134: celam.org/.

[19] Thomas Massaro, SJ, *Mercy in Action: The Social Teachings of Pope Francis* (Lanham: Rowman & Littlefield, 2018), 178.

demonstrate important aspects of his agenda for the church in the world and provide a welcome emphasis on pastoral sensitivity and dialogue with women (*Evangelii Gaudium*, nos. 103–104, 112, 169–175, 179). This approach resonates well with the reproductive justice movement's prioritizing of women of color made vulnerable by the compounding oppressions of racism and sexism.

Finally, a fourth principle that links Catholic social teaching and reproductive justice is the principle of solidarity. John Paul II explained that solidarity is not just a "vague feeling" of compassion or pity for another, but instead is "a firm and persevering determination to commit oneself to the common good" (*Sollicitudo Rei Socialis*, no. 38). If Jesus is the role model for solidarity, then discipleship means being willing to take up one's cross, engage in risk-taking, challenge unjust oppression, and face the consequences of one's actions. Catholic theologian Meghan J. Clark explains that solidarity is not one-way; rather, solidarity is a social virtue because it requires mutuality. We practice solidarity with others, not alone. Solidarity is when we join another's struggle for justice within a community; in Clark's words, neither the individual nor the common good can be eliminated or sacrificed in solidarity that is directed towards its proper end.[20] Since solidarity is so central to the reproductive justice movement, solidarity featured prominently in our virtual table discussions, as we sought to identify how we were being invited, called, and inspired to practice what Catholic theologian Cristina Traina describes as "compassionate solidarity," meaning "compassion in action, urging justice."[21]

Okay, but Why Now?

This volume is timely for a number of reasons. First, the implementation of *Amoris Laetitia* continues to invite Catholic leaders around the world

---

[20] Meghan J. Clark, *The Vision of Catholic Social Thought: The Virtue of Solidarity and the Praxis of Human Rights* (Minneapolis: Fortress, 2014), 114.
[21] Traina, "Between a Rock and a Hard Place," 677.

to enter into the realities of everyday people's lives instead of taking an approach to the moral life that ignores difficult questions or seeks simplistic solutions. Second, nation-states are in flux with regard to laws and policies, and episcopal conferences have been significant actors in shaping public conversation about church teachings on reproduction in particular contexts (not always for the better). Theologians should help to frame these issues in a more nuanced way than bishops often achieve. Third, our collaboration after three years of discussing reproductive justice in a CTEWC virtual table seeks to model respectful engagement of difficult issues even when disagreement emerges. We invite readers to explore complex issues from multiple perspectives and to resist simplistic solutions. It is our hope that seminary students, undergraduate students, theology professors, and vowed religious engaged in work with marginalized populations around the world will find in this text resources for thinking about complex topics in reproductive justice and social ethics.

How is the Book Organized?

The volume is divided into three parts. In the first, scholars lay the groundwork by presenting theoretical and theological categories that inform approaches to ethical analysis of reproduction. These include critical realism, reproductive justice, Catholic social thought, sin-talk, social sin, reciprocity, mutuality, social narrative, virtues of resistance, complementarity, love, and more. The second part of the volume presents two roundtable discussions. In the first roundtable, we asked participants to respond to the questions: "What are the threats to women's dignity and moral agency in your context? Is reproductive justice a helpful framework for addressing those threats?" Authors from the Philippines, United States of America, and Nigeria responded by noting different threats to women's flourishing and some of the possible ways that a framework of reproductive justice can provide meaningful categories for social action. In the second roundtable discussion, we posed the questions: "What should be the role of the Catholic Church in advancing justice with regard to reproduction? In your context, is the Catholic Church a resource or a roadblock?" Scholars from China, the Philippines, United States, India, and the United Kingdom speak to this question from their locations. Teachers may find these particularly useful for course adoption, as they reflect various perspectives on the same question from ethicists in different parts of the world. The roundtable discussions serve as a bridge between the foundations laid out in the first part and the in-depth treatment of particular issues in the third. Here we provide a brief overview of the single-authored chapters in the volume.

Julie Clague (UK), in "Structural Inequality and the Social Determinants of Unintended Pregnancy," analyzes the social drivers of unintended pregnancy and discusses the nature of these inequalities and their consequences for women's health and wellbeing. Since female empowerment can reduce the high numbers of unintended pregnancies, Clague points to what this means in practical terms for women and girls at risk of unintended pregnancies.

Kate Ward (USA), in the essay "Never Just a Choice: Three Theoretical Approaches to Economic Constraints on Family Formation," analyzes the impact of economic realities on decisions around partnership, commitment, and raising children in the US context. She examines three theoretical approaches—critical realist social theory, reproductive justice, and Catholic documentary tradition on families. Pointing out the common ground and distinctions among these three approaches, Ward argues that none of them thoroughly succeeds at describing pursuit of the human good of family formation by persons facing social constraint. Regardless, she proposes a positive vision in light of the contributions made by each of the three approaches that moves beyond the restriction-only approach by the US Catholic Church.

Kathryn Lilla Cox (USA), in "Reproductive Injustice as Social Sin: Mapping Sin Discourse into Debates about Fertility Decisions," suggests that theological work around reproductive justice requires re-thinking sin-talk so that we can more properly name the nature of communal sins that influence individual moral decisions. She unpacks scriptural metaphors for sin, analyzing both the contributions and limitations of these inherited categories. By reflecting on the story of "Miriam," the essay demonstrates how sin-talk matters for vulnerable women.

Hoon Choi (USA/Republic of Korea), in the essay "Fatherhood, Reproductive Justice, and Strategic Invisibility of Men," points to the invisibility of men in women's reproductive stories, while calling for a better response from them to participate in reproductive justice through a genuine reciprocity. He employs an exercise of imagination, where demands faced by women—subjecting them to anguish, enforcement, and torment due to external controls over their bodies and agency—are made on men. By doing so, Choi seeks to evoke distress caused by the absurdity of these demands, so men are motivated to not only recognize the double standards in how society thinks about human bodies and bodily integrity but also acknowledge their role in reproductive justice with all its complexity. Choi proposes that genuine reciprocity called for by Francis in *Amoris Laetitia* provides an opening for the construction of a more just paradigm where men can responsibly contribute to personal and social transformation.

Suzanne Mulligan (Ireland), in the essay "Thinking about Reproductive Justice in Contexts of Violence," examines the relationship between violence towards women and reproductive justice. Drawing on the understanding of social narrative forwarded by Traci C. West and Anne E. Patrick, Mulligan challenges the extent to which human dignity is a genuine social value within our communities. Analyzing the case of Magdalene Laundries in Ireland, Mulligan shows the weaknesses of a Catholic approach to reproduction that fails to address adequately the underlying injustices women experience.

Simeiqi He (China/USA), in the essay "Reconceptualizing Human Reproduction beyond John Paul II," analyzes the evolution of the concept of human reproduction in the teachings of the magisterium, from John Paul II to Francis. She uncovers tensions and inconsistencies within John Paul II's approach to human reproduction and describes how the Church's magisterium has since developed, with a more recent focus on the primacy of love as the central norm. When we reconceptualize human reproduction as part of a holistic anthropocosmic vision then human reproduction becomes the reproduction of love. Such a move invites new reflection on human reproduction ordered to the common good, making space for a deeper understanding of justice in Catholic approaches to reproduction.

Stephanie Ann Puen (Philippines), in the essay "Considerations for a Comprehensive Sex Education Grounded in Catholic Social Thought for Reproductive Justice in the Philippines," reflects on the challenges of implementing the Responsible Parenthood and Reproductive Health Act of 2012 in the Philippines. Puen argues that the Catholic Church—given its teaching on integral human development—should meet the country's need for comprehensive reproductive health education (CRHE). She demonstrates the importance of a CRHE in line with Catholic social thought, while urging an integration of sexual ethics with Catholic social thought, a serious critique on the cultural and religious assumption about women and family and an attention to the value of teaching moral decision-making and discernment.

Karen Peterson-Iyer (USA), in the essay "Reproductive Justice and Agricultural Labor Migrants," gives special attention to migrant farmworker women in the US and their reproductive struggles. Peterson-Iyer employs reproductive justice as an analytical lens to demonstrate the numerous challenges faced by migrant farmworker women, such as family poverty, lack of access to adequate health care and reproductive health care, material precarity, compromised housing and working conditions, sexual harassment and abuse, punitive immigration policies, high degree of exploitation, and risk for the health and safety of their children. Upon examining Catholic teaching on reproductive ethics, labor and immigration ethics, and the importance of family life, Peterson-Iyer argues that Catholic ethics must widen its reproductive lens to incorporate the categories illuminated by reproductive justice. She further offers some preliminary suggestions for concrete policies to promote justice for migrant farmworker women.

Introduction

Mary M. Doyle Roche (USA), in the essay "Rachel is Weeping for Her Children: Theological Reflections on Reproductive Justice and Maternal Health," advocates for an intersectional reproductive justice framework from a Catholic perspective. Calling attention to the devastating reality of morbidity and mortality for Black mothers and children in the United States, Roche demonstrates its root in the history and ongoing impact of white supremacy. She appeals to the biblical image of Rachel, while uniting it with Black mothers and their children harmed by and lost to reproductive injustice. Arguing that the Black Lives Matter movement captures the heart of reproductive justice and a preferential option for the poor and vulnerable, Roche suggests that reproductive justice can serve as a comprehensive approach for Catholic ethics, given the latter's attention to the dignity of the person, the common good, and solidarity with the vulnerable.

Mary Lilian Akhere Ehidiamhen (Nigeria), in the essay "Reclaiming Women's Agency for Reproductive Justice in Nigeria Today: Flourishing for Mother and Child in Situations of Constraints," discusses the importance of reclaiming women's agency for reproductive justice in Nigeria. She points out that Nigerian women face numerous constraints on their agency, and she details patriarchal cultural assumptions and religious teachings, as well as systemic challenges like poverty and conflict, that hinder flourishing. Confronting these constraints and their negative impact on the reproductive life of Nigerian women, Ehidiamhen takes inspiration from Marshall Rosenberg's needs-based theory to advocate a needs-based approach in advancing reproductive justice and the flourishing of mother and child. She contends that a needs-based approach offers women the opportunity to reclaim their reproductive agency in a just and nonviolent way. Observing the deep affinity between the needs-based approach and the teaching of the Catholic Church on human dignity and bodily integrity, Ehidiamhen urges a broader way of being Church that advances reproductive justice in Nigeria.

Eric Marcelo O. Genilo SJ (Philippines), in the essay "Risking Women's Lives, Denying Women's Experiences: CDF Statements on Sterilization in

Catholic Hospitals," conducts a close examination of three documents of the Congregation for the Doctrine of the Faith with regard to sterilization in Catholic hospitals spanning forty-three years. Genilo points out that these documents neglected significant realities that affect the capacity of women to safeguard themselves, their children, and their marriages. He argues that the solidly probable opinion developed by Ford and Kelly to justify the removal of a damaged uterus to prevent a future risky pregnancy acknowledges women's experience and rights and is more consistent with medical standards of care, Christian charity, and common sense than the three CDF responses. Genilo calls for a retrieval and revival of their moral argument and personalist approach in addressing the dire situations women face.

Emily Reimer-Barry (USA), in "Catholic Health Care and Reproductive Justice: Whose Conscience Has Priority When Conscience Claims Collide?," describes the footprint of Catholic health care in the US context and explores the impact of Catholic directives on patient care. In particular, she examines institutional conscience claims that seem to compete with the conscience claims of medical providers and patients. Reimer-Barry forwards the argument that communal discernment is needed in such difficult cases and that bishops should not dictate to the consciences of patients.

Virginia Saldanha (India), in "Religio-Cultural Underpinnings of Gender and Reproductive Injustice and their Impact on Women's Agency in India," utilizes a Catholic feminist methodology to reveal how patriarchal religious teachings within Hinduism and Christianity empower men to dominate over women in the family, in the workplace, and in Indian society. An approach to reproductive justice in India must be holistic and action-oriented. Saldanha forwards the argument that threats to women's flourishing in India are complex but that the women's movement is on the front lines of addressing the needed social transformation.

Introduction

Concluding Reflections

We could not be comprehensive in this volume—a comprehensive treatment would fill libraries—but we sought to use our theological training to help our colleagues, students, and ecclesial leaders see the ways in which the wisdom of the Catholic tradition can fruitfully intersect with and engage the scholarship and activism of the reproductive justice movement. Throughout our discussions, we have been keenly aware that the questions we were raising had been raised by others before us. We knew that our work was building on the work of many brave theologians who had wrestled with the complexities and ambiguities of reproduction and social justice long before virtual tables existed. In our virtual table meeting dedicated to reading and discussing Margaret Farley's trailblazing work in Catholic theological ethics, Simeiqi read aloud from Farley's 1986 book *Personal Commitments*,

> There are, of course, no final answers to most of the questions I have traced and no complete solutions to the life-situations I have described. It is possible, however, to do two things whenever we come face to face with unanswerable questions for which we need answers (without which we cannot go on) and irresolvable situations which we must resolve (or we cannot endure). It is possible, first, to expand our horizons—to push back the dimensions of the problem, gain light by turning it this way and that, broadening its context into a larger world and life. It is possible, second, to enter more deeply into the questions—to take a lantern, as it were, and walk into what may ultimately be a mystery to us, but which we do not deserve to call a mystery until we have entered it as far as we can go.[22]

We can, of course, offer no "final answers" in this collection of essays. Instead, what we have endeavored to do is to look at complex problems

---

[22] Margaret A. Farley, RSM, *Personal Commitments: Beginning, Keeping, Changing* (New York: Harper & Row, 1990), 11.

from multiple perspectives, and to ask how we might proceed in a way that honors what it means to believe in a just and merciful God in the midst of systemic injustice. Farley inspires us to "enter more deeply into the questions" and to trust that by doing so, we will not be alone. We hope this book inspires readers to think critically, lament prayerfully, and seek to collaborate in the transformation of unjust structures. This book is dedicated to our teachers and mentors, who created brave spaces in the guild of Catholic theological ethics, with our deep gratitude.

Emily Reimer-Barry, PhD, is professor in the Department of Theology and Religious Studies at the University of San Diego where she teaches undergraduate courses in Catholic theological ethics. She is the author of two books: *Reproductive Justice and the Catholic Church: Advancing Pragmatic Solidarity with Pregnant Women* (Sheed & Ward, 2024) and *Catholic Theology of Marriage in the Era of HIV and AIDS: Marriage for Life* (Lexington, 2015).

Simeiqi He, PhD, is a Chinese Catholic theological ethicist and social worker. She holds a Ph.D. in Christian ethics from Drew University Theological School, a Master of Arts in Theology and Ministry from Brite Divinity School, a Master of Social Work and a graduate certificate in Women and Gender Studies from Texas Christian University, and a Bachelor of Science in Materials Physics from Sichuan University. Her writings have previously appeared in *Journal of Moral Theology, Catholic Theological Review, Asian Horizons*, and *U.S. Catholic*.

Chapter 2: Structural Inequality and the Social Determinants of Unintended Pregnancy

Julie Clague

The following discussion considers unintended pregnancies, some of the circumstances that give rise to them, and some of the ways to prevent them. It purposely departs from the moral arguments and debates about procreation, contraception, and abortion that have so dominated the field of moral theology. There will be no theological or ethical scholarship brought to bear on the subject matter. The research presented is drawn in large part from the fields of health science and human development, much of it scientific, statistical, data-heavy. No Church teachings are quoted. Instead, global and country-level prevalence rates for unintended pregnancy and abortion are cited. Yet, the questions raised, and evidence presented about unintended pregnancy, are moral to the core.[1] Analysis of the social drivers of unintended pregnancy reveals that deep-seated structural inequalities create the context for women's experiences and decision-making concerning pregnancy and childbearing. The paper discusses the nature of these inequalities and their consequences for women's health and wellbeing.

The first part of the paper draws on the World Health Organization's conceptual framing of the social determinants of health to consider the nature of the structural inequalities implicated in unintended pregnancies. This theoretical section asks: What, precisely, is structural about structural inequality and how does structural inequality affect health outcomes?

---

[1] Essays within this collection that make Catholic theological arguments regarding this and similar data include Suzanne Mulligan, "Thinking about Reproductive Justice in Contexts of Violence," 148–174; Mary Lilian Akhere Ehidiamhen, "Reclaiming Women's Agency for Reproductive Justice in Nigeria Today," 310–333; and Virginia Saldanha, "Religio-Cultural Underpinnings of Gender and Reproductive Justice and Their Impact on Women's Agency in India," 391–410.

Subsequent sections consider the role of income level, access to contraception, gender inequality, and educational access and attainment on the incidence of unintended pregnancy. Since female empowerment can reduce the high number of unintended pregnancies, evidence is provided of what female empowerment means in practical terms for women and girls at risk of unintended pregnancies.

The Social Determinants of Health

Health and wellbeing—including reproductive health and wellbeing—are affected by where people live and the various economic, social, cultural, and politico-legal conditions that form the context for their lives. In medical parlance, these conditions are referred to as social determinants of health. The term determinant can be misleading. Determinants are not destiny; they are usually one of several factors that play a role in health.[2] Determinants of health increase or decrease the risk associated with health conditions. The role played by social factors is significant, often complex or subtle, and not always fully understood. Behavioural determinants play a more evident role in health. Behaviours (e.g., alcohol consumption) are greatly influenced by social context (social determinants) such as social attitudes, availability and access, legal and policy frameworks, religious rules, and so forth. Genetic inheritance, implicated in most diseases, is a major determinant of health risk and explains many population differences in susceptibility to disease. For example, genetic (not social) determinants explain why Africans are more likely than Europeans to develop sickle cell disease. Less obviously, the natural environment is also a health determinant; for instance, where soils lack iodine, inhabitants may become iodine deficient.

Social determinants of health refer to how life context has health consequences. The World Health Organization (WHO) frames this

---

[2] See also Kate Ward, "Never Just a Choice: Three Theoretical Approaches to Economic Constraints on Family Formation," 55–89.

capacious concept as "the full set of social conditions in which people live and work."[3] Multiple aspects of existence come in for scrutiny under this framing. Male circumcision, a cultural practice prevalent in some countries and among certain religious groups, affords some health benefits, including improved genital hygiene and reduced risk of sexually transmitted infections for the circumcised and their sexual partners. Robert Hahn discusses the manufacture of iodised salt to show how society can improve health by deliberately addressing an environmental cause of iodine deficiency.[4]

More often, however, social determinants of health are invoked to draw attention to the harmful effects on health of aspects of social existence. Living in a fragile state, a conflict zone, or a heavily polluted area greatly imperils health and wellbeing. Those in sedentary occupations tend to be less fit and more vulnerable to certain health conditions than people with jobs requiring physical exercise. Child marriage, common in various regions and cultures, which disproportionately affects girls rather than boys, tends to early childbearing, creating various health risks for affected females and their pregnancies.[5] Sub-Saharan Africa's sky-high number of preventable maternal deaths compared to the rest of the globe is socially (rather than behaviourally, genetically, or environmentally) determined.[6]

WHO is invested in better understanding social determinants of health and their role in the causes, prevention, and treatment of health conditions. WHO adopts an intentionally broad description of the social determinants of health: "the non-medical factors that influence health

---

[3] World Health Organization, "A Conceptual Framework for Action on the Social Determinants of Health," 2010, 9, iris.who.int/handle/10665/44489.

[4] Robert A. Hahn, "What is a Social Determinant of Health? Back to Basics," *Journal of Public Health Research* 10, no. 4 (2021): 2, doi.org/10.4081/jphr.2021.2324.

[5] World Health Organization, "Adolescent Pregnancy," June 2, 2023, www.who.int/news-room/fact-sheets/detail/adolescent-pregnancy; UNICEF, "Child Marriage," July 2023, www.unicef.org/protection/child-marriage.

[6] World Health Organization, "Trends in Maternal Mortality 2000 to 2020: Estimates by WHO, UNICEF, UNFPA, World Bank Group and UNDESA/Population Division," 2023 www.who.int/publications/i/item/9789240068759.

outcomes. They are the conditions in which people are born, grow, work, live, and age, and the wider set of forces and systems shaping the conditions of daily life. These forces and systems include economic policies and systems, development agendas, social norms, social policies and political systems."[7] Typically included in lists of social determinants of health are income level, employment status, occupation, educational attainment, gender, ethnicity/race, and class. Also significant are the social values, governance structures, and institutional arrangements that give shape, meaning and order to societies, such as global trade, national healthcare and welfare systems, and laws and policies such as gun, drug, and abortion laws, national speed limits, alcohol taxes, and smoking bans.

Health Inequity

The social determinants of health provide a framework for analysing local, national, and international differences in the health of individuals and groups along with their causes and remedies. When differential health outcomes are the consequence of social injustice or unfairness, these differences are termed health inequities. Health inequity is an inherently moral and evaluative term. In population health, the term health inequality is purely descriptive rather than moral. The distinction between health inequity and health inequality is clarified in the following definitions: "*Health inequality:* A generic term designating differences, variations, and disparities in the health of individuals and groups"; and "*Health inequity:* Those inequalities in health deemed to be unfair or to stem from some form of injustice."[8] According to WHO, "Health inequities are *avoidable* inequalities in health between groups of people within countries and between countries. These inequities arise from

---

[7] World Health Organization, "Social Determinants of Health," www.who.int/health-topics/social-determinants-of-health#tab=tab_1.
[8] David A. Kindig, "Understanding Population Health Terminology" *The Milbank Quarterly* 85, no. 1 (2007): 149, doi.org/10.1111/j.1468-0009.2007.00479.x.

inequalities within and between societies."⁹ WHO's description of health inequities as avoidable reminds us that these human-induced, immoral inequalities can and should be remedied. Clearly, health inequities can only be overcome by tackling the social injustices and unfairness that generate them. There is always, therefore, a moral imperative attached to any attempt to understand the social drivers of health inequity.

WHO's Commission on Social Determinants of Health (CSDH) was established to analyse and address the complex ways that multiple intersecting social factors—structural inequalities—give rise to health inequity. Its conceptual framing of the social determinants of health inequity is highly relevant for any discussion of the underlying causes of unintended pregnancy; it also offers valuable insights concerning the structural character of structural inequality.¹⁰ The Commission explicitly positions health inequities within the moral arena: "Identifying a health difference as inequitable . . . necessarily implies an appeal to ethical norms."¹¹ It declares that "the guiding ethical principle for the CSDH is health equity, defined as the absence of unfair and avoidable or remediable differences in health among social groups."¹² The CSDH's stated objective, therefore, is "to advance health equity, driving action to reduce health differences among social groups, within and between countries."¹³

WHO's analysis of the social determinants of health inequity takes as its starting point a familiar pattern repeated the world over: the worst-off in society have the worst health and those who are well-off have the best health. WHO describes the stratifying effect of health inequities within

---

⁹ World Health Organization, "Social Determinants of Health: Key Concepts," May 7, 2013, www.who.int/news-room/questions-and-answers/item/social-determinants-of-health-key-concepts.

¹⁰ On structural inequality in global health, see also *Prophet to the Peoples: Paul Farmer's Witness and Theological Ethics*, ed. Jennie Weiss Block, M. Therese Lysaught, and Alexandre A. Martins (Eugene, OR: Pickwick Press, 2023).

¹¹ World Health Organization, "A Conceptual Framework," 12.

¹² World Health Organization, "A Conceptual Framework," 14.

¹³ World Health Organization, "A Conceptual Framework," 9.

society as follows: "The poorest of the poor, around the world, have the worst health. Within countries, the evidence shows that in general the lower an individual's socioeconomic position the worse their health. There is a social gradient in health that runs from top to bottom of the socioeconomic spectrum. This is a global phenomenon, seen in low, middle and high income countries."[14] The social gradient in health tracks the socioeconomic gradient that stratifies all societies. Social stratification is a consequence of the way society is organized, which, ultimately, is a reflection of what and who society values.

Social status and value are usually sedimented in social class divisions which, over time, are reinscribed, reorganized, or replaced as a consequence of what society as a whole (or what the most powerful in society) prizes and privileges, such as income level, occupation, educational attainment, gender, ethnicity/race, tribe, religion and so on. These class divisions and differing social identities lead to an ineluctable and often unacknowledged sorting and stratification process that ranks individuals and groups on the spectrum of haves and have-nots, those who are one-of-us and those who are not-of-us, creating social hierarchies of structural inequality. Part and parcel of social stratification is the relative amount of social, economic, and political leverage (i.e., social power) possessed by individuals and groups as compared to others situated on the socioeconomic gradient. The CSDH describes the consequences of social stratification as "the systematically unequal distribution of power, prestige and resources among groups in society."[15] The privileged have more collateral, greater leverage, greater social mobility, and better health than those who are disadvantaged, who generally lack the power, wherewithal, and mobility to change their circumstances. Groups that experience multiple intersecting forms of disadvantage are the most socially marginalized and disempowered; they lack collateral and have the worst health. "In essence," states the CSDH, "health inequities are health

---

[14] World Health Organization, "Social Determinants of Health."
[15] World Health Organization, "A Conceptual Framework," 20.

differences that are socially produced, systematic in their distribution across the population, and unfair."[16] With this statement, it would appear that a signal characteristic of health inequities is identified, namely their predictable, socially stratified arrangement that is reproduced within and across all societies. The CSDH summarizes social stratification and its effects on health as follows: "Social contexts create social stratification and assign individuals to different social positions. Social stratification in turn engenders differential exposure to health-damaging conditions and differential vulnerability, in terms of health conditions and material resource availability. Social stratification likewise determines differential consequences of ill health for more and less advantaged groups (including economic and social consequences, as well differential health outcomes per se)."[17] The health of any society and the health of different population groups within society reveal much about how that society is structured, its value system, who and what is privileged, where power is located, and where resources are directed. The mechanism of social stratification that patterns power and privilege within countries also operates at the international level, producing similar pecking orders of power and privilege and stratified health hierarchies between countries. Social inequity and health inequity go hand-in-hand everywhere, consistently and predictably, within countries and between them.

What Is an Unintended Pregnancy?

We now consider unintended pregnancy, focusing on four social determinants of unintended pregnancy to better understand their role as risk factors for unintended pregnancy and as potential pathways to its prevention. Pregnancy preferences and outcomes are generally described in binary terms: planned or unplanned; intended or unintended; wanted or unwanted. Such either/or categories cannot capture the spectrum of

---

[16] World Health Organization, "A Conceptual Framework," 12.
[17] World Health Organization, "A Conceptual Framework," 24.

possible (sometimes changing) dispositions (such as ambivalence, equanimity, and fatalism) towards future children that some may experience. However, yes/no categories are useful for generating internationally comparable measures of pregnancy intention, which can be further interpreted via a range of economic and human development indicators.

A planned pregnancy is one that is intended and wanted, where attention has likely been paid to the timing and spacing of children. An intended pregnancy is one that was wanted at the time and was almost certainly planned or at least anticipated. The terms planned pregnancy and intended pregnancy are often used synonymously, as are the terms unplanned pregnancy and unintended pregnancy. However, some couples who are open to procreation and/or trying for children resist the connotations associated with family planning. In surveys about future childbearing wishes, this openness to children whenever they arrive is often expressed in the response that a pregnancy is up to God.[18]

Not all pregnancies are wanted. They may be unwanted from day one, or circumstances may lead to a pregnancy becoming unwanted at a later stage. A pregnancy that was unwanted at the time of conception is described as unintended. Many but not all unwanted pregnancies end in abortion. Women may choose to go through with an unwanted pregnancy and keep the child or give it to others (such as via adoption). Infanticide is relatively rare. Wanted and unwanted pregnancies can occur unexpectedly. A wanted pregnancy that occurs unexpectedly is described as mistimed or earlier-than-intended. Mistimed pregnancies count as unintended. Unintended pregnancies, therefore, may be wanted or unwanted. The term unintended pregnancy is used to describe a pregnancy that was unwanted at the time the pregnancy occurred or one that was wanted but mistimed (earlier than planned). The standard

---

[18] See Elizabeth Thomson, "Family Size Preferences," in *International Encyclopedia of the Social & Behavioral Sciences*, ed. James D. Wright, 2nd ed., vol. 8 (New York: Elsevier, 2015), 805–808, 806, dx.doi.org/10.1016/B978-0-08-097086-8.31064-9.

definition of an unintended pregnancy is: "A pregnancy that occurs to a woman who was not planning to have any (more) children, or that was mistimed, in that it occurred earlier than desired"; the definition of an unwanted pregnancy is: "A pregnancy that occurred when a woman did not want to have any children at all, or any more children."[19]

What is the Global Prevalence of Unintended Pregnancy and Abortion?

Jonathan Bearak and colleagues investigated prevalence rates for unintended pregnancy and abortion for the period 1990–94 and 2015–19, producing the first-ever country-level estimates. The prevalence rate is a measure of the number of individuals experiencing a condition within a particular population at a specific point, or within a specific period of time. Unintended pregnancy and abortion rates are expressed in terms of the number of women having an unintended pregnancy or abortion per 1,000 women of reproductive age (age 15 to 49). Bearak and others' findings show that unintended pregnancy and abortion are global phenomena and prevalence rates vary according to national context. In 2015–19, there were 121 million unintended pregnancies annually, equating to 48 percent of all pregnancies. This translates into an unintended pregnancy rate of 64 per 1,000 women of reproductive age (15–49 years) out of a total annual pregnancy rate of 133 per 1,000 women of reproductive age.[20] The country

---

[19] United Nations Population Fund, "State of World Population 2022: Seeing the Unseen: The Case for Action in the Neglected Crisis of Unintended Pregnancy," 2022, 6, www.unfpa.org/swp2022.

[20] Jonathan Bearak, Anna Popinchalk, Bela Ganatra, Ann-Beth Moller, Özge Tunçalp, Cynthia Beavin, Lorraine Kwok, Leontine Alkema, "Unintended Pregnancy and Abortion by Income, Region, and the Legal Status of Abortion: Estimates from a Comprehensive Model for 1990–2019," *The Lancet Global Health* 8, no. 9 (2020): e1152–e1161, e1155; Supplementary Appendix, 9, doi.org/10.1016/S2214-109X(20)30315-6.

estimates for unintended pregnancy rates vary enormously, ranging from 11 in Montenegro to 145 in Uganda.[21]

How many unintended pregnancies end in abortion? Bearak and team estimate that annually, in 1990–94, 25 percent of all pregnancies (51% of unintended pregnancies) ended in abortion, corresponding to an annual rate of 40 abortions per 1,000 women (15–49). In 2015–19, the proportion increased to 29 percent of all pregnancies (61% of unintended pregnancies), an annual total of 73.3 million abortions. Due to population growth, the annual abortion rate remained stable at 39 per 1,000 women (15–49).[22] At country level, abortion rates also varied widely. Singapore had the lowest abortion rate (5), and Georgia the highest (80).[23] Bearak's team did not investigate how marital status relates to the number of abortions. However, Gilda Sedgh and others' earlier study of abortion incidence found that in the period 2010–14, 73 percent of all abortions were obtained by married women (27% by unmarried women).[24] Both studies found that, since 1990, abortion incidence has declined in Europe and Northern America, but not elsewhere.[25] Neither research team found

---

[21] Jonathan Marc Bearak, Anna Popinchalk, Cynthia Beavin, Bela Ganatra, Ann-Beth Moller, Özge Tunçalp, Leontine Alkema, "Country-Specific Estimates of Unintended Pregnancy and Abortion Incidence: A Global Comparative Analysis of Levels in 2015–2019," *BMJ Global Health* 7, no. 3 (2022): 1, dx.doi.org/10. 1136/bmjgh-2021-007151.

[22] Bearak, Popinchalk, Ganatra, Moller, Tunçalp, Beavin, Kwok, Alkema, "Unintended Pregnancy and Abortion by Income, Region, and the Legal Status of Abortion," e1156–e1157; Supplementary Appendix, 9.

[23] Bearak, Popinchalk, Beavin, Ganatra, Moller, Tunçalp, Alkema, "Country-Specific Estimates of Unintended Pregnancy and Abortion Incidence," 1.

[24] Gilda Sedgh, Jonathan Bearak, Susheela Singh, Akinrinola Bankole, Anna Popinchalk, Bela Ganatra, Clémentine Rossier, Caitlin Gerdts, Özge Tunçalp, Brooke Ronald Johnson, Heidi Bart Johnston, Leontine Alkema, "Abortion Incidence Between 1990 and 2014: Global, Regional, and Subregional Levels and Trends," *The Lancet* 388, no. 10041 (2016): 258–267, 258, doi.org/10.1016/S0140-6736(16)30380-4.

[25] Sedgh, Bearak, Singh, Bankole, Popinchalk, Ganatra, Rossier, Gerdts, Tunçalp, Johnson, Johnston, Alkema, "Abortion Incidence between 1990 and 2014," 258; Bearak, Popinchalk, Ganatra, Moller, Tunçalp, Beavin, Kwok, Alkema, "Unintended Pregnancy and Abortion by Income, Region, and the Legal Status of Abortion," e1159.

that legal restrictions on abortion suppressed abortion rates. In countries where access to abortion is relatively unhindered, abortion rates were often lower than in countries where the legal status of abortion makes access more difficult.[26]

Over the 30-year timespan of Bearak's study, unintended pregnancy rates declined from 79 to 64 per 1,000 women (age 15–49).[27] Yet, alarmingly, despite this downward trend, almost half of all pregnancies are unintended and mostly they end in abortion. Equally concerning is the wide variation in unintended pregnancy rates between countries. What factors are driving these disparities? Unintended pregnancies occur for a variety of reasons; their causes are multifactorial. Behavioral determinants clearly play a role. However, the large differences in country-level rates of unintended pregnancy indicate that social context exerts a major influence on the incidence of unintended pregnancy. In the words of Bearak and colleagues, country-level differences in rates of unintended pregnancy suggest "inequality in the ability to determine whether and when to have children."[28] The underlying causes of these inequalities will be investigated by examining four social determinants of health: income level; access to contraception; gender inequality; and education.

---

[26] Sedgh, Bearak, Singh, Bankole, Popinchalk, Ganatra, Rossier, Gerdts, Tunçalp, Johnson, Johnston, Alkema, "Abortion Incidence between 1990 and 2014," 258; Bearak, Popinchalk, Ganatra, Moller, Tunçalp, Beavin, Kwok, Alkema, "Unintended Pregnancy and Abortion by Income, Region, and the Legal Status of Abortion," e1158–e1159.
[27] Bearak, Popinchalk, Ganatra, Moller, Tunçalp, Beavin, Kwok, Alkema, "Unintended Pregnancy and Abortion by Income, Region, and the Legal Status of Abortion," e1152–ße1161, e1155; Supplementary Appendix, 9.
[28] Bearak, Popinchalk, Beavin, Ganatra, Moller, Tunçalp, Alkema, "Country-Specific Estimates of Unintended Pregnancy and Abortion Incidence," 9.

Identifying Twenty-Five Sample Countries for Discussion Purposes

It is not possible to discuss these four social determinants in the abstract. It is necessary to draw on country-level data that relates to income level, contraceptive access, gender inequality and educational access. For illustrative purposes, twenty-five countries have been selected for discussion, offering a snapshot of how social determinants of health play out across a wide geographical range: Africa (Cabo Verde, Democratic Republic of the Congo, Equatorial Guinea, Lesotho, Nigeria); Asia (India, the Philippines, Timor-Leste); Oceania (Papua New Guinea); South America (Argentina, Brazil, Chile, Colombia, Peru, Bolivarian Republic of Venezuela); Central America and Antilles (Dominican Republic, Mexico); North America (United States); Europe (Croatia, France, Germany, Italy, Poland, Portugal, Spain). The countries range in size and relative wealth and, in terms of magnitude and/or proportion are home to large Catholic communities. Most are majority Catholic nations. Together, the selected countries account for 986 million (71 percent) of the global population of 1.4 billion baptised Catholics.[29] Table 1 ranks the twenty-five countries in terms of Catholic population size, indicating, for each nation, the proportion of the population that is Catholic.

---

[29] Vatican Secretariat of State, *Statistical Yearbook of the Church 2022* (Vatican City: Libreria Editrice Vaticana, 2024). Baptism data correct as of 31 December 2022.

Table 1: Number of baptised Catholics (thousands) and proportion of the population that is Catholic (%) for 25 countries, ranked by size of Catholic population[30]

Country	Number of baptised Catholics (thousands) 2022	Proportion of population that is Catholic (%) 2022
Brazil	180,965	84.2
Mexico	118,974	91.4
Philippines	92,851	83.2
United States	75,112	22.5
Italy	57,361	97.2
Democratic Republic of Congo	53,677	49.3
France	49,202	74.9
Colombia	48,374	93.6
Spain	44,229	93.3
Argentina	42,406	91.7
Poland	36,751	97.6
Nigeria	34,241	15.8
Peru	30,489	91.3
Venezuela	29,293	87.8
Germany	24,078	28.9
India	23,174	1.7
Chile	14,680	74.0
Dominican Republic	10,038	94.5
Portugal	9,098	87.9
Croatia	3,394	86.7
Papua New Guinea	2,522	30.6
Lesotho	1,486	63.2
Timor-Leste	1,439	96.0
Equatorial Guinea	1,165	74.8
Cabo Verde	627	94.2
WORLD	1,389,573	17.7

---

[30] Vatican Secretariat of State, *Statistical Yearbook of the Church 2022*.

Social Determinants of Unintended Pregnancy: Income Level

Income level—wealth or the lack thereof—is a major social determinant of health.[31] Prior to discussing the effects of national income levels on unintended pregnancy rates, it is necessary to consider the relative income levels of the twenty-five sample countries and how income is distributed among the members of each nation. The World Bank uses four income groupings to classify countries according to the size of their economies: high-income; upper-middle-income; lower-middle-income and low-income. The classification is based on a comparative measure of a country's Gross National Income (GNI) per capita, which corresponds to the total income received from home or abroad by residents and businesses divided by the number of residents.[32] Nine of the 25 countries are classed as high-income, seven are upper-middle-income, seven are lower-middle-income, one is low-income; Venezuela is unclassified.[33] The global average GNI per capita (2022) is estimated to be $17,254; Liechtenstein has the highest GNI per capita ($146,673), South Sudan the lowest ($691). Of the 25 sample nations, the US is richest ($65,565) and Democratic Republic (DR) of the Congo poorest ($1,080). The disparity in income levels reflects the acute economic inequality that exists between countries.[34]

To gain insights into inequalities that exist in the internal distribution of a nation's wealth, measures of income share are used. Increasing the

---

[31] See World Health Organization, "A Conceptual Framework," 30–31.
[32] Nada Hamadeh, Catherine van Rompaey and Eric Metreau, "World Bank Group Country Classifications by Income Level for FY24 (July 1, 2023–June 30, 2024)," *World Bank Data Blog*, June 30, 2023, blogs.worldbank.org/opendata/new-world-bank-group-country-classifications-income-level-fy24.
[33] World Bank, "World Bank Country and Lending Groups," 2023, datahelpdesk.worldbank.org/knowledgebase/articles/906519-world-bank-country-and-lending-groups.
[34] United Nations Development Programme, "Human Development Report 2023–24: Breaking the Gridlock: Reimagining Cooperation in a Polarized World," 2024, 274–277, hdr.undp.org/content/human-development-report-2023-24.

income share of the poorest 40 percent of the population is a Sustainable Development Goal target (SDG 10.1) relating to SDG 10: "Reduce inequality within and among countries," while lifting people out of poverty corresponds to SDG 1: "End poverty in all its forms everywhere."[35] In 11 of the 25 sample countries, the richest one percent of the population has a greater income share than the poorest 40 percent. In the Dominican Republic, Mexico, and Peru the richest one percent owns more than a quarter of the nation's wealth.[36] In sub-Saharan Africa, many suffer from extreme poverty. Almost one-in-three people in Lesotho and Nigeria and two-thirds of the population of DR Congo live below the international poverty line of $2.15 a day.[37] One-in-ten of the world's female population lives on less than $2.15 a day.[38] SDG target 8.5 aims, by 2030, to achieve equal pay for work of equal value for all women and men. In every country, women's average earnings are less than those of men, highlighting the gendered (i.e., stratified) character of economic inequality. The estimated average annual GNI per capita value is $12,516 for females and $22,035 for males.[39] These economic indicators draw attention to the income inequalities that exist at international and national level and the scale of global poverty. The unjust distribution of wealth within and between countries has a major impact on the relative health of population groups.

How does national income level affect unintended pregnancies? Bearak's team found "substantial differences" in unintended pregnancy

---

[35] See United Nations Department of Economic and Social Affairs, Statistics Division, "SDG Indicators Metadata Repository," unstats.un.org/sdgs/metadata/.

[36] United Nations Development Programme, "Human Development Report 2023–24," 283–287.

[37] United Nations Development Programme, "Human Development Report 2023–24," 298–300.

[38] UN Women and United Nations Department of Economic and Social Affairs, "Progress on the Sustainable Development Goals: The Gender Snapshot 2023," 2023, 8, www.unwomen.org/en/digital-library/publications/2023/09/progress-on-the-sustainable-development-goals-the-gender-snapshot-2023.

[39] United Nations Development Programme, "Human Development Report 2023–24," 288–292.

rates between high-income and low-income countries.[40] Low-income countries had the highest average annual rates of unintended pregnancy (93 per 1,000 women aged 15–49), compared to middle-income and high-income averages of 66 and 34 respectively, showing that economic factors play a significant role in unintended pregnancy rates and that the distribution of unintended pregnancies is stratified across income groups.[41] In general, women in low-income countries are the least able to avoid unwanted pregnancy and women in high-income countries the most able.[42] In the case of abortion, no simple relationship exists between national income levels and abortion rates. Abortion rates are generally highest in middle-income countries, with some of the highest incidences in Asia.[43]

Table 2 gives the World Bank income groupings and 2015–19 estimates for the average annual unintended pregnancy rate and the proportion of unintended pregnancies that end in abortion for women aged 15–49 in the twenty-five sample countries ranked by decreasing size of GNI per capita.[44] Spain has the lowest unintended pregnancy rate (20) and DR Congo the highest (117). The high-income economies of Europe and the US have appreciably lower rates of unintended pregnancy than the low-income and middle-income countries (LMICs) in the sample nations. For the proportion of unintended pregnancies that end in abortion, the picture is

---

[40] Bearak, Popinchalk, Ganatra, Moller, Tunçalp, Beavin, Kwok, Alkema, "Unintended Pregnancy and Abortion by Income, Region, and the Legal Status of Abortion," e1159.
[41] Bearak, Popinchalk, Ganatra, Moller, Tunçalp, Beavin, Kwok, Alkema, "Unintended Pregnancy and Abortion by Income, Region, and the Legal Status of Abortion," e1155–e1156.
[42] Bearak, Popinchalk, Ganatra, Moller, Tunçalp, Beavin, Kwok, Alkema, "Unintended Pregnancy and Abortion by Income, Region, and the Legal Status of Abortion," e1160.
[43] Bearak, Popinchalk, Ganatra, Moller, Tunçalp, Beavin, Kwok, Alkema, "Unintended Pregnancy and Abortion by Income, Region, and the Legal Status of Abortion," e1157; Bearak, Popinchalk, Beavin, Ganatra, Moller, Tunçalp, Alkema, "Country-specific Estimates of Unintended Pregnancy and Abortion Incidence," 7.
[44] Data in columns 1 to 3 are more recent than in columns 4 and 5. Caution is therefore required interpreting data. Columns 2 and 3 are illustrative of general trends in how income group and gender inequality relate to unintended pregnancy rates.

more complex and interpretation of the data more difficult. Values range from 24 percent in Lesotho to 77 percent in India (one of the highest in the world). Europe and the US record some of the lowest annual percentages, though Italy's proportion is much higher (67%), exceeding the global average (61%). There is no apparent association between rates of unintended pregnancy and the proportion of unintended pregnancies that end in abortion. Nor is there an obvious correspondence between income levels and the percentage of unintended pregnancies that end in abortion. Also noteworthy, there is no association between the proportion of unintended pregnancies that end in abortion and the proportion of baptized Catholics in the population.

Social Determinant of Unintended Pregnancy: Access to Contraception

Access to healthcare, including reproductive healthcare, is socially determined.[45] Access to contraception and family planning services depends upon many social factors that vary from country to country, such as laws and policy frameworks, costs, availability and supply, the nature of the provider (state, donor, private sector), prevailing moral and social attitudes (e.g., husband or family pressure, social stigma), ease of travel to sources of supply, and so forth.[46] Family planning services typically include provision of information, advice, and the wherewithal to correctly use what, in medical parlance, are described as modern or traditional methods of family planning. Modern methods include female and male sterilization, intra-uterine devices, implants, injectables, oral contraceptive

---

[45] See World Health Organization, "A conceptual framework for action on the social determinants of health," 39–40; Robert A. Hahn, "What is a social determinant of health?," 3.
[46] See Stephanie Ann Puen, "Considerations for a Comprehensive Sex Education Grounded in Catholic Social Thought for Reproductive Justice in the Philippines," 237–256, in this volume.

Structural Inequality and the Social Determinants of Unintended Pregnancy

Table 2: World Bank income grouping (2024), Gender Inequality Index ranking (2022), estimated annual unintended pregnancy rate (2015–19), and percentage of unintended pregnancies ending in abortion (2015–19) for 25 countries ranked by Gross National Income per capita (2022)

Country (ranked by Gross National Income per capita (2017 PPP $, 2022)[47]	World Bank country classification by income level (financial year 2023–2024)[48]	Gender Inequality Index rank 2022[49]	Average annual number of unintended pregnancies per 1,000 women (aged 15–49), 2015–2019[50]	Average annual proportion (%) of unintended pregnancies ending in abortion, 2015–2019[51]
United States	High	44	35	34
Germany	High	19	21	27
France	High	24	29	50
Italy	High	14	28	67
Spain	High	15	20	43
Portugal	High	21	21	32
Poland	High	31	29	37
Croatia	High	25	33	50
Chile	High	49	70	52
Argentina	Upper-middle	71	69	48
Mexico	Upper-middle	84	60	51
Dominican Republic	Upper-middle	107	84	44
Colombia	Upper-middle	95	63	43

[47] United Nations Development Programme, *Human Development Report 2023-24: Breaking the Gridlock: Reimagining Cooperation in a Polarized World* (New York: United Nations Publications, 2024), 274–277, hdr.undp.org/content/human-development-report-2023-24.
[48] World Bank, 'World Bank Country and Lending Groups', 2024, datahelpdesk.worldbank.org/knowledgebase/articles/906519-world-bank-country-and-lending-groups.
[49] United Nations Development Programme, *Human Development Report 2023–24*, 293–297
[50] Data extracted from Guttmacher Institute Data Center, "Pregnancies", data.guttmacher.org/countries.
[51] Data extracted from Guttmacher Institute Data Center, "Pregnancies."

Brazil	Upper-middle	94	67	48
Peru	Upper-middle	85	90	48
Equatorial Guinea	Upper-middle	..	..	..
Philippines	Lower-middle	92	71	51
Cabo Verde	Lower-middle	75	102	49
India	Lower-middle	108	62	77
Venezuela	Unclassified	134	..	..
Nigeria	Lower-middle	165	68	48
Papua New Guinea	Lower-middle	151	80	46
Lesotho	Lower-middle	141	99	24
Timor-Leste	Lower-middle	103	50	68
Democratic Republic of Congo	Low	152	117	28
World	n/a	n/a	64	61

pills, male and female condoms, vaginal barrier methods (including the diaphragm, cervical cap and spermicidal foam, jelly, cream and sponge), the lactational amenorrhea method, and emergency contraception. Traditional methods refer, chiefly, to withdrawal and rhythm (fertility awareness-based methods, periodic abstinence).[52]

There are 1.9 billion women of reproductive age, of whom 966 million use family planning to postpone or prevent pregnancy. The vast majority (874 million) use modern methods. A small minority (92 million) use

---

[52] United Nations Department of Economic and Social Affairs, Population Division, "World Family Planning 2022: Meeting the changing needs for family planning: Contraceptive use by age and method," 4 UN DESA/POP/2022/TR/NO. 4, 2022, desapublications.un.org/publications/world-family-planning-2022-meeting-changing-needs-family-planning-contraceptive-use. Terminology ("modern", "traditional", "contraceptive") can be misleading and/or divisive. Health scientists categorise rhythm as contraceptive. Barrier methods (classed as modern) have been used for millennia. Supposedly traditional fertility awareness-based methods were developed in the mid-twentieth century and often require use of modern equipment and/or technology.

traditional methods.⁵³ Female sterilization accounts for 219 million (22.9%) of the 966 million contraceptive users, making it the most commonly used form of contraception. Almost half of all sterilized women live in India.⁵⁴ Female sterilization is also prevalent in (Catholic majority) Puerto Rico, Mexico, El Salvador, Colombia, Dominican Republic, and Nicaragua.⁵⁵ The once-and-done permanency of sterilization and its minimal side-effects make it a popular choice among older women who have completed childbearing.⁵⁶ The low cost of sterilization also makes it an attractive option for poorer populations who might otherwise have to pay for a regular supply of contraceptives.⁵⁷ Once the mainstay of large-scale state-sponsored family planning programs, the preference now is for long-acting reversible methods.⁵⁸ The traditional methods of withdrawal and rhythm, that rely for their effectiveness on the willing cooperation of the male partner, are generally less popular and less reliable than most modern methods.⁵⁹ Take-up is low across all regions, accounting

---

[53] United Nations Department of Economic and Social Affairs, Population Division, "World Family Planning 2022," i, 34, 2022, desapublications.un.org/publications/world-family-planning-2022-meeting-changing-needs-family-planning-contraceptive-use.

[54] United Nations Department of Economic and Social Affairs, Population Division, "World Family Planning 2022," 18. See also Virginia Saldanha, "Religio-Cultural Underpinnings of Gender and Reproductive Injustice and Their Impact on Women's Agency in India," in this volume.

[55] United Nations Department of Economic and Social Affairs, Population Division, "World Contraceptive Use 2022," www.un.org/development/desa/pd/data/world-contraceptive-use.

[56] United Nations Department of Economic and Social Affairs, Population Division, "World Family Planning 2022," 18.

[57] Mieke C. W. Eeckhaut and Megan M. Sweeney, "The Perplexing Links Between Contraceptive Sterilization and (Dis)advantage in Ten Low-Fertility Countries," *Population Studies* 70, no. 1 (2016): 39–58, doi.org/10.1080/00324728.2015.1122209.

[58] The history of the practice of female (and male) sterilization is replete with examples of disregard for human rights and ethical norms, including compulsory sterilization of vulnerable populations on racist and eugenicist grounds. Coercion, lack of consent and non-disclosure of the permanency of the procedure remain widespread: United Nations Population Fund, "State of World Population 2022: Seeing the Unseen," 102–103.

[59] United Nations Population Fund, "State of World Population 2022: Seeing the Unseen," 58–59; Mohamed M. Ali, John G Cleland, Iqbal H Shah, World Health Organization,

Structural Inequality and the Social Determinants of Unintended Pregnancy

for less than 10 percent of contraceptive use. Withdrawal is used by 53 million couples worldwide (5.5% of users); 33 million use rhythm (3.5%).[60] Of our 25 countries, Peru (14%), Poland (12%), DR Congo (7.9%) and the Philippines (3.6%) register above average use of rhythm. Italy's prevalence rate for all traditional methods is 13.3 percent.[61] Globally, use of traditional methods is declining.[62]

The availability (and therefore use) of contraceptive methods varies from country to country. In some countries, modern methods are not widely available. In others, there are many available methods, providing greater choice and alternatives that women can switch to for reasons of health, convenience, etc. National family planning programmes or foreign donors sometimes promote one method over others, limiting women's choice of methods. Country-wide prevalence rates for each contraceptive method are tracked annually. Out of the 21 sample countries for which data is available, the pill is the most commonly used form of contraception in Argentina, Brazil, Cabo Verde, Chile, Equatorial Guinea, the Philippines, and Portugal. Female sterilization is preferred in Colombia, Dominican Republic, India, Mexico, and the US. Injectables are the most popular method in Lesotho, Papua New Guinea, Peru, and Timor-Leste. The male condom is the most prevalent method in Italy, Poland, and Spain. Implants are the most used method in Nigeria. In DR Congo, rhythm is the most widely used form of family planning.[63]

"Causes and consequences of contraceptive discontinuation: evidence from 60 demographic and health surveys," 2012, iris.who.int/handle/10665/75429.

[60] United Nations Department of Economic and Social Affairs, Population Division, "World Family Planning 2022," 17–18.

[61] United Nations Department of Economic and Social Affairs, Population Division, "World Contraceptive Use 2022."

[62] United Nations Department of Economic and Social Affairs, Population Division, "World Family Planning 2022," 21.

[63] United Nations Department of Economic and Social Affairs, Population Division, "World Contraceptive Use 2022." Recent data unavailable for Croatia, France, Germany, Venezuela.

Universal access to sexual and reproductive healthcare by 2030 is a specific SDG target (3.7).[64] Currently, however, 164 million (8%) of the 1.9 billion women of reproductive age have an unmet need for family planning.[65] Unmet need is defined as the percentage of married or in-union women of reproductive age (15–49 years) "who are fecund and sexually active, who wish to stop or delay childbearing, but who are not using any form of contraception."[66] Regionally, Oceania (excluding Australia and New Zealand) and sub-Saharan Africa have the highest unmet need and the lowest use of modern methods of family planning.[67] 12 of our sample countries record an unmet need for contraception: Peru (6%); Colombia (7%); US (7%); Mexico (11%); Argentina (13%); Dominican Republic (15%); Lesotho (16%); Philippines (17%); Nigeria (19%); Timor-Leste (25%); Papua New Guinea (26%); DR Congo (29%).[68] The six poorest nations have the highest unmet need and some of the highest unintended pregnancy rates out of the 12 countries.

Demand for family planning varies by country. In high fertility countries, where there is a preference for large families or where couples are open to children whenever they arrive (e.g., Chad, Niger, Burkina Faso), the unintended pregnancy risk and demand for family planning is low. In low-fertility countries, where there is a preference for smaller families, couples must avoid pregnancy for extended periods if they are to achieve their desired family size. In these countries, demand for family

---

[64] United Nations Department of Economic and Social Affairs, Statistics Division, "SDG Indicators Metadata Repository."
[65] United Nations Department of Economic and Social Affairs, Population Division, "World Family Planning 2022," 4.
[66] United Nations Department of Economic and Social Affairs, Population Division, "World Family Planning 2022," 4.
[67] United Nations Department of Economic and Social Affairs, Population Division, "World Family Planning 2022," 6.
[68] United Nations Department of Economic and Social Affairs, Population Division, "World Contraceptive Use 2022."

planning is high because the risk of an unintended pregnancy is high.⁶⁹ In recent decades, across all continents, the desire for smaller families has grown, as reflected in falling birthrates.⁷⁰ Additionally, increasing numbers of women are delaying childbearing to pursue education and careers.⁷¹ As a consequence, increasing numbers of women are at risk of unintended pregnancy, leading to an increased demand for family planning. Despite the push-factors expected to increase rates of unintended pregnancy, Bearak's team found that over the last three decades rates declined, showing that the increased demand for contraception was in large part satisfied: "More people than ever, as a proportion of the population who are at reproductive age, were able to limit or space their childbearing."⁷² That is to say, unintended pregnancy rates declined because access to contraception increased.⁷³

Bearak's study also found an inverse relationship between national income levels and rates of unintended pregnancy. This income-dependent gradient in unintended pregnancy rates suggests that unmet need is not distributed equally across those population groups with a demand for contraception: the burden is disproportionately located in low-income, and to a lesser degree in middle-income, countries. The wider availability of contraceptives in high-income countries (greater met need) contributes

---

⁶⁹ See John Bongaarts and John B. Casterline, "From Fertility Preferences to Reproductive Outcomes in the Developing World," *Population and Development Review* 44, no. 4 (2018): 793–809, doi.org/10.1111/padr.12197.

⁷⁰ See GBD 2021 Fertility and Forecasting Collaborators, "Global Fertility in 204 Countries and Territories, 1950–2021, with Forecasts to 2100: A Comprehensive Demographic Analysis for the Global Burden of Disease Study 2021," *The Lancet*, March 20, 2024, doi.org/10.1016/S0140-6736(24)00550-6.

⁷¹ Global Burden of Disease 2017 Population and Fertility Collaborators, "Population and Fertility by Age and Sex for 195 Countries and Territories, 1950–2017: A Systematic Analysis for the Global Burden of Disease Study 2017," *The Lancet* 392 (2018), 1995–2051, 2007, doi.org/10.1016/S0140-6736(18)32278-5.

⁷² Bearak, Popinchalk, Ganatra, Moller, Tunçalp, Beavin, Kwok, Alkema, "Unintended Pregnancy and Abortion by Income, Region, and the Legal Status of Abortion," e1159.

⁷³ Bearak, Popinchalk, Ganatra, Moller, Tunçalp, Beavin, Kwok, Alkema, "Unintended Pregnancy and Abortion by Income, Region, and the Legal Status of Abortion," e1152.

to the lower rates of unintended pregnancy compared to LMICs, where greater barriers exist to accessing contraceptive services. Economic inequality between countries creates inequality in access to contraception, leading to the national income-related gulf in unintended pregnancy rates. On the link between economic and health inequity, Bearak and others comment: "Our findings suggest that people in high-income countries have better access to sexual and reproductive health care than those in low-income countries . . . . These findings emphasise the importance of ensuring access to the full spectrum of sexual and reproductive health services, including contraception and abortion care, and for additional investment towards equity in health-care services."[74] Universal access to sexual and reproductive health services would reduce the high rates of unintended pregnancy and help address income-related health inequity.

Social Determinant of Unintended Pregnancy: Gender Inequality

Gender inequality is one of the most ubiquitous and enduring of all social injustices, present from womb to tomb, in every nation, throughout every stratum of human existence. It is baked into the structure of all societies; part of the social stratification process that positions people on account of their relative power and assumed value and worth. The interstitial social nature of gender inequality and its systematic expression in forms of gender discrimination is taken up by the CSDH in its discussion of the linkages between gender inequity and health inequity. "Gender," it states, "constitutes a fundamental basis for discrimination." The CSDH refers to the existence of "gender-based social hierarchies" as a consequence of which, "girls and women suffer systematic discrimination in access to power, prestige and resources."[75]

---

[74] Bearak, Popinchalk, Ganatra, Moller, Tunçalp, Beavin, Kwok, Alkema, "Unintended Pregnancy and Abortion by Income, Region, and the Legal Status of Abortion," e1152.
[75] World Health Organization, "A Conceptual Framework," 33.

Structural Inequality and the Social Determinants of Unintended Pregnancy

According to UNESCO, "Gender inequality is strongly correlated with early and unintended pregnancy."[76] Research undertaken for the United Nations Population Fund (UNFPA) using Bearak and colleagues' dataset confirms the positive association between country-level gender inequality and unintended pregnancy: irrespective of income level, countries with higher levels of gender inequality have higher rates of unintended pregnancy.[77] The Gender Inequality Index (GII) is used to investigate the relationship between country-level gender inequality and rates of unintended pregnancy. The GII is a composite indicator used to assign a numerical value to each nation based on its performance against key health and development indicators that, taken together, reflect the degree of gender inequality in society. The GII takes into account a country's achievement in the areas of reproductive health (maternal mortality ratio, adolescent birth rate), female empowerment (percentage of parliamentary seats held by women, percentage of population with at least some secondary education by gender), and the labour market (participation in the labour force by gender).[78] A high GII value corresponds to a high level of gender inequality. The relative performance of each country is reflected in its GII rank. Denmark tops the country rankings as most gender equitable nation; Yemen (ranked 166) is the most gender unequal country. Table 2 displays the 2022 GII rank for the 25 sample countries, showing that LMICs tend to have greater gender inequality than high-income countries. Given the different dates of data collection, the GII rankings cannot be compared directly with unintended pregnancy rates for 2015–19. However, the general trend is clear: more gender equitable nations tend to have lower unintended pregnancy rates.

---

[76] United Nations Educational, Scientific and Cultural Organization, "Early and Unintended Pregnancy and the Education Sector: Evidence Review and Recommendations," 14, 2017, unesdoc.unesco.org/ark:/48223/pf0000251509.

[77] United Nations Population Fund, "State of World Population 2022: Seeing the Unseen," 23.

[78] United Nations Development Programme, "Human Development Report 2023–24," 272.

Recognizing that gender equality is a *sine qua non* for human health and development, SDG 5 ("achieve gender equality and empower all women and girls") has targets and indicators that address a range of social contexts where inequality thrives and that measure progress towards gender equity.[79] Many of these are important for tackling the high incidence of unintended pregnancy. SDG 5.6, for instance, concerns female agency with respect to decision-making about sex and reproduction. Women and girls often lack decision-making power over matters of sex and pregnancy, which can lead to unwanted pregnancies. This can be the case when, for instance, male partners disagree about the frequency of intercourse or the number and spacing of children, and females are expected to accede to the wishes of the male. In sexual matters, girls often have less agency than older females. According to Sarah Bott, "Numerous studies have found an association between forced sexual debut, lack of contraception/condom use, and unintended pregnancy."[80] Diminished agency and duress can arise in any situation of dependency, such as when male gatekeepers control access to vital resources. As a consequence, forced sex and coercion are commonplace. Partners and families may pressure women to abort for social reasons,[81] or to conceive, for instance, to prove fertility prior to marriage,[82] or to obtain a male-child, or to gain the status that a large family confers.[83] Globally, the proportion of women aged 15 to 49 years who make their own informed decisions regarding sexual relations, contraceptive use, and reproductive health care (SDG 5.6.1) is

---

[79] See United Nations Department of Economic and Social Affairs, Statistics Division, "SDG Indicators Metadata Repository."
[80] Sarah Bott, "Sexual Violence and Coercion: Implications for Sexual and Reproductive Health," in *Social Determinants of Sexual and Reproductive Health: Informing Future Research and Programme Implementation*, ed. Shawn Malarcher (Geneva, Switzerland: World Health Organization, 2010), 133–157, 141, www.who.int/publications/i/item/9789241599528.
[81] United Nations Population Fund, "State of World Population 2022: Seeing the Unseen," 46–47, 113.
[82] Sarah Castle and Ian Askew, Contraceptive Discontinuation: Reasons, Challenges, and Solutions (New York: Population Council and FP2020, 2015), 10.
[83] United Nations Population Fund, "State of World Population 2022: Seeing the Unseen," 84.

Structural Inequality and the Social Determinants of Unintended Pregnancy

56 percent. It is estimated that one-in-four women of reproductive age are unable to say no to sex.[84] When women and girls experience diminished sexual and reproductive health decision-making capacity, the risk of unintended pregnancy increases.[85]

Psychological, physical, and sexual violence against women and girls is a scourge affecting every nation (SDG 5.2). Usually inflicted by a current or former husband or male intimate partner, it often goes unchallenged, facilitated by a long-standing culture of social acceptance and inadequate legal protections. The link between intimate-partner violence and unintended pregnancy is drawn out by Sarah Bott: "Evidence suggests that women who live in situations of intimate-partner violence often experience forced sex and are generally less able to negotiate protected sex, leading to higher rates of unintended pregnancies."[86] Globally, the lifetime prevalence of intimate-partner violence (IVP) for ever-married or partnered females age 15–49 is 27 percent, affecting 641 million women and girls. Least developed countries have the highest prevalence, where as many as one-in-two females are victims of IVP. The global prevalence of non-partner sexual violence, perpetrated by friends, relatives, and others, is 6 percent.[87]

Child marriage is almost always a product of gender inequality. Although the practice of child marriage is declining, in many countries it

---

[84] United Nations Department of Economic and Social Affairs, Statistics Division, "Global SDG Indicators Database," 2023, unstats.un.org/sdgs/dataportal/analytics/GlobalRegionalTrends.

[85] See Bright Opoku Ahinkorah, Abdul-Aziz Seidu, Francis Appiah, Linus Baatiema, Francis Sambah, Eugene Budu, Edward Kwabena Ameyaw, "What has reproductive health decision-making capacity got to do with unintended pregnancy? Evidence from the 2014 Ghana Demographic and Health Survey," *PLoS ONE* 14, no. 10 (2019): 1–16 doi.org/10.1371/journal.pone.0223389.

[86] Sarah Bott, "Sexual Violence and Coercion," 141.

[87] World Health Organization, "Violence Against Women Prevalence Estimates, 2018: Global, Regional and National Prevalence Estimates for Intimate Partner Violence Against Women and Global and Regional Prevalence Estimates for Non-partner Sexual Violence Against Women," 2021, viii–xv, www.who.int/publications/i/item/9789240022256.

remains legal or is tolerated.⁸⁸ Globally, 19 percent of females are married or in a cohabiting union before age 18 (SDG indicator 5.3.1).⁸⁹ Child marriage is a problem in the LMIC sample countries, despite laws that prohibit it. In Nigeria, 43 percent of married women are child brides. One-in-three (217 million) of all child marriages occur in India.⁹⁰ UNFPA reports that married girls often experience numerous disadvantages that compound their vulnerability: "Women and girls married as adolescents tend to have less education, less household and economic power and less mobility than unmarried adolescents and older women. They tend to be isolated and lack the knowledge and skills to negotiate situations that are detrimental to their health and well-being—including how many children to have and when."⁹¹ Where child marriage is prevalent, so too is adolescent childbearing (SDG 3.7.2), which carries a greater risk of pregnancy and childbirth complications than in older women.⁹² Most adolescent mothers are married or in a union and they tend to have larger families than women who commence childbearing at older ages.⁹³ Globally, 14 percent of

---

⁸⁸ For the legal status of child marriage across the globe, see Megan Arthur, Alison Earle, Amy Raub, Ilona Vincent, Efe Atabay, Isabel Latz, Gabriella Kranz, Arijit Nandi, Jody Heymann, "Child Marriage Laws around the World: Minimum Marriage Age, Legal Exceptions, and Gender Disparities," *Journal of Women, Politics & Policy* 39, no. 1 (2018): 51–74, doi.org/10.1080/1554477X.2017.1375786; Girls Not Brides, "Child Marriage Atlas," www.girlsnotbrides.org/learning-resources/child-marriage-atlas/.

⁸⁹ United Nations Children's Fund, *The State of the World's Children 2023: For every child, vaccination* (Florence, Italy: UNICEF Innocenti – Global Office of Research and Foresight, 2023), 182, www.unicef.org/media/108161/file/SOWC-2023-full-report-English.pdf.

⁹⁰ United Nations Children's Fund, "Is an End to Child Marriage within Reach?: Latest Trends and Future Prospects," May 5, 2023, data.unicef.org/resources/is-an-end-to-child-marriage-within-reach/?_gl=1*12d8k09*_ga*MTM2NjM0NTY2LjE3MDIyNzk2Njk.*_ga_ZEPV2PX419*MTcwNTI0MzI0Mi4xLjAuMTcwNTI0MzI0Mi42MC4wLjA.

⁹¹ United Nations Population Fund, "State of World Population 2022: Seeing the Unseen," 32.

⁹² World Health Organization, "Adolescent Pregnancy," 2 June 2023, www.who.int/news-room/fact-sheets/detail/adolescent-pregnancy; UNICEF, "Child Marriage," July 2023, www.unicef.org/protection/child-marriage.

⁹³ United Nations Population Fund, "State of World Population 2022: Seeing the Unseen," 30–31.

mothers give birth before age 18,[94] with sub-Saharan Africa recording the highest rates of adolescent fertility.[95] In four of the 25 sample countries one-in-four girls become mothers before their 18th birthday (DR Congo, Equatorial Guinea, Nigeria, Venezuela). Equatorial Guinea has one of the highest prevalence rates in the world for early childbearing (42%).[96] These depressing statistics speak to the second-class status, limited autonomy, and compromised negotiating power of women and girls, compared to males. Too often, females are subject to discriminatory cultural norms that privilege males and circumscribe female choice in matters of sex and reproduction. Intersecting sources and structures of inequality and injustice frequently combine to undermine human dignity, increase vulnerability and disempower large sectors of the female population.

The Demographic and Health Surveys (DHS) program gathers data from LMICs on key development indicators, including those relating to female empowerment. In the familial and interpersonal realm, these include female age at first marriage and sex, the ability to refuse or negotiate about sex and condom use, female attitudes towards wife beating, the extent to which women can choose their spouse, participate in household decisions, control household resources, and manage their own affairs. Sociocultural indicators include male and female rates of educational attainment and mobile phone ownership. Economic indicators include income disparity, property and land ownership, and access to paid work and credit.[97] Esso-Hanam Atake and Pitaloumani Gnakou Ali's research in Francophone Sub-Saharan Africa found that in each of these realms—familial/interpersonal, sociocultural, and economic—female empowerment is associated with lower fertility and lower incidence of unintended

---

[94] United Nations Children's Fund, *The State of the World's Children 2023*, 152.
[95] United Nations Population Fund, "State of World Population 2022: Seeing the Unseen," 142.
[96] United Nations Children's Fund, *The State of the World's Children 2023*, 148–152.
[97] Trevor N. Croft, Courtney K. Allen, Blake W. Zachary, *Guide to DHS Statistics* (Rockville, Maryland: ICF, 2023), 15.1–15.29, www.dhsprogram.com/publications/publication-dhsg1-dhs-questionnaires-and-manuals.cfm.

pregnancy. Of these, economic empowerment is the most important. Independent income improves women's social status. It frees them from their financial dependency on men and equalizes power relations with males. Greater purchasing power allows finances to be directed to control of fertility. Gainful employment also incentivises the avoidance of unintended pregnancy.[98] Economic empowerment buys power (autonomy, influence, control), prestige (mutual respect, social status), and resources (including access to healthcare).

Social Determinants of Unintended Pregnancy: Education (Access and Attainment)

As social determinants, educational access and attainment play beneficial roles in health.[99] Various studies point to the reproductive health benefits conferred on females through educational access and attainment, including greater knowledge and control over fertility and lower unintended pregnancy rates.[100] Educational access is beneficial even when school functions as no more than a safer social environment than out-of-school alternatives. Chung and others' study of adolescent pregnancy in LMICs reports that "a higher level of educational attainment or more

---

[98] Esso-Hanam Atake and Pitaloumani Gnakou Ali, "Women's Empowerment and Fertility Preferences in High Fertility Countries in Sub-Saharan Africa," *BMC Women's Health* 19, no. 54 (2019): 1–14. doi.org/10.1186/s12905-019-0747-9. See Edward Kwabena Ameyaw, Eugene Budu, Francis Sambah, Linus Baatiema, Francis Appiah, Abdul-Aziz Seidu, Bright Opoku Ahinkorah, "Prevalence and Determinants of Unintended Pregnancy in Sub-Saharan Africa: A Multi-Country Analysis of Demographic and Health Surveys," *PLoS ONE* 14, no. 8 (2019): doi.org/10.1371/journal.pone.0220970; Andrew Amos Channon, Jane Falkingham, Zoë Matthews, "Sexual and Reproductive Health and Poverty," in *Social Determinants of Sexual and Reproductive Health: Informing Future Research and Programme Implementation*, ed. Shawn Malarcher (Geneva, Switzerland: World Health Organization, 2010), 73–91, 81, www.who.int/publications/i/item/9789241599528.
[99] See World Health Organization, "A Conceptual Framework," 31–32.
[100] See United Nations Population Fund, "State of World Population 2022: Seeing the Unseen," 43.

schooling is a protective factor against [adolescent] pregnancy. Adolescents who have no formal education or lower level of education, or who are not enrolled in school have a higher likelihood of being pregnant. Long-term school absences, temporary dropout of school, and school failure are also risk factors for pregnancy."[101] Cynthia Lloyd's research on schooling in developing countries also shows the protective effect of education for schoolgirls compared to out-of-school girls who are more exposed to premarital sex, early pregnancy, and child marriage.[102] Lloyd refers to a Kenyan study which found that "the most effective intervention in reducing teen marriage and childbearing was a programme to subsidize the cost of schools through the provision of school uniforms for girls in grades 6–8, thus encouraging school attendance during the teen years and reducing incentives for early dropout and childbearing."[103] Lloyd concludes, "Improved academic performance is associated with delayed sexual initiation and a reduced likelihood of pregnancy."[104] Many factors including poverty, conflict, child marriage, child labour, and gender norms keep girls out of school.[105] Data on out-of-school rates is tracked as part of SDG 4 (universal access to education). Globally, at upper secondary school

---

[101] Hye Won Chung, Eun Mee Kim and Ji-Eun Lee, "Comprehensive Understanding of Risk and Protective Factors Related to Adolescent Pregnancy in Low- and Middle-Income Countries: A Systematic Review," *Journal of Adolescence* 69, no. 1 (2018): 180–188, 184, doi.org/10.1016/j.adolescence.2018.10.007.

[102] Cynthia B. Lloyd, "The Role of Schools in Promoting Sexual and Reproductive Health Among Adolescents in Developing Countries," in *Social Determinants of Sexual and Reproductive Health: Informing Future Research and Programme Implementation*, ed. Shawn Malarcher (Geneva, Switzerland: World Health Organization, 2010), 113–131, www.who.int/publications/i/item/9789241599528.

[103] Cynthia B. Lloyd, "The Role of Schools in Promoting Sexual and Reproductive Health," 128.

[104] Cynthia B. Lloyd, "The Role of Schools in Promoting Sexual and Reproductive Health," 128.

[105] See Andrew Amos Channon, Jane Falkingham, Zoë Matthews, "Sexual and Reproductive Health and Poverty," 84–85.

level, one-in-three girls are out of school; huge disparities exist between nations, ranging from 0% (Singapore; Netherlands) to 89% (Niger).[106]

How does the education of males influence unintended pregnancy rates? Fantu Mamo Aragaw and others' study of the determinants of unintended pregnancy in 61 LMICs found that women whose husbands had no education or education to primary level were more likely to have an unintended pregnancy than women whose husbands had secondary or higher education. In fact, the husband's educational attainment was a better predictor of unintended pregnancy than that of the wife.[107] This finding points to male dominance in sexual and reproductive decision-making: "Partners who have no formal education or a lower level of education are less likely to encourage their wives to use modern contraceptives and a woman's pregnancy intentions and parenting decisions are influenced by her partner's attitude.... [T]he male partner has a strong influence on most household decisions, including the timing of pregnancy and the number of children desired."[108] UNFPA's study of the relative contribution of female and male educational attainment on unintended pregnancy rates found that the rates were correlated with the overall country-wide level of educational attainment for both sexes, rather than with female educational attainment alone.[109]

Comparing national data on mean years of schooling (SDG 4.4) shows how educational opportunity varies worldwide and how females in LMICs suffer educational disadvantage compared to females in high-income nations. The value for mean years of schooling for girls ranges from 1.3 (Niger) to 14.3 (Germany); the global average is 8.7 completed years of

---

[106] United Nations Children's Fund, *The State of the World's Children 2023*, 174–178.

[107] Fantu Mamo Aragaw, Tsegaw Amare, Rediet Eristu Teklu, Biresaw Ayen Tegegne, Adugnaw Zeleke Alem, "Magnitude of Unintended Pregnancy and Its Determinants Among Childbearing Age Women in Low and Middle-income Countries: Evidence from 61 Low and Middle Income Countries," *Frontiers in Reproductive Health* 5 (2023): 1–10, doi.org/10.3389/frph.2023.1113926.

[108] Fantu Mamo Aragaw, Tsegaw Amare, Rediet Eristu Teklu, Biresaw Ayen Tegegne, Adugnaw Zeleke Alem, "Magnitude of Unintended Pregnancy," 5–6.

[109] United Nations Population Fund, "State of World Population 2022: Seeing the Unseen," 23.

education.[110] Educational inequity intersects with income inequity and gender inequity, creating a perfect storm of disadvantage for women and girls in poorer parts of the world, with negative consequences for health, including higher incidences of unintended pregnancy (health inequity). At the same time, access to quality education is not only educationally beneficial; its benefits extend to the intersecting areas of life that might otherwise hold back females, lifting them out of income-related, gender-related, and health-related disadvantage. The large international research team that comprises the Global Burden of Disease (GBD) 2021 Fertility and Forecasting Collaborators detail some of these extensive benefits: "Quality education increases the knowledge, skills, and self-confidence needed to challenge traditional gender roles, and equips women to make more informed decisions about their health, careers, and lives as a whole. It also improves women's decision-making power in the household and lowers their risk of exposure to abuse in the home. Furthermore, higher female educational attainment is associated with higher paid labour-force participation and higher wages."[111] In short, education is empowering.

Conclusion

Females in low-income and middle-income countries have more unintended pregnancies and abortions than do females in high-income countries. These disparities are caused by interlocking and compounding structural inequalities, which cement injustice into the *status quo*. Gender equity and redistribution of social power and resources would contribute greatly to reducing the inexcusably high rates of unintended pregnancy among some of the world's most disadvantaged and vulnerable women

---

[110] United Nations Development Programme, "Human Development Report 2023–24," 274–278.
[111] GBD 2021 Fertility and Forecasting Collaborators, "Global Fertility in 204 Countries and Territories, 1950–2021," 33. Cf. Kien Le and My Nguyen, "How Education Empowers Women in Developing Countries," *The B.E. Journal of Economic Analysis & Policy* 21, no. 2 (2021): 511–536, doi.org/10.1515/bejeap-2020-0046.

and girls. This requires a change process in which female empowerment is an essential component. Female empowerment not only challenges the power inequity and socioeconomic stratification that positions females at a disadvantage to males but it also reduces a range of inequity-generated vulnerabilities, including vulnerability to unintended pregnancy. In the words of WHO: "Health equity depends vitally on the empowerment of individuals to challenge and change the unfair and steeply graded distribution of social resources to which everyone has equal claims and rights."[112]

Julie Clague, MTh, is lecturer in Catholic theology at the University of Glasgow (UK). She edits the European writers' forum of Catholic Theological Ethics in the World Church and serves on various editorial boards for journals, including *Ecclesial Practices: Journal of Ecclesiology and Ethnography*, *Theology in Scotland*, and *Acta Universitatis Carolinae Theologica*, and for the book series Studien der Moraltheologie (Aschendorff) and Ecclesiological Investigations (Bloomsbury). She was editor of the journals *Political Theology* and *Feminist Theology* for over a decade. She co-edited *Moral Theology for the Twenty-First Century* (Bloomsbury 2008). Julie is a Director of the Joint Learning Initiative on Faiths and Local Communities.

---

[112] WHO, "Social Determinants of Health: Key Concepts."

Chapter 3: Never Just a Choice: Three Theoretical Approaches to Economic Constraints on Family Formation

Kate Ward

This article attempts to understand how economic realities influence decisions around forming and raising a family for US people, whether poor or well-off.[1] By forming a family, I mean the decision to have children and decisions around how many children one has, as well as commitment to a partner. Critical realist social theory, reproductive justice, and the Catholic documentary tradition on families all assist in understanding these realities and articulating solutions to the challenges they pose. Part of this essay's work will be to reveal a surprising amount of common ground among the three approaches. Still, none of the three, in my view, thoroughly succeeds at describing pursuit of the human good of family formation by persons who are themselves socially constituted, as are the options from which they choose. The fact that each of these theoretical approaches recommends similar political responses to family formation serves to highlight critical distinctions between the affordances and drawbacks of each approach. In addition, reading these traditions in concert allows us to see and critique a discrepancy between the ways Catholic tradition understands economic

---

[1] I am grateful to the CTEWC Reproductive Justice and the Common Good Virtual Table and the other contributors to this volume for helping shape my thoughts on reproductive justice and Catholic thought and specifically for their invaluable feedback on this essay. I also thank the Women Shaping Theology discussion group, particularly Jessica Coblentz and Elyse Raby, for supportive and helpful feedback, and Leah Wakefield for research assistance. This research was supported by a fellowship grant from Marquette's Institute for Women's Leadership. I am grateful to the IWL leadership and affiliates for the supportive community they provide in service of the flourishing of women scholars.

constraints on family formation and the way present US church leadership responds to them.

The critical realist tradition describes the complexities of family and reproductive decision-making amid economic constraint better than the Catholic tradition, with its less precise but equally communal understanding of personal agency, or reproductive justice, which defaults to an individualist framework when it speaks in terms of rights. However, the descriptive critical realist tradition cannot offer a normative moral vision, while reproductive justice and Catholic thought find surprising common ground on their own—both describing family formation as a positive good and encouraging society to support a greater range of genuinely attainable options. Each tradition, in turn, critiques the others in the service of the shared goal of articulating family formation as a positive good and calling for society to meaningfully support it. Catholic thought, with those other two traditions, understands family formation decisions, like all other personal actions, as taking place within a social context which shapes the environment of human action. However, the public rhetoric of US church leaders shrinks that communal understanding of the person to individual agency, prescribing personal dispositions like "openness to life" and advocating vociferously for laws that restrict individual choices like abortion and birth control. By so doing, the public witness of the US church fails to be a prophetic witness in the context of the dominant US culture, unfortunately ascribing to that culture's individualistic understanding of family formation decisions.

Economic Realities

The dominant US culture tends to understand family formation as a matter of individual agency, envisioning parents "choosing" whether and how many children to have. This consumerist framing is evidenced in the rhetoric of "choice" surrounding reproductive decisions and the widespread understanding that at higher income levels, families with more children function as status symbols for their parents.[2] As dominant US culture highly prizes individuality and remains uncomfortable with morally normative claims, viewing family formation as a "choice" may be the best it can do in terms of expressing that families are a good in human life (since if it is a choice, at least some people must consider it choice-worthy.) However, this insipid popular rhetoric obscures the fact that concrete economic realities in the US constrain people's freedom to found their families, to have as many children as they hope to, and to exercise their right to bodily integrity by avoiding pregnancy. While people in poverty face the starkest constraints, even fairly well-off people find their choices around family size and pregnancy restricted by economic realities.

Sadly, poverty is not an aberrant experience for US families. The most recent relevant Census report showed 24.1 percent of single parent families living in poverty. The data for this report came from 2017, a year otherwise notable for record stock market highs and low unemployment. Significantly, 18.4 percent of these single parents raising families below the poverty line were employed full time.[3] It is often suggested that the reason families are in poverty is that parents are not working; allegedly, encouraging them to work, or making more job opportunities available, will solve the problem. Over two million single parents, working full time and still raising their

---

[2] For a critique of "choice" language from Dorothy Roberts, a legal scholar within the reproductive justice framework, see "Reproductive Justice, Not Just Rights," *Dissent Magazine*, Fall 2015, www.dissentmagazine.org/article/reproductive-justice-not-just-rights. See also Dorothy Roberts, *Killing the Black Body: Race, Reproduction, and the Meaning of Liberty, Twentieth Anniversary Edition* (New York: Vintage Books, 1997), 6–7. Regarding larger families as status symbols for the wealthy, see Ronald Bailey, "Kids as Status Symbols," *Slate*, June 28, 1997, slate.com/news-and-politics/1997/06/kids-as-status-symbols.html; and Emily Hales, "This Used to Be a Sign of Poverty; Now It's a Status Symbol," *Deseret News*, July 9, 2014, www.deseret.com/2014/7/9/20544454/this-used-to-be-a-sign-of-poverty-now-it-s-a-status-symbol.

[3] Timothy Grall, "Custodial Mothers and Fathers and Their Child Support: 2017," US Census Bureau, 2020, 5, www.census.gov/content/dam/Census/library/publications/2020/demo/p60-269.pdf.

children in poverty, testify that it is not so simple.[4] The US could easily reduce or eliminate poverty for children and their families with redistribution programs, but only occasionally summons the political will to institute programs that effectively do so. An expanded child tax credit intended to support families through the economic shock of the Covid-19 pandemic drove child poverty to a record low in 2021, but the program was ended after just one year.[5]

While not all families are founded by married partners, it is worth noting that a growing "marriage gap" in the US describes the reality that those with college degrees are significantly more likely to marry and less likely to divorce than those with less education.[6] It has been alleged that poor people marry less because they value marriage less; perhaps they have a different culture than those who are better off. Sociologists disagree. In fact, poor women value marriage a great deal. Unfortunately, they struggle to find partners who meet their completely reasonable standards. Sociologists Kathryn Edin and Maria Kefalas found that the widely known lower rates of marriage among women in poverty are not evidence that poor women do not value marriage. Rather, they do, but in general the partnerships they find available to them do not live up to their standards

---

[4] Grall's report identifies 12.9 million single parent families. By my calculations, that means at least 2,373,600 families are living in poverty while working full-time.

[5] Kalee Burns, Liana Fox, and Danielle Wilson, "Expansions to Child Tax Credit Contributed to 46% Decline in Child Poverty Since 2020," Census.gov, September 13, 2022, www.census.gov/library/stories/2022/09/record-drop-in-child-poverty.html; Ben Casselman, "Child Tax Credit's Extra Help Ends, Just as Covid Surges Anew," *New York Times*, January 2, 2022, www.nytimes.com/2022/01/02/business/economy/child-tax-credit.html; Jason DeParle, "The Expanded Child Tax Credit Is Gone. The Battle Over It Remains," *The New York Times*, November 25, 2022, www.nytimes.com/2022/11/25/us/politics/child-tax-credit.html.

[6] Victor Tan Chen, "America, Home of the Transactional Marriage," *The Atlantic*, August 20, 2017, www.theatlantic.com/business/archive/2017/08/marriage-rates-education/536913/; The related phenomenon of "assortative mating," marrying those with similar education and income, contributes significantly to economic inequality. Jeremy Greenwood et al., "Marry Your Like: Assortative Mating and Income Inequality," National Bureau of Economic Research, January 2014, www.nber.org/papers/w19829.

for marriage: trust, freedom from abuse, responsibility, and maturity and financial stability on the part of both partners.[7]

While shaky economic prospects hinder marriage, they can incentivize the pursuit of successive short-term partnerships out of financial necessity. Economists Anne Case and Angus Deaton observe that "repeated re-partnering in the US is often driven by the need for an additional income, something that is less true in Europe with its more extensive safety net."[8] Contrary to claims that marriage can be a magic solution for poverty, one in four US families consisting of married parents with children qualifies as low income, living on less than thirty-eight thousand dollars per year for a family of four.[9]

Economic constraints profoundly affect when, if ever, US people will feel ready to become parents and how many children they will end up having.[10] Many US people experience the postpartum period as a time of increased economic desperation, due to the fact that only 13 percent of workers have access to paid leave, and many fear career consequences if they actually use it.[11] The Family and Medical Leave Act (FMLA) guarantees unpaid leave, which does precious little good when families depend on that parent's paycheck. This helps explain why nearly a quarter of new mothers in the US return to work within a shocking *two weeks* after

---

[7] Kathryn Edin and Maria Kefalas, *Promises I Can Keep: Why Poor Women Put Motherhood before Marriage* (Berkeley: University of California Press, 2005), 130–131, 216–217.

[8] Anne Case and Angus Deaton, "Mortality and Morbidity in the 21st Century," *Brookings Papers on Economic Activity* (Spring 2017): 397–476, 414.

[9] Shawn Fremstad, "Partnered but Poor," Center for American Progress, March 11, 2016, www.americanprogress.org/issues/poverty/reports/2016/03/11/131968/partnered-but-poor/; Rebecca J. Rosen, "Marriage Will Not Fix Poverty," *The Atlantic*, March 11, 2016, www.theatlantic.com/business/archive/2016/03/marriage-poverty/473019/.

[10] Pope Francis notes that young people considering starting families face competing pressures: economic limitations in some cases, too many tempting choices in others. Pope Francis, *Amoris Laetitia*, nos. 40–42.

[11] Jay L. Zagorsky, "Divergent Trends in US Maternity and Paternity Leave, 1994–2015," *American Journal of Public Health* 107, no. 3 (2017): 460, doi.org/10.2105/AJPH.2016.303607; Sharon Lerner, "The Real War on Families: Why the US Needs Paid Leave Now," *In These Times*, August 18, 2015, inthesetimes.com/article/18151/the-real-war-on-families (13%: BLS figure).

giving birth.[12] In many states, single mothers of infants receiving state cash assistance encounter equally draconian work expectations during their postpartum period.[13] That any mother of a newborn should be compelled by family financial realities or state assistance requirements to reenter the workplace this soon after giving birth ought to be a national scandal. At two weeks postpartum, many new mothers are still healing from the physical labor of birth themselves and all are adjusting to the physical, mental, and spiritual demands of caring for a newborn. Most daycares will not accept infants before six weeks of age, potentially leaving mothers with no safe option for childcare, and protective vaccines are not given until two months of age or later. When financial circumstances compel postpartum mothers to return to work so early, they endanger the health and safety of mother and baby alike.

When welcoming children can devastate a family's finances and health, why do poor women continue to found their families, even, most frequently, outside marriage?[14] Sociologists explain that poor women are well aware their economic prospects are constrained. They know implicitly what economists confirm: economic inequality in the US is "sticky" at the top and the bottom, meaning someone who is born poor will likely stay that way.[15] When professional careers seem out of reach, "children offer a tangible source of meaning," leading to early parenthood

---

[12] Lerner, "The Real War on Families." A moving story of a new mother returning to work as an Uber driver is detailed in Danielle Paquette, "She Was Pregnant and Broke. She Signed up for Uber—and Fell into Debt.," *Washington Post*, April 8, 2017, www.washingtonpost.com/business/economy/she-had-a-newborn-and-no-money-signing-up-for-uber-drove-her-into-debt/2017/04/07/b5ee9510-05d1-11e7-b9fa-ed727b644a0b_story.html.

[13] We expect the same of single moms, mothers of infants, receiving welfare: Heather Hahn, David Kassabian, and Sheila Zedlewski, "TANF Work Requirements and State Strategies to Fulfill Them," Urban Institute, March 2012, 2, www.acf.hhs.gov/sites/default/files/opre/work_requirements_0.pdf.

[14] Chen, "America, Home of the Transactional Marriage."

[15] Kate Ward and Kenneth R. Himes, "'Growing Apart': The Rise of Inequality," *Theological Studies* 75, no. 1 (2014): 124, doi.org/10.1177/0040563913519045.

for many poor women.[16] If a "culture of life" means one where babies are welcomed without counting the cost, as it often seems to in Catholic discourse, then a culture of life does exist in the United States. It exists among poor women who welcome children despite their own poor economic prospects and even with little social support, and who are less likely to practice birth control than their wealthier sisters.

While there is clearly a genuine openness to life among poor US women, it is also the case that poverty affects access to birth control, natural family planning, and abortion. In the US, without guaranteed health care, birth control may be paid for out of pocket or require copays for doctors' visits even if covered by insurance. Abortion may be covered by insurance in some cases, but never for recipients of Medicaid or others whose health care is paid for by the federal government, for example through the military or Indian Health Services.[17] In the case of abortion, depending on the circumstances, clinic fees, the cost of caring for other children or dependents, and lost wages and travel fees may be part of the economic picture. As legal restrictions post-*Dobbs* shrink the geographic areas where abortion can be obtained, many will face higher costs in order to access it.

Methods of family planning permitted by the Catholic Church also pose economic barriers to access. Catholic teaching permits heterosexual couples to avoid pregnancy through the use of fertility awareness or natural family planning (NFP) methods.[18] Catholic author Simcha Fisher, perhaps the leading commentator on the social and spiritual realities of these methods, notes that the costs for training and practicing many types of fertility awareness place it out of reach for many couples: "Fairly or not, NFP in the United States is often perceived as a privileged spiritual lifestyle." More reliable NFP methods require significant upfront and

---

[16] Edin and Kefalas, *Promises I Can Keep*, 49.
[17] Loretta J. Ross and Rickie Solinger, *Reproductive Justice: An Introduction* (Berkeley, CA: University of California Press, 2017), 80.
[18] See John Paul II, *Evangelium Vitae*, no. 97.

Three Theoretical Approaches to Economic Constraints on Family Formation

ongoing costs for medical devices or training and are often not covered by health insurance, leading to the sad irony that "couples who can least afford the most highly effective forms of N.F.P. can also least afford an unplanned pregnancy."[19]

While abortion costs money, as mentioned above, many people who pursue abortion see it as a family formation choice driven by economic necessity. A significant majority (75%) of US people who seek abortions are poor or low-income, and most of those already have at least one child.[20] Sociologist Gretchen Sisson found that people pursuing abortion almost unilaterally preferred to parent their child and believed they would have been able to do so given a relatively small amount of money, less than $5,000.[21] Along similar lines, a Pennsylvania nonprofit offers abortion-seeking women $3,000 to carry their child to term. The fact that they claim to have prevented over 100 abortions this way starkly demonstrates that family formation decisions are never as simple as individual choice, since that relatively small economic incentive can apparently empower or compel women who had intended to abort to instead bear the child.[22] When women seeking abortion believe bearing another child will financially harm their current family, their views appear to be justified by a study that compared women who were turned away from a wanted abortion with those who were able to have the abortion they sought. "Women denied an abortion were more likely than were women who received an abortion to experience economic hardship and insecurity lasting years," including the sobering finding that women who sought an

---

[19] Simcha Fisher, "Natural Family Planning Can Be Hard and Expensive to Use. Can New Tech Help?," *America Magazine*, January 24, 2020, www.americamagazine.org/faith/2020/01/24/natural-family-planning-can-be-hard-and-expensive-use-can-new-tech-help.

[20] Guttmacher Institute, "Induced Abortion in the United States," May 3, 2016, www.guttmacher.org/fact-sheet/induced-abortion-united-states.

[21] Irin Carmon, "Amy Coney Barrett's Adoption Myths," *Intelligencer*, December 3, 2021, nymag.com/intelligencer/2021/12/amy-coney-barrett-adoption-myths.html.

[22] Jana Kasperkevic, "The Price of Being Pro-Life: Meet the Woman Who Pays $3,000 to Prevent Abortions," *The Guardian*, November 30, 2015, www.theguardian.com/money/2015/nov/30/pro-life-activist-pays-to-stop-abortions-laura-merriott-financial-support.

abortion and were unable to attain one were more likely, over the following years, to become the only adult in the household—that is, to lose the support of other family members or partners.[23]

The cost of avoiding childbirth ranges between perhaps hundreds of dollars yearly for some NFP or birth control methods to several thousand for an abortion requiring out of state travel. However, with the US's limited social safety net for children, and many mothers forced to look for work rather than caring for children in order to receive any benefits in the first place, the cost of avoiding pregnancy obviously shrinks in comparison to the costs of raising a child to young adulthood. Poor US women do not involve abortion in their family formation decisions because they do not value life or do not wish to parent their children. They are making heartbreaking economic calculations.

We might think that limiting family size to fewer children than one prefers is a choice primarily made by poor parents, those whose economic calculations might turn on figures as small as $3,000. However, the reality of limiting family size due to economic concerns reaches across the income spectrum in the US. Across income levels, many US Americans have fewer children than they prefer.[24] Demographers consistently find that US "ideal" fertility outstrips actual or completed fertility, meaning that falling

---

[23] This study, the Turnaway study, was conducted pre-Dobbs. Women were turned away due to restrictions on gestational age for obtaining abortion in their location. Diana Greene Foster, "Socioeconomic Outcomes of Women Who Receive and Women Who Are Denied Wanted Abortions in the United States," *American Journal of Public Health* 108, no. 3 (2018): 407–413, doi.org/10.2105/AJPH.2017.304247. See also Diana Greene Foster, *The Turnaway Study* (New York: Scribner, 2020), 21–22.

[24] Lyman Stone, "American Women Are Having Fewer Children Than They'd Like," *The New York Times*, February 13, 2018, www.nytimes.com/2018/02/13/upshot/american-fertility-is-falling-short-of-what-women-want.html: "As a result, the gap between the number of children that women say they want to have (2.7) and the number of children they will probably actually have (1.8) has risen to the highest level in 40 years." Men tend to desire the same as women, per the article.

birthrates indicate unachieved dreams on the part of aspiring parents.[25] In a *New York Times* survey, scarcity of money and time, including little or no access to paid family leave, were the primary reasons respondents mentioned for having fewer children than they wanted or having no children at all.[26] Strikingly, the fact that birth rates for poor women remain higher than those for women better off suggests that scarcity of money and time is a contributing factor to having fewer children than one wants, even for women who are well off.[27] There are good reasons for this paradoxical situation.

First, in a country where health insurance and paid parental leave are contingent on employers, even relatively well-off couples hoping to welcome a child may have to time pregnancy and birth around an opportunity to change jobs or incur significant reductions in family income in order to bear and take time off with a newborn. A 2022 study found that the average out of pocket cost, with insurance, for giving birth in a hospital was nearly $3000. Of course, uninsured patients risk incurring far greater charges, and all birthing people undergo significant bodily transformations that can incur future need for medical treatment.[28] With data suggesting that higher health care costs contribute to declining birth rates, and 10 percent of *insured* US adults reporting difficulty paying

---

[25] Lyman Stone, "How Many Kids Do Women Want?," *Institute for Family Studies*, June 1, 2018, ifstudies.org/blog/how-many-kids-do-women-want; Karen Benjamin Guzzo and Sarah Hayford, "US Birth Rates Are at Record Lows—Even Though the Number of Kids Most Americans Say They Want Has Held Steady," *The Conversation*, January 12, 2023, theconversation.com/us-birth-rates-are-at-record-lows-even-though-the-number-of-kids-most-americans-say-they-want-has-held-steady-197270; Stone, "American Women Are Having Fewer Children Than They'd Like."

[26] Claire Cain Miller, "Americans Are Having Fewer Babies. They Told Us Why," *The New York Times*, July 5, 2018, www.nytimes.com/2018/07/05/upshot/americans-are-having-fewer-babies-they-told-us-why.html.

[27] Erin Duffin, "Birth Rate by Poverty Status in the US 2021," *Statista*, December 12, 2022, www.statista.com/statistics/562541/birth-rate-by-poverty-status-in-the-us/.

[28] "Health Costs Associated with Pregnancy, Childbirth, and Postpartum Care," *Peterson-KFF Health System Tracker*, www.healthsystemtracker.org/brief/health-costs-associated-with-pregnancy-childbirth-and-postpartum-care/.

Three Theoretical Approaches to Economic Constraints on Family Formation

medical bills, it is reasonable to assume that health care costs contribute to economic anxiety even for families in the relatively fortunate position of having employer-provided health insurance.[29] Even for well-resourced, educated and well-off parents to be, threading the needle of professional and educational commitments, the limitations and time frames of employer health care coverage, and stark calculations of the impact of time off on the family budget, can make a joyous event feel like a ticking time bomb.

For heterosexual couples experiencing infertility, and for many same-sex couples, welcoming children can incur significant costs, with fees for private adoption or certain fertility methods running into the tens of thousands of dollars. Same-sex couples in particular encounter significant financial constraints on welcoming children for reasons at the intersection of biology and bias. They may choose costlier fertility methods due to legal bias against same-sex adoptive parents in many US states and the obvious reason that while conceiving via intercourse may be an option for some, it requires sex with someone outside the couple. However, insurance may not pay for fertility methods for same-sex couples in cases where it does for heterosexual couples. A nonprofit study of family formation methods being considered by LGBTQ+ couples found stark disparity in the methods considered by couples who desired to welcome children, with only couples in the top income bracket feeling able to consider private adoption.[30]

In contrast with their poorer compatriots, wealthier parents often delay children for many years as they complete their education and establish careers. This engenders different anxieties, including pressure to marry and

---

[29] Arleen Leibowitz, "The Response of Births to Changes in Health Care Costs," *The Journal of Human Resources* 25, no. 4 (1990): 697–711, doi.org/10.2307/145672; "Problems Paying Medical Bills," *Peterson-KFF Health System Tracker*, www.healthsystemtracker.org/indicator/access-affordability/problems-paying-medical-bills/.

[30] Family Equality, "Building LGBTQ+ Families: The Price of Parenthood," www.familyequality.org/resources/building-lgbtq-families-price-parenthood/.

concerns with later-in-life fertility.[31] A couple can be fortunate enough to be well-educated and married and still find that starting a family demands excruciating attention to timing. The demanding schedules required to build careers in medicine, politics, business or law accommodate poorly if at all to the physical and mental needs of bearing and caring for young children, so women with the privilege of considering a professional career confront a different set of dilemmas. Some leave their professional track to care for family, perhaps never to return, whereupon what John Paul II called the "indispensable contribution" of women's professional work is forever diminished in US society.[32]

When both parents do stay in the labor market, they need childcare, another source of economic pressure that may result in couples having fewer children than they intend. In 30 US states, according to the advocacy organization Zero to Three, center-based child care costs more than public college tuition.[33] Nearly two-thirds of US people have limited their family size below what they see as ideal due, among other factors, to the high cost of child care.[34] While that study did not break out reasons for limiting family size by income level, it is reasonable to assume that many families gain higher incomes, in part, by sending two parents to work, making child care costs a very real concern for higher income families. Furthermore, US families at the upper end of the income spectrum engage in more intensive parenting practices compared to poorer families now and to wealthier families in previous generations, another likely contributing factor to choosing family size below what the parents regard as ideal.[35]

---

[31] Jean M. Twenge, "How Long Can You Wait to Have a Baby?," *The Atlantic*, August 2013, www.theatlantic.com/magazine/archive/2013/07/how-long-can-you-wait-to-have-a-baby/309374/.

[32] John Paul II, "Letter to Women," June 29, 1995, www.vatican.va/content/john-paul-ii/en/letters/1995/documents/hf_jp-ii_let_29061995_women.html.

[33] Madeline Daniels Benderev, "Infant-Toddler Child Care Fact Sheet," *ZERO TO THREE*, www.zerotothree.org/resource/infant-toddler-child-care-fact-sheet/.

[34] Miller, "Americans Are Having Fewer Babies. They Told Us Why."

[35] Robert D. Putnam, *Our Kids: The American Dream in Crisis* (New York: Simon & Schuster, 2015).

While both poor and middle-class parents are affected by US economic constraints on family formation and rearing, the burden absolutely does not fall equally. College-educated parents are often praised for their "wise decision" to delay parenthood, and they reap financial and professional rewards as well. While it is undoubtedly stressful to balance two professional careers with the demands of young children at home, parents in poverty face tougher challenges and starker choices. Struggling to raise children on limited resources, they can expect not praise, but often derision, for accepting the life-changing commitment to raise a child.[36] To our shame as a society, stigmas of poor parents carelessly reproducing persist.[37] In 16 states, this stigma is written into law in the practice of welfare "family caps," where additional children in a family beyond a certain number have no right to receive state benefits.[38] Reproductive justice theorist and legal scholar Dorothy Roberts writes that such laws "enforce the view that childbearing by poor women is pathological and should be deterred through social policy," pointing to statements by lawmakers that articulate this view openly.[39] Our culture proclaims, through economic structure and regrettably, through explicit public discourse, that children are only gifts and blessings if their parents are well-off.[40]

---

[36] E.g., Kevin Williamson at *National Review* describing working-class white Americans "whelping of human children with all the respect and wisdom of a stray dog" in "The Father-Führer," *National Review*, March 28, 2016, www.nationalreview.com/nrd/articles/432569/father-f-hrer.

[37] Kenneth J. Neubeck and Noel A. Cazenave, *Welfare Racism: Playing the Race Card against America's Poor* (New York: Routledge, 2001), chap. 5.

[38] Jamelle Bouie, "The Most Discriminatory Law in the Land," *Slate*, June 17, 2014, www.slate.com/articles/news_and_politics/politics/2014/06/the_maximum_family_grant_and_family_caps_a_racist_law_that_punishes_the.html.

[39] Dorothy Roberts, "Welfare's Ban on Poor Motherhood," in *Whose Welfare?*, ed. Gwendolyn Mink (Ithaca, NY: Cornell University Press, 1999), 152–170, 153.

[40] Ross and Solinger, *Reproductive Justice*, 171–172.

Critical Realist Social Theory and Economic Constraints on Family Formation

Critical realist social theory offers a way to understand the relationship of economic realities to family formation that evades the twin errors of erasing personal agency or closing our eyes to societal impacts on individual choice. To begin with, there are many wrong ways to understand the relationship of social factors to moral agency. We sign individual agency over to social factors with linguistic framings such as "Economic concerns *drive* couples to choose smaller families." While it's a common enough way to express a correlative relationship, it is too deterministic. Human persons are not cars or livestock to be *driven* without any agency of their own. A more accurate framing which retains personal agency might be, "Weighing economic factors, couples choose smaller family sizes." Unfortunately, Church leaders fall into the same trap—not merely a linguistic error—when they urge families to have more children, or to remain "open to life," without taking economic and social factors into account.[41] This presumes a world in which individual choice and agency is all that matters, denying the reality that when humans with free will weigh their options, they may be adding up very different lists of factors which will contribute to their decision.

Critical realist social theory offers a way past these naïve and inaccurate framings. Formulated by sociologist Margaret Archer, critical realist social theory aims to describe the influence of social factors on human choice

---

[41] Such blithe dismissal is seen in the USCCB's letter *Love and Life in the Divine Plan*, where "serious economic and social burdens" on couples are contrasted with implicitly graver "fundamental challenges to the nature and purposes of marriage," including contraception and cohabitation (17). Pope Francis received criticism for comments that seemed to ascribe the choice to have fewer children in wealthy Western societies to selfishness, although philosopher Sam Rocha pointed out that in context he seemed to be commenting on the comparatively luxurious treatment of pets in a world of human poverty. "What Did Pope Francis Actually Say about Having Pets or Kids?," *America Magazine*, January 7, 2022, www.americamagazine.org/faith/2022/01/07/pope-francis-pets-kids-242164.

while retaining individual agency and acknowledging the real ways social factors influence decisions. As described by theologian Daniel K. Finn, critical realist social theory sees *social structures* as systems of relations among social positions which emerge from human individual and collective activity.[42] Social structures do not control individual choice or behavior, but they do influence individual choice and behavior through the opportunities, incentives and restrictions generated within the system of relations among social positions that makes up every social structure. Decisions made within a given social structure will usually tend to reproduce the structure as it is, but social structures can be changed through human action, whether the action is expressly intended to change the structure or not intended to at all.[43] Finn concludes that "people are, of course, the cause of their own decisions, but this claim is incomplete without acknowledging that the decisions may have been made differently had no restriction or opportunity been present."[44]

Therefore, we can clearly articulate how people respond to economic factors in their family formation decisions. The US political economy is a social structure that offers few opportunities and incentives to have children. Financial support for children is rarely available. Most US people obtain the majority of their children's necessities through the market, including formula, diapers and paid child care. These necessities are expensive for working families and subject to shortages that may place them out of reach.[45] In contrast, the United States offers few incentives for family formation, such as the generous paid leave and financial support for

---

[42] Daniel K. Finn, *Consumer Ethics in a Global Economy: How Buying Here Causes Injustice There* (Washington, DC: Georgetown University Press, 2019), 68.
[43] Finn, *Consumer Ethics in a Global Economy*, 71–74.
[44] Finn, *Consumer Ethics in a Global Economy*, 69–70.
[45] PBS NewsHour, "Simultaneous Shortages of Formula, Tampons and Child Care Hit Parents Hard," June 16, 2022, www.pbs.org/newshour/economy/simultaneous-shortages-of-formula-tampons-and-child-care-hit-parents-hard.

parenting available in most other developed nations.[46] As we will see, both reproductive justice theory and Catholic thought advocate for economic support to families to enable parents to realize their family formation goals. Critical realist social theory helps us see why such supports are, indeed, likely to work as incentives. Some would argue that there are few restrictions on having children in the US social structure. To be sure, there are not blatant penalties such as China's one-child law, and forcible government sterilization is a thing of the (tragically recent) past.[47] However, restrictions generated within US social structures include the "baby penalty," which affects working mothers' wages and employability, and the aforementioned welfare "family caps."[48]

Using critical realist social theory to assess US family formation helps us understand the paradoxical finding that poorer US parents are often more willing to welcome children: the incentives and opportunities educated, well-off adults enjoy when they delay parenthood are much less available to poor US people. Certainly, people remain free to choose and many continue to form families and welcome life even in the face of strong economic headwinds. But using critical realist social theory to envision restrictions, opportunities and incentives makes it clear that the US political economy, as a social structure, strongly disincentivizes forming families and welcoming as many children as one may want. In this light, findings of falling US fertility should come as no surprise. Moreover, consumerist framings of family formation as a personal choice obscure the real restrictions on this meaningful life pursuit that critical realist social theory helps reveal.

---

[46] Kalee Burns, Liana Fox, and Danielle Wilson, "Expansions to Child Tax Credit Contributed to 46% Decline in Child Poverty Since 2020."

[47] Rickie Solinger, *Pregnancy and Power: A Short History of Reproductive Politics in America* (New York: New York University Press, 2005), 192–200.

[48] Shelley J. Correll, Stephen Benard, and In Paik, "Getting a Job: Is There a Motherhood Penalty?," *American Journal of Sociology* 112, no. 5 (2007): 1297–1339, doi.org/10.1086/511799.

Reproductive Justice Theory and Economic Constraints on Family Formation

The present question of how economic realities affect family formation, and how to make normative claims about that reality, is one reproductive justice has asked and answered from its inception. Far from uninformed claims that "reproductive justice" is disingenuous code for abortion rights, Loretta Ross wrote of the 1994 gathering where she and other Black women framed reproductive justice theory: "While abortion was a crucial resource for us, we also needed health care, education, jobs, day care, and the right to motherhood."[49] This is much broader than the agenda of white feminism in which reproductive rights begin and end with legal abortion. Ross and Solinger rightly critique this white feminist framework for viewing reproductive justice as secured with *Roe* v. *Wade*'s legal guarantee of a negative right, rather than focusing on "enabling conditions" for family formation, including ending racial discrimination and broadening the social understanding of "legitimate motherhood."[50] In contrast with individualist rights accounts, "Reproductive justice rests on claims for both negative and positive human rights," asking whether people are genuinely able to live into their "reproductive possibilities" "without coercion and with social supports."[51] Thus, the framers of reproductive justice describe it as defined by three pillars: "(1) the right not to have a child; (2) the right to have a child; and (3) the right to parent children in safe and healthy environments."[52] They advocate for "enabling conditions" that would allow all women to realize those rights.[53] As a normative goal, Ross wrote elsewhere: "Reproductive Justice is the complete physical, mental, spiritual, political, social and economic well-being of women and

---

[49] Ross and Solinger, *Reproductive Justice*, 64.
[50] Ross and Solinger, *Reproductive Justice*, 120.
[51] Ross and Solinger, *Reproductive Justice*, 169.
[52] Ross and Solinger, *Reproductive Justice*, 65.
[53] Ross and Solinger, *Reproductive Justice*, 121.

girls, based on the full achievement and protection of women's human rights."[54] As the framers of reproductive justice consistently express, whether or not one can realize the rights to form a family and parent a child is profoundly affected, in each case, by economic factors.

On the face of it, the framing of "the right to have a child" strikes me as problematic.[55] Parenting is a relationship with a specific, unique other individual; it strains the mind to think about enjoying a "right" to a relationship with a specific, unique other individual.[56] For example, feminists rightly reject proposals of "rights" to sex among adults, on the grounds that one cannot have a right to interact with the body of another

---

[54] Loretta Ross, "Understanding Reproductive Justice: Transforming the Pro-Choice Movement," *Off Our Backs* 36, no. 4 (2006): 14.

[55] *Catechism of the Catholic Church*, no. 2211 and the Yogyakarta Principles articulated by international human rights experts both articulate a right phrased differently: "the right to found a family." "Relating to the Right to Found a Family (Principle 24)," yogyakarta principles.org/relating-to-the-right-to-found-a-family-principle-24/. I am grateful to Agnes Brazal for introducing me to the Yogyakarta Principles, which assisted greatly in clarifying my thinking on this question. This framing can be used to describe a variety of family structures and clarifies that adoption may be a means of founding a family. However, in my view, it does not escape the questions I raise above about the appropriateness of articulating a right to relationship with a specific other person. Envisioning adoption as a means of founding a family also raises additional concerns about the duty-bearer of rights. For example, if there is a right to found a family, can there be any just restriction on who is eligible to adopt a child? A recent case in Washington state, where a woman is suing after being rejected as a foster parent when she would not agree to support the identity of a potential LGBTQ+ child, raises this question. While "the right to found a family" may be regarded as protecting the right to form kinship networks among adults, it is not clear that this practice is threatened in a way that needs articulation as a right in order to protect it.

[56] Mary Doyle Roche and Cristina L. H. Traina have both contributed important bodies of work to thinking about the rights of children related to, but not totally identified with, the rights of parents within a Catholic theological perspective. As representative examples, see Mary Doyle Roche, "Children and the Common Good: Protection and Participation," in *Prophetic Witness: Catholic Women's Strategies for Reform*, ed. Colleen M. Griffith (New York: Herder and Herder, 2009), 123–131, and Cristina L. H. Traina, "For the Sins of the Parents: Roman Catholic Ethics and the Politics of Family," *Prophetic Witness*, 114–121. My thinking here is informed by their contributions on children's rights, but I do not mean to imply that they would agree with what follows.

person. Another objection is one raised in the case of economic rights: if speaking of a right implies a "duty-bearer" whose job it is to ensure that persons can realize that right, who occupies that role for the right to have a child?[57] It is true that reproductive justice does not only frame its analysis in terms of individual rights. In fact, Ross and Solinger thoroughly criticize the limited US vision of personal, negative rights in *Reproductive Justice*.[58] In keeping with the movement's recognition of the power and limitations of rights language, I investigate what the framework achieves and what it communicates less successfully through its description of reproductive justice through three key rights.

Reproductive justice insists on "the right to have a child" because of specific, historical events in which societies have used the power of their criminal justice systems to interfere with the healthy fertility and desire to parent of women that society judges inadequate, usually related to patterns of unjust oppression. Reproductive justice points a finger at the state and the ways it uses its militarized power to prevent people from forming and raising their families, including forced sterilization of incarcerated US women, removal of Native American children from their parents' homes, and other force-based interventions in which the family members in question would agree they have no choice.[59] Framing "having a child" as a right also highlights the truth that, in these violations of rights, persons have been stripped of goods that are not fully protected via appeals to other rights. For instance, sterilization is a violation of bodily autonomy, as would be, for example, permanently severing someone's finger. However,

---

[57] Darryl M. Trimiew, "The Economic Rights Debate: The End of One Argument, the Beginning of Another," *The Annual of the Society of Christian Ethics* 11 (1991): 90. Catholic social thought has demonstrated beyond a doubt, in my view, that communities are "duty-bearers" for the economic rights of their members and that states are legitimate agents of communities in realizing those rights through taxation and redistribution, if necessary.

[58] For example, they criticize the Constitution for focusing on "intentions, not effects," which means that rights are not effectively guaranteed. *Reproductive Justice* prefers to focus on "enabling conditions" (22–23).

[59] Ross and Solinger, *Reproductive Justice*, 89–90, 92.

unlike the loss of a finger, sterilization removes a unique *future, affective* possibility for that person—the possibility of carrying and nurturing a relationship with her child—against her will. While any bodily violence denies human dignity, forcible sterilization is uniquely derogatory of human dignity, as it is done intentionally to enforce stereotypical ideas of unfit motherhood on the body of a particular, unique individual.

That said, what reproductive justice successfully establishes by articulating "the right to have a child" is the idea of children and childrearing as positive goods. To name something as a right is to claim it as a good worth defending, including for those not currently able to achieve or access this good. As earlier mentioned, neither mainstream consumerist choice models of family formation nor the merely descriptive critical realist social theory is able to articulate family formation as a human good in this way. By so doing, the reproductive justice movement achieves a goal articulated by Linda Hogan as retrieving human rights traditions to better respond to "the obligating features of human nature" in light of the feminist realization that earlier rights traditions' assumption of an independent, autonomous human self excludes many important aspects of human experience.[60] I agree with this project and with the insight of reproductive justice that welcoming and raising children is a positive good, and in this spirit I retain the framework's language of "the right to have a child" despite my concerns mentioned above.

Once we understand the reproductive justice articulation of the right to have a child, interventions of government force—including removing children from their parents' protection or eliminating women's fertility against their will—are easily recognized as signal examples of violations of this right.[61] However, I believe this language is not best suited for describing our topic at hand, which concerns economic constraints on

---

[60] Linda Hogan, *Keeping Faith with Human Rights* (Washington, DC: Georgetown University Press, 2015), 94–95, 31.

[61] Dorothy Roberts describes such rights violations in *Torn Apart: How the Child Welfare System Destroys Black Families and How Abolition Can Build a Safer World* (New York: Basic Books, 2022).

Three Theoretical Approaches to Economic Constraints on Family Formation

family formation. The young couple who decide to remain childless for economic reasons, or the mother who has an abortion in order to continue to support her other children, are exercising choice in a way that is simply not the case for Native American women whose children were ripped away into boarding schools, for parents separated from children by the family courts system, or those sterilized without their knowledge or consent. Critical realist social theory again offers a more accurate framing. A society that accepts high rates of childhood poverty, provides no paid family leave or childcare assistance, and one where simply giving birth to a child can cost tens of thousands of dollars, certainly *disincentivizes* and *constrains* the choice to found a family and raise a child. Certainly, the right to have a child continues to be violated within the US sociopolitical system, but this particular right is more often directly violated by government action than by economic constraints.[62] At the same time, we have seen the repeated evidence and multiple reasons that both higher- and lower-income people have fewer children than they want for economic reasons. This demonstrates the complex nature of family formation decisions when constrained by poverty, even if economic realities do not constrain choice to the same degree as government interventions through force.

Rights language, however, connects directly to economic constraints in another right proclaimed by reproductive justice: *The right to parent the children we have in safe and healthy environments*. This expression of the rights of parenthood encompasses two desiderata: the right to parent the children we have, that is, the right to continue raising one's child without unjust disruptions to that relationship; and the right to raise one's family in safe and healthy environments. The Reproductive Justice framework correctly draws attention to violations of parental rights by government systems that remove children from families for reasons that can be racist, biased in other respects, and that can systemically mistake poverty for

---

[62] Examples include removing the children of women who give birth while imprisoned or family separation policies for immigrants to the United States enforced by both Republican and Democratic administrations.

neglect. Most reports to child welfare are not about physical or sexual abuse but rather about neglect. Physician and public policy expert Mical Raz comments,

> Reporting a family for not having what a child needs to thrive essentially amounts to reporting a family for being poor. Often children are removed and placed in foster homes where foster parents get funding from the government. Had that funding instead been given to the original family, they would have been able to provide what their child needs at home.[63]

Reproductive justice would call for a social safety net to provide financial health care and other material supports in way that support parents in raising their own children without recourse to the traumatic disruption of child removal when more consistently accessible material support would have addressed the issue.

By calling for the right to raise children in safe environments, the founders of reproductive justice highlight the fact that many dangers to children are disproportionately present when children live in poverty. For example, while parents at all income levels worry about bullying and anxiety, low-income parents are much more likely to worry that their neighborhood is a poor place to raise kids, that their children will be the victim of violence, get in trouble with the law, or even be shot.[64] Pollution is another source of danger in children's environments that disproportionately affects poor families, for example, contributing to elevated rates of dangerous asthma in children.[65]

---

[63] Sandra Knispel, "Child Services Targets Poor Families for Biased Reasons," *Futurity*, December 16, 2020, www.futurity.org/child-protective-services-welfare-parents-poverty-2488042-2/.

[64] Pew Research Center, "Parenting in America: Outlook, Worries, Aspirations Are Strongly Linked to Financial Situation," December 17, 2015, www.pewsocialtrends.org/2015/12/17/parenting-in-america/.

[65] Philip J. Landrigan, Virginia A. Rauh, and Maida P. Galvez, "Environmental Justice and the Health of Children," *The Mount Sinai Journal of Medicine, New York* 77, no. 2 (2010): 178–187, doi.org/10.1002/msj.20173.

Three Theoretical Approaches to Economic Constraints on Family Formation

We have discussed above how poverty can affect people's ability to access birth control, abortion, and natural family planning, affecting the ability to exercise what Reproductive Justice articulates as the right *not to have a child*. I do not elaborate this further here because it seems to me that the Reproductive Justice approach is unique in its desire to lift up the goodness and desirability of parenting children, even amid multiple intersecting oppressions. While few US thought leaders promote the right to have children and raise them for Black and Brown, disabled, or poor would-be parents,

> Reproductive justice maintains that people should be able to have the number of children they want, when they want, in the way they want to have them. Individuals must have the ability to raise their children with the social supports they need to provide safety, health, and dignity. ... Since feminists of color have historically fought population-control strategies... in the United States and worldwide, reproductive justice underscores the crucial and complex matter of safe and dignified parenthood.[66]

The Reproductive Justice framers rightly highlight that, in fact, the right not to have a child has often been twisted into eugenic impositions on the desires for parenthood and family among communities of color.[67] The need remains to insist on the goodness of welcoming and parenting children, not simply as an individual consumerist choice, but as a critical, foundational part of personhood which society has a duty to support for each of its members.

---

[66] Ross and Solinger, *Reproductive Justice*, 170–171.
[67] Roberts, "Welfare's Ban."

Catholic Tradition and Economic Constraints on Family Formation

Catholic thought on society and the family would strongly oppose the framing of family formation as a private choice. Rather, children are a good to all of society and raising them a significant way to contribute to the common good. Equally, society has a responsibility to support parents in doing so. The fact that many US people continue to start and raise families amid significant economic headwinds and a profoundly workaholic culture is reason to observe that US people affirm the many goods, joys and responsibilities Catholic thought discerns in family life (*Gaudium et Spes*, no. 47–52). However, this theoretical perspective finds much to lament in the economic realities that interfere with having children, with having as many children as parents hope for, and with raising them in secure and stable comfort.

Papal Catholic teaching on the family has always seen the goods and duties of the family and of society as intertwined. Raising a family is a means of participating in society, which is both a right and a duty of every person. If the family is "the first and vital cell of society," where parents raise children to become responsible community participants, so too societies, and in particular the state, have a duty to support families in fulfilling their purpose of raising children in health, safety and security (*Catechism*, 2208–2211). When this support is lacking, the Church laments the situation and charges societies with failing to fulfill their duties to families. As Pope Francis observed in his apostolic exhortation *Amoris Laetitia*:

> In many ways, the present-day economic situation is keeping people from participating in society. Families, in particular, suffer from problems related to work . . . Workdays are long and oftentimes made more burdensome by extended periods away from home. This situation does not help family members to gather together or parents to be with

their children in such a way as to nurture their relationships each day (no. 44).

Cultural factors, such as the idolization of "market logic," can "prevent authentic family life and lead to discrimination, poverty, exclusion, and violence" (no. 201). Market-based thinking on the economic responsibilities of parenthood leads to stigma and exclusion of children from poor families, a great scandal. Francis writes, "There are those who dare to say, as if to justify themselves, that it was a mistake to bring these children into the world. This is shameful! . . . How can we issue solemn declarations on human rights and the rights of children, if we then punish children for the errors of adults?" (no. 166).[68]

Catholic papal teaching consistently holds that a society that claims to value children should provide the necessary material resources to help each child flourish and never be content for children born to impoverished parents to suffer worse outcomes than children from wealthy families. In earlier teaching by popes and theologians, the method advocated was a family-supporting wage paid to a presumably male breadwinner. Recently, Christine Firer Hinze updated the economic teaching of John A. Ryan to call for economic policies guaranteeing "sufficiency" to families, whether they have one, two or no wage-earning adults.[69] Given the tradition's strong support for women's engagement in public life, I have argued that government-supported child care is another method of societal support for families that the Catholic tradition can and should support.[70] Pope

---

[68] Some of the broader context discusses the family's welcome of a child, but society's responsibility is clear in that poor parents generally do not issue human rights declarations. One might in fairness say that this scorching critique fails to indict the US for hypocrisy, since the sole non-signatory to the UN Convention on the Rights of the Child at least does not accompany its disdain for children's needs with declarations of their rights.

[69] Christine Firer Hinze, *Radical Sufficiency: Work, Livelihood, and a US Catholic Economic Ethic* (Washington, DC: Georgetown University Press, 2021).

[70] Kate Ward, "America's Child Care Crisis and Catholic Social Teaching," *America Magazine*, October 2021, www.americamagazine.org/politics-society/2021/09/16/childcare-work-catholic-social-teaching-241381.

Three Theoretical Approaches to Economic Constraints on Family Formation

Francis is on record as supporting universal basic income, not a policy limited to families, obviously, but one with significant potential to alleviate the economic challenges that affect freedom in family formation. Broadly speaking, the Catholic tradition would advocate any method of social support that provides families material assistance without unduly constraining parents' freedom to welcome and raise children as they see fit.

The Catholic tradition recognizes the complexity of decisions surrounding family formation and the insight, expressed above through critical realist social theory, that social structures incentivize, restrict, and reward decisions, but never fully take away agency. For example, in *Evangelium Vitae*, John Paul II wrote:

> Decisions that go against life [that is, contraception and abortion] sometimes arise from difficult or even tragic situations of profound suffering, loneliness, a total lack of economic prospects, depression and anxiety about the future. Such circumstances can mitigate even to a notable degree subjective responsibility and the consequent culpability of those who make these choices which in themselves are evil (no. 18).

"Mitigated responsibility" is another way of expressing constrained freedom, a way the Church understands and describes our ability to exercise choice amid the constraints, incentives and opportunities of social structures which may themselves be sinful. "Mitigated culpability" refers to the person's guilt for sin before God. In a document that has become totemic for opposition to abortion and birth control and popularizing the phrase "culture of death," John Paul II expresses notable empathy and understanding that people choose abortion and birth control because they feel they, functionally, have no other choice. By speaking of mitigated culpability, he makes it clear that God understands this, too.

Unfortunately, it is difficult to locate this empathetic, contextual understanding of families who make the difficult choice to avoid pregnancy or even have an abortion due to challenging economic circumstances in the public communications and actions of the contemporary United States Conference of Catholic Bishops (USCCB). In its lobbying activity, the USCCB has opposed multiple attempts to provide universal health care in order to oppose public funding of abortion; applauded the elimination of access to abortion even in cases that endanger the mother's life; and fought with equal vigor against legal requirements for employer-provided health insurance to cover contraception.[71] If their public action focuses on eliminating individual choices, so do their public communications ignore the pressures of economic restrictions while framing family formation as a matter of individual choice and dispositions.

An example is their treatment of "openness to life," a disposition mentioned only twice in *Evangelium Vitae*, where it clearly means openness to all of human life, not simply welcoming children.[72] In contrast, the USCCB's most recent pastoral letter on marriage and family discuss a disposition called "openness to children."[73] A stance that opposes euthanasia, inequality, and loneliness and connects the goods of the family with defense of life on all these grounds has become shrunk into opposition to birth control and abortion and pressure to welcome children into a marriage at all costs. By transforming "openness to life" to "openness to children" and removing it from the context of social structures in which it originated, the US bishops buy into American ideas of personal striving to overcome obstacles and obtain merit. Regardless of your personal challenges or circumstances, they seem to be saying, you can be open to life if you just try hard enough.

---

[71] Jeanine Kraybill, "Catholic Church Advocacy and the Affordable Care Act," *Oxford Research Encyclopedia of Politics*, 2019, doi.org/10.1093/acrefore/9780190228637.013.823.

[72] In no. 24, "love, openness and service to human life" are contrasted with materialism and economic self-sufficiency which rejects the vulnerable and suffering, as discussed in no. 23. In no. 97, a couple's "openness to life" is even compatible with "choos[ing] to avoid a new birth for the time being or indefinitely," provided they use NFP methods of avoiding pregnancy.

[73] United States Conference of Catholic Bishops, "Marriage: Love and Life in the Divine Plan," nos. 4, 18.

Another example of disregard for economic restrictions impacting family formation decisions is found in the treatment of cohabitation in the same USCCB document. As we saw earlier, cohabitation (a couple living together without being married) is a family formation choice more frequently made by lower-income people, while marriage is increasingly becoming an upper-middle-class lifestyle practice in the US. Without addressing these realities, the bishops label the family formation choice pursued by many US people, disproportionately poor ones, "gravely immoral" and warn that it "can have a negative impact on children."[74] With their continued emphasis on individual choices and dispositions to the exclusion of structures surrounding them which may lessen the free exercise of agency, the US bishops sadly buy into the US cultural understanding of family formation as solely a matter of individual agency. This individualist view of family formation feeds consumerist attitudes such as viewing more children as a status symbol.

Catholic thinkers who disagree with the extremist positions of the USCCB on access to abortion and birth control do so through the analysis of the broader Catholic tradition that freedom is not removed, but can be significantly constrained by social factors, including economic ones. Cristina Traina diagnoses how both "pro-choice" and "pro-life" advocates in the US context adopt individualistic framings that obscure the need for structural solidarity with women facing unwanted pregnancies. "Structural evil, not necessity, is the primary driver of forced pregnancy choices that injure women and their children both materially and morally."[75] Seeking "Catholic common ground" on abortion, Julie Hanlon Rubio suggests the possibility of contraception as a "cooperation with the good" strategy, in that contraceptive use obviously reduces the need for abortions. On the other hand, the presence or absence of access

---

[74] USCCB, *Marriage*, nos. 26–27.
[75] Cristina L. H. Traina, "Between a Rock and a Hard Place: Unwanted Pregnancy, Mercy, and Solidarity," *Journal of Religious Ethics* 46, no. 4 (2018): 658, doi.org/10.1111/jore.12240.

to contraception is not the final word on whether one uses it or later chooses abortion or not, so this strategy may ultimately be "insufficient."[76]

For Catholic thought, family formation is a positive good through which parents have the opportunity to shape the common good and grow in virtue. Catholic social thought strongly disagrees with consumerist framings of family formation as an individual choice. As a positive good, family formation should be available to all regardless of income, and society has a duty to support it through affirmative material assistance. However, the leadership of the Catholic Church does not succeed in expressing this socially embedded view of family formation decisions in its public communication and actions, embracing an individualist view which fails to affirm the good in family formation models, such as cohabitation, that fall short of the married, middle-class ideal which many low-income US people find to be an opportunity out of their reach to choose.

A Positive Vision

I will now offer some reflections on what our three strands of thought can contribute to a positive vision for family formation amid US economic realities. As I mentioned above, critical realist social theory is primarily descriptive; it does not attempt to offer a vision of the way things should be, but simply to help us see the way they are. To the extent that it contributes to our positive vision, it will be with the reminder that social structures can be changed by the actions of the people choosing within them. Critical realist social theory can assist in articulating the social and economic structures which constrain, incentivize and restrict forming and raising a family so that our society can offer different opportunities, restrictions, and incentives that better support all people in founding the families for which they long.

---

[76] Julie Hanlon Rubio, *Hope for Common Ground: Mediating the Personal and the Political in a Divided Church* (Washington, DC: Georgetown University Press, 2016), 172–174, 179.

The reproductive justice framework links family formation decisions to bedrock human identity and makes visible the fact that challenges to family formation do not stop with the decision to have or not have a child. In particular, reproductive justice is able to understand economic constraints on family formation, even those that affect the well-to-do, better than common US rhetorics of "choice" or popular Catholic frameworks of "openness to life." The movement advocates not only for removing barriers to accessing reproductive health care and welcoming children, but also for robust financial supports that might enable women in poverty to raise their children in stable comfort, including paid maternity leave for the poorest workers.[77]

The reproductive justice and Catholic traditions of thought find surprising common ground on a positive vision for the family. Both begin with similar basic definitions, naming family foundation as among the rights of human beings. By asserting that "the political community . . . has a duty to ensure...the freedom to establish a family" (no. 2211), the *Catechism of the Catholic Church* echoes the framing chosen by Reproductive Justice and the Yogyakarta Principles, naming family formation as a right. By naming something as a right, each framework defines human goods which persons must be free to pursue and locates a duty of communities and authorities to protect persons in seeking and achieving that good. Thus, there is a clear anthropology expressed in naming something as a right. Another area of agreement is that both the reproductive justice framework and Catholic teaching on the family regard the family as a unit as possessed of economic rights and view economic well-being as part and parcel of the well-being of the family unit.

Reproductive justice, Catholic thought, and even critical realist social theory all highlight the fact that family decisions are not made in a vacuum, and the first two theories propose a positive vision of the family supported by the broader society. Exercising one's rights to have a child and raise them in safe and secure conditions requires a robust network of social

---

[77] Ross and Solinger, *Reproductive Justice*, 161.

supports to caregivers and children, including medical care for pregnancy and postpartum, financial assistance, safe and healthy living conditions, and quality public education. Furthermore, when we evaluate the restrictions, incentives and opportunities facing US family formation in light of the positive moral vision furnished by reproductive justice and Catholic thought, we realize that supporting family formation ought to lead to a re-evaluation of work which recognizes family care as work and involves society in supporting it financially. Given that child care costs and income concerns are the two biggest reasons US people cite for having fewer children than they aspire to, policies which make it possible to pay parents to stay home with young children or provide free child care would address both of these restrictions.[78] The fact that each tradition promotes the importance of economic support to enable raising children in dignity and comfort makes the lack of such support for most US families an especially stark omission.

Placing our three theories in conversation, we also notice that Catholic thought pays attention to opportunities, incentives, and restrictions framed by critical realist social theory when it comes to economic realities around family formation, urging support to promote the opportunity to have as many children as one wants. However, when it comes to limiting the number of one's children through birth control or abortion, the US Church only pursues restrictions, and those quite stringently—fiercely opposing not just abortion, but even the most remote material cooperation in providing birth control, for example, through taxpayer-funded health care.[79]

---

[78] See Ward, "America's Child Care Crisis," for an evaluation of some recent proposals.

[79] It is true that when social safety net legislation is discussed, the USCCB will post messages on its website endorsing it in terms of support for the family. However, I believe any honest observer of the US Catholic Church's public messaging would admit that its public opposition of abortion and birth control, from the 1970s to the present day, exceeds by orders of magnitude in volume, passion, and use of ecclesiastical power its promotion of economic family support policies. For example, bishops encourage and even require their priests to denounce legislation related to abortion and birth control (in the case of the Affordable Care

The restrictions-only approach pursued by the US Catholic church is a problem for the Church's credibility and for its effective promotion of family formation as a positive good. Most obviously, it falls short of proclaiming the full truth of the Church's teaching that society has a positive duty to support family formation through reliable material resources—and indeed, it undermines this vision. It seems that Church leaders do not trust the communitarian vision of family formation to bear the fruits they want it to by encouraging people to welcome children and forgo abortion. Instead, in public rhetoric and activism, the bishops fall back on an individualistic framework that treats complex, socially structured decisions as nothing more than the result of individual choice. It is now a truism to point out that limiting access to abortion does little to ensure an environment where a woman confronted by economic or other constraints will feel herself able to bear and raise that child. Critical realist social theory helps us better articulate why that is.

While advocating better economic supports to incentivize avoiding abortion has reached the level of truism, new ideas from within the Catholic tradition articulate limits to the good achievable by a restriction-only approach to abortion. Kathleen Bonnette incisively observes that while the Catholic tradition considers abortion an intrinsic evil—an action that can never under any circumstances be done for a good purpose—it applies the same moral category to violations of bodily integrity. "If violating bodily integrity is an intrinsic evil, then it is never permissible to use a woman's body against her will, regardless of the good we hope to attain," Bonnette writes. "This is precisely why it can be logically consistent to be 'morally but not legally' opposed to abortion: laws prohibiting abortion may violate a woman's bodily integrity and thus, be

---

Act) in Sunday homilies. I am not aware of a similar mandate in any diocese regarding support for an economic family support policy. See Timothy Byrnes, *Catholic Bishops in American Politics* (New Jersey: Princeton University Press, 1991), chapters 6 and 8, for discussion of the 1980s environment that established abortion as the preeminent political issue of the USCCB.

seen as intrinsically evil."⁸⁰ Catholic attorney Jacqui Oesterblad similarly worries that restrictions on when abortions can be performed in emergency cases unjustly impose government restriction on the safety of women's bodies.⁸¹ And jurist and theologian Cathleen Kaveny observes that the current legal framework of abortion in the US falls short of standards for good law in the Anglo-American tradition, where bodily integrity is a highly prized value, and those set forth by Thomas Aquinas, who observed that law must be "possible to nature" and avoid imposing unequal burdens, even in pursuit of the common good. For Kaveny, "prioritizing the creation of the social safety net [over restricting abortion] puts pedagogical priority on nurturing the positive gift of family life, which requires care and commitment that cannot be forced by law."⁸²

The restrictions-only approach pursued by the US Catholic bishops in their public lobbying and communications against abortion clearly conveys that human life is precious and worthy of defense from its very earliest stages. Less credible has been an equally vociferous restrictions-only approach pursued with regard to birth control, which most US people not only use but also regard as entirely compatible with family formation.⁸³ In my judgment, these restrictions-only approaches have not succeeded in communicating the positive vision that Catholic teaching shares with reproductive justice: that family formation is a positive good for persons which society should materially support. Moreover, the intense public focus on the choices of individual mothers rather than society's duty to support all families participates in what reproductive

---

⁸⁰ Kathleen Bonnette, "Holding the Tensions: Female Bodily Integrity as an Intrinsic Good," *Journal of Moral Theology* 12, no. 1 (2023): 114, doi.org/10.55476/001c.66245.

⁸¹ Jacqui Oesterblad, "We Need to Talk about 'Life of the Mother' Exceptions in Abortion Law," *America Magazine*, June 27, 2022, www.americamagazine.org/faith/2022/06/27/abortion-dobbs-catholic-exceptions-243163.

⁸² M. Cathleen Kaveny, "Abortion and the Law in the United States: From *Roe* to *Dobbs* and Beyond," *Theological Studies* 84, no. 1 (2023): 134–156, doi.org/10.1177/00405639231153868.

⁸³ Guttmacher Institute, "Contraceptive Use in the United States by Demographics," January 22, 2020, www.guttmacher.org/fact-sheet/contraceptive-use-united-states.

justice identifies as stigma around "legitimate motherhood," in which mothers who are poor or nonwhite or who welcome children outside marriage are depicted as less competent mothers and targeted by punitive state policies.[84] While lodging a defense of unborn children, therefore, the restrictions-only approach fails to convey the full truth of the goodness of family life and family formation.

In several ways, the restrictions-only approach participates in an individualist anthropology which is not accurate to the Catholic Church's teaching about personhood. It presumes an individualistic, atomized understanding of family formation which sees abortion or birth control not in their complex social context informed by restrictions, opportunities and incentives, but rather as a simplistic choice. If the choice is removed, this logic suggests, the incentives to pursue it will no longer trouble or restrict the person. But critical realist social theory shows us why this belief is false. Reproductive justice, by framing having children and raising them as rights, effectively communicates that welcoming children is a positive human good which society must materially support. While Catholic social thought shares this identical belief, the restrictions-only approach of the US bishops, by treating family formation as an individual choice, conveys the view of the dominant US culture in which family formation is a good *for those individuals who choose it*, imposing no responsibilities and conveying no benefit to society at large. The failure of the leadership of the US church to convey the truth of its belief that family formation is a positive good for parents and for society as a whole is not simply an oversight, it is a tragedy.

By pursuing restrictions without using their power and platform equally to promote incentives for family formation, US Catholic leadership falls prey to the dominant US view of family formation as solely an individual choice. The same view, at different extremes, regards more children as a status symbol for wealthy parents or refuses to acknowledge that a woman might grieve an abortion that was, after all, "her choice."

---

[84] Ross and Solinger, *Reproductive Justice*, 42–43, 122, 171–172.

Three Theoretical Approaches to Economic Constraints on Family Formation

Applying our three-theory approach to economic constraints on US family formation recommends a new approach to practice for the US Church. A vociferous defense of economic supports for families in any form, coupled with a clear explanation of the anthropological and social justifications for such support, will more effectively communicate this positive vision. Most importantly, examining economic constraints on family formation through the lenses of critical realist social theory, reproductive justice, and Catholic social thought should bind anyone who comments on family formation, including Catholic leaders, to intellectual honesty in our understandings of moral agency. According to Catholic thought, the family teaches each of us, from the beginning of our existence, that at the core of our being we are constituted by others. We depend on others and they on us. To treat discussions of family as if this were not true—as if people engage in family formation as rugged individuals—harms women, their families, and the proclamation of the Catholic faith.

Kate Ward, PhD, is associate professor of theological ethics at Marquette University and the author of *Wealth, Virtue and Moral Luck: Christian Ethics in an Age of Inequality* (Georgetown University Press, 2021). She is completing a book on work in Catholic social thought.

Chapter 4: Reproductive Injustice as Social Sin: Mapping Sin Discourse into Debates about Fertility Decisions

Kathryn Lilla Cox

Narrative[1]

In the early 1990's I taught high school in New York City, where I met Miriam during one summer school session.[2] She needed summer school to finish her high school graduation requirements after missing a semester to have a baby. Miriam juggled school, work, and child-care needs. She dealt with conflicting familial, societal, and ecclesial responses to her teen pregnancy, parenthood, and unmarried status. Miriam experienced desires for a good life, further education, and to be like other teens, love for her child, and the weight of her responsibility. She felt confusion, shame, anger, and distress about being treated as a single teen mother by society, some family members, and her church community.

Miriam asked and wondered: "Yes, I had sex. But I didn't use birth control and I didn't have an abortion. Why am I being punished?" Miriam experienced whispers about herself, roadblocks to finishing school set up

---

[1] I would like to thank the Reproductive Justice and the Common Good Virtual Table members for years of conversation, for their work, and their generous reading of and suggestions regarding this essay. Special thanks to Simeiqi He and Emily Reimer-Barry for their leadership midwifing this project to completion including their generous editorial eyes.

[2] Her name has been changed to the name of another teen mother, Miriam of Nazareth. Miriam of Nazareth is from a different era and a different culture, yet the stories of Miriam of Nazareth's pregnancy carry echoes of how unmarried women of all ages and centuries have been treated. It bears prayerful reflection and consideration, asking 1) if her fleeing to see Elizabeth was an ancient version of escaping gossip; 2) if faith, history and hindsight help us uplift one teen mother as a model for motherhood (even if overidealized), can we consider what models of grace contemporary teen mothers offer?

by others, stigma for being an unmarried mother, trouble getting food stamps, and little aid from her church. Despite various difficulties, she succeeded in summer school, finishing her high school requirements.

Introduction

German theologian Klaus Demmer argues that moral theologians have a responsibility to carry forward, reflect upon, and incorporate into their theologizing stories from people's lives.[3] To what and whom we attend shapes our theological imaginations, providing embodied reality to our moral norms. Embodied reality tests our moral norms' capacity to foster justice, mercy, compassion, love, and healing. Demmer's invitation to consider how people's lives intersect with, inform, and illuminate moral theory leads me back to Miriams's story as a framing narrative for this essay. Miriam's story is both unique and universal. Considered through the lens of social sin, it yields new insights detailing communal responsibility, the need for communal conversion, and the urgency of reproductive justice.

Decades later, I am struck anew by Miriam's resilience, dedication, courage, shame, anger, questions, and faith. Back then, I was focused on teaching the course material and accompanying Miriam in her goal to finish high school. Now Miriam's insights and questions regarding how she broke one Church teaching (no sex outside of marriage) and abided by other Church teachings (no birth control and no abortion) become important in the reproductive justice discussion. For me, Miriam's story raises many questions. Among them: How do we hold together the complexity of a constellation of norms and teachings with their effect on our lives? Why do communities emphasize an individual's sin while often neglecting graced actions? Why do communities often highlight their communal "charitable actions" while ignoring their own sinful complicity in social sin?

---

[3] Klaus Demmer, MSC, *Living the Truth: A Theory of Action*, trans. Brian McNeil (Washington, DC: Georgetown University Press, 2010), 1–5.

Reproductive Injustice as Social Sin: Debates about Fertility Decisions

In Miriam's case, people focused on the fact she had sex, got pregnant, and did not marry her child's biological father—the sins, if you will. Yet, most ignored that she also abided by two other Church teachings—no birth control and no abortion. Her Catholic high school administrators chose to emphasis the sins rather than how Miriam followed Church teachings. Seeing her decision to have the baby as problematic, they barred her from attending her graduation ceremony, fearing it would send the wrong message. I wonder, who gave and who received the wrong message?

The messages Miriam received included: Do not have sex. If you have sex do not use birth control and do not get pregnant. If you have sex and get pregnant, do not have an abortion. Staying pregnant will be hard. Keep your pregnancy out of high school, but do not drop out. Be ready to work for your food stamps, housing vouchers, and other forms of social support because, as a mother receiving social support, you must not be lazy.[4] Attending school does not count for your work requirement.[5] By barring Miriam from graduation at her all-girls Catholic high school, the other high schoolers received the same message.[6]

The way Miriam became a mother broke the societal and ecclesial norms for motherhood for contemporary late twentieth-century US life: finish high school, maybe go to college, get married, then enter into

---

[4] On the stereotype of the welfare queen, see Dorothy Roberts, *Killing the Black Body: Race, Reproduction, and the Meaning of Liberty* (New York: Vintage, 1997, 2017), 17–20.

[5] Another option in the 1990's for young women in the U.S. context, was 'go visit' relatives usually for 6 to 9 months. For a sociological analysis of social changes affecting how people looked at teenage pregnancy over a period of decades in the twentieth century, see Kristin Luker, *Dubious Conceptions: The Politics of Teenage Pregnancy* (Cambridge, MA: Harvard University Press, 1996). For a critique of women's experiences in Ireland, see Suzanne Mulligan's chapter in this volume, "Thinking about Reproductive Justice in Contexts of Violence," 148–177.

[6] This was the same message my classmates and I received at our all-girls Catholic high school in Michigan in the early 1980's. Some classmates of mine had abortions, and others hid their pregnancies; those who concealed their pregnancies avoided the public discipline and shame of missing graduation, which had been imposed for other "perceived" infractions such as too many absences due to illness. This concern about sending the wrong message still exists in the twenty-first century.

parenthood. If you get pregnant and are unmarried, you should get married to the biological father. Like many women before her, Miriam stepped outside of approved boundaries and norms. Because she did, her pregnancy was less celebrated than those mothers whose pregnancies stayed within the prescribed boundaries. Miriam, herself, was less celebrated. Like other women who step outside the "proper scripts" for motherhood, Miriam experienced attempts at shaming, scapegoating, and dismissing of her story and insights.[7] In other words, Miriam's teen motherhood was seen as problematic, not sanctified. Miriam embodied two different binaries for women: 1) good mother/bad mother and 2) women as pure virgin (Mary) or the cause of sin (Eve).[8]

Nevertheless, Miriam told me her story, like other women continually tell their stories. By doing so, she shattered these binary options imposed by sexism. The experiences of women and their theological insights are taken seriously in some spaces. Subsequently, women contribute to a more robust, encompassing framework for the theological work of rectifying reproductive injustice and bringing forth life-affirming healing. Implicit in Miriam's story is the reality of sin: her sins, the sins of individuals who interacted with her, and the sins of the communities to which Miriam belonged. Accurately naming reproductive injustices and advocating for reproductive justice requires more comprehensive attention to the various

---

[7] Variations of Miriam's experience appear for unmarried women working in Catholic institutions when they get pregnant. They must worry that they will be fired, losing their livelihood, along with any shaming, judgement, and lack of support for their pregnancy. The story of Naiad Reich is an example of an unmarried pregnant woman fired from a Catholic institution. See Emily Reimer-Barry, "Another Pro-Life Movement is Possible," *Catholic Theological Society of America Proceedings* 74 (2019): 21–41, 21.

[8] Rachel Sophia Baard, *Sexism and Sin-Talk* (Louisville, KY: Westminster John Knox, 2019), 57–107. Baard in two chapters explores how perspectives on Eve and Mary are shaped by patriarchy. They become a "dual image of the patriarchal feminine," which when allowed and followed "also participates in the dehumanization of women." See also, Elisabeth T. Vasko, "'Mad Mothers, Bad Mothers': Resisting Stigma and Embracing Grace as Dis-ease," *Journal of the Society of Christian Ethics* 37, no. 1 (2017), 141–159. Vasko does not discuss Eve or Mary, but she deftly defines and challenges the heteropatriarchal vision of 'good mothers.'

sins underlying reproductive injustice. Therefore, the theological work around reproductive injustice includes re-thinking sin-talk.[9] Specifically, it involves naming as concretely as possible the intersecting network of communal sins influencing individual moral decisions.

Considering sin-talk's import for all reproductive injustice remains impractical. Therefore, I will not provide ethical analyses related to individual reproductive decisions. Nor will I classify different moral reproductive quandaries women navigate into distinct sin categories. Instead, I apply feminist theologian Elizabeth A. Johnson's insight that the symbol of God functions,[10] shaping our theological imaginations and worldviews to the question of sin and reproductive injustice. The symbols of sin function. Therefore, seeking reproductive justice necessitates moving beyond categorizing individual sins for confession and instead analyzing how sin-talk functions to shape our moral-theological imaginations and subsequent attempts to address reproductive injustice.[11] Considering how sin-talk functions can deepen our understanding of intersecting realities that lead to reproductive injustice, thus opening new possibilities for justice.

The argument of this essay moves from category to cartography to seek clarity about what is at stake in conversations about sin and reproduction within the Catholic context. Section one outlines theological landscape changes that influenced discussions of reproductive justice and sin-talk. Section two provides the background on the metaphorical nature of language, how it works, and why it matters for theology. By way of example, I delineate how several words in this essay's title capture layers of meaning, assumptions, and frameworks about reproduction. Section three explores changes in sin-talk in the new theological landscape. Specifically,

---

[9] Baard, *Sexism and Sin-Talk*. I adopt this language of sin-talk from Baard.
[10] Elizabeth A. Johnson, *She Who Is: The Mystery of God in Feminist Theological Discourse* (New York: Crossroad Publishing Co., 1997).
[11] On categorizing sin for confession, see John Mahoney, "The Influence of Auricular Confession," *The Making of Moral Theology: A Study of the Roman Catholic Tradition* (Oxford: Clarendon, 1987), 1–36.

it investigates how sin-talk functions metaphorically in scripture and is followed by a theological grappling with the complex interplay between individual and communal sin. The conclusion argues that employing a metaphorical structure for sin-talk reveals new possibilities for honoring women's moral agency. It maintains the reality of individual sin, while holding communities culpable for their sins of fostering and permitting reproductive injustice. Throughout sections three and four, I propose options for a communal examination of conscience to better foster reproductive justice.

Section One: Sin and Changing Theological Landscapes[12]

Conceptually, 'sin' attempts to describe multi-faceted and complex aspects of the human condition and of human behavior. Sin has been categorized as mortal, venial, omission, or commission, and described as sinning in thought, word, and deed.[13] While valuable, our understanding of these categories and how they often shape our imaginations rely on an older theological landscape. While an incomplete description, this older theological matrix includes the following features: visions of women as misbegotten males,[14] whose essential nature is motherhood;[15] categorizing sinful actions to prepare for confession;[16] Catholic theologians who are almost exclusively priests and male;[17] a patriarchal, hierarchical ecclesiology

---

[12] While each shift or movement named below has significance, listing the various features of the older and new landscapes must suffice for this essay.

[13] Richard M. Gula, S.S., *Reason Informed by Faith: Foundations of Catholic Morality* (New York: Paulist Press, 1989), 106–122. See the Catholic prayer, the *Confiteor*, for the description of sinning in thought, word, and deed.

[14] Thomas Aquinas, *Summa Theologiae* I, q. 92, a. 1.

[15] John Paul II, *Mulieris Dignitatem*. Note: Pope John Paul II's letter is only one example of essentializing women as mothers.

[16] Mahoney, *The Making of Moral Theology*, 1–36. Mahoney looks at rise of the manuals detailing sins to aid confession.

[17] Charles E. Curran, *The Catholic Theological Society of America: A Story of Seventy-Five Years* (New York: Paulist Press, 2021). While this book chronicles one professional society of

and an inward facing church with a defensive posture to the world;[18] and the initial development of Catholic social thought (CST) aimed at addressing social injustice.[19] In this worldview, despite CST, individual sin is the primary focus.

Theological movements from the nineteenth to the twenty-first century began to question and even challenge these theological foundations.[20] While the effects have not been fully realized or manifested, changing assumptions about women, ecclesial authority, conscience, and power invite us to question whether we are using outdated maps while the landscape around us is changing. This newer theological landscape challenges the older one and can result in different responses to injustice.[21] Women are recognized as created in *imago Dei*, worthy of respect with full moral agency and a plurality of vocations.[22] There is a renewed emphasis on conscience development and aiding moral decision-making by people.[23] Acts matter in the context of a person-centered approach, and naming sins helps identify areas for growth in discipleship. Catholic theologians are

---

theologians, its trajectory as a theological society of mostly male clerics to mostly lay theologians can be traced in other societies as well.

[18] Bishop De Smedt of Bruges, Belgium, critiqued this view of the church on December 1, 1962, during the first session of the Second Vatican Council. In Xavier Rynne, *Vatican Council II* (Maryknoll, NY: Orbis Books, 1999), 113.

[19] For an overview of the development of Catholic social teaching and its documents, see Thomas Massaro, *Living Justice* (New York: Rowman & Littlefield, 2024), 35–56.

[20] See John W. O'Malley, *What Happened at Vatican II* (Cambridge, MA: Harvard University Press, 2008), 1–92.

[21] See for example, Christina A. Astorga, *Catholic Moral Theology and Social Ethics: A New Method* (Maryknoll, NY: Orbis, 2014).

[22] Ann O'Hara Graff, ed. *In the Embrace of God: Feminist Approaches to Theological Anthropology* (Maryknoll, NY: Orbis, 1995); M. Shawn Copeland, *Enfleshing Freedom: Body, Race, and Being* (Minneapolis, MN: Fortress Press, 2009); Mary Catherine Hilkert, *Speaking with Authority* (Mahwah, NJ: Paulist Press, 2008); Susan Abraham and Elena Procario-Foley, eds., *Frontiers in Catholic Feminist Theology: Shoulder to Shoulder* (Minneapolis, MN: Fortress Press, 2009).

[23] See *Amoris Laetitia*, nos. 37, 42, 222, 300–303; Anne E. Patrick, *Conscience and Calling* (London: Bloomsbury T & T Clark, 2013); and Kathryn Lilla Cox, *Water Shaping Stone: Faith, Relationships, and Conscience Formation* (Minneapolis: Liturgical Press, 2015).

increasingly lay and experience various types of committed partnerships and family responsibilities (including parenting children).[24] The church is lurching toward living a global, synodal, dialogical participation of the People of God ecclesiology.[25] Vatican II advocated and encouraged more openness to the world, to other academic disciplines, and to other religions and the truths they offer.[26] Catholic social teaching articulates how institutions constrain moral agency even as the principles of Catholic social teaching offer support, structure, and wisdom for social justice.[27] Other shifts influencing theology include neo-capitalist constructions of the family in the USA, growing acknowledgment of sexism in Catholicism, the sex abuse crisis in the Catholic Church,[28] increasing awareness of Catholic complicity in racism,[29] and more in-depth medical knowledge of how the reproductive systems and pregnancy work, complicating reproductive decisions. There is also increasing attention to how culture functions to promote or hinder moral formation.

---

[24] For a description of the changing demographics of moral theologians, see James F. Keenan "What Happened at Trento 2010?," *Theological Studies* 72, no. 1 (2011): 131–149. Katarina Schuth has documented changes in seminary faculty over the decades. See, for example, Katarina Schuth, *Seminaries, Theologates, and the Future of Church Ministry* (Collegeville, MN: Liturgical Press, 1999).

[25] The Synod on Synodality with meetings in Rome in October 2023 and 2024 represents this halting ecclesial change post-Vatican II. See Gerard Mannion, "Beyond Hierarchiology: Congar, Pope Francis and the Council's Unfinished Liberation of Ecclesiology," in *The Promise of Renewal: Dominicans and Vatican II*, ed. M. Attridge, D. Dias, OP, M. Eaton, and N. Olkovich (Adelaide: ATF Theology, 2017), 51–77.

[26] See *Gaudium et Spes*, nos. 36, 42, 44, and 54; *Nostra Aetate*, no. 2.

[27] For example, Christine Firer Hinze, *Radical Sufficiency: Work, Livelihood, and a U.S. Catholic Economic Ethic* (Washington DC: Georgetown University Press, 2021); Daniel J. Daly, *The Structures of Virtue and Vice* (Washington DC: Georgetown University Press, 2021).

[28] Julie Hanlon Rubio and Paul Schutz, *Beyond 'Bad Apples': Understanding Clergy Perpetrated Sexual Abuse as a Structural Problem & Cultivating Strategies for Change*, 2022, www.scu.edu/ic/programs/bannan-forum/media--publications/beyond-bad-apples-/.

[29] Bryan N. Massingale, *Racial Justice and the Catholic Church* (Maryknoll, NY: Orbis, 2010); Vincent W. Lloyd and Andrew Prevot, *Anti-Blackness and Christian Ethics* (Maryknoll, NY: Orbis, 2017).

These new and still emerging theological landscapes shape and influence how we conceptualize and respond to reproductive injustice. I argue that the newer theological landscape holds possibilities for more just reproductive policies and norms. Therefore, bracketing venial or mortal sin-talk and stressing sin-talk that illuminates both personal and communal complicity in reproductive injustice are important. Theological ethicists have begun bridging Catholic social teaching about the common good and moral theology's attention to individual sin informed by the feminist insight that the personal is political (communal) and the political (communal) is personal. Attention and respect are given to experiences of intersectionality and interconnection, with analysis of what mutual self-sacrifice, self-gift, and the importance of self-love in a Christian worldview means.[30]

Within this shifting landscape, where theology speaks to and advocates for reproductive justice, the facts of fertility and pregnancy matter. Older theological frameworks paid little attention to the fact that menstrual cycles, pregnancy, and menopause bring with them consequences on various bodily systems (circulatory, endocrine, digestive, to name a few). Women recognize and experience the reality that their reproductive capacity is also about health care. In some newer theological frameworks, scientific advances and understanding about reproduction inform theological work. However, recent political decisions and laws in the US around reproduction point to scientific ignorance at best, and even worse, willful disregard of scientific knowledge to further both political and theological agendas. Sadly, the fact that reproduction is about women's healthcare is still too often ignored in many discussions of reproductive injustices.[31]

---

[30] Grace Ji-Sun Kim and Susan M. Shaw, *Intersectional Theology* (Minneapolis, MN: Fortress Press, 2018); Erin Lothes Biviano, *The Paradox of Christian Sacrifice: The Loss of Self, the Gift of Self* (New York: Herder & Herder, 2007).

[31] See the chapter in this volume by Emily Reimer-Barry, "Catholic Health Care and Reproductive Justice: Whose Conscience has Priority when Conscience Claims Collide?," 358–390.

Furthermore, the belief held by many people in societal, cultural, and ecclesial circles that women can easily get pregnant, stay pregnant, and bring the pregnancy to term, giving birth to a healthy new human being needs correction. Women's stories of pain, loss, suffering, and hardships around getting pregnant, staying pregnant, bringing a pregnancy to term, or the ambiguity around pregnancy and whether pregnancies are even wanted, prove the myth of pregnancy's ease wrong.[32] Additionally, infertility inflicts upon women a different tension around motherhood, church teaching, and societal expectations.[33]

Discussions, laws, and theological norms regarding reproductive justice must remain grounded in biological facts for both pre-natal life and women, effects on women's health, and their moral agency in reproductive decisions. Anything less diminishes and objectifies women.

This objectification and diminishment of women's agency starkly appears in the United States of America's tortured history legislating women's fertility. On the one hand, some women have been seen as incompetent and incapable of being mothers, leading to coerced sterilization either forcibly or without their knowledge.[34] On the other hand, courts or state assemblies legislate that women must be mothers by severely limiting or outlawing abortion.[35] Thus, they negate women's own

---

[32] Nadine Pence Frantz and Mary T. Stimming, *Hope Deferred: Heart-Healing Reflections on Reproductive Loss* (Cleveland, OH: Pilgrim Press, 2005).

[33] Mercy Amba Oduyoye, "A Coming Home to Myself: The Childless Woman in the West African Space," in *Liberating Eschatology: Essays in Honor of Letty M. Russell*, ed. Margaret A. Farley and Serene Jones (Louisville, KY: Westminster John Knox, 1999): 105–120; Kathryn Lilla Cox, "Toward a Theology of Infertility and the Role of *Donum Vitae*," *Horizons* 40, no. 1 (2013): 28–52.

[34] See Roberts, *Killing the Black Body*, 8–10, 56–103; Harry Bruinius, *Better for all the World: the Secret History of Forced Sterilization and America's Quest for Racial Purity* (New York: Knopf, 2006); Rebecca M. Kluchin, *Fit to be Tied: Sterilization and Reproductive Rights in America, 1950–1980* (New Brunswick, NJ: Rutgers University Press, 2009); John J. Clifford, SJ, "Marital Rights of the Sinfully Sterilized," *Theological Studies* 5, no. 2 (1944): 141–158.

[35] Guttmacher Institute, "Abortion Policy in the Absence of Roe," April 24, 2023, www.guttmacher.org/state-policy/laws-policies.

determination in consultation with healthcare professionals about their health conditions or readiness and ability to be mothers. In both instances other people control women's reproductive potential, diminish women's moral agency, and promote women's dehumanization.

Despite patriarchal attempts to control women's reproductive capabilities under the guise of 'celebrating motherhood' and protecting the unborn, pregnancy, motherhood and children are insufficiently envisioned and supported. Unwed pregnant women and pregnant teens are usually shamed, as Miriam experienced.[36] Pregnant working women frequently lack needed accommodations like extra bathroom breaks with easy accessibility. Paid parental leave in the US is either non-existent or woefully

---

[36] Moving beyond rhetoric, the federal government of the United States of America in 2022 included in the Consolidated Appropriations Act of 2023 the Pregnant Workers Fairness Act (PWFA). Signed by President Biden, the PWFA went into effect on June 27, 2023. The PWFA guarantees "reasonable accommodations" for pregnant workers working for employers with more than fifteen employees. However, reasonable accommodations cannot cause "undue hardship" for the employer. Texas Attorney General Ken Paxton sued the federal government over the PWFA saying 1) it puts an undue financial burden on the Texas government to enact this law and 2) the law was unconstitutionally passed. On February 27, 2024, the *Texas Tribune* reported that the federal court in Lubbock, Texas, ruled in favor of Texas AG Ken Paxton stating that the Pregnant Workers Fairness Act was unconstitutionally passed and thus invalid. The Federal government should appeal this ruling. This lawsuit, along with other recent Texas actions related to abortion and medical procedures needed by pregnant women, indicate a disregard for women, their agency and health while pregnant, as well as pre-natal life. See U.S. Equal Employment Opportunity Commission, "What You Should Know About the Pregnant Workers Fairness Act," 2023, www.eeoc.gov/wysk/what-you-should-know-about-pregnant-workers-fairness-act; Liz Morris and Cynthia Thomas Calvert, "Pregnant Workers Fairness Act," American Bar Association, September 7, 2023, www.americanbar.org/groups/labor_law/publications/labor_employment_law_news/issue-summer-2023/pregnant-workers-fairness-act/; Matthew Choi, "Federal Judge Rules Against Pregnant Workers in Win for Paxton," *The Texas Tribune*, February 27, 2024, www.texastribune.org/2024/02/27/ken-paxton-proxy-votes-congress/.

inadequate.[37] Food insecurity affecting children is on the increase.[38] More recent theological writing on CST speaks to the dynamic between cultural, structural systems, and the interweaving and interrelatedness of the human beings that make up these communities.[39]

Our theological landscape includes the concepts used to describe human reality. How we name, describe, and analyze experiences and actions matter. Thus, examining how language functions in naming, describing, and analyzing reproductive injustice in a shifting theological landscape is the next step.

Section Two: The Metaphorical Nature of Theological Language and Why It Matters

Anselm's definition of theology as faith seeking understanding has value.[40] However, difficulties arise with Anselm's definition when 1) the propositions themselves are not questioned and are presumed to fully capture reality, and 2) it is believed that precise enough language for norms and faith statements provides clear instructions for discipleship. These difficulties obscure how language functions, in general, and the effort to fully grasp or describe encounters with God.

As theologian Robert Masson writes, "Words prompt for meaning rather than capture it. Language is an underspecified tip of a giant iceberg of underlying and mostly unconscious cognitive processes of

---

[37] See two chapters in this volume: Kate Ward, "Never Just a Choice: Three Theoretical Approaches to Economic Constraints on Family Formation," 55–89, and Karen Peterson-Iyer, "Reproductive Justice and Agricultural Labor Migrants," 257–289.

[38] M.P. Rabbitt, L.J. Hales, M.P. Burke, and A. Coleman-Jensen, "Household Food Security in the United States in 2022," U.S. Department of Agriculture, Economic Research Service, 2023, www.ers.usda.gov/webdocs/publications/107703/err-325.pdf?v=7814.4.

[39] See Kate Ward, "Never Just a Choice."

[40] St. Anselm, *Proslogion*, in *Anselm of Canterbury: The Major Works*, ed. Brian Davies and G. R. Evans (Oxford: Oxford University Press, Reissue Edition, 2008)

categorization and metaphorical mapping."[41] This iceberg includes the various relationships and encounters with people, the intricate reality we call culture, values we hold, things we have been taught, feelings, wounds we carry, dreams, longings, and everything that encompasses a person's worldview. Metaphorical mapping shows and teases out the various ways ideas and concepts overlap, influencing each other and our views in previously unforeseen ways. Sometimes this mapping creates new landscapes of meaning, subsequently shifting our worldviews.

God-talk and its accompanying theological disciplines seek to elucidate these revelatory shifts in comprehension and worldviews within religious frames. Thus, Masson argues that "[t]heology can be thought of as the effort to make sense of the revelatory understanding in terms of its tectonic and novel mapping."[42] Geologically, when the tectonic plates under the earth's surface shift, visible landscapes can change. Likewise, when our theological language changes, our internal and external landscapes transform in both subtle and drastic ways. Initially, any difference might go unrecognized. Yet, when we encounter something new that disrupts our current worldview, rearranging the ground beneath us, we need to make sense of it and to reconstruct a worldview that provides meaning, structure, and purpose.[43] Transformation or conversion can occur with implications for action.

Where Masson explores the implications of metaphorical thinking and conceptual blends for systematic theology, moral theologian Thomas Kopfensteiner analyzes the implications of metaphorical thinking for moral norms. Following Paul Ricoeur, Kopfensteiner applies the insight

---

[41] Robert L. Masson, "Foreword," in *Putting God on the Map: Theology and Conceptual Mapping*, ed. Erin Kidd and Jacob Karol Rinderknecht (Lanham, MD: Lexington Books/Fortress Academic, 2018), xii.

[42] Masson, "Foreword," xiv.

[43] See, for example, Robert L. Masson, *Without Metaphor, No Saving God: Theology after Cognitive Linguistics* (Leuven: Peeters Press, 2014); Also see the whole collection of essays in *Putting God on the Map*. Another alternative is to retreat and reinforce prior worldviews that cannot hold newness.

that metaphors both reveal and conceal something about the reality or truth they are ascribing to normative claims. Kopfensteiner argues that normative claims reveal and conceal insights about reality, how we are to act, and what being a disciple means. Norms contain an element of indeterminacy because of their metaphorical structure and the need to be applied in new situations with new contexts. Therefore, norms require ongoing interpretation, often yielding new insights.[44] Thus, passive reception of normative claims is insufficient. We must arrive at, understand, and apply a norm in our lives within the confines of human fulfillment understood as the call to discipleship. This ongoing endeavor, fashioning and deepening lived discipleship, contains individual and communal components.

Such a task is not new for Christian disciples. As Klaus Demmer points out, the first disciples constructed meaning regarding God's revelation in Jesus. So, too, must today's disciples for a new era and new people. While Christians believe that God reveals the fullness of truth, our finitude means our grasp of truth is partial, mediated, and incomplete.[45] Therefore, our lives of discipleship require a continual process by which we evaluate meaning, our value system, and obligations to God, others, and self, ultimately manifested in our actions.[46]

While past experiences and awareness ground and yield moral insight, insight also develops through new experience.[47] Certain experiences, whether positive or negative, tear the fabric of people's lives, rippling beyond one moment. They disrupt a worldview, touch us deeply, and involve some form of reweaving the fabric of our lives in the attempt to structure a meaningful way to re-engage the world. Our capacity for critically examining and reflecting on our experiences helps us recognize

---

[44] Thomas Kopfensteiner, "The Metaphorical Structure of Normativity," *Theological Studies* 58, no. 2 (1997): 335–336.
[45] Cf. 1 Corinthians 13:12.
[46] Klaus Demmer, "Sittlich Handeln aus Erfahrung," *Gregorianum* 59 (1978): 661–690, 686.
[47] Demmer, "Sittlich Handeln aus Erfahrung," 662.

how certain events disrupt worldviews and structures of meaning. Critical examination and reflection also facilitate the necessary reweaving and meaningful re-engagement with the world. However, we must remain mindful that seemingly common or similar experiences can yield different moral interpretations or applications of relevant norms. Our capacity for analysis of, reflection upon, and acknowledgement of varied applications of norms remains crucial for moral dialogue.[48] Hopefully, attentiveness to these features of developing moral insights opens us up to moral insights that expand beyond our own experience.[49]

Masson, Kopfensteiner, and Demmer remind us that our theological language, moral norms, knowledge, and grasp of revelation remain partial and incomplete. No one holds all answers to reproductive injustice or moral truth. This fact necessitates ongoing mutual reflection and discernment when seeking a deeper, richer, more textured approach to reproductive justice.

This reflection and discernment include consideration of how language functions in reproductive conversations. For example, the original title for this essay used the phrase 'fertility choices.' Choice means to select among options, the act of choosing a thing. While women do choose a course of action related to their reproductive capacity, naming this as a 'choice' does not fully capture this reality. This is because 'choices' also frequently reference daily activities like which fruit to buy or what I am having for dinner. Consequently, using 'choice' language when theologically analyzing reproductive injustice contributes to minimizing the contexts, circumstances, and the depths of thought, emotional wrestling, and considerations women bring to bear on their reproductive decisions. 'Choice' language allows people to argue wrongly that women do not think deeply or have the capacity to make their own decisions around reproductive matters. Labeling a life-altering event a 'choice,' rather than a moral decision, gives different weight to the action being undertaken.

---

[48] Demmer, "Sittlich Handeln aus Erfahrung," 680, n. 49.
[49] Demmer, "Sittlich Handeln aus Erfahrung," 681.

My increasing discomfort with the language of 'choices' when discussing reproductive injustice, led to the phrase 'fertility decisions' in the title. Even if only implicitly aware of our internal perspectival shift, saying 'fertility or reproductive decisions' acknowledges that women are not simplistically choosing between 'options.' 'Fertility decisions' language requires refocusing on and considering women's moral agency in their complex, arduous reproductive decision-making processes.

On the other hand, the title retains the term 'debate' despite my preference for the term dialogue. Dialogue indicates a willingness to hear, consider, and be influenced by the truth of what others say about their experiences, perspectives, and thoughts when engaging in conversation or decision making. However, women who bear the burden of health risks, economic effects, and other challenges from reproductive injustice find themselves participating in 'debates' rather 'dialogue' to arrive at reproductive justice. Too many people in various social settings, legislative halls, and theological conversations still arrive with preset perceptions of women, their thoughts, experiences, and how their agency should be used. The term 'debate' captures the fact that too many people think they have the answers to others' reproductive decisions. They dictate what is to be done and see their role as mandating courses of action rather than listening to the people most affected. While 'debates' look different depending on the reproductive area under consideration, 'debates' obscure women's anguished stories of reproductive injustice, and how their stories are all too often ignored, even in ecclesial spaces.[50]

More fundamental than the words used in this essay's title is a needed re-examination of our language around reproductive injustice and sin. Comprehending that the symbolic (Johnson) or metaphorical (Masson) language for God functions in shaping understandings of God and revelation also means considering the implications of language for sin-talk. Analyzing reproductive sin-language as metaphorical reveals what hides in our shared words—differing worldviews, life experiences, positionality,

---

[50] See Kate Ward, "Never Just a Choice."

cultures, hopes, and more. These undercurrents, when exposed, help explain existing tensions when applying norms and principles in the pursuit of reproductive justice.

The next section begins with sin-metaphors in scripture because scripture is a foundational text for a Judeo-Christian worldview. Stepping back and identifying scriptural metaphors, rather than simply scriptural definitions, provides a different starting point for sin-talk. Metaphors shape our imagination and provide insights into our reality. Scriptural metaphors with their tributaries and filaments provide additional insight into the human condition we call sin.[51] The additional perspectives provided by scriptural metaphors for sin open new venues for analyzing reproductive injustice. For example, the metaphors highlight the more personal component of communal sin embedded in the structural sin that CST addresses. The next section concludes by using theological work that explores the interconnection between individual moral agency and communal structures that limit, constrain, and culturally shape our moral agency.

Section Three: New Sin-Talk: Pathways from Scripture and Theological Ethics

Feminist theologian Rachel Baard writes, "God-talk and grace-talk cannot bypass sin-talk, since God speaks the word of grace into the concrete pathologies we encounter in human existence and is heard from within those experiences. The theologian therefore cannot bypass reflection on the painful matters that go by the name of 'sin.'"[52] Her work is "premised upon the recognition that words have power, and perhaps more so when those

---

[51] Terry Wardlaw argues that this approach has implications for translating the various notions for sin in the Hebrew Bible and for understanding their transition into the New Testament. See Terry Wardlaw, "Translating 'Sin:' What Does the Old Testament Have to Say?," *Notes on Translation* 15, no. 4 (2001): 17–36.

[52] Baard, *Sexism and Sin-Talk*, 3.

words have doctrinal status." For Baard, "feminist conversation on sin-talk is therefore centered on the question, how does sin-talk create a script that people perform?"[53]

A metaphorical approach to sin-talk provides one method for interrogating the script that people perform. Consciously attending to the metaphorical structure of sin-talk language illuminates a network of concepts generating a worldview. Or as Joseph Lam notes, "Sin is a cultural notion, constructed within the norms of a particular society, and deriving its significance from a place in a broader linguistic-conceptual framework."[54] This broader linguistic-conceptual framework is both spoken and written.

Therefore, Gary A. Anderson can argue that scripture contains "metaphorical pictures" of sin and forgiveness that shape and arise from specific "cultural and linguistic circumstances." This in turn yield narratives that are related yet "not predetermined by their underlying metaphors."[55] In other words, biblical narratives can be interrogated for their relevance and import given the underlying metaphors. Our interpretations of the narratives and their foundations can vary, subsequently affecting actions and decision-making by moral agents. Ideally, then, various metaphors for sin and forgiveness will be placed in conversation with each other. This provides a more comprehensive map of sin, forgiveness, and the narratives they tell us, with important implications for reproductive justice.

Four metaphorical schemas for sin in the Hebrew Bible are particularly pertinent to reproductive justice conversations: 1) sin as a burden, 2) sin as

---

[53] Baard, *Sexism and Sin-Talk*, 3.
[54] Joseph Lam, *Patterns of Sin in the Hebrew Bible: Metaphor, Culture, and the Making of a Religious Concept* (New York: Oxford University Press, 2016), 2.
[55] Gary A. Anderson, "From Israel's Burden to Israel's Debt: Towards a Theology of Sin in Biblical and Early Second Temple Sources," in *Reworking the Bible: Apocryphal and Related Texts at Qumran*, ed. Esther G. Chazon, Devorah Dimant, and Ruth Clements (Boston: Brill, 2005), 3.

a stain, 3) sin as debt or accounting, and 4) sin as directional.[56] Burden describes human experience of sin as a weight, heavy, and transferable by us. Scripture tells us God has the capacity to and does ease or relieve the burden. The burden can also be transferred to another and carried away.[57] Lam notes that sin as a burden is multi-faceted, speaking to actions, guilt by the actor, and potential punishment.[58] Considering sin as a burden within the context of oppression, injustice, and social sin raises questions. For example, what burdens do we put on others or which sins of ours do we transfer to others? How do we translate the belief that we are created as *imago Dei*—in the image of a God who relieves burdens, who shares burdens, who accompanies the suffering—into actions relieving, sharing, and accompanying women with their burdens related to reproductive decisions? For in a system of injustice and oppression, women's burdens are often placed on them by others—whether by people or by the way institutions and systems operate.

Sin as debt or account contains the idea of keeping a record with God as the record-keeper, the one who passes judgement. Sin as debt or account reminds us that sins endure and require payment. God is the judge, and only God decides what constitutes repayment or whether to forgive the debt.[59] However, not all suffering is the result of our own actions. Some suffering is put upon us by others, despite our innocence.[60] When we judge reproductive sins, do we account for the way our actions cause suffering? What accounting does the community need for their inability to support mothers and all parents with paid parental leave, a living wage, adequate food, shelter, and other necessities to raise the children society and

---

[56] See Joseph Lam, *Patterns of Sin in the Hebrew Bible*, and Gary A. Anderson, "From Israel's Burden to Israel's Debt."
[57] Anderson, "From Israel's Burden to Israel's Debt," 3–9.
[58] Lam, *Patterns of Sin in the Hebrew Bible*, 5, 208.
[59] Anderson, "From Israel's Burden to Israel's Debt," 18–20; Lam, *Patterns of Sin in the Hebrew Bible*, 5, 208–209.
[60] Anderson, "From Israel's Burden to Israel's Debt," 16–18.

churches deem intrinsically good? What debt is owed to those suffering injustice at the hands of others?

Directional metaphors include time, space, and movement. They focus on the moral agent's progress, regression, or conversion to following God and God's ways. They can capture intentionality as well.[61] Using this lens, missing the mark is both a definition and a directional metaphor.[62] The community can ask: Where have we missed the mark in fighting reproductive injustice? Where have we failed to live the corporal and spiritual works of mercy in the context of suffering due to reproductive injustice?

Lam explains that "metaphors of 'stain' or 'impurity' present sin as inherent intrusions into some defined sphere or as disruptions of a pristine state." These metaphors "work implicitly by conveying sin's approval and disapproval, its consequences and remedies."[63] Blood is used as an image for sin as a stain and as a source of life within Hebrew Scriptures and New Testament theologies. For example, Jesus' giving of his life blood is seen as purifying and cleansing, a sacrifice for our collective sins, and the giving of new life. Yet, for women, sin, stain, and women's embodied experience of reproductive bleeding are conflated.[64] Women's blood which can give life, also renders her unclean. Hence rituals exist(ed) for women's purification and cleansing. As a result, any women's pregnancy, talk of reproductive bleeding, or reproductive changes, transgresses the patriarchal taboos regarding blood and challenges the mythical ideal of female sexual purity as non-bloody. Reproductive justice movements also help destigmatize and normalize pregnancy and menstruation.

However, sin as stain reminds us of the enduring nature of sin—it is hard to extricate, to get out. It lives on through generations and in

---

[61] Lam, *Patterns of Sin in the Hebrew Bible*, 15, 208.

[62] Wardlaw, "Translating 'Sin,'" 23, 30–33.

[63] Lam, *Patterns of Sin in the Hebrew Bible*, 15, 209.

[64] For a positive retrieval of menstruation and female bleeding, see Doris M. Kieser, "The Female Body in Catholic Theology: Menstruation, Reproduction, and Autonomy," *Horizons* 44, no. 1 (2017):1–27.

embodied form. We see this enduring nature of sin in systemic, generational racial injustice. Because of the enduring nature of sin, we must confront it and its lingering effects. Enduring sin slowly eviscerates individuals and communities leading to death. Only by acknowledging sin's endurance can we begin moving from death to life.

Rachael Baard writes that "authentic sin-talk is the language of *pathos* and not only of pathology, born from a prophetic *ethos*, aimed at denouncing that which is death dealing, and at affirming life."[65] Contemporary moral theologians grappling with sinful complicity in social structures shape sin-conversation in new ways, illuminating alternative possibilities for acting well and addressing injustice. A few examples will need to suffice.

Julie Hanlon Rubio retrieves the principle of cooperation with evil from moral manuals to analyze complex questions of complicity in far-flung, world-wide systemic systems of injustice.[66] Some manualists used the language of cooperation with evil, others cooperation with sin. The manualists are concerned with helping people determine if and how their engagement with the sins of others might be cooperation and sinful too.[67] The manualists with the principle of cooperation were attempting "to balance the reality of limited power and influence with the desire of individuals not to participate in the sins of those with whom they interact in public life."[68]

Rubio's retrieval of the principle of cooperation with evil shifts the context from confession and individual contexts to accountability for public, political advocacy aimed at resisting and transforming social sin and

---

[65] Baard, *Sexism and Sin-Talk*, 153.
[66] Julie Hanlon Rubio, "Moral Cooperation with Evil and Social Ethics," *Journal of the Society of Christian Ethics* 31, no. 1 (2011): 103–122, and "Cooperation with Evil Reconsidered: The Moral Duty of Resistance," *Theological Studies* 78, no. 1 (2017): 96–120.
[67] The manualists do not spend time precisely defining the category evil even though many use the term. Their concern is defining when cooperation is sinful. Thank you to Julie Hanlon Rubio for an email exchange about the manualists and their use of the term "cooperation with evil."
[68] Rubio, "Cooperation with Evil Reconsidered," 105.

sinful structures—the very social and sinful structures within which we act and participate. Rubio considers how individuals can make moral decisions for acting in spaces of communal sinfulness as well as foster much needed transformation. Drawing on the incisive work of womanist theologians and Black Catholic theologian M. Shawn Copeland, Rubio highlights their challenging reminders that we have a responsibility to do more than avoid sin. We must resist evil.[69] Because when it comes to structural sin "we bear some responsibility for the evil even when we cannot eradicate it alone." Thus, any talk of solidarity with others means we have an "obligation to act."[70] This means individuals and communities must ask what troubles them about structural evil, interrogate the structural evil they accept, and reflect upon what they fail to resist.[71] Other questions include: Who suffers and is oppressed?[72] What is our complicity in systemic reproductive injustice? How can we limit our participation in injustice? What acts of resistance do particular injustices demand?

The questions about troubling, accepting, resisting, and complicity directly reference actions, while implicitly pointing behind the actions

---

[69] Rubio in her work uses the language of social sin, structural sin, and evil when talking about social issues. The womanists and black theologians also use the language of evil when discussing social injustices. Thus, evil in these instances refers to the pervasive, embedded, systemic sinfulness, oppression, injustice in our structures, institutions, cultures, and societies. Therefore, the language of evil captures a depth of corruption requiring transformation different than a single instance of a sinful act.

[70] Rubio, "Cooperation with Evil Reconsidered," 104–112.

[71] The three questions about troubling, accepting, and resisting come from Rubio's reading of womanist theology. Rubio, "Cooperation with Evil Reconsidered," 110.

[72] The Korean notion of *han* also explores the oppression resulting from social sin in a specific context. A more in-depth study is beyond this essay. See Andrew Sung Park, *The Wounded Heart of God: The Asian Concept of Han and the Christian Doctrine of Sin* (Nashville: Abingdon Press, 1993); Kevin Considine explores intercultural implications of *han* for understandings of sin and addressing various forms of injustice for the sinned-against. See for example, Kevin Considine, "*Han* (恨) and Salvation for the Sinned Against," *New Theology Review* 26, no. 1 (2013): 87–89, and "Kim Chi-Ha's Han Anthropology and its Challenge to Catholic Thought," *Horizons*, 41, no. 1 (2014): 49–73. I want to thank Hoon Choi for introducing me to the scholarship on *han*.

towards motivations, affections, and attitudes. Darlene Fozard Weaver, arguing that sin is irreducibly relational,[73] looks beyond sinful behaviors to sinful dispositions and attitudes. She contends that sins of omission have roots in various sinful attitudes shared by all because of a communal moral worldview and expectations.[74] Where Rubio's questions help us identify sins of omission, Weaver connects the roots of individual sins of omission in shared (communal) worldviews and expectations. Therefore, individuals and communities must ask: What dispositions, attitudes, perspectives, and theological concepts contribute to sins of omission and need uprooting? And what dispositions, attitudes, perspectives, and theological concepts contribute to transformation, thus needing cultivation?

In both moral and immoral actions, we enact our human freedom. In her 2023 CTSA plenary address, Weaver explores the role of freedom in a morally diverse world.[75] Weaver discusses freedom and various elements required or affecting freedom's enactment: charity, justice, honesty, self-examination, forbearance, fortitude, and building a culture of nuance. It seems to me that these same features are some of the dispositions, attitudes, perspectives, and theological concepts needed for reproductive justice.

Arguing that our freedom is both individual and communally situated and enacted, Weaver writes: "Human freedom is yoked to responsibility to, for, and with others, and this dynamic of freedom and responsibility lies at

---

[73] Darlene Fozard Weaver, "Sin and the Subversion of Ethics: Why the Discourse of Sin is Good for Theological Anthropology," in *T & T Clark Handbook of Theological Anthropology*, ed. Mary Ann Hinsdale and Stephen Okey (London: Bloomsbury Publishing Plc., 2021), 100; Darlene Fozard Weaver, "Freedom in a Morally Diverse World," *CTSA Proceedings* 77 (2023): 23, ejournals.bc.edu/index.php/ctsa/article/view/16959.

[74] Weaver, "Sin and the Subversion of Ethics," 105. A sin of omission means sinning by inaction.

[75] Weaver, "Freedom in a Morally Diverse World," 19. She defines moral diversity as including "not only the fact of moral disagreements but the plurality of ways of life, which our conceptions of goodness too often fail to convey." Furthermore, "Moral diversity is both a consequence of and an occasion for the exercise of freedom. . . . [O]ne's decision about what to make of instances of moral diversity is always also a decision about one's own moral commitments and a decision about how to relate to moral others."

the heart of freedom's integral relation to an objective moral order."[76] In other words, we have responsibilities and obligations towards each other for bringing about a just, moral order. This includes the sphere of reproduction.

Weaver examines fundamental frameworks for communal worldviews. Megan K. McCabe contextualizes the influences of communal worldviews, expectations, and sins on individual actions when she analyzes rape culture. McCabe writes, rape "is the extreme manifestation of gender norms and expectations that construct femininity as sexual availability and masculinity as sexual aggression and dominance."[77] Rape is an individual sin contextualized by the social sin of a rape culture.[78]

McCabe's analysis and questions regarding rape culture apply to reproductive injustice. Reproductive injustice has both individual and social sin manifestations. Social conditions and patterns normalize and obscure instances of reproductive injustice. Women are to be sexually available and bear the burdens of unwanted and unasked for pregnancy, even when raped.[79] Male sexual aggression and dominance extends beyond physical violence into the very enacting of laws that protect their violence. When lawmakers pass laws restricting abortion access to women whose pregnancy's result from rape, this both normalizes pregnancy from rape and obscures the violence endured by females of all ages.[80] Gendered norms

---

[76] Weaver, "Freedom in a Morally Diverse World," 22.

[77] Megan K. McCabe, "A Feminist Catholic Response to the Social Sin of Rape Culture," *Journal of Religious Ethics* 46, no. 4 (2018): 635.

[78] Pope John Paul II, despite essentializing tendencies in his theological anthropology, also says rape is an individual sin, with complicity by society. John Paul II, *Letter to Women*, no. 5. See also Francis, *Amoris Laetitia*, nos. 54, 282.

[79] See Erika Bachiochi, "The Uniqueness of Woman: Church Teaching on Abortion," in *Women, Sex, and the Church: A Case for Catholic Teaching*, ed. Erika Bachiochi (Boston: Pauline, 2010), 37–55, at 50: "Aborting an unborn child conceived through rape makes the child, rather than the rapist, ultimately responsible for the grievous violence perpetrated on the woman."

[80] Normalizing pregnancy from rape means we do not understand how prevalent rape is, how many pregnancies result from rape, and thus do not grasp the insidious way violence is woven

and patterns of normalized violence and injustice also appear in ecclesial treatment of women's reproductive health, in the inability of female migrant workers to receive adequate health care and protection from sexual aggression, in sex trafficking where victims are criminalized.[81]

McCabe's contention that social transformation of rape culture "requires theological and ethical treatment in order to consider what is necessary to make possible social transformation away from beliefs, behaviors, and expectations that place women in the role of the desired object"[82] also applies to reproductive injustice. Lawmakers, ecclesial leaders, and community members are shaped by a reproductive injustice culture that prevents meaningful acknowledgement that structures, norms, and laws foster injustice and harm.[83] This makes change difficult but not impossible. Social transformation fostering reproductive justice must also dismantle beliefs, behaviors, and expectations that place women in the role of passive receivers of reproductive decisions made for them by others and focused on women's "individual sin." Social transformation would recognize women's full human dignity, capacity, and capability to discern and make moral decisions. Additionally, communities would commit to support the financial, spiritual, mental, and social needs of women around their reproductive decisions. Social transformation would eliminate laws that penalize women for pregnancy and/or limit their

---

into the fabric of reproductive decisions by women. Given the recent push for no exception abortion laws, there are attempts to quantify the number of pregnancies resulting from the rape of women. See Selena Simmons-Duffin, "Raped, Pregnant and in an Abortion Ban State? Researchers Gauge How Often it Happens," *National Public Radio*, January 24, 2023, www.npr.org/sections/health-shots/2024/01/24/1226161416/rape-caused-pregnancy-abortion-ban-states.

[81] See in this volume Eric Genilo, SJ, "Risking Women's Lives, Denying Women's Experiences: CDF Statements on Sterilization in Catholic Hospitals," 334–357. and Peterson-Iyer, "Reproductive Justice and Agricultural Labor Migrants," 257–289.

[82] McCabe, "A Feminist Catholic Response to the Social Sin of Rape Culture," 646.

[83] McCabe, "A Feminist Catholic Response to the Social Sin of Rape Culture," 651, n. 10. I adopt her insight about changing rape culture to reproductive justice.

agency and would pass laws that hold men accountable for acts of dominance and gender-based violence.

McCabe offers the themes of interruption, solidarity, and conscience as a means of changing culture. She applies Edward Schillebeeckx's concept of negative contrast experiences and Johann Baptist Metz's dangerous memory as forms of interruption that can help transform a toxic culture of sexual violence.[84] These concepts also work for transforming a culture of reproductive injustice, a transformation to which this collection of essays contributes. The essays interrupt narratives that reproductive injustice does not exist. They disrupt narratives that moral decisions around reproduction are easily decided. They challenge the myopic focus on the unborn developing human being, arguing for concrete facts rather than idealized abstractions when advocating for women's agency and reproductive moral decisions. The essays within this collection offer dangerous memories of alternative narratives of women's experiences, challenging everyone to see differently, to notice a different landscape requiring new responses. Hoon Choi's essay provides an alternative narrative from a male perspective helping cultivate a new landscape that demands attention to men's responsibilities.[85]

McCabe's second offering, solidarity, requires something of the community. Standing by, doing nothing in the face of injustice belies our complicity as Rubio, following womanist theologians, points out. Rubio writes, "There is a strong sense of the duty to act, not to avoid culpability, but to avoid cooperating with the social structures that harm vulnerable persons whose connections to me are undeniable. I cannot be in right relationship with God if I am involved in denying the rights of others. It is impossible to disconnect their lives from mine."[86] Solidarity requires practices that disrupt and resist the cultural beliefs and standards that

---

[84] McCabe, "A Feminist Catholic Response to the Social Sin of Rape Culture," 652–653.
[85] See in this volume Hoon Choi, "Fatherhood, Reproductive Justice, and Strategic Invisibility of Men," 122–147.
[86] Rubio, "Cooperation with Evil Reconsidered," 111.

support reproductive injustice. The call for resistance to evil and cooperation with injustice referenced above would be one practice to adopt. For example, not firing single pregnant women from their jobs in identifiable Catholic spaces would be a disruptive practice and a step towards accompaniment of women in their reproductive decisions.[87]

Likewise, Weaver's work on attitudes and dispositions provides guidance for living in solidarity. What in our communities' worldviews foster our complicity and inaction? What attitudes and dispositions provide venues for relieving burdens, generosity of spirit, and compassionate accompaniment? Weaver challenges us to practice interrogating our beliefs and attitudes that hinder solidarity. For example: Do we think single or teenage mothers deserve no financial support, and if so, why? We must ask what communal dispositions, attitudes, worldviews, and expectations about women, unmarried pregnancy, infertility, or abortion decisions contribute to stigma rather than understanding, support, and reproductive justice.

McCabe follows many contemporary theologians when she argues that conscience helps moral agents navigate what is practically required to implement practices that work toward changing a toxic, harmful culture. Listening to conscience "is the mature expression of moral agency to make real the commandment to love God, self, and neighbor in the particular, concrete circumstances of day-to-day life."[88] Conscience connects the work of interruption to the work of solidarity and thus it "challenges and guides individuals to pursue their role" in the work of transforming a culture of reproductive injustice.[89] This conscience work cannot remain the work of

---

[87] Single pregnant women in Catholic institutions often risk losing their jobs, jeopardizing their capacity to care for themselves and the pre-natal life they carry. See, for example, Maria Sole Campinoti, "New Jersey Supreme Court Rules in Favor of Catholic School that Fired a Teacher for Having Premarital Sex," *CNN*, August 16, 2023, www.cnn.com/2023/08/15/us/new-jersey-catholic-school-premarital-sex-firing/index.html.

[88] McCabe, "A Feminist Catholic Response to the Social Sin of Rape Culture," 654.

[89] McCabe, "A Feminist Catholic Response to the Social Sin of Rape Culture," 655. Again, I apply her insights to reproductive injustice.

individuals. We need to develop practices of communal discernment and formation of conscience. As scripture and the theologians used in this section have shown, communities shape culture, influencing and forming the individuals in them who act. Thus, individuals and communities must work to transform the cultures and structures enabling reproductive injustice.

Conclusion

I began with Miriam's experience of reproductive injustice, as a single, teen mother. Her experience and the questions raised about navigating the sins of both individuals and communities in reproductive justice conversations highlighted the limitations of traditional sin talk in the context of reproductive injustice. An overview of changing theological landscapes influencing sin-talk indicated the value of considering the metaphorical nature of language, specifically sin-talk. This led to a review of several scriptural metaphors for sin with implications for sin-talk when analyzing and seeking solutions to reproductive injustice. Using various theologians, who describe various dimensions of social sin, I argued for seeing reproductive sin as a form of social sin. Perceiving reproductive sin as social sin necessitates social transformation for reproductive justice.

Social transformation is required because the dehumanization of women and ignoring of their moral agency has been institutionalized in social systems and laws, as well as in ecclesial teachings and structures. This results in part from an intellectual tradition where sin-talk and conscience formation primarily focus on individual avoidance of sin instead of a focus on communal fostering of justice, prudential judgement about acting in conflict situations, or navigating disagreements about magisterial teaching. For Christians, this means revisioning discipleship as individuals in community and in relationship, also recognizing that communities act collectively as disciples.

Discipleship's demands are rigorous, challenging, and ongoing, as we are called to love all and from this love pursue justice. We can start by listening to people most affected by unjust laws, practices, and cultural norms, seeking their knowledge about what structures need transformation. Authentic listening and dialogue means turning away from fixating on another's named or perceived sin which permits me to ignore the complexity surrounding reproductive injustice and my contribution to unjust structures, systems, and cultures. While seeking justice, we need to contextualize individual decisions within communal spaces, acknowledging systems of oppression and the harm they do to people's moral agency.

Jesus challenges the community 'judges' and 'onlookers' to examine the planks in their own eye, their hearts and motives, and their sins (e.g., Matthew 7:3–5, Luke 16:14–15, John 8:2–11). Jesus's invitation to examine assumptions, motives, and sin extends to us. Considering how we, as 'onlookers' and 'judges,' contribute to reproductive injustices illuminates our communal malformation. Mapping communal complicity shows what needs conversion. Individual women cannot navigate reproductive injustice alone. Eradicating injustice and creating more just cultures for people making reproductive decisions is a communal endeavor.

Returning to Miriam's story we can ask: What does a revised sin-talk that pays as much attention to communal complicity in reproductive injustice and social sin as to individual sin do for her?[90] What would a changed vision look like for her? What new message might she receive? The community might ask her: What burdens are you carrying? Which ones can we lift or help you carry? She would find a community reflecting upon and rectifying their contributions to her burdens. Her burdens would be lightened and shared by her community. They would provide childcare, assistance with food, and other necessities, so she could focus on school and her child, rather than worry about their survival. However, this support would need appropriate dispositions and attitudes by those

---

[90] Thank you to Mary M. Doyle Roche who suggested returning to Miriam's story in the conclusion and asking what a revised sin-talk would do for her.

providing aid so that Miriam's sense of isolation and punishment would be lifted as well.

It can be argued that Miriam missed the mark and strayed from the moral path of avoiding pregnancy as an unmarried teen. Did her school need to keep her from graduation as a form of accounting and payment for her sins, sins she perceived as offset by her decision to become a mother? Being allowed to attend graduation would function as a form of solidarity—a sign that her community stands with her to continue with her education while raising a child. New sin-talk means that Miriam's school administrators would also consider how they strayed from the path of discipleship. The administrators strayed by adding to Miriam's burdens instead of easing them, and by not acknowledging and supporting her hard decision to become a teen mother once pregnant.

The questions posed in section three and in this brief revisiting of Miriam's story can form the basis for a communal examen of conscience around reproductive justice.[91] Additional examen questions include: What ideas, norms, conceptions, ideologies, theologies, values, commitments, attachments, obligations, and emotions frame and shape the rules and regulations we put in place? Who benefits? Who is left out? Who is marginalized? Who is put front and center? How are we socialized (formed) to view each other, to view what matters in terms of reproductive injustice? What have we overlooked in our considerations? Participating in an examen of conscience helps in naming and analyzing how communities 1) sin, 2) bear culpability for and contribute to another's sin, and 3) participate in unjust systems. All three have valuable repercussions for addressing reproductive injustices. Examens form the basis for asking for forgiveness and enacting change for justice. These examens could find

---

[91] Ignatian discernment with its examen offers one model that can be adapted for communal discernment. See Jesuit Conference of Canada and the U.S., "The Ignatian Examen," www.jesuits.org/spirituality/the-ignatian-examen/ for various applications of the examen. Various religious communities who have structured communal practices for discerning new leadership, such as the Benedictines, could provide education and models for ecclesial and other communities for discerning new directions around reproductive justice.

liturgical expression for example, in the penitential act, the prayers of the faithful, communal rites of reconciliation, Stations of the Cross, or retreats structured around reproductive concerns.

We are in a liminal space with the opportunity to see our past truthfully for what it was, to name as accurately as possible our present reality, and decide to shape a more just, equitable future around reproductive decisions. We continue to live in this liminal space—a space filled with relief, hope, compassion, empathy, commitment to truth, and a focus on justice. It is also a space fraught with trepidation, despair, anger, anxiousness, fear, lies, deceit, and death. It is a space that requires undertaking attempts to answer the question of how we learn to recognize, name, acknowledge, and begin repairing our malformation, especially when the systems that form us also contribute to our malformation and to our sinfulness.

While broken and sinful, we all yearn to belong in community. And one purpose of sin-talk is healing, bringing people back into community, creating wholeness and re-connection.[92] When we forget our own broken sinfulness by seeing others as more sinful, barring them from communities and Eucharistic communion, we are not disciples calling all to Christ.[93] Instead, we rupture the community. Boundaries and norms can provide a life-giving and protective service. However, they can prevent solidarity and authentic encounters that transform people. Boundaries and norms can

---

[92] Baard, *Sexism and Sin-Talk*, 153.

[93] Reconsidering sin-talk has both liturgical and sacramental implications. For example, how does the sacrament of confession or reconciliation need adaptation for communal sins? How can the clerical dynamics which structure our sacraments be reconceived? Exploring these and other questions is beyond the scope of this essay. However, the Dicastery for the Doctrine of the Faith recently provided specific guidance regarding single mothers and the sacraments in a letter responding to an email from Bishop Ramón Alfredo de la Cruz Baldera. Single mothers should have access to the sacraments and the support of their pastors and ecclesial communities. See Prefect Víctor Manuel Cardinal Fernández, "Letter to His Excellency, the Most Reverend Ramón Alfredo de la Cruz Baldera, Bishop of the Diocese of San Francisco de Macorís (Dominican Republic) Regarding Access to Eucharistic Communion for Single Mothers," December 13, 2023, www.vatican.va/roman_curia/congregations/cfaith/documents/rc_ddf_doc_20231213_risposta-madri-single_en.html. Thank you to Emily Reimer-Barry who sent me the link to this letter as it came out during the revisions of this essay.

bar people from communion with each other. Boundaries can thus render the Body of Christ an incomplete wasteland instead of the fertile space of life-giving possibilities in the Spirit. May the Miriams in our midst find in us, individually and communally, life-affirming spaces.

Kathryn Lilla Cox, PhD, is a research associate in the Department of Theology and Religious Studies at the University of San Diego. Her research interests include fundamental moral theology, marriage and infertility, moral formation, and Benedictine approaches to moral theology. She authored *Water Shaping Stone: Faith, Relationships, and Conscience Formation* (Liturgical Press, 2015). Authored essays appear in *Horizons*, *Journal of Moral Theology*, and several edited collections.

5. Fatherhood, Reproductive Justice, and the Strategic Invisibility of Men

Hoon Choi

The story of the "woman caught in adultery" in John 7:53–8:11 famously leaves out any details about the man involved in the adultery. As the story begins, the woman alone is accused. Even as she is "forgiven" by Jesus, the man accused of sharing his bed with her receives no public shaming and no scrutiny from generations of Christians who have retold and interpreted this story. Perhaps for many women who have heard this story proclaimed from the pulpit, what resonates most with their lived experiences is the fact that women continue to be shamed while their sexual partners flee from any responsibility from their actions. To hear such a story preached as "The Gospel of the Lord" may indeed be triggering for survivors of relationship violence.[1]

Today, we clothe this absence and the exoneration of men differently, but they remain intact in the stories of heterosexual experiences of sexual activities. There are double standards between men and women that exonerate men because of their invisibility. Every time a person asks what she was wearing, what kind of personality she had, or how she was behaving, the focus of the offense—whether it is neglect, harassment, assault, or abuse—shifts from the perpetrator to the victim. Men can, and often do, simply walk away from it all. Society does not ask the same questions to, does not demand the same scrutiny of, or place the same

---

[1] This chapter does come with a trigger warning. It has subjects dealing with abuse, abortion, pregnancy, adoption, and irresponsible, neglectful, and abusive behaviors of fathers, boyfriends, and/or men. If you are experiencing relationship violence, you do not have to suffer alone. In the United States, the National Domestic Violence Hotline is a 24/7 service that provides callers with confidential support. Call 1-800-799-7233, Text START to 88788, or visit thehotline.org.

blame on men. Because men have often bought into these double standards, these norms go unchecked for them. By exonerating men from culpability, men often occupy and enjoy the center stage of society without the burden of accountability.[2] This reality is not limited to sexual and gender violence but extends more broadly to many facets of life in general, including issues concerning reproductive justice.

Reproductive justice (RJ) encompasses many overlapping components related to reproduction: medical and legal ethics, theological teachings and beliefs, personal values and principles, family upbringing and cultural norms and expectations, bodily and biological integrity, socio-global setting and situational challenges, and laws and policies, to name a few. The questions that often arise through discussion of these wide-ranging issues concern the status and viability of the fetus, whether one has the right *not* to have a child, and/or what happens when one is forced to carry an unwanted, ill-timed, or dangerous pregnancy to term. What is missing in that conversation, however, is the responsibility of men in those pregnancies.

Thus, I aim to decenter men from infiltrating the realms of women's bodies, experiences, and agencies and, in turn, insert men back in their own realms to take responsibility in ways most appropriate to their roles. My method is to help men imagine and acknowledge their role in RJ so that men may discern in charity and compassion rather than simply casting judgment or blame on women.

Nonetheless, this aim requires caution because it is to "talk about men" yet again. After all, men often dominate and occupy the center of our *his*tories, rendering women's presence and experiences invisible and peripheral. Placing men back in these stories related to RJ, however, makes visible the strategic invisibility that conveniently hides men's decisions,

---

[2] See Kathryn Lilla Cox's analysis of the story of "Miriam" in her essay within the present volume, "Reproductive Injustice as Social Sin: Mapping Sin Discourse into Debates about Fertility Decisions."

actions, and accountability.[3] Doing so also restores the agency of women to its rightful owner.

Admittedly, it is difficult to motivate men to unlearn and undo these incoherent and inconsistent standards, much less inspire them to encourage one another for social transformation. This unwillingness to behave differently often comes down to the failure of moral imagination. In *Moral Discernment*, Richard M. Gula S.S. finds that people "can't act any differently because they can't imagine what it would be like to be someone else."[4] When we decide to act or not act, it is "not as much motivated by our fundamental convictions and reasons as it is by our imagination" and "our reasons will be convincing only if they are consistent with the world of images [that] we are using to interpret our experiences."[5] Such images and imagination shape and clarify what we see and envision as possible.[6]

It is suitable, therefore, to use an exercise of imagination to help men see the current reality and to urge them towards personal and social transformation. Such an exercise exposes the double standards and the lack of coherence and consistency surrounding the issue of reproduction, all of which contribute to restore moral agency back to women.[7]

---

[3] Here, I am using a liberative literary strategy, perhaps like the approach used by the author of the Gospel of John, to evoke a certain reaction in the readers to make a point. See Rita Felski, *Uses of Literature* (Oxford: Wiley-Blackwell, 2008); Leticia A. Guardiola-Sáenz, "Border-Crossing and its Redemptive Power in John 7:53–8:11: A Cultural Reading of Jesus and the Accused," in *Transformative Encounters: Jesus and Women Re-Viewed*, ed. Ingrid R Kitzberger (Leiden, The Netherlands: Brill, 2000).

[4] Richard M. Gula S.S, *Moral Discernment* (New York: Paulist Press, 1997), 97.

[5] Gula, *Moral Discernment*, 94.

[6] Gula, *Moral Discernment*, 95.

[7] Cathleen Kaveny finds this lack of coherence manifested as too narrowly focused almost exclusively on outcome in the discipline of moral theology. Simplistic questions like "Do you or do you not defend magisterial teaching?" suggest that complex Catholic tradition "can be reduced to a multiple-choice test." Because of the complexity of Catholic (moral) tradition, moral theology must also be multidimensional. Cathleen Kaveny, *Ethics at the Edges of Law Christian Moralists and American Legal Thought* (New York: Oxford University Press, 2018), 30–31.

This chapter moves in four parts to achieve this aim. First, it sets up the conversation by placing the RJ movement in its proper historical and current context with its intent, definition, and meaning. Then, it moves into the Catholic realm and places RJ in a context that is already fundamentally essentialist,[8] uneven, and sexist. Despite this contextual limitation, however, the concern about a society without fathers and the required discernment that Pope Francis uplifts in *Amoris Laetitia* (AL) can be key aspects of the moral life for a "genuine reciprocity" in relationships. Thirdly, while Pope Francis's call is an effort to put men back into the story for a true and genuine reciprocity, it does not do enough to imagine a world in which men experience the kinds of scrutiny that women endure. Thus, this chapter introduces an exercise of imagination, employing a visceral method and a tongue-in-cheek provocation by making similar demands on men as those faced by women. It is meant to evoke distress caused by the sheer absurdity of these demands, so readers recognize that if the demands are unreasonable for men, then they are certainly unreasonable for women, too. The purpose of this exercise is not to demonize men. Rather, it is to build empathy, which in the context of "contact hypothesis" (a concept I address later) may behoove men to take appropriate responsibilities. Such a method reveals the double standards in how society thinks about human bodies and bodily integrity. Finally, identifying the double standards exposes the simplistic nature of our policies, laws, and teachings and leads to the recognition of the complex and intersectional implications for RJ. Thus, the chapter concludes that the response from RJ perspective must not only be personal and on the level of social and personal support but also address its relations to global male dominance and white supremacy.

---

[8] For a definition of gender essentialism in theology, see Adrian Thatcher, *God, Sex, and Gender: An Introduction* (West Sussex, UK: Wiley-Blackwell Publishing, 2011), 20: "In theological discussions of gender, essentialism is the doctrine that God created humanity in two distinct sexes. Each is made for the other. Our created nature is to be either male or female. Our nature cannot change. Our desires are intended to be for the opposite sex. Same-sex desire cannot conform to our created nature."

What I suggest is that the most adequate solution must include continued conversations about the systemic, structural, ecclesial, intersectional, and global variables and determinants that play important roles in the conversation about RJ. However, I maintain that none of that can occur adequately without enfranchised women's presence, voices, and experiences at the table of conversation about RJ. All of this, however, must begin by men taking responsibilities for their actions.

Restoring Men into the History of RJ

As mentioned throughout this volume, the term Reproductive Justice—coined by twelve Black women in 1994 at a conference in Chicago—"is a political movement that splices reproductive rights with social justice to achieve reproductive justice," which at its heart claims that, "all fertile persons and persons who reproduce and become parents require a safe and dignified context for these most fundamental human experiences."[9] Right away, RJ, properly understood, is not a simple and divisive conversation about being Pro-choice or Pro-life and moves beyond them to the broader context as it relates to human dignity. Thus, the twelve Black women activists and scholars were suspicious of any movements that gave "the primacy of abortion, but not its necessity." They viewed this issue from an intersectional lens that "made the case that while abortion was a crucial resource for [them], [they] also needed health care, education, jobs, day care, and the right to motherhood."[10] Thus, it has "three primary values, 1) the right *not* to have a child; 2) the right to *have* a child; and 3) the right to *parent* children in safe and healthy environments."[11]

What is historically missing, however, is the role of men and the lack thereof in these movements/frameworks. To uphold these values of RJ,

---

[9] Loretta Ross, and Rickie Solinger, *Reproductive Justice: An Introduction* (Oakland CA: University of California Press, 2017), 9, 63. For a further discussion on these three primary values, see Kate Ward's chapter in this volume.

[10] Ross and Solinger, *Reproductive Justice*, 64.

[11] Ross and Solinger, *Reproductive Justice*, 65.

the discussion of men is essential first because sperm vitality is important in considering fertility. Thus, considering all fertile persons and persons who reproduce must include men. Second, men are a necessary part of the equation in addressing the context of the intersecting social elements—including health care, education, jobs, day care, and the right to motherhood and singlehood—that makes real choices possible. Relatedly, one cannot adequately discuss social needs in a context that is disproportionate for people of color and transgender folks without considering men and their roles. Thus, while mindful of the different aspects of these inferences, men's vantage point is my focus of this chapter because it is sometimes a missing link in the existing conversation about RJ.

Using a method rooted in the Catholic understanding of mutual responsibility, which I discuss in the next section, rather than an approach rooted in retrieval of patriarchal gender relations,[12] one can begin to underscore this inextricable link. In the three primary values outlined by the RJ movement, one can apply men's roles in them, both in terms of accountability and support. That is, to take responsibility for the right of a woman *not* to have a child, men must be equally responsible and present and contribute to what is required when she decides not to have the child. To take responsibility for the right of a woman to *have* a child, men must be present in supporting prenatal care, childbirth expenses, parental care, the raising of a child, and so on. To take responsibility for the right to parent children in safe and healthy environments, men must contribute to providing and sustaining such environments, to the extent that they are able, and fight for social structures and systems that enable the condition for the possibility of such parenting alongside women. Suffice it to say that in the context of the history of the reproductive justice movement, RJ conversations should include men. That is not to say, however, that men

---

[12] See Anne M. Clifford, *Introducing Feminist Theology* (Maryknoll, NY: Orbis, 2002), 16–21; see also "Male Supremacy," *Southern Poverty Law Center*, www.splcenter.org/fighting-hate/extremist-files/ideology/male-supremacy.

should dominate pregnancy discernments. The concept of "reciprocity" helps bringing men into the discussion without having them dominate the discussion.

Catholic "Genuine Reciprocity" for Men and Reproductive Justice

AL offers a different vision of reciprocity, which subverts that gendered power dynamic, not by completely turning it on its head but at least starting an *initial step* towards an egalitarian approach with respect to RJ. Francis claims that "a rigid approach turns into an over-accentuation of the masculine or feminine and does not help children and young people to appreciate the genuine reciprocity incarnate in the real conditions of matrimony" (AL, no. 286). This flexibility enables men to do their part towards the "genuine reciprocity" and feel connected by the bond created by the sexual relationship well beyond the physical act of sexual activity. It opens possibilities for men to imagine in reciprocal, connected, and responsible ways to think about the (sexual) relationship generally and as it pertains to RJ more particularly.

This reciprocal imagination is important because most men—and more particularly cisgender men in heterosexual (married) relationships—find it difficult to navigate through the issue of RJ while often feeling awkward and lost when talking or thinking about it. Part of this unease is understandable as the issues involve women's bodies and experience, of which cisgender men have no direct experience. However, another important reason may be the fact that men feel removed from the issue given the physicalist mindset rooted in a long-standing dualistic tradition of the Western philosophy and culture. In other words, once men are "done" with the physical sexual activity, he can "walk away" from the interconnected and multiple responsibilities of that act and treat it as if it is an isolated physical incident. Moreover, the dualistic categorization is related, if not directly, to heteronormative and (toxic white) masculine maintenance of power. Reciprocal imagination, then, helps men not only to realize the inextricable link beyond the physical but also to combat against unjust maintenance of power.

Regardless, this reciprocal imagination hinges on what reciprocity is. Francis did not really present an understanding of reciprocity nor did he clearly define what genuine reciprocity means. He did, however, claim that one cannot achieve it through "a rigid approach" or "an over-accentuation of the masculine and feminine." In *Mutuality: A Formal Norm for Christian Ethics*, Catholic ethicist Dawn M. Nothwehr notes that "in a relationship characterized by reciprocity, there are clearly defined boundaries between parties involved, and any action, influence, giving/receiving is conditioned by the expectation by the other party(ies) that what is received is of equal value to what is given."[13] Relatedly, in *Just Love: A Framework for Christian Sexual Ethics*, Catholic ethicist Margaret A. Farley claims that human sexuality, which is fundamentally relational, requires "double reciprocal incarnation" in the context of sexual activity and desire, and seeks mutuality of desire and embodied union.[14] One can apply reciprocity, double reciprocity, and mutuality for men in these ways and fulfill the expectation of giving justifiable and appropriate due consideration

---

[13] Ultimately, Nothwehr rightly supposes mutuality as a better term/concept than reciprocity since in mutuality "boundaries are distinct, but the critical difference is that they are determined *with* the other(s) and thus, they are more flexible and fluid." Between cis-gender persons, it means "sharing of 'power-*with*' by and among women and men in a way that recognizes the full participation of each in the *imago Dei*, embodied in daily life and through egalitarian relationships." Dawn M. Nothwehr, *Mutuality: A Formal Norm for Christian Ethics* (Eugene, Oregon: Wipf & Stock Publishers, 1998), 4–5, 233.

[14] Margaret A. Farley, *Just Love: A Framework for Christian Sexual Ethics* (New York: Continuum, 2006), 220–222. See Jean-Paul Sartre, *Being and Nothingness*, trans. Hazel E. Barnes (New York: Philosophical Library, 1966). Like Nothwehr, Farley also uses the notion of mutuality as a preferred term.

for men not only for mutual respect but also for men's accountability to women.[15]

How would a reciprocal approach evaluate Francis's concern about "a society without fathers" (AL, no. 176)? One would immediately recognize that fathers are missing from the conversation even though it "takes two to tango" and fathers are only inserted into the conversation to tell women what they can or cannot do. Imagine what would happen if fathers were not only recognized as mutual and loving interlocutors of their partners but also put through the same kind of scrutiny that women experience (without adequate social support). How might such an exercise help men to empathize through imagination and learning and caring about other vulnerable populations that are more likely to be denied a full range of social services and protections necessary for RJ, namely BIPOC, LGBTQIA+, persons with disabilities, and young people.

In other words, while acknowledging the existence of the deep-rooted physicalism and essentialism in AL, one can still build upon Francis's teaching, as it opens the vision of genuine reciprocity towards achieving RJ. In this way, AL is a development and an advancement from the more rigid physicalism and essentialism present in previous papal teachings. Within such a framework, one can begin to address the concern about a society without fathers by placing men back in the conversation about RJ. In this sense, then, (Catholic) men may play a crucial role in the discussion of RJ.

Empathy through Contact Hypothesis

To invite and convince men to join the difficult conversation of RJ and to learn from women about their experiences and bodies from women's vantage points, I propose that we take the approach of "contact

---

[15] It is important to note that while the issue of gender complementarity is lurking in the background of all of this, Nothwehr and Farley's notions of reciprocity and mutuality are markedly different from it.

hypothesis," according to which, intergroup contact or interaction under appropriate conditions can reduce prejudice between members especially if one recognizes the common humanity as an "in-group."[16] Through this approach, men may be more open to conversation and quicker to respond when the issues are perceived as *their* issues. For instance, the problem of impotence has been quickly resolved not only with the accidental invention but, more importantly, the wide distributions of Viagra (Sildenafil).[17] The aim of this exercise, then, is to help men treat the issue of RJ in a socially just and urgent manner by imagining it as experienced by men in their bodies, so they can empathize with women's experiences and perspectives. In other words, men can learn from and center women's experiences by imagining "being in their shoes." Centering women's experience in this way can be transformative.[18]

But how? My suggestion is for men to imagine going through the similar kind of scrutiny through which women experience the world. Authors in this volume point to various kinds of scrutiny that women face—whether because of economic constraints (Ward), cultural practices (Saldanha and Ehidiamhen), educational policies (Cox), institutional racism (Roche), immigration laws (Peterson-Iyer), or hospital regulations (Reimer-Barry). Many women around the world are forced to acquiesce to (patriarchal) laws and moral regulations. Often these policies and regulations require pregnant people to carry-to-term, simplistically

---

[16] See Gordon W. Allport, *The Nature of Prejudice: 25th Anniversary Edition*, 2nd ed. (Reading, MA: Addison-Wesley, 1980), especially chapter 3. Taschler and West found that such interactions could be a potential tool to combat sexism, rape myth acceptance, intentions to rape in men, and sexualization of rape by women. Miriam Taschler and Keon West, "Contact with Counter-Stereotypical Women Predicts Less Sexism, Less Rape Myth Acceptance, Less Intention to Rape (in Men) and Less Projected Enjoyment of Rape (in Women)," *Sex Roles* 76, no. 7 (2017): 473–484, doi.org/10.1007/s11199-016-0679-x.

[17] Abi Berger, "The Rise and Fall of Viagra," *British Medical Journal* 317, no. 7161 (1998): 824, doi.org/10.1136/bmj.317.7161.824.

[18] For instance, it could allow our culture, which teaches girls to wait for boys to grow up, to teach boys to learn from girls because girls mature faster. My challenge is simply that men learn from women about women's experience and women's bodies from women's vantage points.

expecting them to place the baby for adoption if they do not have the means to raise the baby, or force abortion without their consent. In the cases of pregnancy complications and/or fetal genetic anomalies, some laws force women to wait until the life of the mother is in danger to perform a procedure that would address the pregnancy complications. The reason for this delay is either so that this "proof requirement" confirms no "attack" on the "viable fetus" or that it is considered a permissible "indirect abortion" via the principle of double effect.[19] Even after the abortion (and presumably in early pregnancy losses), laws can potentially require the hospitals and mothers to bury or cremate the fetal remains, as it is deemed to be a human death.[20] Meanwhile, men disappear from the original stories and only appear as enforcers of these regulations, policies, rules, and theologies.[21]

What if men can imagine, as they should, these issues as "their issues" and share appropriate responsibility? What would happen if men, and their bodies, had to go through such anguish, enforcement, and torment because of an external control over their bodies and agency? Would it not highlight the complexity and the absurdities? If men are appalled, would it not help them see and be outraged by the preposterous demands on women, too? Thus, while the following exercise of imagination will or should feel outlandish, such a response is the point of it. One ought to feel indignation and imagine what women experience in real life.

Imagine, then, applying similar kinds of conditions and external control to men and their bodies. Take, for instance, the possible scenario of coerced male sterilization to minimize unwanted pregnancies and babies. If unwanted pregnancy is a social problem and if it takes two people's genetic material for pregnancy to be achieved, then preventing

---

[19] David Kelly, Gerard Magill, and Henk ten Have, eds., *Contemporary Catholic Health Care Ethics*, 2nd ed. (Washington DC: Georgetown University Press, 2013), 104–121.
[20] Brandon Smith, "Legal Battle over Indiana Fetal Remains Law Over as U.S. Supreme Court Declines Appeal," *WFYI* PBS-NPR affiliate in Indianapolis, May 1, 2023, www.wfyi.org/news/articles/legal-battle-over-indiana-fetal-remains-law-over-as-us-supreme-court-declines-appeal.
[21] Michelle Goodwin, *Policing the Womb* (New York: Cambridge University Press, 2022).

unwanted pregnancy could warrant mandatory vasectomies for men. Such a policy would require men/boys to have a vasectomy and only reverse the procedure when they are ready to be responsible.[22] What about the physical, emotional, mental toll of a vasectomy? There are some possibilities for complications from the outpatient surgical procedure that can cause this strain. Stress may also result from the law requiring vasectomy because it would not need to attend to the patient's informed consent but merely to the application of the law in the patient's life. Men would simply have to withstand them in similar manner that woman had to endure in cases of uncertain fetal viability.

Moreover, how would one determine whether they are ready to be responsible? One would have to prove it. Such a "proof requirement" would force men to demonstrate that they have financial means to support a child, mental stability, and maturity to parent, and familial or communal support (both physical and emotional) necessary to bring a child into the world responsibly.[23] While this is quite a narrow opening for bringing a child into the world, rules based on women's biological cycle, with

---

[22] Yelena Dzhanova, "An Oklahoma State Rep Proposed Legislation that Would Mandate Young Men Get Mandatory Vasectomies," *Business Insider*, May 21, 2022, www.businessinsider.com/oklahoma-state-rep-proposed-legislation-mandating-vasectomies-for-men-2022-5. Similar, tongue-in-cheek arguments were made for requiring vasectomy at age fifty or after three children. Of course, the US Supreme Court ruled that forced sterilization is unconstitutional, "but during the 20th century, the federal government funded coerced sterilization of people of color, disabled people and poor people in 32 states, PBS reported." Kristin Lam, "Mandatory Vasectomy at Age 50? Alabama Lawmaker Proposes Response to Abortion Ban," *USA Today*, February 18, 2020, www.usatoday.com/story/news/nation/2020/02/17/mandatory-vasectomy-alabama-proposal/4791335002; See also Emily Reimer-Barry's discussion of Dorothy Roberts' report about forced sterilization of Black men in Indiana in 1902. Dorothy Roberts, *Killing the Black Body* (New York: Vintage Books, 2017), 66–68.

[23] These requirements often do not have the desired effect. Cf. Ximena Bustillo, "Congress Created Changes to Food Assistance. Here's What They Mean" *NPR*, June 2, 2023, www.npr.org/2023/06/02/1179633624/snap-food-assistance-work-requirements-congress-debt-ceiling.

additional external consideration of married life, limit such an opportunity in similar ways.

However, Catholic persons might object on the grounds of artificiality. That is, one might argue that vasectomy is not natural continence, unlike NFP or the rhythm method. The *Catechism of the Catholic Church* claims that part of parental responsibility "concerns the regulation of procreation" (no. 2368) that can be achieved by "periodic continence . . . based on self-observation and the use of infertile periods" (no. 2370). To be faithful to these teachings on "naturality" and if applied just as strictly to men, such continence and regulation could not only be based on women's biological cycle but also based on men. Why would such continence not manifest in terms of limiting the number of times men can engage in sexual activity per month or only certain days of the week? It is within the means of what is often considered "natural" or not artificial and the forced control over men's bodies is consistent with the restrictions on women.

Moreover, since there are restrictive measures accessing mifepristone and misoprostol, which were widely available for women who sought to terminate a pregnancy, why not restrict men from getting and using Viagra (sildenafil) to further safeguard and get to the core of the "problem" by limiting it until men go through a "proof requirement" of responsibility? After all, mifepristone use is a lot less risky (one death per every one million usage) than Viagra (forty-nine deaths per every million usages).[24] Furthermore, if we are serious about men's responsibility for pregnancy, what is

---

[24] Mike Mitka, "Some Men Who Take Viagra Die—Why?" *Journal of the American Medical Association* 283, no. 5 (2000): 590–593, doi.org/10.1001/jama.283.5.590-JMN0202-2-1; Analysis of Medication Abortion Risk and the FDA report "Mifepristone US Post-Marketing Adverse Events Summary through 6/30/2021," *Advancing Standards in Reproductive Health* Issue Brief, November 2022. Note that according to FDA, these events not only "cannot with certainty be causally attributed to mifepristone," but also the latest update through June 2022 shows even less risk for Mifepristone (www.fda.gov/media/164331/download); See Annette Choi and Will Mullery, "How safe is the abortion pill compared with other common drugs?" *CNN Health,* April 21, 2023, www.cnn.com/2023/03/15/health/abortion-pill-safety-dg/index.html.

stopping these regulations from going so far as to require the biological father to pay half of the cost related to the mother and the (actual and potential) child after the sexual encounter, no matter what their relationship status is?[25] According to one opinion, such support includes "medical costs, living costs, education—all the costs a father normally assumes for his child. In addition, the child should have a full share of the father's estate when the father dies. If women cannot decide whether to carry a child, fathers should not be able to decide whether... to support the woman and the child."[26] At the very least, financial support should be required regardless of the outcome. And how would we know who the father is? One can use "DNA as a verification," to establish "paternity for every embryo." In this way, men can assume "responsibility for the consequences of their pleasure."[27]

To be sure, these are not just hyperbolic sardonicism. There are legal and existential implications. If men are rightly linked to every heterosexual sexual activity then they would also be implicated in laws that punish women for the violations concerning pregnancy and terminations. Instead of convicting only women of "murder" for carrying out abortion in the states where abortion is illegal, the legislation would concurrently introduce a bill that can implicate men as the accomplices or conspirators of that "crime." The only mention of the "husband" that I can find in these bills is in terms of not exonerating women with "presumption that a woman is subject to compulsion when acting in the presence of her

---

[25] For example, the Catholic Diocese of Salt Lake City supports such measure in Utah, calling it a "positive pro-life measure to help women who want to keep their baby but feel overwhelmed by the costs." Rachel Treisman, "Utah Law Requires Biological Fathers to Pay Half of Pregnancy-Related Medical Costs," *NPR*, April 7, 2021, www.npr.org/2021/04/07/985089967/utah-law-requires-biological-fathers-to-pay-half-of-pregnancy-related-medical-co. Notably, there is a concern that "the bill could tie women financially to an abusive partner," although its supporters are confident that the law would "not open doors for anything that could put a survivor of domestic violence in any fear."

[26] Robert Veitch, "Readers Write: Abortion: Women Deserve Better," *Star Tribune*, May 3, 2022, www.startribune.com/readers-write-abortion/600170244.

[27] Veitch, "Readers Write: Abortion: Women Deserve Better."

husband." Thus, even though one of these bills in question is called "equal protection act," referring to the Fourteenth Amendment, there is not the same equality in prosecuting all responsible parties, most certainly including men.[28]

If there are men who decide to stay unmarried—which through the eyes of the Church is not fulfilling their natural duties unless it is for religious reasons—could the Church demand that they become adoptive parents? It would not only fulfill their natural duty and inclination towards fatherhood and contribute to finding homes for "unwanted" babies but also it would deter men from staying single for "selfish" reasons and would allow them to be more "totally giving" of themselves.

All these regulations and expectations are consistent with the typical regulatory ethos men advance and force upon women. Here, what makes the difference is that such an attitude is applied also to men. If these suggestions seem far-fetched or even absurd then they serve the aim of this exercise. While it in no way replaces women's experiences or grasps the anxiety, toll, and even fear of dying during pregnancy, labor, delivery, and postpartum complications, it does give men a visceral perception, a state of mind, if only vicariously and temporarily, of what it is like when external entities regulate their bodies, decisions, agencies, and bodily integrity. They are not unreasonable scenarios both because men are involved in *all* unwanted pregnancies and because these expectations are already normatively applied to women. If coerced sterilization, forced adoption, disregard of informed consent, applying the law without due consideration for the human aspect of the problem, proof requirement or establishing paternity for every embryo through DNA verification (justified in the name of making the world safer for babies) are all too excessive for men, then they are excessive for women, too.

---

[28] Logan Sparkman, Brian Lawson, and Jess Grotjahn, "New Alabama Bill Wants Abortion to Carry Murder Charge," CBS 42, May 11, 2023, www.cbs42.com/alabama-news/new-alabama-bill-wants-abortion-to-carry-murder-charge/amp.

Towards Genuine Reciprocity

If indeed there are double-standards and discrepancies in how societies evaluate and apply rules, regulations, laws, and practices concerning our bodies then one can apply the notion of genuine reciprocity both to highlight such inconsistencies and to suggest more consistent evaluations and applications. Such work has been done in the past, but it often does not explicitly name men in that reciprocity. Genuine reciprocity would require such explicit naming and the development of a more just paradigm. However, all of that would require a short but important digression on bodily integrity because it will underscore and name the discrepancy and highlight the need for empathy and reciprocity.

In other words, if male readers are understandably opposed to coerced sterilization, for example, on what moral grounds do they assert the necessity of their bodily autonomy and the necessity of their informed consent? Might those principles be relevant to women discerning whether they can continue to provide bodily life support for a prenatal life or not? Drawing on the resources of Catholic feminist theology could provide a compelling rationale for why readers should justifiably reject men's forced sterilization and—to avoid double standards—why one would need to extend the argument to women's discernments as well.

In comparing organ donation and abortion, Catholic ethicist Patricia Beattie Jung asserts that the human body, unlike other possessions, is an embodied reality and, as such, bodily integrity must be a condition necessary for agency.[29] That is, while beneficence may require agents to give or share possessions as gifts that contribute to overall benefit and human flourishing, "it can never require of agents so pure and personal a gift as the gift of one's body" because "the more personal the gift, the more 'gifty' and discretionary it becomes." After all, what type of gift is more

---

[29] Patricia Beattie Jung, "Abortion and Organ Donation: Christian Reflections on Bodily Life Support," *Journal of Religious Ethics* 16, no. 2 (1988): 286.

personal and intimate than the gift of one's bodily self?[30] As such, even as Christian love (self-giving agape) preaches selflessness in response to the needs of the human community, bodily forms of giving (e.g., bodily life support) are "highly discretionary gifts, and ought only be encouraged" for the sake of the other and human community and not required or forced.

Thus, organ donation and transplantation, against which Catholic medical ethics once argued using a restricted individualistic interpretation of the principle of totality, are now morally permissible in Catholicism using a broader understanding of the "body" as the human community within the same principle. By a broader understanding of the body, Bert Cunningham means "the mystical body of Christ" which "might serve as the basis for a wider interpretation of 'totality.' The totality would be corporate and not individual and hence organ transplantation would be licit."[31] However, David F. Kelly is careful and clear not to impinge on the respect for the individual person and their agency and claims that "we need to guard against it precisely by using individualism and corporatism as correctives to each other's excesses."[32] And there are many other complex problems of administering the process and the procedures of organ donation and transplantation.[33] Those procedural problems notwithstanding, a similar kind of step can be taken in terms of abortion and bodily integrity if we understand the body as the Mystical Body of Christ, as long

---

[30] Jung, "Abortion and Organ Donation: Christian Reflections on Bodily Life Support," 287, 289.

[31] Kelly, Magill, and ten Have, *Contemporary Catholic Health Care Ethics*, 37; Bert Joseph Cunningham, *The Morality of Organic Transplantation* (Washington DC: Catholic University of America Press, 1944).

[32] Kelly, Magill, and ten Have, *Contemporary Catholic Health Care Ethics*. See Kelly's original argument in his "Individualism and Corporatism in a Personalist Ethics: An Analysis of Organ Transplants," in *Personalist Morals: Essays in Honor of Professor Louis Janssens*, ed. Joseph A. Selling (Leuven: Leuven University Press, 1988).

[33] For example, Senator Elizabeth Warren, among others, is highly critical of the agency that monopolizes and mishandles many organ transplantation and transportation procedures. Blake Farmer, "Transplant agency is criticized for donor organs arriving late, damaged or diseased" *NPR*, August 17, 2022, www.npr.org/sections/health-shots/2022/08/17/1118009567/damaged-and-diseased-organs-the-agency-overseeing-transplants-faces-intense-scru.

as we are always cognizant of the similar danger of the excesses of individualism and corporatism.

However, while Christian ethicists agree that no one ought to "be forced to donate an organ or submit to other invasive physical procedures for however good cause," some pro-life feminists disagree and claim that this principle cannot be extended to childbearing and abortion. Catholic ethicist Sidney Callahan, for example, says that in the case of pregnancy, "this right to bodily integrity does not apply" because "one's own body no longer exists as a single unit but is engendering another organism's life" when pregnant.[34] Catholic ethicist Lisa Sowle Cahill described childbearing as "a *prima facie* duty or obligation mandated by the natural requirements of justice."[35]

These disagreements may be irreconcilable. Firstly, even when there is a *prima facie* duty to bear a child, the principle is only binding if it does not come in conflict with another moral principle, in which case one must choose between the two. For that reason, sometimes *prima facie* duty is referred to as "conditional duty."[36] In the case of childbearing, the health, well-being, and the life of the mother may come in conflict with, and therefore may override, the original obligation.[37] Secondly, there are fundamental differences in their vision and understanding of life in the womb and outside of the womb. The pro-life Catholic feminists regard the fetus as a person, which makes it a fundamentally different case than organ

---

[34] Jung, "Abortion and Organ Donation," 287.

[35] Jung, "Abortion and Organ Donation," 280.

[36] See W.D. Ross, *The Right and the Good* (Oxford: Clarendon Press, 2002), 19: "I suggest '*prima facie* duty' or 'conditional duty' as a brief way of referring to the characteristics (quite distinct from that of being a duty proper) which an act has, in virtue of being of a certain kind (e.g. the keeping of promise), of being an act which would be a duty proper if it were not at the same time of another kind which is morally significant."

[37] Margaret Farley makes similar arguments about the release of obligations. "When another obligation comes into conflict with and supersedes the obligation to keep a commitment, a just love may require that the commitment be broken or changed." See Margaret A. Farley, *Personal Commitments: Beginning, Keeping, Changing* Revised Edition (Maryknoll, NY: Orbis Books, 2013), 92–100, 126–136.

donations, as removing it before viability would threaten the life of the fetus. Organ donation is different, they would argue, because while not requiring organ donation may lower the chance of survival for the needy patient, the potential donor is not directly and immediately implicated in the survival and death of the patient *and* because they might come across other willing and able donors elsewhere.

Jung, however, sees the similarity between childbearing and organ donation since both protect another person's life. So, while recognizing and agreeing that childbearing is an "other-regarding activity and that this other can be intelligibly regarded as a person, whose very life is dependent upon maternal bodily support," the "good cause" in organ donation is also "the preservation of another person's life."[38] In other words, they may share the same *finis operantis* of preserving another person's life, but the pro-life feminists differ on the *finis operis*, as the *act* of removing the fetus itself is deemed immoral.[39] Jung would still claim that there is a common end sought in removing the fetus and in organ donation, namely preservation of another person's life and that life outside the womb is just as sacred as life inside it.

Notwithstanding the differences, and while they may differ on their evaluation of the women's bodily integrity, what remains in common is that men have a choice about what they want or do not want to do with their bodies and pregnant women often do not. Men (and non-pregnant women) might have a choice to give bodily life support by the virtue of tissue or blood type in organ donations.[40] Pregnant women providing bodily life support for the fetus, on the other hand, do not have choice in the same way, irrespective of the condition leading to and during

---

[38] Jung, "Abortion and Organ Donation," 287.

[39] However, as Ward reminds us in this volume, violating bodily integrity can also be an intrinsic evil. See Kathleen Bonnette, "Holding the Tensions: Female Bodily Integrity as an Intrinsic Good," *Journal of Moral Theology* 12, no. 1 (2023): 114, doi.org/10.55476/001c.66245. Then, there can be a competing *finis operis* that comes in conflict, in which case either one can override the prior obligation, or one faces a truly impossible choice like *Sophie's Choice*.

[40] Jung, "Abortion and Organ Donation," 273.

pregnancy. In other words, whether it is the case of mutual sexual encounter, incest, rape, or complications in pregnancies, women can be involuntarily bound, unlike men. Thus,

> Persons find themselves linked—by virtue of blood or tissue type, of rape, of their sexual or social nature—to other persons in need of bodily life support. These needy others are experienced as unalterable "givens" in an agent's life. Their burdensome and difficult presence is experienced as totally beyond voluntary control. It is not now, even if it might be in the future, humanly possible to reverse in all cases the process of renal failure or prevent in all cases the rape-induced or otherwise unwelcome conception…. These are part of the radically involuntary necessities which ground and limit human freedom. Though such givens are unalterable they need not crush human freedom because like other brute facts of life, they are not only unalterable but also received. Agents have a choice about how they are going to respond to such burdens and difficulties. This choice informs and is informed by the dispositional stance the agent has assumed in relation to the finitude and frailty of human existence in general.[41]

When all that is said and done, it means that men do not bear the burden of involuntary and compulsory pregnancy and have the freedom to make decisions about their bodies. Such an uneven ethos or teaching can make (and has made) it easier for men to walk away irresponsibly from these and related situations.

Bodily integrity, therefore, is an important requirement in evaluating and understanding genuine reciprocity. It allows the observer to recognize *that* there is a double standard about one's (bodily) autonomy as it relates to RJ. Once one can see this discrepancy, one can expose how simplistic and one-sided our policies, laws, and teachings are. By recognizing the complex and intersectional implications, then, one can usher in a more just paradigm for RJ.

---

[41] Jung, "Abortion and Organ Donation," 292.

Complexity, Nuances, and Intersectionality

I can think of at least two ways in which inadequate, unsophisticated, and unjust consequences may result from not acknowledging the complexity of RJ. First, defending the life of the fetus is not so simple. The implication for the broad definition of personhood of the fetus is quite complex. Should the Church develop special funerary rites—as a matter of fact, not make any distinctions with other funerals—every time there is an early pregnancy loss? To be extra careful "not to kill an innocent," since we do not know the precise *moment* when the "moment of conception" happens, should there be a funeral service every time a heterosexual sexual activity does not lead to a pregnancy? Relatedly, what happens when a law enforcement officer pulls over a pregnant woman in the states with High-Occupancy Vehicle (HOV) lanes reserved for vehicles with a driver and one or more passengers?[42] Would she be exonerated if she is "alone" but pregnant (therefore, not alone)? If she is not "visibly pregnant," how would one prove that she is? Would law enforcement need to carry a pregnancy kit? Would pregnant people need to at least carry a certificate? In a wrongful death lawsuit, should the fetus that died on the job inadvertently be considered a life, thereby linking them to the lawsuit, even to the point of designating it as an employee?[43] Insofar as the fetus is considered a person, could the state not only give rights and affirm the sanctity of life but also enforce restrictive regulations regarding preserving/freezing of eggs? If it is regulated, why is masturbation not regulated in similar ways? Why is it that in those countries with restrictions

---

[42] Vanessa Romo, "Pregnant woman who claimed her fetus was an HOV lane passenger gets another ticket," *NPR*, September 2, 2022, www.npr.org/2022/09/02/1120628973/pregnant-woman-dallas-fetus-hov-lane-passenger-ticket.

[43] St. Louis had a case where the Missouri Department of Transportation (MoDOT) faced a lawsuit for the wrongful death of an unborn baby. Susan El Khoury, "Loophole in Missouri Law Means Employers May Be off the Hook if You Die on the Job," *KMOV*, August 30, 2022, www.kmov.com/2022/08/30/loophole-missouri-law-means-employers-may-be-off-hook-if-you-die-job/.

on freezing eggs, it is often *not* illegal to freeze the sperm?[44] To highlight the complexity (even absurdity) further, if we are consistent here, one could also claim that male masturbation, which wastes potential opportunities for fecundity, to be a greater crime or sin than cases of rape, which preserves life. Why are men and their bodily integrity not under the similar kind of scrutiny? Why is masturbation not regulated? Why is the status of the sperm not cross-examined? Why are male bodily elements not controlled? Why else other than blatant sexism?

Second, one must also recognize how this complexity is markedly different once they examine the intersecting contexts. For instance, men in the traditional Asian heterosexual households (especially of previous and older generations) occupy and hold different social, familial, and financial space and power than women. In that context, disenfranchised and disempowered women find it difficult simply to walk away from the married relationship even if it is uneven, unjust, and downright abusive. To complicate the matter, many live in tightly knit communities where their community members frown upon abortion or divorce because of the stigma attached to them and the expectation for the collective, parental, and marital roles over the individual, independent, expressive culture, contributing to the absence of agency and personal control.[45] I have

---

[44] Phoebe Zhang, "Single Women Cry Foul as China Doubles Down on Egg Freezing Ban, Accusing Authorities of Gender Bias and Forcing Women into Marriage," *South China Morning Post*, February 2021, www.scmp.com/news/people-culture/gender-diversity/article/3123213/china-reinforces-ban-single-women-freezing.

[45] "Lack of openness around sexual and reproductive health (SRH) topics contributed to stigma and influenced most participants' decision not to disclose their abortion to family members, which resulted in participants feeling isolated throughout their abortion experience." Sruthi Chandrasekaran, Katherine Key, Abby Ow, Alyssa Lindsey, Jennifer Chin, Bria Goode, Quyen Dinh, Inhe Choi, and Sung Yeon Choimorrow, "The Role of Community and Culture in Abortion Perceptions, Decisions, and Experiences among Asian Americans," *Frontiers in Public Health* 10, no. 982215 (2023), doi.org/10.3389/fpubh.2022.982215. There is a good indication that things are changing. However, even when they are, they do not always result in positive outcomes. "The increased economic role of Asian wives and the associated decline in their husbands' economic power and social status have contributed to marital conflicts." "Marriage and Divorce Statistics of Asian and Pacific Islanders," *National Healthy Marriage Research*

witnessed this dearth manifested in my own community, especially for the reality of the older and first-generation immigrant wives, many of whom rely heavily on their husbands for written and spoken English and family finances to sustain their daily lives. The lack of agency, coupled with the deprivation of it in these ethnic and culturally specific realities, incapacitate women doubly or triply for any chance at their bodily integrity and full human agency.

Furthermore, the anti-abortion movement in the US context is closely linked to racial segregation and the stronghold of whiteness in its Christian contexts. While anti-abortion advocacy is closely linked to the Roman Catholic Church today, its political origins in America may be more strongly tied to the evangelical Religious Right movements. For the US evangelical movement, the New South, which championed racial equality and social justice, acquiesced in the rise of the Religious Right rooted in nationalism, individualism, and free-market capitalism.[46] Randall Balmer suggests that the court case that galvanized the Religious Right was the 1971 decision in *Green v. Connally*, which threatened the tax-exempt status of religious institutions that discriminated based on race. In other words, Southern white evangelicals could no longer protect the white space in their private schools. Religion and politics were (and are) about white (male) control and domination of their (now threatened) positions of power. Balmer suggests that it was the issue of abortion that became the central political issue to mobilize and successfully galvanize the grassroots white evangelical voters. It became *the* central issue to maintain whiteness in their white spaces.[47] This strategy is in the same vein of controlling

---

Centers, www.healthymarriageinfo.org/research-policy/marriage-facts-and-research/marriage-and-divorce-statistics-by-culture/asian-and-pacific-islanders/.

[46] Randall Herbert Balmer, *Redeemer: The Life of Jimmy Carter* (New York: Basic Books, 2014).

[47] Randall Herbert Balmer, *Bad Faith: Race and the Rise of the Religious Right* (Grand Rapids, MI: Eerdmans, 2021), especially Part II. Thus, whiteness is associated with possession, control, and mastery by white men characterized by rationality and self-sufficiency. Willie James Jennings, *After Whiteness: An Education in Belonging* (Grand Rapids, MI: Eerdmans

power in non-consensual human subject research, forced sterilization, and other injustices committed against Black people and their bodies in the United States. Abortion regulations have been a political tool for the maintenance of white superiority and supremacy. The throttlehold of white men usurps the agency of women and people of color for the maintenance of their slowly eroding status quo. Wherever one stands on the highly complex and polarizing issue of abortion, then, it cannot be adequately understood without interrogating the white supremacist underpinning that undergirds the issue. If we continue to recognize the myriad ways women are bound, the non-life affirming invisible hand that takes away the agency of women will become more visible.

It is always tricky to construct a paradigm about reproduction from exclusively men's vantage points because the panels, narratives, and social scripts are often dominantly about and controlled by men. However, in the case of RJ, it may be necessary because men's disappearance from these stories contributes to the lack of their moral accountability. Because of this convenient disappearing act and because of the predominance of blaming the victims in our societies, descriptions must restore men as inter-subjects of RJ discussions, rather than veiling them behind passive voices.[48]

Genuine Reciprocity, therefore, begins by "finding missing fathers" and placing them as partner-subjects of RJ not only in married and separated relationships but relationships in general. Then, by equipping men with egalitarian and reciprocal vision, as I attempted to do here, men might rightly begin considering RJ not only with empathy about mothers but also as their own issue.[49] Once it is imagined and acknowledged as their

---

Publishing, 2020), 6; See also J. Kameron Carter, *Race: A Theological Account* (New York: Oxford University Press, 2008), chapter 2.

[48] Nancy M. Henley, Michelle Miller, and Jo Anne Beazley, "Syntax, Semantics, and Sexual Violence: Agency and the Passive Voice," *Journal of Language and Social Psychology* 14, no. 1-2 (1995): 60–84, doi.org/10.1177/0261927X95141004.

[49] An important resource for conceiving of mutual "sexual projects" between two people who both retain autonomy within the sexual interaction is elaborated upon in Jennifer S. Hirsch

issue, men may discern in charity and compassion rather than judgment or blame. Any institution can initiate such a process. The Catholic Church with its global infrastructure is uniquely positioned to do just that. It can disseminate directives for fathers of the world to be involved, supportive, and responsible. But as Hille Haker argues, individual healing is inadequate when unjust conditions also produce genuine moral dilemmas.[50] Thus, the Church can also circulate directives for social engagement to bring about structural change. While structural justice by itself will not eliminate unwanted pregnancy, Cristina L.H. Traina suggests that structural justice through "higher wages, cheaper housing, improved access to health care, and better preschool programs" would "reduce unwanted pregnancy's collateral moral damage to women and to society generally."[51]

However, one can also start at the diocesan or even on the individual-parish level. One might reimagine how men's organizations—The Men of St. Joseph, Knights of Columbus, That Man is You, Fraternus, Exodus 90, and so forth—could directly address these issues. Through them, men may (re)interpret the Biblical stories, including the story this chapter identifies as part of the problem. Men could be encouraged to imagine "*men* caught in adultery" for instance. In doing so, men in Catholic parish life could come to see how double standards currently function, and could be encouraged to see a better way, a way that fosters empathy and solidarity with women. It might propel other discussions in general, but certainly discussion about relationships and RJ more particularly, to a merciful, graceful, charitable, compassionate, congenial, and loving common ground in justice. Only on these honest, loving, and just grounds can any discussion about RJ become hopeful. If men are not accountable partners of the discussion, then none of it can be genuinely reciprocal.

---

and Shamus Khan, *Sexual Citizens: Sex, Power, and Assault on Campus* (New York: W.W. Norton & Company, 2020), xvi, 250.

[50] Hille Haker, "Compassion for Justice," *Concilium* 4 (2017): 54–64.

[51] Cristina L.H. Traina, "Between a Rock and a Hard Place: Unwanted Pregnancy, Mercy, and Solidarity," *Journal of Religious Ethics* 46, no. 4 (2018): 676, doi.org/10.1111/jore.12240.

Hoon Choi, PhD, is an associate professor of theology and religious studies at Bellarmine University. He received his PhD from Loyola University Chicago on *Catholic Masculinities* and Master of Divinity and B.A. from Yale Divinity School and Boston College, respectively. His teaching and research interests intersect among race, ethnicity, gender, sexuality, and Catholic moral and contextual theology with a particular attention to the spectrum of masculinities and post-colonial methods vis-à-vis (masculine) white supremacy and Western imperialism. Those interests came together in a recent article, "A Case for Intersectional Theology," in the *Journal of Moral Theology*.

6. Thinking About Reproductive Justice in Contexts of Violence

Suzanne Mulligan

One cannot properly advocate for reproductive justice without considering its connection to sexual violence. I am not suggesting that only females are victims of this type of violence, but women and girls are disproportionately affected, with wide-ranging implications for their reproductive health. Sexual violence is something that traverses economic, social, racial, and ethnic divides, but we know that poorer women are at greater risk globally. The World Health Organization (WHO) defines violence against women as: "any act of gender-based violence that results in, or is likely to result in, physical, sexual, or mental harm or suffering to women, including threats of such acts, coercion or arbitrary deprivation of liberty, whether occurring in public or in private life."[1] In addition, "intimate partner violence" is defined as violence by an intimate partner or ex-partner that results in psychological, sexual and/or physical harm. This includes all forms of physical aggression, sexual coercion, and various types of controlling behavior.[2] According to WHO, "sexual violence" refers to "any sexual act, attempt to obtain a sexual act, or other act directed against a person's sexuality using coercion, by any person regardless of their relationship to the victim, in any setting. It includes rape, . . . attempted rape, unwanted sexual touching and other non-contact forms."[3]

WHO data indicates that between 2000 and 2018, across 161 countries, almost one in three (30%) women were subjected to physical and/or sexual violence by an intimate or non-intimate partner or both. More than a

---

[1] World Health Organization (WHO), "Violence Against Women: Key Facts," March 25, 2024, www.who.int/news-room/fact-sheets/detail/violence-against-women.
[2] World Health Organization (WHO), "Violence Against Women: Key Facts."
[3] World Health Organization (WHO), "Violence Against Women: Key Facts."

quarter of females aged between fifteen and forty-nine years have endured physical and/or sexual violence by an intimate partner on at least one occasion in their life,[4] and approximately 38% of all murders of women globally are committed by an intimate partner.[5]

Gender-based violence[6] is exacerbated by several factors, including low levels of education, a history of family violence, substance abuse, and social attitudes that condone violence more generally. In addition, a woman's economic disempowerment can heighten her sexual vulnerability, for she may be less able to negotiate safe sex or refuse sex to her partner. Gender-based violence remains a largely invisible and unspoken reality in many communities.[7] Cultural and religious norms often reinforce harmful gender stereotypes, and there is urgent need for religious leaders of all faiths to condemn gender-based violence. Moreover, some cultures place priority on family honour and sexual purity, beliefs used to justify violence towards women and control their sexual freedom. Societal norms that emphasize male sexual entitlement are deeply problematic here too and are usually accompanied by inadequate legal penalties for perpetrators of sexual violence.[8] Unjust power dynamics within the sexual/marital relationship regularly lead to sexual abuse, but, ironically, these same power imbalances can be a reason why some women feel compelled to remain in abusive and dangerous relationships.[9] Thus, intersectional understandings of, and

---

[4] World Health Organization (WHO), "Violence Against Women: Key Facts."
[5] World Health Organization (WHO), "Violence Against Women: Key Facts."
[6] Gender-based violence can happen to someone of any gender, but typically women and girls experience violence on a more frequent and sustained scale. For the purposes of this chapter, I use the term "gender-based violence" in relation to female victims of violence. On this point see WHO, "International Day for the Elimination of Violence Against Women," 2023, www.un.org/en/observances/ending-violence-against-women-day.
[7] World Health Organization (WHO), "Violence Against Women: Key Facts."
[8] World Health Organization (WHO), "Violence Against Women: Key Facts." See also the chapters in this volume by Virginia Saldanha, Mary Lilian Akhere Ehdiamhen, and Eric Genilo.
[9] UN Women, "Facts and Figures: Ending Violence Against Women" (2024), www.unwomen.org/en/what-we-do/ending-violence-against-women/facts-and-figures.

responses to, sexual violence globally are urgently needed.[10] Churches, political leaders, and a wide range of civil society organizations have a vital role to play here. But key to any response must be the creation of spaces where the lived experiences of women, especially those who are most marginalized, help shape policy in this field.[11]

The health implications of a sexual attack are often devastating. Unintended pregnancies, serious gynaecological injury, and infection with sexually transmitted infections (STIs) such as HIV are commonplace in the aftermath of such attacks. Moreover, physical violence during pregnancy increases the chance of miscarriage, stillbirth, or pre-term delivery. And of course, it is unsurprising that sexual attacks often leads to depression, post-traumatic stress disorder, sleep difficulties, eating disorders, and suicide attempts among women and girls.[12]

Moreover, forced sexual encounters contribute to increase in occurrence of disease, especially STIs. For example, in 2021, 54% of all people living with HIV were women and girls. In that same year, approximately 4900 young women aged between fifteen and twenty-four years became infected with HIV every week. In sub-Saharan Africa, six in seven new HIV infections among people aged fifteen to nineteen years are among girls. And females aged fifteen to twenty-four years are twice as

---

[10] Julie George, SSpS, "Intersectionality at the Heart of Oppression and Violence against Women in Law: Case Studies from India," *Journal of Moral Theology* 12, special issue 1 (2023): 108–131.

[11] There is an awakening in the tradition of the importance of human experience as a source of moral wisdom. This is reflected in the new interest in the *sensus fidei* and synodality. If synodality is about *journeying together*, listening to those on the margins, then human experience becomes a vital font of morality. But we are only beginning to consider the implications of this for the whole area of sexuality. The International Theological Commission alludes to the role of human experience when it says: "This lack of reception [of official teaching] may indicate a weakness or a lack of faith on the part of the people of God. . . . But in some cases it may indicate that certain decisions have been taken by those in authority without due consideration to the experience and the *sensus fidei* of the faithful, or without sufficient consultation of the faithful by the magisterium." See International Theological Commission, *Sensus Fidei in the Life of the Church*, no. 123.

[12] UN Women, "Facts and Figures: Ending Violence Against Women."

likely to be HIV positive than men in the same age category. Women and girls accounted for 63% of all new HIV infections in Sub-Saharan Africa in 2021.[13] These figures indicate a correlation between gender and HIV. In fact, a document from Concern Worldwide opens with the following statement: "40 years on, women and girls are the most impacted [by HIV/AIDS]—the face of HIV in 2021 is an adolescent girl."[14]

Responses will therefore require multi-faceted strategies, able to address complex and inter-connected crises and ought to be founded on intersectional research, something especially needed in Catholic teaching. In addition, incorporating intersectional scholarship allows space for the voices of those most affected to be heard. The goal of achieving reproductive justice for women and girls, including tackling sexual violence, will be more effectively realized if we listen to the stories of survivors. Strategies aimed at securing better reproductive justice for females will need to be founded on sophisticated thinking that recognizes the nuances and the challenges involved and understands that reproductive justice is won in contexts of broader social, economic, and human rights gains.

This chapter is divided into four sections. First, we consider how sexual violence is rooted in social narrative; next we explore the connection between institutional violence and reproductive health outcomes, taking Ireland as a case study; thirdly, we consider how virtue ethics—especially the virtues of resistance and resilience—might act as a valuable resource for the issues discussed here; and finally, some implications for Catholic teaching will be considered.

---

[13] UN Women, "Facts and Figures: Ending Violence Against Women."
[14] Concern Worldwide, "Gender Inequality," November 30, 2021, www.concern.net/news/gender-inequality-leaving-women-and-girls-more-vulnerable-hiv-and-aids. See also Melissa Browning, *Risky Marriage: HIV and Intimate Relationships in Tanzania* (Lanham, MD: Lexington, 2013).

Sexual Violence and Sinful Social Narratives

How can we better promote the reproductive rights of women and work to improve reproductive health globally? Structural reform aimed at improving educational opportunities for girls is one crucial element. Evidence confirms that improved educational opportunities for girls is directly linked to family size. In other words, better-educated girls tend to have fewer children than those who leave formal education at a younger age. Moreover, structural reform that aims to economically empower women can improve sexual health and family well-being. The Grameen Banking system in Bangladesh provides a vivid illustration of the positive outcomes that can be achieved through improving women's economic freedoms, even in modest ways.[15]

But there is another dimension that must be addressed, and that is the way in which social narratives perpetuate injustices against females. If we wish to improve reproductive health then we must dismantle damaging narratives about women, their bodies, and their "function" in society. Thus, wider educational initiatives aimed at re-examining dominant social narratives and the values/virtues that underpin them are crucial. For as Christian ethicist Traci West puts it, "This broader collective pattern of intuitive knowledge reveals lessons about how moral harm is generated."[16] Catholic feminist theologian Anne Patrick, who has written extensively about this, observes:

---

[15] For more on this, see Aminur Rahman, *Women and Microcredit in Rural Bangladesh: An Anthropological Study of Grameen Bank Lending* (Oxford: Westview Press, 2001). Also see the work of Amartya Sen, who examines the connections between women's economic empowerment and human capabilities, including his *Development as Freedom* (Oxford: Oxford University Press, 1999).

[16] Traci C. West, *Disruptive Christian Ethics: When Racism and Women's Lives Matter* (Kentucky: Westminster John Knox Press, 2006), 45.

> Narrative . . . plays a key educational role by communicating and reinforcing the values and virtues esteemed by a culture. Moreover, narrative also serves to criticize views of value and virtue once their favored status in a society is seen as ambiguous. The critical role of narrative, in fact, is an important part of the dynamics of change where value and virtue are concerned.[17]

Who decides which traits of character are important and why? We know that our ability to grow in virtue is influenced by the social groups to which we belong and by the stories and norms that underpin them.[18] So, deciding which virtues are or are not desirable within a social group must be open to continued scrutiny. In the case of Catholic teaching, Patrick believes that a patriarchal paradigm has contributed to the marginalization of women, facilitating patterns of thinking and acting that are characterized by misogyny, sexism, and a general mistrust of the female sex. These ways of thinking then become enshrined in the structures, laws, and processes of the institution over time. For much of its tradition, the Catholic faith has provided narratives of exclusion rather than narratives that nourish, support, and encourage women, Patrick argues. She calls for an "egalitarian paradigm" which recognizes the radical equality of the sexes.[19] Such a shift in emphasis would see control being replaced with respect for all human beings. It is a paradigm, she believes, that would allow us to see the value of the body and the humanity of women. Furthermore, like many scholars, Patrick says that sexuality and social justice are connected and

---

[17] Anne Patrick, "Narrative and the Social Dynamic of Virtue," in *Virtue*, ed. Charles E. Curran and Lisa A. Fullam (New York: Paulist Press, 2011), 79.

[18] Patrick, "Narrative and the Social Dynamic of Virtue," 80.

[19] See also Anne E. Patrick, "His Dogs More Than Us: Virtue in Situations of Conflict between Women Religious and Their Ecclesiastical Employers," in *Conscience and Calling: Ethical Reflections on Catholic Women's Church Vocations* (London: Bloomsbury, 2013); and "Framework for Love: Toward a Renewed Understanding of Christian Vocation," in *A Just and True Love: Feminism at the Frontiers of Theological Ethics: Essays in Honor of Margaret A. Farley*, ed. Maura A. Ryan and Brian F. Linnane, SJ (Notre Dame: University of Notre Dame Press, 2007), 303–337, 310–311 and 329.

that sexuality is not just a matter of personal virtue. In other words, the exercise of authentic moral agency is dependent on complex social, economic, and cultural factors. It is imperative, therefore, that this paradigm of equality would include a commitment to the wellbeing of oneself and others, as well as a commitment to establishing just social relations based on mutuality, respect, and equality.[20] Patrick believes that an egalitarian paradigm would also acknowledge the impact of long-established power imbalances within relationships, something that especially harms the dignity of women and places women and girls at risk of intimate violence.[21] She calls for deeper understanding of how society, economics, and politics affects a person's freedom to make responsible choices and argues that special attention must be given to the impact of race, gender, and religion on moral agency.

Social narratives can provide motivation and inspiration, but malformed narratives can weaken our moral sensibilities to the extent that we may not even be able to properly see the moral parameters of a situation. By way of illustration, Patrick recounts the murder of a Catholic nun, Marie Clementine Anwarite, by soldiers during Zaire's civil war. Sr. Marie chose to be killed rather than surrender her virginity to her aggressors, and when putting forward the case for her canonization, Pope John Paul II praised the "primordial value accorded to virginity" that Sr. Marie displayed in the face of impending danger.[22]

Among the many things revealed by this terrible incident is a lack of appreciation by John Paul II of the physical danger in which Sr. Marie found herself. Nor do we find any recognition of the fact that this sort of violence is visited upon millions of women daily. It was an opportunity missed. For it *was* an opportunity for the head of the Catholic Church to raise awareness of gender-based violence and to condemn it in the strongest

---

[20] Patrick, "Narrative and the Social Dynamic of Virtue," 83.
[21] Patrick, "Narrative and the Social Dynamic of Virtue," 84.
[22] Homily of Pope John Paul II, "Beatification of Marie Clementine Anwarite," August 15, 1985, www.vatican.va/content/john-paul-ii/fr/homilies/1985/documents/hf_jpii_hom_19850815_beatificazione-kinshasa.html.

terms. It *was* an opportunity for a pope to stand firmly in solidarity with women across the world who routinely endure sexual violence. Instead, it appeared that the priority was to reinforce the "traditional feminine virtues" of obedience, docility, and submissiveness.[23] In addition, John Paul II forgave the man who murdered Sr. Marie, raising further concerns about a lack of understanding of gender-based violence among some leaders in the Church. In contexts where "feminine" virtues like submissiveness, meekness, or docility are prized and where virginity is considered more important than the life of a woman, one starts to see how malformed narratives can distort our moral sensibilities. As Patrick puts it:

> What women in patriarchal society need are not exhortations to humility and self-sacrifice, or stories of saints who preferred death to rape. Women need instead new models for virtue and new stories that communicate them . . . [What are needed] are new narratives that go beyond criticism and theory to provide models that demonstrate—with a power scholarly prose can never attain—the goodness and beauty of lives governed by the egalitarian paradigm for virtue.[24]

Social narrative and social sin are connected.[25] For social narratives legitimize our sense of self, they give meaning to our lives, and they shape our views of the world. But, of course, some narratives serve to undermine human dignity, and aid the construction of "structures of violence,"[26] or what we call "structural" or "social sin" in theological parlance. As we will see in the next section, this coming together of social narrative and social sin was evidenced in Ireland through the establishment of institutions that

---

[23] Patrick, "Narrative and the Social Dynamic of Virtue," 85.
[24] Patrick, "Narrative and the Social Dynamic of Virtue," 91.
[25] See also Kathryn Lilla Cox, "Reproductive Injustice as Social Sin: Mapping Sin Discourse into Debates about Fertility Decisions," in this volume.
[26] This phrase is borrowed from the work of Paul Farmer. See, "Women, Poverty, and AIDS," in *Women, Poverty, and AIDS: Sex, Drugs, and Structural Violence*, ed. Paul Farmer, Margaret Connors, and Janie Simmons (Monroe, ME: Common Courage Press, 2011), 26.

directly denied women many of their basic human rights, including their reproductive rights. Control of women's bodies was justified by narratives that blended Catholic moral norms with notions of nationalism and patriotism. But there are many other ways of identifying how structural violence affects women's reproductive health; unjust legal, religious, economic, or cultural structures increase the risk of disease and premature death among the poor, contribute to the economic and sexual exploitation of women and girls, and legitimize gender norms that do harm to women. Sinful structures are maintained by humans, so these structures need their "apologists," as Paul Farmer put it.[27] Structural sin also implies the existence of a *pervasive culture* that supports formal expressions of injustice. It refers to the creation of a culture, a way of seeing and living, that legitimizes the oppression of others.[28] It creates a kind of moral "disorientation" within us, as Anna Rowlands describes it.[29]

What are the consequences for women's reproductive justice? In addition to physical and psychological harms, Black feminist theologian Traci West speaks of how women's "becoming"[30] is denied: "It should be apparent that when they are sexually violated women's well-being is denied, and, in the language of liberative Christian ethics, their 'personal and communal becoming' is thwarted. As their bodies are violated, their dignity and worth are demeaned on a personal level."[31] West continues by explaining that they are further devalued on a communal level because of the "insufficient manner" in which their injury and victimization are taken seriously by society, Church, and state institutions.[32] Thus, we need to

---

[27] Farmer, "Women, Poverty, and AIDS," 26.

[28] See for example, Anna Rowlands, *Towards a Politics of Communion: Catholic Social Teaching in Dark Times* (London: T & T Clark, 2021), chapter four in particular.

[29] Rowlands, *Towards a Politics of Communion*, 85. For an excellent account of the application of "structural sin" to the migrant crisis, see Kristin E. Heyer, *Kinship Across Borders: A Christian Ethic of Immigration* (Washington, DC: Georgetown University Press, 2012), chapter 2.

[30] We return to this idea of "becoming" below.

[31] West, *Disruptive Christian Ethics*, 51.

[32] West, *Disruptive Christian Ethics*, 51.

understand more fully the reasons why misogyny and sexism persist and how this militates against the dignity of women. One might ask whether Catholic magisterial teaching goes far enough in naming the structures of violence that place women in danger and deny them their reproductive rights.

If the institutional Church wishes to become a stronger advocate for women's rights, then it must begin by listening to the lived experiences of women. Traci West echoes this point. She argues that Christian theology must be shaped by the stories and struggles of women; the trauma as well as the joy faced by women ought to inform how we do and understand our theology. Part of what is needed, therefore, is an honest examination of existing practices and attitudes *within* Christian communities "that inhibit and assault the social and spiritual well-being of persons." In addition, she states that it is imperative to identify how these practices "should be transformed to provide or support socially just and spiritually nurturing relations among us."[33] But much more needs to be done here. West concludes:

> Attention to how we generate public perceptions of the moral and spiritual worth of women in conjunction with public practices that sanction their sexual abuse, assault, and harassment is especially salient in developing social ethics . . . . [The] intimate, private aspects of women's selves are inescapably linked to public responses. . . . The subject of sexual violation and its attendant public practices, therefore, provides a useful and rigorous test of the extent to which human dignity is a genuine social value within our communities.[34]

The task of critical, honest reflection, hopefully leading to positive social confrontation, is not a solitary one. Faith communities ought to support each other, *and* they must hold each other accountable. Many ecclesial communities and churches are only beginning this painful process. But for

---

[33] West, *Disruptive Christian Ethics*, 38.
[34] West, *Disruptive Christian Ethics*, 38.

West, this "ethical work requires a visceral recognition of the meaning of body invasion, body assault, and body-demeaning speech, for women and for the whole of society."[35] Moreover, acquiring knowledge of these realities will mean going beyond rational categories and theological concepts; it will mean that we confront our personal biases and our malformed understandings of womanhood, victimization, and how we value human bodies. We will see below how this is especially true in the Irish context in the aftermath of institutional gendered violence towards women.

Although West calls for the strategic priority of women's voices in theological ethics, she cautions against thinking of women's voices in a singular way. To put it differently, including "women's experiences" in our discourse is not enough. These voices need careful discernment, investigation, and articulation. Otherwise, we risk creating a different set of problems or new forms of discrimination. This is because "women" do not constitute a homogenous group. And we know that some women are the instigators of gender oppression. Therefore, inequalities within power relations, including those among women, must be carefully understood.[36]

Sinful Social Narratives and Institutional Gendered Violence: Lessons from Ireland

In recent decades, Ireland has been coming to terms with its deeply troubling past. The extent of abuse perpetrated against women, children, and vulnerable adults by both church and state raises many ethical questions. It is an uncomfortable history that is only slowly being acknowledged. We know that social narrative played its part here too, a narrative that amalgamated Catholic identity with nationalism, and one which prized virtues of sexual purity, submissiveness, and obedience in women. In the case of Magdalene Laundries and Mother and Baby

---

[35] West, *Disruptive Christian Ethics*, 42.
[36] West, *Disruptive Christian Ethics*, 48–49.

homes,[37] both church and state colluded in the violation of women's basic rights. It was strengthened by a national narrative that suggested both church and state had the right to control of women's sexual and reproductive agency.[38] Scholars of law Claire Hamilton, Lynsey Black, and Sinéad Ring explain:

> Anxious to create and preserve its identity as different to and better than the colonizer, the new Irish state inscribed a repressive Catholic gender order on the bodies and lives of women and girls. It did so by using the network of massive Victorian institutions run by Catholic religious orders which had provided basic levels of relief to the poor in the wake of the famines of the 19th century."[39]

---

[37] For more on these institutions see Clara Fisher, "Gender, Nation, and the Politics of Shame: Magdalen Laundries and the Institutionalization of Feminine Transgression in Modern Ireland," *Signs* 41, no.4 (2016): 821–843. These institutions were named after Mary Magdalene and the Biblical misinterpretation which depicted her as a whore, sex worker, and fallen woman. Importantly, Fisher notes that these types of institutions were not peculiar to Ireland, although they flourished in Ireland in the twentieth century at a time when other countries were beginning to dismantle these asylums. "Often called Magdalen laundries because the women were put to work washing clothes, by the early twentieth century there were at least twenty-three such institutions unlike in earlier times, they seemed to be more preoccupied with 'wayward daughters' and unmarried mothers than prostitutes," according to Diarmaid Ferriter, *Occasions of Sin: Sex and Society in Modern Ireland* (London: Profile Books, 2009), 32. It is believed that approximately thirty thousand women were incarcerated in these institutions throughout the nineteenth and twentieth centuries in Ireland.

[38] The Christian moral tradition acknowledges the fact that true moral agency can only be exercised in contexts of freedom and knowledge, and that a variety of factors can impact both. See Richard M. Gula, *Reason Informed by Faith* (New York: Paulist Press, 1989), 75, where he describes freedom and knowledge as "two indispensable conditions of being a moral subject," and claims that "freedom is so central to the moral life that without it we cannot properly speak of being moral persons at all." Today we have a more acute awareness of the numerous cultural, societal, intergenerational factors that can limit freedom and diminish moral culpability.

[39] Claire Hamilton, Lynsey Black, Sinéad Ring, "Historical Gendered Institutional Violence: A Research Agenda for Criminologists," *Journal of Contemporary Criminal Justice* 39, no. 1 (2023): 20.

Following independence, the Irish Free State, later to become the Irish Republic, relied on Catholic-run institutions for the policing of gender norms. Women who were forced into these laundries and homes were stigmatized: they were "fallen" women who not only violated Catholic moral teaching but also betrayed the nationalistic vision of a pure Ireland. These women became a source of free labor, providing considerable economic benefits for both church and state. Reasons for incarceration were broad, ranging from being in an "unsuitable" relationship, being considered too attractive, being a victim of a sexual attack, or being involved in sex work. Catholic authorities also incarcerated women who were deemed to be a burden on their families, or who were thought *likely* to become sexually promiscuous.[40] "Suspect women" were sometimes placed in laundries even though they had not transgressed any sexual moral codes at all. This included women with mental health issues, poor women, girls growing up in broken families, and so forth. As Lynsey Black explains:

> Early in the life of the new state, sexual immorality had been identified as a threat to the nation. This 'threat' was especially located within the bodies of young women of the working and labouring classes. . . . [M]arginalised women and families experienced significant state and Church intervention, particularly in matters of morality and sex. While the sanctity of the family was respected, for lone women who posed a threat to this, there was no such protection.[41]

It is important to say that Magdalene Laundries were highly visible throughout Ireland and were an integrated, crucial part of the Irish economy. People knew of their existence. Moreover, most women and

---

[40] On this see also Hamilton, Black, and Ring, "Historical Gendered Institutional Violence," 17–37.

[41] Lynsey Black, *Gender and Punishment in Ireland: Women, Murder and the Death Penalty, 1922–64* (Manchester, England: Manchester University Press, 2022), 2, doi.org/10.7765/978 1526145291.

girls were incarcerated with the cooperation of family members and the broader community. The social norms of the time, and the Catholic/nationalistic narratives that bolstered them, meant that a significant portion of the population were compliant when it came to the running of these institutions. As Black puts it, societal attitudes facilitated these injustices, especially paternalistic attitudes towards women: "Paternalism imagined women as childlike, inferior in rationality and lacking the capacity for full citizenship. This was particularly so for younger unmarried women who became pregnant."[42] In fact, Black goes further and argues that the incarceration of so many women in Ireland during this period demonstrated the highly conditional nature of "citizenship," not to mention the limited concept of reproductive rights and freedoms.[43]

So, if social virtue and social narrative depend on compliance from a significant portion of the population, what role do women play as oppressors of other women? As mentioned, one disturbing feature of Ireland's Magdalene laundries and Mother and Baby Homes was the extent to which society—including other women—cooperated in the incarceration of these vulnerable women and girls. It is important to acknowledge, therefore, the ways in which women do harm to other women, often in ways that impact of their reproductive and sexual rights.

Women contribute to, and collude in, structures that are oppressive others for several reasons. Fear of violence can lead some to remain silent in the face of injustice. Others internalize so-called "feminine virtues" such as obedience and submission, which further adds to a culture of silence. And some women exploit others for profit, for example in the human trafficking and sex industries. Shawnee M. Daniels-Sykes explores how women and girls at times contribute to their own oppression.[44] She

---

[42] Black, *Gender and Punishment in Ireland*, 42.

[43] Black, *Gender and Punishment in Ireland*, 42.

[44] Shawnee M. Daniels-Sykes, "A Feminist Ethical Perspective on Women/Girls as Oppressors: The Cycle of Oppressor-Internalized Oppression," in *Feminist Catholic Theological Ethics: Conversations in the World Church*, ed. Linda Hogan and A.E. Orobator (New York: Orbis Books, 2014), 269–279.

explains that for females living in patriarchal contexts, a cycle of injustice is generated; women are oppressed, and because of this oppression become the oppressor of other females.[45] Hopelessness, despair, powerlessness, poverty, and marginalization contribute to circumstances in which women either remain silent in the face of oppression or participate in the sinful structures that cause their oppression in the first place.[46] To illustrate the point, Daniels-Sykes mentions how women are often involved in the organization of human trafficking, in facilitating female genital mutilation, and in the bullying of other females. "In order to transform this cycle of oppressor-internalized oppression, the persons involved must understand that a glimpse of the living God requires a profound rebirth."[47]

Daniels-Sykes draws on the work of Paulo Freire and Elizabeth A. Johnson, noting that, for Johnson, acquiring the dispositions and traits that will halt the oppressor-internalized oppression cycle is vital. For Freire, we must "unlearn" and dismantle the cycle of oppressor-internalized oppression if we are to build relationships of mutuality, respect, and love. Redemption of the oppressor is as important as freeing the oppressed, and for Daniels-Sykes, this must include the conversion of female oppressors.[48]

Resisting social sin requires inner transformation; it requires a new way of seeing and interacting. Paul Wadell describes injustice as a failure of moral imagination, and our efforts to *reimagine* a more just world will inevitably require a radical and unsettling change in attitude.[49] This is especially crucial where the oppression of women is caused by women oppressors. Virtue ethics, with its attention on moral growth, the formation of character, and personal conversion has a vital contribution to make here. As Daniels-Sykes and Wadell observe, the achievement of sexual wellbeing and the establishment of just sexual relationships depends

---

[45] Daniels-Sykes, "A Feminist Ethical Perspective on Women/Girls as Oppressors," 269.
[46] Daniels-Sykes, "A Feminist Ethical Perspective on Women/Girls as Oppressors", 270.
[47] Daniels-Sykes, "A Feminist Ethical Perspective on Women/Girls as Oppressors," 270.
[48] Daniels-Sykes, "A Feminist Ethical Perspective on Women/Girls as Oppressors," 276.
[49] Paul J. Wadell, "Reimagining the World: Justice," in Curran and Fullam, *Virtue*, 189.

on profound personal conversion as much as reform of sinful social structures.

The Virtues of Resistance and Resilience

There exists the moral responsibility to resist unjust social structures to help create better communities. It is vital, therefore, for individuals and groups to cultivate a critical consciousness, since it is through this awareness that we can critique the values and practices of our own culture. Furthermore, a critical consciousness empowers oppressed groups to see that injustice can be transformed and overcome. The virtue of resistance helps contest unjust power relations, so for Kochurani Abraham, this virtue becomes an integral part of any "ethic for change."[50]

Let us consider the ways a virtue of resistance might positively address the question of reproductive justice. Abraham explores how this virtue might be applied to women's rights in India. In a culture where modesty and submission in females is glorified, people are nevertheless daring to resist norms that threaten their dignity. "Thanks to the political underpinnings of the feminist movement, women are finding ways and means to give vent to their anger at whatever is distorting their human dignity."[51] The situation in India is exacerbated by cultural norms that prioritize "feminine virtues" such as submission, self-sacrifice, and passivity, while social narratives reinforce the notion that preservation of the family is primarily a woman's responsibility.[52] These stereotypes heighten female vulnerability since they make women feel less able to speak

---

[50] Kochurani Abraham, "Resistance: A Liberative Key in Feminist Ethics," in Hogan and Orobator, *Feminist Catholic Theological Ethics*, 105.

[51] Abraham, "Resistance," 98. See also Virginia Saldanha, "Religio-Cultural Underpinnings of Gender and Reproductive Injustice and their Impact on Women's Agency in India," 391–410 in this volume.

[52] Stephanie Ann Y. Puen expresses similar concerns about the messages that form women in Filipino culture. See Puen's "Considerations for a Comprehensive Sex Education Grounded in Catholic Social Teaching for Reproductive Justice in the Philippines."

out for fear of familial breakup. The cost of this to women is seen in many ways; for some, it is utter helplessness in the face of violence, for others it is an increasing vulnerability to violence within the "feminine space" of the home.[53]

But through the virtue of resistance, women can reclaim their agency, their subjectivity, and their sense of self, Abraham argues. It is through the virtue of resistance that power relations are critiqued and even dismantled. Abraham believes that in order to challenge sinful attitudes and structures we must first develop "a critical consciousness." Forming this critical consciousness would help women see that oppression is not final, that resistance offers hope, and that current injustices can be overcome. I would argue that this critical consciousness needs to be cultivated by Church leadership also and that the Magisterium's teaching on the family ought to more clearly take account of the injustices endured by women and girls across the world. Narratives of domination need to be unmasked and rejected. And as already mentioned, women's voices must be heard and their experiences taken seriously if we are to enrich our understanding of how best to live in right relationship with each other.

The virtue of resistance is a crucial step towards sexual self-care, but resisting unjust sexual norms can be both difficult and dangerous. Prudence helps determine if, and when, resistance is called for.[54] The precarity of a woman's situation may make it unwise, indeed dangerous, to challenge societal norms. Although we bear a responsibility to create more just communities conducive to the flourishing of all peoples, we have a duty of self-care also. The virtue of resistance, accompanied by courage and prudence, plays a key role in positive social transformation, but one must also be cognizant of the precarious lives of many women. In these circumstances, resistance may need to be entrusted to others. Still, this

---

[53] Abraham, "Resistance," 99.

[54] In Catholic virtue ethics, prudence is the ability to apply right reason to action. Aquinas developed what Aristotle had previously described as practical wisdom. See Thomas Aquinas, *Summa Theologiae* I–II, q. 57, a. 5. See also Stephen J. Pope, "Overview of the Ethics of Aquinas," in *The Ethics of Aquinas* (Washington, DC: Georgetown University Press, 2002), 34.

virtue remains a critical tool for social change, especially for those most affected by injustice. It requires the courage to defy established systems of oppression and challenge patterns of domination and control. And although this brings with it enormous risk, we see women resisting deep-rooted injustice in creative, sustained ways across the world.[55]

Others like Nuala Kenny prefers to speak of the virtue of resilience. "The promotion of resilience is crucial in responding to trauma and abuse and healing from it. The word's origins are in the Latin *resilere*, meaning 'to recoil or spring back.' In psychology it has come to mean the ability to respond effectively to and cope with trauma, adversity, and failure. It is never returning to normal but a positive adaptation resulting in an ongoing protective capability."[56] Writing about clerical sexual abuse in the Catholic Church, Kenny calls for both a recognition of the harms done and a need to tackle the systemic and cultural causes of abuse. The latter will require confronting cultural norms and narratives that encourage various forms of violence. She calls for a deeper understanding of human vulnerability, arguing that this is crucial for the prevention of sexual violence in particular and helps foster resilience in the face of harm.[57] Vulnerability is part of our common embodied existence, she tells us, but also belongs to each unique and personal situation. However, Kenny warns against thinking of vulnerability in paternalistic or oppressive terms, for we risk stigmatizing the person or group when we do so: "There are strong ethical implications of vulnerability. It can be patronizing and paternalistic or unifying and socially transformative. Acknowledging

---

[55] For more on this point, see Julie Hanlon Rubio, "Cooperation with Evil Reconsidered: The Moral Duty of Resistance," *Theological Studies* 78, no. 1 (2017): 96–120.

[56] Nuala Kenny, "Clergy Sexual Abuse, Trauma-Informed Theology, and the Promotion of Resilience," in *Doing Theology and Theological Ethics in the Face of the Child Abuse Crisis*, ed. Daniel J. Fleming, James F. Keenan SJ, and Hans Zollner, SJ (Eugene, OR: Pickwick Publications, 2023), 373.

[57] Kenny, "Clergy Sexual Abuse," 364.

mutual vulnerability allows us to be aware of others and their dignity and capabilities."[58]

Constructing ethical responses that promote autonomy and resilience helps individuals and communities overcome a sense of powerlessness and loss of agency in the aftermath of violence.[59] Importantly for Kenny, recovery from trauma requires accompaniment, which in turn depends on "truth-telling and wound healing." As Christians, we take hope, strength, and courage from the belief that "the Resurrection demonstrates the ultimate resilience after trauma," as Kenny puts it.[60]

In a way, this leads us back to an earlier point by West, namely the notion of *becoming*. If we think of this idea alongside resistance and resilience, we find in Kenny and West's work a hopeful view of what the future might hold for women's sexual and reproductive lives. Seen through a Christian lens, an "ethic of becoming" is future-orientated while simultaneously grounded in a critique of present realities. West writes:

> Becoming reflects hope about solidarity that should inform (*become* a part of) our communal relations ... [It] also depicts a process of struggle upon which this hopeful vision depends. It describes an ethic that is not concerned with achieving a finite goal or with a place that one aspires to reach in order to be finished with certain ethical problems. Instead, hope for ethical relationships is only found in one's participation in the process of becoming a more compassionate society, in confronting the multiple patterns of denial, devaluation, and abuse or assaults like those produced in the sexual violation of poor women sex workers.[61]

As West understands it, *becoming* is an unfinished task. An ethic of becoming forces us to ask, what are we becoming and why? For our practices reveal to the world the nature of our moral commitments. They

---

[58] Kenny, "Clergy Sexual Abuse," 366.
[59] Kenny, "Clergy Sexual Abuse," 366.
[60] Kenny, "Clergy Sexual Abuse," 370.
[61] West, *Disruptive Christian Ethics*, 52.

make known our stance towards others. In the context of this chapter, we can say that our practices are a reflection of how committed we are to the dignity of women. Our concern for women's reproductive agency must be accompanied by critical self-reflection and accountability when norms are violated. West believes that "A liberative Christian social ethic ... ignites a commitment to find ideas for resisting societal practices that violate bodies, devalue worth and dignity, and treat dismissively the gifts, hopes, and struggles of peoples."[62] Among other things, such an ethic must include the scrutiny of institutions, including religious institutions; seeking out, and hearing from, those who dwell on the margins; and developing methods of strategic resistance.[63] This idea of becoming, and the liberative Christian social ethic that West refers to, also points to deep theological truths that guide and sustain our efforts in this life. Becoming captures a vision of the person as always imperfect, journeying towards betterment, and in need of God's mercy. It suggests that the human condition is fragile and that moral growth is gradual. It reminds us that discipleship is dynamic and ongoing, always working (becoming) towards the building up of God's Kingdom in the here and now.

Implications for Catholic Teaching

What, then, are the implications for magisterial teaching regarding women's reproductive rights? Most Catholic ethicists today recognize the need for balanced, informed dialogue about the complex realities of reproductive health and sexuality. None of this is at the expense of the rich tradition that sustains and guides Catholic ethical discourse, but intersectional and inclusive research is vitally important here. For these reasons, I argue that Church leadership ought to address the complexity of reproductive health in a more nuanced and integrated way. The many dimensions of women's reproductive rights need careful attention,

---

[62] West, *Disruptive Christian Ethics*, 69.
[63] West, *Disruptive Christian Ethics*, 69.

underpinned by an understanding of how this question is tied to other human rights and social justice issues affecting women. Singular approaches will not yield hopeful answers for the millions of women and girls who find themselves in dangerous or crisis situations.

Poverty, lack of education, and social and cultural marginalization are leading causes of women's sexual and reproductive disempowerment. In addition, gender-based violence is not just a serious violation of human rights; it increases crisis situations in the lives of women and girls. Thus, to think of reproductive justice in singular terms fails to acknowledge the complicated nature of human relationships or the ways in which our socio-economic and cultural contexts often shape the decision-making of women. Securing greater empowerment and agency for females is a critical step towards reproductive justice, but this cannot be done without addressing the structures of violence that oppress women and girls globally.

And yet this is a weakness of magisterial teaching. Commonly, issues of reproductive health are dealt with in ways that fail to recognize the difficult realities of many women's lives. Church teaching ought to name more explicitly the underlying injustices that affect the health and wellbeing of women. Instead, discussions about the empowerment of women are regularly met with suspicion and mistrust and unfairly equated with a pro-choice agenda. Moreover, magisterial teaching would benefit from greater inclusion of intersectional thinking in the area of reproductive justice. Above all, the voices and experiences of women need to be heard, especially in teaching that details the most intimate concerns of women's lives. Finally, the dangers faced by females *within* the family present challenges for Church teaching on marriage. Does Catholic teaching offer any hope to women in abusive relationships or to women and girls who are forced into (often early) marriage? Would it not be a more credible witness to the Gospel if magisterial teaching were as renowned for its condemnation of child marriage and gender-based violence as it is for its opposition to artificial contraception?

Confronting Harmful Gender-Stereotypes

The Church must renounce harmful gender-stereotypes if it is to promote reproductive justice. The reliance on limiting gender stereotypes that we find in magisterial teaching endanger the health and security of women in some contexts. For example, an emphasis on caregiving as a feminine quality might reduce women's agency and freedom, especially if caregiving is not a free choice but something imposed through social or religious expectation. In many cultures, caregiving is thought of almost exclusively as a feminine virtue and can serve to reduce women's freedoms outside the home.

A criticism of Pope Francis's teaching to date has been his failure to address the question of women's agency in a detailed way. It is disappointing to see that, like his predecessors, he falls back on romanticized notions of womanhood. Lisa Sowle Cahill says that in Pope Francis's documents "women's agency is essentialized, romanticized, politically subordinated, or entirely neglected."[64] And Kristin Heyer argues that although the teaching of Francis shows development, "there remains anxiety about the weakening of sexual differences, maternal presence, and mothers' self-sacrificial responsibilities."[65]

The way magisterial teaching discusses women is problematic, and even dangerous. For ideals of womanhood that emphasize self-sacrifice within the home can create contexts of danger for millions of women globally. What is needed from Church leadership is strong, clear condemnation of sexism and misogyny in all its forms, as well as a commitment to hear the voices of women and learn from their experiences. In addition, it is important to confront malformed notions of masculinity that place females at risk of violence.

---

[64] Cited in Kristin Heyer, "Walls in the Heart: Social Sin and *Fratelli tutti*," *Journal of Catholic Social Thought* 19, no. 1 (2022): 37–38.
[65] Heyer, "Walls in the Heart," 38.

Re-thinking Culture, Consent, and Agency

Catholic teaching must also consider more deeply the ways in which culture, consent, and agency impact the sexual and reproductive agency of women. Karen Peterson-Iyer explores the idea of agency in the context of the hookup culture in America, teen sexting, sex trafficking, and the commercial sex industry.[66] Although writing mostly from the American (and Western) context, her work raises vital questions that extend to other geo-political locations and is a valuable resource for the purposes of this chapter. For Peterson-Iyer, hyper-individualism, freedom of choice, and agency are regularly cited in defense of the hookup culture, so any critique must also include the broader socio-cultural attitudes and assumptions that underpin it. Importantly, she explains how hyper-masculinity, the objectification of women's bodies, a lack of self-care for one's own body or the bodies of others, create damaging sexual expectations among people. Peterson-Iyer contends that the hookup culture must be confronted through an emphasis on *authentic* human agency. Here too, we see how damaging expectations contribute to malformed ideas of agency and freedom; instead of liberating women, they create expectations that increase personal risk for females. She argues that what is needed is a "holistic understanding of human flourishing animated by the demands of justice."[67]

Consent, of course, is complicated, and can be compromised in several ways. Poor communication, fear of violence, intoxication, peer pressure, and gendered cultural expectations serve to diminish consent. Moreover, cultural expectations that discourage women from expressing true agency are highly problematic.[68] The human subject, and her agency, must contend with the tensions that broader culture brings. Our sense of "self"

---

[66] See Karen Peterson-Iyer, *Reenvisioning Sexual Ethics: A Feminist Christian Account* (Washington, DC: Georgetown University Press, 2022), in particular chapter 3.
[67] Peterson-Iyer, *Reenvisioning Sexual Ethics*, 56.
[68] Peterson-Iyer, *Reenvisioning Sexual Ethics*, 63–64.

is conditioned by a host of factors that converge to shape and form us, including societal narratives.

One area that Peterson-Iyer is particularly critical of is the growing cultural narrative around hyper-masculinity. We have seen above how restrictive gender norms harm the wellbeing of women. Interestingly, Peterson-Iyer notes that a 2016 meta-review of seventy-eight studies on masculinity and mental health concluded that men who place value on power, strength, and dominance over women are more likely to suffer from mental health problems such as depression and anxiety and have body image difficulties, and are likely to suffer from substance abuse.[69] Thus, social narratives contribute to harmful messages for men as well as women. The virtues of self-care, resistance, and resilience are as important to cultivate among men as among women.

We perhaps think of agency and consent as something relatively straightforward, and yet our ability to exercise authentic agency is influenced by many things. Much of this chapter has focused on the ways poorer women are disempowered through poverty and harmful gender norms and the impact that these have on their reproductive well-being. Discourse around sexual and reproductive rights must be nuanced, informed, and above all compassionate if we are to effect positive change. Echoing an earlier point, Michelle Becka explains that "while respect for relational and vulnerable autonomy of the human person has become a nucleus of theological ethics more recently, it is still given too little consideration in the church's debate about sexual violence."[70] Drawing from the work of Hille Haker, Judith Butler and others, Becka discusses the notion of "vulnerable agency," an idea that reminds us that autonomy and agency coexist with vulnerability and relationality.[71]

---

[69] Peterson-Iyer, *Reenvisioning Sexual Ethics*, 69.

[70] Michelle Becka, "Sexual Abuse in the Church and the Violation of Vulnerable Agency," in *Doing Theology and Theological Ethics in the Face of the Abuse Crisis*, 11.

[71] Becka, "Sexual Abuse in the Church and the Violation of Vulnerable Agency," 12. See also James F. Keenan, SJ, "Vulnerability," in *The Moral Life: Eight Lectures* (Washington, DC: Georgetown University Press, 2023), 19–37.

Vulnerable agency can be understood in three interconnected ways. The first is ontological vulnerability, whereby human beings by their very nature are "touchable by others and open to the world."[72] It refers to the human condition of being receptive to others, being open to the world and relationships, and allowing ourselves to accept the risk that this entails. The second dimension that Becka highlights is moral vulnerability. This refers to our susceptibility to be harmed by someone else and recognizes the fragility of human interactions. "The subject is at the same time a free agent *and* vulnerable. Because the self-determination and agency that constitutes the human being is always at risk, it requires special protection."[73] This brings us to the third dimension of vulnerable agency, namely structural vulnerability. It is what Judith Butler describes as "precarity" and refers to the "situations and structures in which people lack security and social freedom [that] other groups have."[74]

We know that our understanding of human flourishing is historically and culturally situated and therefore in need of constant, robust scrutiny. As Becka and others demonstrate, our understanding of agency, freedom, and consent must also include recognition of human fragility, including the vulnerability and precarity that connects us all.[75] Peterson-Iyer argues that any sexual ethic interested in fostering genuine sexual agency and promoting human flourishing must encourage environments conducive to mature sexual discourse and true sexual self-knowledge. In other words, what is needed are supportive contexts in which integration of the sexual into our overall identity can be achieved, encouraging an ethic of care for both the individual and those with whom we share our intimate lives. An ethic that takes seriously sexual and reproductive agency "will actively call people to consider their values, their histories, and their emotions as they make sexual choices, being honest with themselves about their fears,

---

[72] Becka, "Sexual Abuse in the Church and the Violation of Vulnerable Agency," 15.
[73] Becka, "Sexual Abuse in the Church and the Violation of Vulnerable Agency," 15.
[74] Becka, "Sexual Abuse in the Church and the Violation of Vulnerable Agency," 15.
[75] For more on this see James Keenan, "The World at Risk: Vulnerability, Precarity, and Connectedness," *Theological Studies* 81, no. 1 (2020): 132–149.

desires, and goals. . . . A Christian ethic will seek to articulate and promote what might count as supportive, safe contexts for sex—contexts that foster human wholeness and therefore emotional, psychological, and spiritual well-being."[76]

Conclusion

This chapter began with sobering statistics from the WHO that demonstrate the stark realities of gender-based violence and its devastating consequences for women and their reproductive agency. The Irish context provided a vivid illustration of how social and religious narrative can become intertwined with institutions that oppress females and deny them their fundamental rights. Magdalene Laundries and Mother and Baby Homes serve as a reminder of the Catholic Church's collusion in violence against women. The virtues of resistance and resilience are needed precisely because of the social sins that continue to oppress females today, both within society and within Church institutions. Resisting patriarchal norms is critical for women's reproductive agency; new ways forward must be rooted in justice and reflect the lived experiences of women.

Moreover, Catholic discourse on women's reproductive rights ought to be conducted with compassion and gentleness rather than seen as a weapon to crush and control women's bodies. Magisterial teaching would be strengthened if it more deeply incorporated the complexities of reproductive justice, learning from the testimonies of women. Intersectional scholarship provides a valuable resource for Church teaching, something which could enrich its approach to these matters. As every chapter within this volume details, reproductive justice is connected to a host of other justice issues. If we are committed to the flourishing of all human beings and to the protection of human dignity, the bodily integrity and reproductive wellbeing of women must be an integral part of such a

---

[76] Peterson-Iyer, *Reenvisioning Sexual Ethics*, 75.

commitment. This will require sophisticated thinking as well as efforts to dismantle the harmful structures and damaging narratives that oppress women. It will also require us to appreciate the precarity and vulnerability that accompanies reproductive agency in a more thoughtful way. And above all, it will require patience and understanding as we journey with others towards responsible, just moral decision-making.

Suzanne Mulligan, STL, PhD, teaches at the Center for Social Concerns, University of Notre Dame, USA. She is a member of the Planning Committee of Catholic Theological Ethics in the World Church.

7. Reconceptualizing Human Reproduction beyond John Paul II

Simeiqi He

What is human reproduction? Does it only mean the production of individual human offspring and giving birth to children? Or could it have a more expansive meaning? What do the rich resources of magisterial teaching provide us? Are they only unreasonable demands for uncritical obedience? Or are they invitations to further the spirit of inquiry through an ongoing faith seeking understanding that demonstrates a creative fidelity to the tradition? These questions sit at the heart of this chapter as I take a deep dive into the question of reproduction and its evolving conceptualization in the Church's magisterium.

John Paul II played an indispensable and authoritative role in shaping the magisterial teaching on the meaning and ethics of human reproduction. Within the modern papacy, John Paul II provided the most substantial elaboration on the concept of reproduction—which is among the central concerns of his entire pontificate—by first formulating its philosophical and theological foundation in the 1960 book *Love and Responsibility*. During the Second Vatican Council, the then Archbishop Karol Wojtyła participated in the drafting of what would later become *Gaudium et Spes*. He was also instrumental in the formulation and development of *Humanae Vitae* by Paul VI,[1] who was reportedly reading *Love and Responsibility* when writing the 1968 encyclical.[2] A staunch advocate of *Humanae Vitae*, John Paul II dedicated his most carefully elaborated work, *Man and Woman He Created Them: A Theology of the*

---

[1] George Weigel, *Witness to Hope: The Biography of Pope John Paul II* (New York: Cliff Street Books, 1999), 207.

[2] Janet Smith, *Why Humanae Vitae Was Right: A Reader* (San Francisco: Ignatius, 2014).

Body to its defense.³ John Paul II's conceptualization of reproduction and its implication for reproductive practices are repeatedly reiterated in the *Catechism of the Catholic Church*, the *Compendium of the Social Doctrine of the Church*, and two documents related to the issue of reproduction published by the Congregation for the Doctrine of Faith—*Donum Vitae* and *Dignitas Personae*.

Underlying the magisterium's rejection of artificial contraception, sterilization, abortion, and assisted reproductive technology is the normative understanding of human reproduction as the birthing of children resulting directly from heterosexual conjugal intercourse. Any deviation from such a narrow norm is considered an offense against justice and morally illicit. With regard to guidelines for human reproductive methods provided by the *Compendium of the Social Doctrine of the Church*, only rejections and condemnations are issued and no positive proposals are substantiated (nos. 233–235). However, as contributors in this volume argue, such a negative assessment with regard to human reproduction is not only inadequate but diminishes flourishing—especially for women[4]—and further instigates injustices in the contexts of unintended pregnancies,[5] economic constraints,[6] gender relations,[7] gender

---

[3] John Paul II, *Man and Woman He Created Them: A Theology of the Body* (Boston: Pauline Books & Media, 2006), 100.

[4] In this volume, see Mary Roche, "Rachel Is Weeping for Her Children: Theological Reflections on Reproductive Justice and Maternal Health," 55–89, Karen Peterson-Iyer, "Reproductive Justice and Agricultural Labor Migrants," 257–289, Mary Lilian Akhere Ehidiamhen, "Reclaiming Women's Agency for Reproductive Justice in Nigeria Today: Flourishing for Mother and Child in Situations of Constraints," 310–333, Eric Marcelo O. Genilo, SJ, "Risking Women's Lives, Denying Women's Experiences: CDF Statements on Sterilization in Catholic Hospitals," 334–357, and Virginia Saldanha, "Religio-Cultural Underpinnings of Gender and Reproductive Injustice and Their Impact on Women's Agency in India," 391–410.

[5] Julie Clague, "Structural Inequality and the Social Determinants of Unintended Pregnancy," 21–54.

[6] Kate Ward, "Never Just a Choice: Three Theoretical Approaches to Economic Constraints on Family Formation," 55–89.

[7] Hoon Choi, "Fatherhood, Reproductive Justice, and Strategic Invisibility of Men," 122–127.

violence,[8] sex education,[9] and health care.[10]

Thus, John Paul II's normative proposal regarding the conceptualization of human reproduction first laid out in *Love and Responsibility* is insufficient in addressing the complex realities of the topic. To grapple with such difficulty requires a re-evaluation and revision of the concept of reproduction beyond the narrow scope propagated by John Paul II. A careful examination of magisterial teaching on human reproduction offers a clue, revealing a rather steady evolution of the concept toward an expansive horizon, where a reconceptualization of reproduction can be attained.

This chapter begins with a close analysis of the concept of reproduction in the seminal text *Love and Responsibility* by the then Archbishop Karol Wojtyła. The first section examines Wojtyła's proposal of "procreation" in conceptualizing human reproduction and the struggle to distinguish the two concepts of "procreation" and "reproduction" while revealing inconsistencies in Wojtyła's argument, along with an anthropocentric outlook. The second section provides a thorough investigation of Wojtyła's notion of justice with regard to human reproduction. It argues that there exists a fundamental tension within Wojtyła's prescription of normative human reproduction. Demonstrating Wojtyła's influence in subsequent magisterial development, I point out that the recent shift of magisterial teaching's attention toward the advancement of social love demands that John Paul II's normative prescription for human reproduction be re-evaluated and revised. The last section proposes that Francis's social doctrine where human reproduction is viewed from the vantage point of love and its fruitfulness provides a novel opening for the reconceptualization of reproduction as the reproduction of love in human

---

[8] Suzanne Mulligan, "Thinking about Reproductive Justice in Contexts of Violence," 148–174.
[9] Stephanie Ann Puen, "Considerations for a Comprehensive Sex Education Grounded in Catholic Social Thought for Reproductive Justice in the Philippines," 237–256.
[10] Emily Reimer-Barry, "Catholic Health Care and Reproductive Justice: Whose Conscience Has Priority When Conscience Claims Collide?," 358–390.

societies through diverse forms, moving away from John Paul II's anthropocentric outlook to conceive an anthropocosmic vision. I conclude the chapter with an overview of my arguments, while presenting an open horizon by reconceptualizing reproduction as the reproduction of love.

Reproduction and Procreation

John Paul II's most extensive conceptualization of reproduction is found in *Love and Responsibility*, where the concept of reproduction is viewed through the varying orders of the supernatural, the personal, the natural, and the biological. The then Archbishop Karol Wojtyła differentiated the two concepts—"reproduction" and "procreation"—by pointing out that the word "procreation" expresses more fully the content and natural finality of human conjugal intercourse than the word "reproduction," given that the meaning of the latter is "purely biological."[11] Earlier in the book, Wojtyła expressed a rather negative assessment of what he calls the "biological order" by distinguishing it with the order of nature. He stressed that the two expressions cannot be confused, given that the order of nature "remains in relation to God the Creator,"[12] and together with the supernatural order, is the divine order; while the "biological order" is a "work of the human mind . . . [and] has man as its immediate author."[13] Though signifying[14] the order of nature, the "biological order" separates

---

[11] Karol Wojtyła, *Love and Responsibility*, trans. Grzegorz Ignatik (Boston: Pauline Books & Media, 2013), 211.

[12] Wojtyła, *Love and Responsibility*, 40.

[13] Wojtyła, *Love and Responsibility*, 41.

[14] Wojtyła's understanding of sign and expression is analogical and eminent. Signifying the order of nature, the "biological order" is considered by Wojtyła as an abstraction of the natural order. The French philosopher Gilles Deleuze's description seems to speak to Wojtyła's notion of sign and expression. When delineating the difference between eminent and immanent expression, Deleuze points out that abstractions are images and extrinsic signs that are indicative but not expressive of truth. They arise when our capacity for being affected is exceeded and we no longer seek to understand but are instead content with imagining, setting up as an essential trait while disregarding the others. See Gilles Deleuze, *Spinoza: Practical*

some elements of this order from "what really exists"[15] and denotes the order of nature "only inasmuch as it is accessible for the empirical-descriptive methods of natural sciences, and not as a specific order of existence with a clear relation to the First Cause, to God the Creator."[16]

As a work on sexual ethics, Wojtyła's treatment of reproduction in *Love and Responsibility* confines itself to the issue of human heterosexual conjugal intercourse. He conceived the human sexual drive as pertaining not only to the "biological order" but also the order of nature, while setting his whole sexual ethics to address the distinction between the two. Wojtyła argued that the confusion of the order of nature with the "biological order" erases the link between the sexual drive with the divine work of creation, where "the sexual drive is only a sum of functions, which from the biological point of view undoubtedly tend to a biological end, to reproduction."[17] In Wojtyła's view, the human sexual drive concerns not only the biological order alone but the order of nature, which "constitutes a group of cosmic relations that occur among beings that really exists," for the latter is the order of existence and "the whole order present in existence finds its basis in the one who is the unceasing source of this existence, in God the Creator."[18] For Wojtyła, the order of nature is "first and foremost the order of existing and becoming - of procreation."[19] Human sexual drive is "linked in a particular way with the order of existence," which according to him, "is the *divine order* inasmuch as it is realized under the continuous influence of God the Creator."[20] Human conjugal intercourse becomes the gateway through which human beings enter into the orbit of the order of nature.[21]

Philosophy (San Francisco: City Lights Books, 1988), 45.
[15] Wojtyła, *Love and Responsibility*, 41.
[16] Wojtyła, *Love and Responsibility*, 40.
[17] Wojtyła, *Love and Responsibility*, 41.
[18] Wojtyła, *Love and Responsibility*, 41.
[19] Wojtyła, *Love and Responsibility*, 211.
[20] Wojtyła, *Love and Responsibility*, 40.
[21] Wojtyła, *Love and Responsibility*, 211.

That is, in John Paul II's early conceptualization of human reproduction, human heterosexual conjugal intercourse pertains to the order of nature, which is the divine order. It is not to be confused with the "biological order," which is considered as only an abstraction of the natural order resulting from the scientific endeavor of the human mind. To remedy the tendency to collapse the two orders, Wojtyła preferred the term "procreation" instead of "reproduction" in defining human reproduction, stating that "it is evident that in this case the point is not merely the beginning of life in a purely biological sense, but the beginning of the existence of the person; hence it is better to say 'procreation.'"[22]

In distinguishing the concept of "procreation" with "reproduction," Wojtyła further introduced the concept of the personal order that differs from both the natural order and the biological order, while viewing human procreation more in the context of the former than the latter. According to Wojtyła, unlike the pure biological meaning of "reproduction," "procreation" as *procreatio* denotes a more profound philosophical and theological significance, as "when a man and a woman within marriage consciously and freely choose sexual intercourse, then together with it they choose at the same time the possibility of procreation; they choose to participate in creating (to apply the proper meaning of *procreatio*)."[23] Such significance pertains to the concept of the person reserved only for human persons, as evident in his writing where he argues,

> Reproduction is connected with biological fertility, by the power of which the mature individuals of a given species become parents by bringing into the world their offspring, i.e., new individuals of that species. The case is similar within the species *Homo sapiens*. [Human being], however, is a person, and, therefore, a simple natural fact of becoming a father or a mother possesses a deeper meaning: not only

---

[22] Wojtyła, *Love and Responsibility*, 211.
[23] Wojtyła, *Love and Responsibility*, 213. There lacks a robust discussion in John Paul II of the various situations when the freedom of sexual intercourse and procreation is less attainable, especially for women.

'biological,' but also personal.[24]

Thus, the concept of procreation pertains to the order of the person. It also pertains to the complete objectivity of human conjugal intercourse as it is by its essence a union of persons in relation to *procreatio*—concerning the objective order of nature, in which God the Creator is expressed.

The introduction of the personal order to delineate the distinction between "reproduction" and "procreation" posed a difficulty for Wojtyła as it resulted in the separation between the order of nature and the order of person. To further define the boundary between "reproduction" and "procreation," while at the same time attempting to establish the relation between the natural order and the personal order, Wojtyła appealed to the supposed difference between animals and human beings, considering the concept of reproduction as only pertaining to the animal world, which he argued is dominated by instinct.[25] Wojtyła contended that in the animal world, "There are no persons here, hence there is neither the possibility for nor the demands of the personalistic norm proclaiming love."[26] According to Wojtyła, for human persons, "instinct alone does not solve anything, and the sexual drive, so to speak, enters the gates of consciousness and the will, providing not only the conditions of fertility but at the same time the specific 'material' for love."[27] He stressed that if the question of human sexual drive is to be solved on a human level, the two orders—the personal order and the natural order—must be held together.[28]

Perhaps unintended by Wojtyła himself, conceptualizing reproduction as pertaining to animals and instinct moves away from the view of the "biological order" as an abstraction from the natural order produced by the human mind through scientific endeavors. Reproduction now bears directly upon the order of nature, where both in animals and in humans

---

[24] Wojtyła, *Love and Responsibility*, 213.
[25] Wojtyła, *Love and Responsibility*, 212.
[26] Wojtyła, *Love and Responsibility*, 212.
[27] Wojtyła, *Love and Responsibility*, 212.
[28] Wojtyła, *Love and Responsibility*, 212.

the role of instinct cannot be completely negated. That is, by considering reproduction as pertaining to animals and instinct, Wojtyła located "reproduction" in the order of nature, which is previously said to be the order of "procreation" that expresses the divine order.

Without re-evaluating the "biological order," nor further investigating the value of evolving scientific understanding undertaken by the human mind, its meaning as relating to the natural and divine order, Wojtyła hastened to collapse the concepts of "reproduction" and "procreation" into the order of nature, while maintaining its distinction with the personal order and devoting his whole sexual ethics to achieving an integration between the two orders. However, in doing so, Wojtyła introduced a fragmentation in the conceptualization of the natural order as well as that of "procreation."

While pointing out that the order of nature "aims at reproduction," Wojtyła argued that the personal order "is expressed in the love of persons and strives to realize this love as fully as possible."[29] As previously mentioned, Wojtyła emphasizes that the two orders cannot be separated, rather "one depends on the other, and particularly the relation to reproduction (*procreatio*) conditions the realization of love."[30] Only when viewed together, "Both, i.e., procreation (reproduction) as well as love, are realized on the basis of the conscious choice of persons."[31] That is, by distinguishing the order of nature from the order of person, Wojtyła also removed love from reproduction (procreation), leading to a fragmented understanding of procreation (reproduction) that is non-human and loveless. Though the stress to integrate human reproduction with personal love presents an honest struggle for Wojtyła, the analysis so far has shown that the initial separation between the natural order and the personal order—between reproduction and love—is in fact a direct result of Wojtyła's own problematic conceptualization.

---

[29] Wojtyła, *Love and Responsibility*, 211.
[30] Wojtyła, *Love and Responsibility*, 212.
[31] Wojtyła, *Love and Responsibility*, 212–213.

Moreover, Wojtyła's normative argument for human reproduction (procreation) as the process of heterosexual conjugal sexual intercourse leading to the birth of children with no "artificial interference" is defined by what is a fundamentally anthropocentric outlook that separates the reproduction of human beings from that of animals.[32] Conceptualizing reproduction as located in the order of nature and directly connected with "the sexual life of animals remaining under the power of instinct," Wojtyła distinguished the process of human reproduction (procreation) from that of animals by considering the former's "conscious share in the work of creation" as transcending animal instinct.[33]

Wojtyła's confused conceptualization of human reproduction and his anthropocentric outlook are further reflected in *Gaudium et Spes*. Without explicitly mentioning Wojtyła's language of the personal order and personalistic norm, *Gaudium et Spes* put forward a more personalistic understanding of marriage, where "marriage to be sure is not instituted solely for procreation; rather, its very nature as an unbreakable compact between persons, and the welfare of the children, both demand that the mutual love of the spouses be embodied in a rightly ordered manner" (no. 50). By invoking the concept of procreation, *Gaudium et Spes* did not attend to its nuanced meaning—and its tension with the concept of reproduction—present in the earlier work of Wojtyła. Rather, it emulated Wojtyła's collapse of the two concepts by claiming that human reproduction, intimately connected with human sexual characteristics, is a human faculty that "wonderfully exceed[s] the dispositions of lower forms of life" (no. 51).

By doing so, *Gaudium et Spes* overlooked Wojtyła's struggle to first conceptualize reproduction in the order of nature. Having now insisted that human reproduction is procreation and is situated in the natural order, *Gaudium et Spes* also reproduced Wojtyła's anthropocentric outlook by teaching that human reproduction (procreation) exceeds the function

---

[32] Wojtyła never considered the reproductive processes of plants nor fungi.
[33] Wojtyła, *Love and Responsibility*, 234.

of the natural order as the domains of animal instinct. Underlying its appeal to mutual spousal love is Wojtyła's personal order and the personalistic norm that exists outside of the natural order. Following Wojtyła's lead, *Gaudium et Spes*—by locating human procreation (reproduction) in the order of nature—removed procreation (reproduction) from the order of person, while arbitrarily inventing two mutually exclusive orders: the "order of person" that transcends the natural order and the "order of nature" that is alien to love and human persons. The former pertains to the "authentic conjugal love," while the latter pertains to "the transmission of life" (no. 51).

Moreover, *Gaudium et Spes* went further than Wojtyła and hastened to define these two aspects as divine law pertaining to the divine order (no. 51), without serious attention to the unresolved fundamental tension with regard to the conceptualization of the natural order and the personal order and their infinite distance from the divine order found in Wojtyła's own argument. It warns married couples "in their manner of acting . . . should be aware that they cannot proceed arbitrarily, but must always be governed according to a conscience dutifully conformed to the divine law itself, and should be submissive toward the Church's teaching office, which authentically interprets that law in the light of the Gospel" (no. 50).

Nonetheless, *Gaudium et Spes* is not blind to the contradiction between the two proposed aspects, insisting that "a true contradiction cannot exist between the divine laws pertaining to the transmission of life and those pertaining to authentic conjugal love" (no. 51). Such statement presupposes the existence of a contradiction, one that was first noticed by Wojtyła himself. He was committed to integrate the order of nature and the order of person, insisting that only heterosexual marital intercourse leading to the birth of children—as the norm for human reproduction (procreation)—constitutes the remedy for the contradiction, a point that will be further investigated in the next section.

However, the contradiction was never a logical one, given that following Wojtyła's own conceptualization, where "procreation"—as "reproduction"—pertaining to at once the personal order, the order of nature, the divine order, and even the "biological order," there should be no need for integration. The contradiction appears to be a product of Wojtyła's introduction of the personal order reflecting a transcendental personalism. The assumption that heterosexual conjugal intercourse resulting in the birth of children constitutes the whole norm and the sole defining character for human reproduction (procreation) is predetermined in Wojtyła's analysis, as both its premise and its conclusion. Such an approach undercuts the legibility of his own conceptualization on human reproduction and procreation. Further, with the magisterium's presumption that certain reproductive (procreative) practices do not measure up to such a norm, the forced elevation and integration of the two orders by a hasty invocation of the divine law held significant sway in the magisterium's sanctions regarding sexual ethics and the ethics of human reproduction. The impact of such a confused divine mandatory norm came into full force in light of Paul VI's publication of the controversial document *Humanae Vitae* as it served as the rationale to denounce all artificial interference with conception.

Regardless, it is worth affirming that Wojtyła and the magisterium's approach to the issue does indicate an aspiration to arrive at a vision of human reproduction (procreation) that integrates the biological order, the personal order, the natural order, and the divine order. Such aspiration, though holding tremendous moral power, was quickly circumscribed with detrimental ethical implications by a narrow and flawed conceptualization of human reproduction (procreation), a rigid understanding of justice with regard to the matter, and a lack of effort in conceptualizing human reproduction (procreation) beyond the process of heterosexual marital intercourse leading to the birth of children without "artificial" interference. However, with more recent magisterial developments under the leadership of Francis, we are moving closer to reconceptualize reproduction beyond John Paul II that affirms the oneness of God, human, and nature, an argument I will propose in the last section.

Reproduction and Justice

The theoretical foundation underlying the magisterium's approach to justice with regard to sexual ethics and human reproduction was first laid out by Wojtyła in terms of "justice with respect to the Creator" in *Love and Responsibility*. According to Wojtyła, "With respect to the Creator, the rational creature, man, is just by striving in his action toward precisely this human value, by conducting himself as *particeps Creatoris*."[34] He argued that given its creatureliness, human beings should *first* remain in conformity with the law of nature, "*[only] then* will man be just with respect to the Creator."[35] The sequential nature of Wojtyła's argument implies that human beings do not have direct access to the divine law. It is only through their conformity with the law of nature, human beings are able to fulfill the divine law which is justice.

As mentioned in the previous section, Wojtyła—when distinguishing "reproduction" from "procreation"—considered "procreation" both in the order of nature (which differs from the "biological order" concerning "reproduction") and the order of person (as the coming into existence of persons). There, the order of nature is the divine order serving as the source of human moral acts. However, after collapsing the two concepts, Wojtyła reduced the concept of procreation (reproduction)—along with the order of nature—to the domain of animal instinct, while instilling a personal order that transcends it. Inventing a separate personal order governed by reason and will subjected to what is the moral order, Wojtyła erased morality from instinct and the natural order. The latter became alienated from the moral order and the morality of human reproduction (procreation) no longer concerns the order of nature. Instead, it emphasizes the personal order over and against the natural order.

The hierarchal relation between the personal order and the natural

---

[34] Wojtyła, *Love and Responsibility*, 233.
[35] Wojtyła, *Love and Responsibility*, 233. Italics my own to highlight the sequential nature of the argument.

order underlies Wojtyła's ethical argument regarding human reproduction. While insisting on the conformity of human acts with the law of nature regarding human reproduction, Wojtyła considered justice with respect to the Creator as comprising two elements—"the preservation of the order of nature" and "the manifestation of the value of the person"[36]—corresponding respectively to the order of nature and the personal order. Only the latter concerns the value of the created person as *particeps Creatoris* through participation in the thought of the Creator.[37] Wojtyła argued that it is this personal order—constituting the personalistic norm—that "causes [man] to possess a correct relation to the whole of reality in all its constituent parts, in all elements."[38] In emphasizing the significance of the personalistic norm to justice, Wojtyła stated that "[b]y being the Creator of the person, God is the source of the whole personal order, which *rises above* the order of nature thanks precisely to the person's capacity for understanding the latter and for his conscious self-determination within it. Justice with respect to the Creator demands from man *above all* the preservation of the personal order."[39] Here, it is apparent that in Wojtyła's treatment of the natural order and the personal order on the issue of justice regarding human reproduction, the two orders do not bear equal weight. Rather, what justice demands pertains to the personal order (not necessarily the natural order) and its superiority over the natural order.

According to Wojtyła, such superiority is precisely manifested and justified through his normative proposal for human reproduction, where the transcending character of human reason over and against animal instinct is carried out through the process of heterosexual conjugal intercourse directly resulting in the birthing of the human offspring. Pointing out that reproduction alone does not fulfill the obligation of

---

[36] Wojtyła, *Love and Responsibility*, 233.
[37] Wojtyła, *Love and Responsibility*, 233.
[38] Wojtyła, *Love and Responsibility*, 233.
[39] Wojtyła, *Love and Responsibility*, 234.

justice in relation to the Creator, Wojtyła explained that "[the] person *transcends* the world of nature, and the personal order is not completely contained in the order of nature. Therefore, a man and a woman who have conjugal relations fulfill their obligations with respect to God the Creator only when they place all these relations on the…level of a truly personal union."[40] That is, Wojtyła's understanding of justice with regard to human reproduction is fundamentally dependent upon the moral distinction between human and animals and the personal order and the order of nature. It demands the transcendence of the personal order over the natural order, human beings over animals, and reason over instinct. For Wojtyła, it is the personal order alone that fulfills the requirement of justice as far as the moral law is concerned. The order of nature is relegated to the world of animals dominated by an amoral (or immoral) instinct.

Underlying Wojtyła's account of justice with regard to human sexual ethics and reproduction is an anthropocentric moral outlook. It is achieved through the personalistic norm, which fundamentally concerns the personal order distinct from the natural order and in an *indirect* relation to the divine order. Central to the conception of the personalistic norm is "a kind of love" that is "not only a love of the world, but also a love of the Creator."[41] Wojtyła stressed that the love of the Creator is included in this relation *"only in an indirect way"* and "the man who has a correct relation to the whole created reality by that very fact *indirectly* has a proper relation to the Creator, is simply and fundamentally just with respect to him."[42] Wojtyła did not directly address the divine order with regard to human reproduction nor inquire further into the love of the Creator and how it might shed new light into our understanding of human reproduction. Rather, his invocation of the love of the Creator only harks back to the argument for his already determined personalistic norm that "the personalistic norm is a substantiation for the commandment of the Gospel"

---

[40] Wojtyła, *Love and Responsibility*, 234–235.
[41] Wojtyła, *Love and Responsibility*, 233.
[42] Wojtyła, *Love and Responsibility*, 233.

and "the order of justice is more fundamental than the order of love."[43]

Given Wojtyła's own argument that justice with respect to the Creator is ultimately achieved through the conformity with the law of nature (and not the personalistic norm), the order of nature cannot be so easily transcended. As previously mentioned, Wojtyła himself recognized that—with regard to human reproduction (procreation)—the preservation of the natural order together with the manifestation of the personal order constitute the two elements of justice with respect to the Creator. Noticing the contradiction between what justice demands of the two orders, Wojtyła argues that the only remedy is to prescribe heterosexual marital intercourse leading to the birth of children without "artificial" interference as the definite ethical norm for human reproduction. He elaborated this solution in *Love and Responsibility*, writing,

> The sexual intercourse of a man and a woman in marriage possesses its full value of a personal union only when it contains the conscious acceptance of the possibility of parenthood. This is a plain result of the synthesis of the two orders: the order of nature and the order of the person. A man and a woman in conjugal intercourse do not remain only and exclusively in a reciprocal relation to each other, but, as a matter of fact, they remain in relation to the new person who can be created (*procreatio*) thanks precisely to their union.[44]

In Wojtyła's understanding, human heterosexual conjugal intercourse rises to the level of a personal union only when the couple demonstrate the attitude of "I can be a father" and "I can be a mother." The potential character of the relation with the child—as a "a new property and a new state" in which the husband and wife as father and mother participate[45]—at once justifies the sexual intercourse and enriches the personal communion of the husband and wife, thus fulfilling both the elements of

---

[43] Wojtyła, *Love and Responsibility*, 26.
[44] Wojtyła, *Love and Responsibility*, 213–214.
[45] Wojtyła, *Love and Responsibility*, 214n.

justice with regard to the Creator. Wojtyła's solution is intended not only to bring the order of nature and the order of the person together but also to maintain the hierarchy, where "man wins a victory over nature and masters it."[46]

Regardless, by insisting that both elements of justice need to be met and the only way to meet them is through his prescription of a normative human reproduction, Wojtyła moves toward a direction where the hierarchical relation between the personal order and the natural order—and the moral superiority of the former over the latter—is at stake. By claiming that "everywhere man masters nature by adapting to its immanent dynamic," Wojtyła advocates a view where the personal order is said to transcend the natural order by being based on nature, which is also immanent to human persons. This view cannot be logically sustained, for *one cannot transcend something that is immanent to it*.[47] Considering human sexual drive as nature, Wojtyła argues that man wins a victory over nature only by "adapting it its immanent finality thanks to understanding the laws that govern that drive" and sexual intercourse is based on the drive by engaging with which the moral value of the person is formed.[48] He claims that all of this is based on "the presupposition according to which there is a close link between the order of nature and the person as well as the realization of human personhood."[49] Redeeming the natural order from its moral demise, Wojtyła now admits that the power of the order of nature is "constitutive for morality and thus also for the realization of human personhood, inasmuch as behind this order one perceives the personal authority of the Creator."[50] Wojtyła did not go further to

---

[46] Wojtyła, *Love and Responsibility*, 215.

[47] An appropriate response could be drawn from Maurice Merleau-Ponty, who stresses that sexuality is "continuously present in human life as an atmosphere" and is coexistent with life. Sexuality cannot be transcended. See Maurice Merleau-Ponty, *Phenomenology of Perception*, trans. Donald A. Landes (London & New York: Routledge, 2014), 172, 174.

[48] Wojtyła, *Love and Responsibility*, 216.

[49] Wojtyła, *Love and Responsibility*, 216.

[50] Wojtyła, *Love and Responsibility*, 217.

investigate this renewed relationship between the two orders nor what precisely is the "close link." Rather, he asserts that "man must reconcile himself to his natural greatness" precisely by not forgetting that he is a person "when he so deeply enters into the order of nature, when he immerses himself, as it were, in the vehement processes of nature."[51] Wojtyła returns to his previous argument that human sexual life needs to be justified, not by nature, for "instinct alone will not solve anything in him," but by the personal responsibility for procreation.[52]

Thus, there exists a fundamental tension within Wojtyła's proposal of the ethical norm for human reproduction that was not and cannot be easily resolved. The analysis in this section has shown that Wojtyła's investigation of justice with regard to reproduction is largely based on an anthropocentric distinction between the natural order and the personal order and the moral superiority and transcendence of human intellect over against animal instinct. It demonstrates also that, given Wojtyła's own argument that justice is achieved through the conformity with the law of nature, such moral hierarchy cannot be maintained. Rather than further investigating his proposition with regard to the two orders and re-assessing his proposal for the ethical norm of human reproduction, Wojtyła exercised a confused integration of the two orders to justify his normative proposal, a move that risks the integrity of his own reasoning.

Such confused reasoning, far from being resolved by subsequent magisterial development up until the pontificate of John Paul II, was further intensified. As I have demonstrated in the previous section, a similar confusion was present in *Gaudium et Spes*, especially through its elevation of normative human procreation (reproduction) as pertaining directly to the divine law, which can only be authentically interpreted by the Church's magisterium. Its claim that there exist two divine laws pertaining to the transmission of life and those pertaining to authentic conjugal love finds its prototype in Wojtyła's proposition of the two

---

[51] Wojtyła, *Love and Responsibility*, 222–223.
[52] Wojtyła, *Love and Responsibility*, 223.

elements mentioned earlier in the section that comprise justice with respect to the Creator—"the manifestation of the value of the person" and "the preservation of the order of nature."[53] *Gaudium et Spes* hastened to define these two aspects as divine laws pertaining to the divine order, without attending to Wojtyła's own argument that the moral order is foreign to the order of nature and is only relevant to the order of person, which stands in an *indirect* relation with the divine order.

The tension was further exacerbated through *Humanae Vitae* where the relation between natural law, moral law, and divine law with regard to human reproduction became further confused. Reiterating Vatican II's declaration that the Church magisterium *alone* is entrusted the task to teach the divine law (no. 19), *Humanae Vitae* reminds its audience that the Church magisterium is competent and indisputable in its interpretation of the natural moral law, acting as the "authentic guardians and interpreters of the whole moral law, not only, that is, of the law of the Gospel but also of the natural law" (no. 4). It claims that the natural law "declares the will of God, and its faithful observance is necessary for men's eternal salvation" and the magisterium's moral teaching on marriage is "based on the natural law as illuminated and enriched by divine Revelation" (no. 4). That is, to define and execute the ethical norm for human reproduction concerns the authority of the magisterium to authentically interpret and teach the divine law, the moral law, and the natural law. This authority is confirmed by its doctrinal affirmation of "responsible parenthood" and the denunciation of artificial contraception and its supposed objection to the "natural law of God" (no. 23).

The influence of Wojtyła can be readily observed in *Humanae Vitae* where it says the biological reproductive process must be respected, while at the same time human reason and will must exert control over the human being's innate drives and emotions (no. 10). By stressing that "in the procreative faculty the human mind discerns biological laws that apply to the human person" (*Humanae Vitae*, no. 10), Paul VI follows Wojtyła in

---

[53] Wojtyła, *Love and Responsibility*, 233.

the latter's distinguishing of procreation from reproduction.

However, Paul VI's doctrinal proposal of responsible parenthood as the ethical norm for human reproduction already signaled a development away from Wojtyła's rigid (and confused) division of reproduction and procreation. Unlike Wojtyła, who considered the biological order as an abstraction of the natural order and an arbitrary product of the human mind, having the human being as its immediate author, Paul VI spoke of a "biological law" that is integral to the natural law. Not only did he call spouses to discern the biological law as they observe the natural law in carrying out responsible parenthood, Paul VI also entrusted such task to scientists. He explicitly acknowledged "the inherent difficulties of the divine law" (*Humanae Vitae*, no. 17). Paul VI affirmed the value of scientific discovery regarding the biological process of human reproduction and its role not only in furthering human knowledge of the order of nature and the divine order but also in providing moral insights into the procreative process (*Humanae Vitae*, no. 24). However, in keeping with the ethical conclusion of Wojtyła and *Gaudium et Spes*, Paul VI, when speaking of medical science, only considered the study of natural rhythms as an observation of the natural law without acknowledging that underlying any medical advancement, including artificial contraception, abortion, and assisted technology, is the inherent function of the biological law integral to the natural law. Regardless, Paul VI, by acknowledging the difficulties with regard to the two divine laws and appealing to scientists, already implies a revision of Wojtyła's sharp moral distinction of the divine order, the natural order, and the personal order.

What can also be readily observed in *Humanae Vitae* is Paul VI's expansion of the discussion of human reproduction far beyond the narrow scope of sexual ethics prescribed by Wojtyła and found in *Gaudium et Spes* to consider it as a social concern. Paul VI addressed the issue of human reproduction and the regulation of birth as pertaining to the creation and advancement of a truly human civilization (*Humanae Vitae*, nos. 18, 22). He made appeals to not only married couples themselves but also public authorities, scientists, doctors and nurses, priests and bishops, and ultimately all people of good will, calling it the "great work" of education, progress and charity.

During the papacy of John Paul II, the social dimension of "responsible parenthood" was further elaborated. In *Evangelium Vitae*, John Paul II approached the issue of responsible procreation as a part of his appeal to offer the world "new signs of hope, and work to ensure that justice and solidarity will increase and that a new culture of human life will be affirmed, for the building of an authentic civilization of truth and love" (no. 6). The *Compendium of the Social Doctrine of the Church* states that the unified aspect of procreation's physical and spiritual dimensions pertains to the "communion of generations" and provides "essential and irreplaceable support for the development of society" (no. 237).

The intimate connection between human reproduction, integral human development, and the creation of a new civilization was well established by Benedict XVI. In *Caritas in Veritate*, he points out that Paul VI's *Humanae Vitae* forged a strong link between life ethics and social ethics, "ushering in a new area of magisterial teaching" (no. 15), one that is further carried out by John Paul II's *Evangelium Vitae*. Benedict XVI affirmed that responsible procreation "has a positive contribution to make to integral human development" (no. 44). Capturing the central message of Paul VI, Benedict XVI considered his social teaching as pointing to "the indispensable importance of the Gospel for building a society according to freedom and justice, in the ideal and historical perspective of a civilization animated by love" (*Caritas in Veritate*, no. 13).

However, in spite of the magisterium's expansion of social vision with regard to human reproduction, the earlier work of John Paul II continues to serve as the functioning apparatus for conceptualizing reproduction and the primary rationale for upholding heterosexual conjugal sexual intercourse directly resulting in the birth of human offsprings as the exclusive ethical norm. The tension and incoherency existing within John Paul II's argument for normative human reproduction and his understanding of the natural order, the personal order, and the divine order remain unresolved. Further, the recent shift of magisterial teaching's attention toward the advancement of social love demands that John Paul II's framework for understanding human reproduction and justice be re-evaluated and revised. Such revision, though already present during John Paul II's papacy, is reaching the height of its promise through Francis's vision of universal love and its fruitfulness.

Reproduction and Love

Unlike John Paul II, who started the conceptualization of human reproduction from the process of heterosexual conjugal sexual intercourse leading to the birth of children and eventually arrived at the conclusion that defined it as the exclusive ethical norm for human reproduction, Francis opened a new beginning by envisioning human reproduction from the openness and fruitfulness of love itself.

Though appealing to Paul VI and John Paul II in speaking of marriage and parenthood, the regulation of birth, and gender differences, Francis through *Amoris Laetitia* put forward a much more expansive vision of fruitfulness, one that is centered upon love and not limited to the rigid understanding as having children resulting directly from heterosexual conjugal sexual intercourse. In chapter five, "Love Made Fruitful," Francis stresses that it is love that gives life (no. 165). For Francis, the discussion of fruitfulness reflects "the primacy of the love of God" (no. 166). While acknowledging that having children is an expression of the fruitfulness of love (nos. 166, 167), Francis does not consider it as the only expression nor a superior one for marriage. Exalting the joy of motherhood, he nonetheless cites the General Conference of the Latin American and Caribbean Bishops to emphasize that "motherhood is not a solely biological reality, but is expressed in diverse ways" (no. 178) and "the maternal vocation is fulfilled through many kinds of love, comprehension, and service to others."⁵⁴ Francis envisioned "an expanding fruitfulness," where fruitfulness finds its expression in many ways, through adoption (nos. 179, 180), foster care (no. 180), and ultimately through "[binding] the wounds of the outcast, [fostering] a culture of encounter and [fighting] for justice" (no. 183).

Thus, Francis conceptualizes the expression of fruitfulness through human reproduction from the vantage point of social love, a framework he further developed in his two social encyclicals, *Laudato Si'* and *Fratelli Tutti*. In *Laudato Si'*, Francis notes that social love "is the key to authentic development" and "moves us to . . . encourage a 'culture of care' which permeates all of society" (no. 231). He continues in *Fratelli Tutti* to consider that social love "makes it possible to advance towards a civilization of love" and is a "force capable of inspiring new ways of approaching the problems of today's world, of profoundly renewing structures, social organizations and legal systems from within" (no. 183).

Such renewed attention to love, with a civilization of love as its horizon, has been developing steadily since the Second Vatican Council and is now central to Catholic social teaching. John Paul II noted in the 1991 social encyclical *Centesimus Annus* that Paul VI had expanded the previous concepts of Leo XIII's "friendship" and Pius XI's "social charity" to speak of a civilization of love in addressing questions confronted by modern society (no. 10). In the 1995 encyclical *Evangelium Vitae*, John Paul II repeatedly called for the effort to build an authentic civilization of love. The entire *Compendium*—much of it is a reiteration of what was previously articulated by John Paul II—concluded on this call, while exalting the primacy of love as shedding light on the fundamental principles of the Christian view of social and political organization (no. 580). It made clear that the full truth of the human identity "makes it possible to...open up...for justice the new horizon of solidarity and love," stressing that justice alone is not enough but must "open to that deeper

---

[54] Fifth General Conference of the Latin American and Caribbean Bishops, *Aparecida Document*, no. 457.

power which is love" (no. 203). The *Compendium* called for the reconsideration of love "in its authentic values as the *highest and universal criterion* of the whole of social ethics" (no. 204) and urged that "in every sphere of interpersonal relationships justice must...be *corrected to a considerable extent by that love* which . . . possesses the characteristics of that merciful love which is so much of the essence of the Gospel and Christianity" (no. 206). That is, the *Compendium* put forward love as a more fundamental ethical norm and provided the opening for the re-evaluation and revision of previous concepts of justice in light of love.

Such primacy of love was further developed by Benedict XVI in the context of the global society and radically universalized by Francis. In the 2009 encyclical *Caritas in Veritate*, Benedict XVI spoke of the new and creative challenge brought by love, which urges a broadening of "the scope of reason and making it capable of knowing and directing these powerful new forces [of globalization], animating them within the perspective of that 'civilization of love' whose seed God has planted in every people, in every culture" (no. 33). He considered a kind of "ethical convergence" among diverse cultural traditions as the natural law (no. 59). Calling it the "universal moral law," Benedict XVI states that it provides "a sound basis for all cultural, religious and political dialogue" and ensures "a wonderful opportunity for encounter between cultures and peoples" (no. 59). He notes that "every culture has burdens from which it must be freed and shadows from which it must emerge" (no. 59).

Francis's reconceptualization of human reproduction from the fruitfulness and openness of love is conceived within this tradition of Catholic social teaching, its primacy of love and its vision for a civilization of love. Rather than narrowing its scope to prescribe an exclusive form, Francis breaks open the conceptual bonds of human reproduction to expand toward a new universal horizon. Exalting the family, Francis looks not to the rigid form of the heterosexual nuclear family, but the human family and the entire creation as a whole, urging us to recognize the wisdom of creation and the vocation of family to "domesticating" the world in helping each person to see fellow human beings as brothers and sisters (*Amoris Laetitia*, no. 183). He stresses that the current transition in civilization demands a new covenant of love that "should …guide politics, the economy and civil coexistence" and "decides the habitability of the earth, the transmission of love for life, the bonds of memory and hope."[55] Francis explains that the Church set before the world the ideal of a civilization of love because love is at once civic and political, personal and social (*Laudato Si'*, no. 231). It impels us towards universal communion (*Fratelli Tutti*, no. 95). While evoking this universal vision, Francis in *Laudato Si'* appealed to the mystery of the universe where creation is a gift and a reality illuminated by love (no. 76). He points out that such love calls us into a deep communion with all creation, where everything is connected (*Laudato Si'*, nos. 91–92). In *Fratelli Tutti*, Francis advanced a universal horizon where each particular group belongs in the fabric of universal communion (no. 149). He called for "the growth of a culture of encounter capable of transcending . . . differences and divisions" (no. 215). Such encounter is again fostered through love (no. 190), which, with its impulse to universality, is capable of building a new world (no. 183).

Such a new culture and new world is given the name of "open societies" by Francis in *Fratelli Tutti*. Evoking the concept of "open society," Francis's approach to situating human reproduction in the context of love also implies a new direction towards a convergence of the biological order, the natural order, the moral order, the personal order, and the divine order that is to remedy the previous confusions inherent in John Paul II's conceptualization. Francis called for the realization of open societies that integrate everyone with a universal openness in love (no. 97). He declared that "charity is at the heart of every healthy and open society" (no. 184) and all our acts of love "encircle our world like a vital force" (no. 195). It is the fruitfulness of this love that Francis calls us to actualize in all our micro- and macro- relationships (nos. 193–197). Human reproduction

---

[55] Pope Francis, "General Audience," September 16, 2015, www.vatican.va/content/francesco/en/audiences/2015/documents/papa-francesco_20150916_udienza-generale.html.

reconceptualized beyond the narrow scope of heterosexual conjugal sexual intercourse leading to the birth of children with no "artificial" interference now concerns "the hidden power of the seeds of goodness we sow" and the initiation of processes "whose fruits will be reaped by others" (no. 196). The politics of human reproduction becomes a "good politics [that] combines love with hope and with confidence in the reserves of goodness present in human hearts" (no. 196). It is generative as it is "constantly renewed whenever there is a realization that every woman and man, and every generation, brings the promise of new relational, intellectual, cultural and spiritual energies" (no. 196).

The concepts of "open society" and "vital force" central to Francis's proposal are to be attributed to the French philosopher Henri Bergson, one of the most influential philosophers of the twentieth century.[56] Coining the term "open society" in his final book *The Two Sources of Morality and Religion*, Bergson pointed out that "[t]he open society is the society which is deemed in principle to embrace all humanity."[57] It embodies on every occasion something of itself in creations through transformation and is a creative effort, "opening what was closed" and bringing every closed society "back every time to humanity."[58] For Bergson, an open society, by nature of its openness, is a spiritual society where "societies of this kind might multiply; each one, through such of its members as might be exceptionally gifted, would give birth to one or several others…until such time as a profound change in the material conditions imposed on humanity by nature should permit, in spiritual matters, of a radical transformation."[59] The diverse efforts of actualizing open societies, according to Bergson, can be summed up into one and the

---

[56] I have previously established the connection between Francis's use of the term "open society" and Bergson's final work. See Simeiqi He, "Towards Universal Communion," *Journal of Moral Theology* 12, no. 1 (2023): 101–104, doi.org/10.55476/001c.6624.1.
[57] Henri Bergson, *The Two Sources of Morality and Religion*, trans. R. Ashley Audra and Cloudesley Brereton (Notre Dame: University of Notre Dame Press, 2013), 267.
[58] Bergson, *The Two Sources of Morality and Religion*, 267.
[59] Bergson, *The Two Sources of Morality and Religion*, 236.

same thing as "an impetus" which is carried forward through the medium of persons who are able to develop the "mystic life."[60] For Bergson, this impetus is a "mystic impetus" that is to be imparted in persons forming a spiritual society.[61] It is an "impetus of love" that drives the lifting of humanity up to God and the completion of divine creation.[62] Such impetus is what is preserved and continued through generations of human societies.[63]

Bergson first introduced the concept of impetus—the French word is *Élan vital* and is often translated as "vital impetus" or "vital force" in English—in his 1907 book *Creative Evolution*. He conceived an "original impetus of life" that "[passes] from one generation of germs to the following generation of germs through the developed organisms which bridge the interval between the generations."[64] Such impetus culminated in the human species, in social life, in a system of habits that bears a resemblance more or less to *instinct*.[65] Unlike John Paul II, who deemed that "instinct does not solve anything" and that human reason must rise above the instinct that dominated animals to provide a justification for personhood and moral act, Bergson presented a different and more reasonable conceptualization of intellect and instinct, noting,

> The intellect is characterized by a natural inability to comprehend life. Instinct, on the contrary, is molded on the very form of life. While intelligence treats everything mechanically, instinct proceeds, so to speak, organically. If the consciousness that slumbers in it should awake, if it were wound up into knowledge instead of being wound off into action, if we could ask and it could reply, it would give up to us the most intimate secrets of life. For it only carries out further the work by which life organizes matter—so that we cannot say, as has often been shown,

---

[60] Bergson, *The Two Sources of Morality and Religion*, 268.
[61] Bergson, *The Two Sources of Morality and Religion*, 236.
[62] Bergson, *The Two Sources of Morality and Religion*, 236.
[63] Bergson, *The Two Sources of Morality and Religion*, 236.
[64] Henri Bergson, *Creative Evolution* (Mineola, NY: Dover Publications, 1998), 87.
[65] Bergson, *The Two Sources of Morality and Religion*, 55.

where organization ends and where instinct begins.⁶⁶

For Bergson, "instinct is . . . coextensive with life," and social instinct is "nothing more than the spirit of sub-ordination and co-ordination animating the cells and tissues and organs of all living bodies."⁶⁷ He considered social life as "immanent in instinct as well as in intelligence."⁶⁸ According to Bergson, while intelligence is "made to utilize matter, to dominate things, to master events," left to itself, intelligence "would simply realize its ignorance."⁶⁹ Instinct, on the other hand, give rise within intelligence to imagination.⁷⁰ Bergson declared that "instinct is sympathy." It is *intuition* that leads us to "the very inwardness of life"⁷¹ and "is proved by the existence in [human beings] of an aesthetic faculty along with normal perception."⁷² Intuition is mind itself, life itself. We can only recognize the unity of spiritual life through intuition, "[placing] ourselves in intuition in order to go from intuition to the intellect, for from the intellect we shall never pass to intuition."⁷³ To reabsorb intellect in intuition gives us power to act and to live, for "with it, we feel ourselves no longer isolated in humanity, humanity no longer seems isolated in the nature that it dominates."⁷⁴ Rather, all the living is held together, "as the smallest grain of dust is bound up with our entire solar system."⁷⁵

By appealing to Bergson's concepts, Francis invoked an alternative understanding of instinct and moved beyond the anthropocentric outlook of John Paul II to arrive at an anthrpocosmic vision. Human moral life is no longer viewed as a domination over and struggle against animal life and

---

⁶⁶ Bergson, *Creative Evolution*, 165.
⁶⁷ Bergson, *The Two Sources of Morality and Religion*, 121.
⁶⁸ Bergson, *The Two Sources of Morality and Religion*, 21.
⁶⁹ Bergson, *The Two Sources of Morality and Religion*, 163.
⁷⁰ Bergson, *The Two Sources of Morality and Religion*, 164.
⁷¹ Bergson, *Creative Evolution*, 176.
⁷² Bergson, *Creative Evolution*, 177.
⁷³ Bergson, *Creative Evolution*, 268.
⁷⁴ Bergson, *Creative Evolution*, 270.
⁷⁵ Bergson, *Creative Evolution*, 270.

its instinct but is conceived in the process of creative evolution and returned to the immensity of the universe, where "creation is of the order of love" (*Laudato Si'*, no. 77). No more is the personal and moral order justified by a despairing war against the natural and biological order. Rather, biology is given "the very wide meaning it should have...that all morality...is in essence biological."[76] Beginning with intuition, moral perception returns to life, which "appears in its entirety as an immense wave...starting from a centre, spreads outwards."[77]

Thus, human life no longer begins with conception but is coexistent with the universe. Human reproduction is recaptured not merely as the birthing of human offspring but as the pulsation of cosmic life. The personal order, the moral order, the natural order, the biological order are one. Such oneness is not realized through a narrow definition of human procreation as heterosexual conjugal intercourse leading to the birth of children so human sexual life is justified with regard to the Creator. It is accomplished in love, which is the Creator and the divine order itself. Love is divine substance and the "eternal law which creates and governs the universe."[78] It is the common good itself and the fulfillment of the law.[79] The eternal law, the natural law, and human law form a continuous series comparable to a living tree with "the eternal law for its root, the natural law for its trunk, and the different systems of human law for its branches."[80] It is in love—which is life—that the coherence of orders and the law is accomplished. God, as noted by Bergson, is "unceasing life, action, freedom," and creation is experienced by us in ourselves when we act freely.[81] Freedom is not achieved as a triumph over animal instinct.

---

[76] Bergson, *The Two Sources of Morality and Religion*, 101.

[77] Bergson, *Creative Evolution*, 266.

[78] Bernard and Emero S. Stiegman, *On Loving God* (Kalamazoo, MI: Cistercian Publications, 1995), 37.

[79] John C. H. Wu, *Fountain of Justice: A Study in the Natural Law* (New York: Sheed and Ward, 1955), 46. Regarding the common good, see ST I, q. 44, a. 4.

[80] Wu, *Fountain of Justice*, 24–25.

[81] Bergson, *Creative Evolution*, 248.

Rather, novelty and creation are inherent in the free act.[82] Love, by virtue of its nature, is essentially free, creative, and fruitful. It reproduces itself—fulfilling itself through diverse forms—and alone is the ethical norm immanent to all acts with love as their expression. Perceived in this way, reproduction is expansive. It is a reproduction of love—the original impetus, the vital force, and the mystic impetus—that preserves, sustains, and generates the love of God as "the fundamental moving force in all creation" (*Laudato Si'*, no. 77).

Conclusion

Beginning with a thorough investigation of the concept of reproduction in the seminal text *Love and Responsibility* and the argument for prescribing heterosexual conjugal intercourse directly resulting in the birthing of human offspring as the exclusive norm for human reproduction, I demonstrated that there exist internal inconsistencies, fragmentations, and tensions within John Paul II's conceptualization of reproduction. The latter is characterized by a struggle to integrate the natural order and the personal order in the justification of human sexual acts, while maintaining that human reason must master animal instinct. I argued that underlying John Paul II's prescription of normative human reproduction is an anthropocentric moral outlook, which has exercised no small influence in subsequent magisterial developments.

However, the development of Catholic social teaching and the increasing attention to the primacy of love offers a novel opening to re-evaluate and revise previously rigid conceptualizations of reproduction. I proposed that Francis has taken the necessary steps in expanding human reproduction from the vantage point of love and its fruitfulness. His invocation of the Bergsonian concepts "open societies" and "vital force" provides us with an invitation to reconceive the nature of instinct, moving

---

[82] Bergson, *Creative Evolution*, 270.

away from John Paul II's anthropocentric outlook to arrive at an anthropocosmic vision. I argued that viewed within this universal horizon, love becomes the constituting norm for reproduction, accomplishing the oneness of God, human, and nature.

Thus, human reproduction is defined far beyond the narrow scope of heterosexual conjugal intercourse directly resulting in the birthing of human offspring and is capable of taking diverse forms. It is conceived as the reproduction of love, where the reproductivity of love is preserved through the generation of open societies, in which souls freely discern the mystic impetus of love. The reproduction of human life is coexistent with cosmic life and demonstrates an eternal continuity of creation and the duration of love. It is essentially a creative and solidary endeavor. Considering the universe as "the confluence of universal life in the mode of perpetual creativity,"[83] the Chinese philosopher Thomé H. Fang notes that "life of all forms is fulfilled and the value of all kind is achieved through the spirit of love,"[84] as the "embodiment of the felicity of life."[85] The unceasing creative transformation—that is life[86]—manifesting through human reproduction represents nothing other than the fecundity and reproductivity of divine love which expresses itself immanently as "an emerging world of subjective intercommunion"[87] and solidarity. It is also the driving force for the transformation of human society to an absolutely open one, where the vital force—the impetus of love—slowly gives shape to a true culture of life as a new civilization of love. Thus, human reproduction—by reproducing love—ushers us towards the actualization of the common good, which is God, inviting us to participate in the creativity of divine life through universal communion, so humanity could be lifted up to God and divine creation reach its final consummation.

---

[83] Thomé H. Fang, *The Chinese View of Life: The Philosophy of Comprehensive Harmony* (Hong Kong: The Union Press, 1957), 71.

[84] Fang, *The Chinese View of Life*, 76.

[85] Fang, *The Chinese View of Life*, 78.

[86] Bergson, *Creative Evolution*, 230–231.

[87] Thomas Berry, *The Dream of the Earth* (Berkeley: Counterpoint, 2015), 136.

Simeiqi He, PhD, is a Chinese Catholic theological ethicist and social worker. She holds a Ph.D. in Christian ethics from Drew University Theological School, a Master of Arts in Theology and Ministry from Brite Divinity School, a Master of Social Work and a graduate certificate in Women and Gender Studies from Texas Christian University, and a Bachelor of Science in Materials Physics from Sichuan University. Her writings have previously appeared in *Journal of Moral Theology*, *Catholic Theological Review*, *Asian Horizons*, and *U.S. Catholic*.

Part 2

Theo-Ethical Roundtable Discussions

8. On Threats to Women's Flourishing

Stephanie Ann Puen (Philippines), Karen Peterson-Iyer (USA), Mary M. Doyle Roche (USA), Emily Reimer-Barry (USA), and Mary Lilian Akhere Ehdiamhen (Nigeria)

Note from the Co-Editors: In this first roundtable, we asked participants to respond to the questions: "What are the threats to women's dignity and moral agency in your context? Is reproductive justice a helpful framework for addressing those threats?" Authors from the Philippines, United States of America, and Nigeria responded by noting different threats to women's flourishing, and some of the possible ways that a framework of reproductive justice can provide meaningful categories for social action.

Stephanie Ann Puen (Philippines)

In September 2023, the Senate Committee on Women, Children, Family Relations, and Gender Equality in the Philippines approved "a consolidated measure that provides for absolute divorce based on various grounds, including five years of separation, whether continuous or broken, and the commission of the crime of rape before or after marriage."[1] Journalists noted that the bill faced an uphill battle because of the role of religious leaders in the Philippines.[2] Discussion of legal divorce in the Philippines comes a decade or so after the signing of the reproductive health bill into law in 2012, which was also fraught with controversy in a country where the Catholic church is still a strong institution, especially in

---

[1] Cecille Suerte Felipe, "Divorce Bill An Uphill Battle – Tulfo," *Philippine Star*, September 25, 2023, www.philstar.com/headlines/2023/09/25/2298815/divorce-bill-uphill-battle-tulfo.
[2] Felipe, "Divorce Bill An Uphill Battle – Tulfo." The state does recognize and allow Islamic law and its provisions for divorce to apply to Muslims within the country.

the more rural areas outside of the metropolitan cities.[3] Leaders of the Catholic church in the Philippines fought fiercely to keep this prohibition of legal divorce in place, as there was a feeling that the church lost power and influence when the reproductive health bill was signed into law. They feared the same result if divorce were to be declared a legal right for Catholics.[4]

The concern with divorce and reproductive health is connected and stems from the injustice Filipino women face in marriage and the family. Husbands often force wives to have sex in marriage, claiming there is no such thing as rape in marriage, as marriage entitles the man to sex. When the woman becomes pregnant and has children, the man is not really expected to care for them, and often the woman is left to care for their children. Should the man leave for someone else, laws that require fathers to support their biological children are not strictly enforced, if enforced at all, and women are left to be solo parents in a country where dual incomes are needed to survive. In Filipino culture, men can also have several mistresses and sire children with them, with this phenomenon being seen as a sign of virility and a badge of honor, whereas women are still seen as "sluts" or "whores" if they are found to have had multiple partners. The opposition to divorce and reproductive health and contraception measures has contributed to the growing number of "illegitimate" children in the country, who have no stable home or care and who are shamed for their "illegitimate" status. Women thus become reduced to objects, essentialized to particular gender roles as mothers or mistresses, and

---

[3] Michael Lipka, "5 Facts About Catholicism in the Philippines," *Pew Research Center*, January 9, 2015, www.pewresearch.org/short-reads/2015/01/09/5-facts-about-catholicism-in-the-philippines/.
[4] The only countries in the world in which divorce is illegal are the Philippines and the Vatican City State. See Rowalt Alibudbud, Alexander Smith, Michael Liebrenz, and Janet M. Arnado, "Reframing Divorce as a Mental Health Policy Issue in the Philippines," *The Lancet* 11, no. 4 (2024): doi.org/10.1016/S2215-0366(24)00002-6.

unjustly treated, especially when they deviate from these roles. Women are not regarded as human persons with inherent God-given dignity.[5]

Reproductive justice as a framework is helpful in that it can clarify further what justice can and should look like in the reproductive health law and the proposed divorce bill. Reproductive justice goes beyond consent and individual agents' choices and rights because it includes the structural factors that affect issues of sex, gender, marriage, and reproductive health.[6] In the Philippines, where relationality and community are important, reproductive justice can be a more welcome framework to use as it highlights the relationships of the people, particularly women, and what is needed to care for their well-being.

A justice-based framework is superior to a legalistic framework because it can help flesh out the guidelines of divorce in the country while still being sensitive to the concerns of Filipino culture. If we review the grounds for divorce in the proposed bill—physical violence against a spouse or child, imprisonment of a spouse for more than six years, abandonment for more than a year, sexual infidelity or perversion, bigamy, homosexuality, or drug addiction—we will see that these grounds reflect a desire to address cases of injustice within family relationships. Analysts explain that a "cooling off period" is built in to the proposal which says that, except in cases that involve violence against women or children, the court would not be allowed to take any action for six months after the initial filing.[7] The bill also obliges the court to "take steps toward the reconciliation of the spouses" before granting the final decree.[8] Most importantly, the bill

---

[5] For a provocative analysis of gender-based violence and the question of women's humanity, see Catharine A. MacKinnon, *Are Women Human? And Other International Dialogues* (Cambridge, MA: Belknap Press, 2007).

[6] Loretta J. Ross and Rickie Solinger, *Reproductive Justice: An Introduction* (Oakland: University of California Press, 2017), 56.

[7] Tom Hundley and Ana P. Santos, "The Last Country in the World Where Divorce is Illegal," *Foreign Policy*, January 19, 2015, foreignpolicy.com/2015/01/19/the-last-country-in-the-world-where-divorce-is-illegal-philippines-catholic-church/.

[8] Hundley and Santos, "The Last Country in the World Where Divorce is Illegal."

provides guidelines for the division of assets, child support, and payment of damages to "the innocent spouse."[9]

As for the reproductive health law, reproductive justice is a good framework for a comprehensive sex education, as comprehensive sex education is part of the reproductive health law but has not been as well-implemented.[10] Reproductive justice can be the foundation of an age-appropriate comprehensive sex education that is not just about consenting to sex, but also helping people be responsible by learning the implications of engaging in sex, pregnancy, contraception, and marriage and its impact on one's reproductive and overall health and relationships, as well as its relationship to other social issues such as poverty. Attention to the flourishing of women and children in the Philippines remains an important priority for people of faith; while certainly this is a complex issue, a lens of reproductive justice can help Catholic leaders see that a prohibition of legal divorce can create suffering for women and children.

Karen Peterson-Iyer (USA)

As Stephanie Ann Puen highlights in the context of the Philippines, feminist ethical scholarship (and indeed any good ethical scholarship) must not ignore the concrete structural power dynamics of a given practice. In other words, it is not enough to promote certain practices (marriage, childbearing, and so forth) in the abstract, apart from the concrete struggles and injustices such women face in the real world. For in that real world, sexual double standards prevail, responsibility for caregiving tends to fall to women, and women are frequently the recipients of unwanted sexual attention or of sexual violence—both at home and in the workplace. Reproductive justice, then, must attend to these real

---

[9] Hundley and Santos, "The Last Country in the World Where Divorce is Illegal."
[10] For elaboration, see Stephanie Ann Puen, "Considerations for a Comprehensive Sex Education Grounded in Catholic Social Thought for Reproductive Justice in the Philippines," 237–256, in this volume.

struggles and challenges that women face in order to attain (or even to move in the direction of) genuine reproductive flourishing. Moreover, approaches to envisioning women's well-being must take account of those women in their concrete, relational—that is, their REAL—contexts.

For women (and girls) who labor in agricultural contexts in the US,[11] it is simply not enough to ensure access to reproductive health care, envisioned only or even primarily as accessible abortion. This may be one piece of the puzzle, but it is only one piece—and a piece that comes rather late in the game. These women deserve a full-throttle affirmation of their dignity and moral agency from the start, one that addresses them honestly and squarely in the midst of their relational complexity and concrete struggles.

Women—particularly younger women—who work on most farms frequently struggle to care for their born children, to feed and clothe them, to keep them safely sheltered and educated, and to ensure that they can play and grow. This constitutes a major set of hurdles to familial well-being. Moreover, the low wages and grinding poverty, the substandard and notoriously unsafe housing, and the disproportionate exposure to pesticides constitute massive challenges to these women's dignity, agency, and ability to care for their families. To make matters worse, illiteracy and innumeracy, the well-grounded fear of encountering the US immigration system, and a general lack of access to reliable transportation make it difficult for such women to access the social supports necessary to bolster their dignity and agency. Finally, a reasonable fear of violence—both at home and in the fields—leads many women to endure injustice and maltreatment at additional levels, all in the name of supporting their families.

What these women need are approaches to health and well-being that bolster their ability to protect and care for themselves and their (born) children. They need access to culturally competent medical care such that they genuinely understand their own health situation and experience an

---

[11] For elaboration, see Karen Peterson-Iyer, "Reproductive Justice and Agricultural Labor Migrants," 257–289, in this volume.

authentic sense of empowerment vis-à-vis their choices and their rights. They need to be empowered, by way of interactions *within their own communities*, that help them to shore up their social, legal, and educational options and opportunities. They need safe and affordable housing and childcare, and they need nearby high-quality educational opportunities for their children. They need to know that they may work safely in the fields and live safely in their homes, free from the dangers of domestic violence and sexual abuse that currently haunt them in both places. They need the US government not only to fortify these various social and legal supports; they need it to *reform the broken immigration system*—replacing it with meaningful immigration reform that includes pathways to citizenship for women and their children and spouses. Such changes themselves must be accompanied by efforts (on the part of individuals, religious communities, and governments) to confront and reject the xenophobia that characterizes far too much of immigrant experiences today.

All of these changes can rightly be addressed within the framework of reproductive justice. Reproductive justice, by offering a social and structural approach to analyzing human struggle, begins to take seriously the concrete struggles and genuine relationships of migrant women who labor in America's fields. In this way it represents a compelling conceptual tool for bolstering their flourishing, their agency, and ultimately their human dignity.

Mary Doyle Roche (USA)

As Stephanie Ann Puen and Karen Peterson Iyer have highlighted in this exchange, women's dignity and agency are deeply entwined in a complex web of social determinants. Even when women's dignity and agency might be protected technically, as when laws recognize their basic political rights, they are frequently denied the goods that they require to meaningfully exercise those rights. In the US context, as I suspect in other parts of the world, the denial of those goods has been deliberately and systematically orchestrated in ways that benefit white supremacist patriarchy.[12] Even the measured progress of civil rights movements for people of color, women, LGBTQIA+ persons, and migrants is being met with what scholar Terry Smith and journalist Wesley Lowery have described as "whitelash."[13] Fear has rallied proponents of white supremacist patriarchy and white Christian nationalism in the US, giving them an outsized voice in electoral politics that has resulted in the steady erosion of rights that include access to reproductive healthcare and the vote.

The particular slice of US culture in which I place myself each day is a small, liberal arts, Catholic and Jesuit college in the northeast. I am particularly attuned to and worried about how the education of young people can honor dignity and advance agency or undermine it. The 2022 Supreme Court decision in *Dobbs v. Jackson Women's Health Organization* is an assault on women's dignity, rights, and agency. The movement for reproductive justice has made this clear and has also moved the conversation beyond access to abortion services to include the real ability to have children and raise them in a just and healthy world. Women's agency rests on *both* immunity from undue interference on the part of governments and other institutions *and* positive claims for basic needs like healthcare, housing and nutrition, education, a livelihood, and security.

Whitelash has also taken the form of school curricular changes, book challenges, and book bans. In the US, the American Library Association's list of frequently banned and challenged books includes books that feature LGBTQIA+ experiences, sexual content, as well as the struggles and achievements of Black people and other minoritized groups. Many of these

---

[12] On this point, see Dorothy Roberts, *Killing the Black Body: Race, Reproduction, and the Meaning of Liberty*, 2nd ed. (New York: Vintage, 2017); Harriet A. Washington, *Medical Apartheid: The Dark History of Medical Experimentation on Black Americans from Colonial Times to the Present* (New York: Anchor, 2006); M. Shawn Copeland, *Enfleshing Freedom: Body, Race, and Being* (Minneapolis: Fortress, 2010).

[13] Terry Smith, *Whitelash: Unmasking White Grievance at the Ballot Box* (New York: Cambridge University Press, 2020); Wesley Lowery, *American Whitelash: A Changing Nation and the Cost of Progress* (Boston: Mariner Books, 2023).

books look squarely at racism, sexism, homophobia, and abuse from the "coming of age" vantage point.[14] It is already the case that many young people lack access to adequate sex education, and young people in Catholic and other religiously sponsored schools may be at a particular disadvantage in this regard.[15] Not only is some basic scientific and historical information kept from them or misrepresented, the banning of books can leave them without stories to help them make sense of their sexual lives, gender identities, and intimate relationships. Such censoring is proposed in the guise of protecting children, but these efforts will, in the end, undermine their development and agency, leaving them more vulnerable to harm.[16] Book banning can stifle the kind of imagination that reproductive justice requires for biological and social reproduction. Such censoring ignores the value of embodied experiences, the lessons of history, and ways of knowing passed on among indigenous peoples and marginalized communities. This white supremacist and white nationalist project to circumscribe access to experience, science, history, and imagination thwarts the dignity and agency of women, girls, LGBTQIA+ persons, and people of color. The reproductive justice framework and movement provides the intersectional analysis needed to unmask the intentions of book banners. Reproductive justice advocates reach back into the past and look ahead to the future in a kind of intergenerational solidarity that honors dignity, agency, and interdependence.

---

[14] American Library Association Office for Intellectual Freedom, "Banned and Challenged Books: 2023," www.ala.org/advocacy/bbooks/frequentlychallengedbooks/top10.

[15] For further elaboration, see Stephanie Ann Puen, "Considerations for a Comprehensive Sex Education Grounded in Catholic Social Thought for Reproductive Justice in the Philippines," in this volume.

[16] Some feminist scholars are concerned, for example, that many young people learn about sex and sexuality from pornography, which contains scripts of violence and can undermine a sexual ethics rooted in intimacy and mutual well-being. See, for example, Karen Peterson-Iyer, *Reenvisioning Sexual Ethics: A Feminist Christian Account* (Washington, DC: Georgetown University Press, 2022), 68, 86–88; Gail Dines, *Pornland: How Porn Has Hijacked Our Sexuality* (Boston: Beacon, 2011).

Emily Reimer-Barry (USA)

I will take as my starting point what Karen Peterson-Iyer describes as the "concrete structural power dynamics" that undermine reproductive justice in my context. I live in California, one of the epicenters of mass incarceration in the United States.[17] Mass incarceration refers to a network of policing, prosecution, incarceration, surveillance, debt, and social control that reproduces social inequalities.[18] The challenges faced by incarcerated women are different than the ones faced by incarcerated men. A gendered analysis can prove especially fruitful because it enables us to see how women's experiences of sexual abuse, pregnancy loss, and motherhood are criminalized in US society, especially for poor women and women of color.

First, we must look at the prison pipeline for women and girls. It is not the case that all incarcerated women have been convicted of violent crimes. The cash bail system in the US criminalizes poverty because people who cannot afford to pay bail face detention while they await trial. 60 percent of women in local-jurisdiction jails are in pre-trial detention because they cannot afford bail. Research by the Prison Policy Initiative found that the typical bail amounts to a full year's income for women, and many find that even though they are the primary caregivers of children, they are stuck in jail awaiting trial. 58 percent of all women in US prisons are mothers, as are 80 percent of women in jails.[19] Most of these women are incarcerated for

---

[17] Christopher Kaiser-Nyman, Michelle Parris, and Brandon Sixto, "California: The State of Incarceration," Vera Institute of Justice (2023): www.vera.org/california-state-of-incarceration/. Vera is an organization dedicated to end overcriminalization and mass incarceration of people of color, immigrants, and people experiencing poverty. See "About Us," www.vera.org/who-we-are/about-us.

[18] See Institute to End Mass Incarceration, "What We Mean by Mass Incarceration," 2024, endmassincarceration.org/what-is-mass-incarceration/. See also Michelle Alexander, *The New Jim Crow: Mass Incarceration in the Age of Colorblindness* (New York: New Press, 2020).

[19] Wendy Sawyer and Wanda Bertram, "Prisons and Jails Will Separate Millions of Mothers from their Children in 2022," *Prison Policy Initiative*, May 4, 2022, www.prisonpolicy.org/blog/2022/05/04/mothers_day/.

drug and property offenses.[20] But an alarming number of women and girls encounter the criminal justice system for other reasons. In Ohio, thirty-three-year old Brittany Watts was charged with abuse of a corpse after she miscarried at twenty-one weeks of pregnancy.[21] In Connecticut, Sanna Dilawar, mother of an eleven-week old daughter, was arrested when she reported her husband's domestic abuse.[22] In Missouri, a judge sentenced Tamarae LaRue, a single mother, to jail for fifteen days when her kindergartner missed fourteen days of school.[23] In what researchers call a "perverse twist of justice," many girls who experience sexual abuse are routed into the juvenile justice system because of their victimization.[24] Children previously incarcerated within the juvenile justice system can violate their probation for infractions such as failing to make their bed or missing curfew.[25] Under fetal personhood laws, pregnant women who are

---

[20] To learn more about a faith-based organization working to address the criminalization of Black motherhood, see the work of Dr. Nikia Smith Roberts at Abolitionist Sanctuary, www.abolitionistsanctuary.org/.

[21] Julie Carr Smyth, "A Black Woman Was Criminally Charged After a Miscarriage," *AP News*, December 16, 2023, apnews.com/article/ohio-miscarriage-prosecution-brittany-watts-b8090abfb5994b8a23457b80cf3f27ce.

[22] Sarah Smith, "In Connecticut, Calling for Help Carries Risk for Domestic Violence Victims," *CT Mirror*, February 19, 2017, ctmirror.org/2017/02/19/in-connecticut-calling-for-help-carries-risks-for-domestic-violence-victims/.

[23] Donna St. George, "Some Parents Are Prosecuted or Fined When Children Miss School," *The Washington Post*, January 2, 2024, www.washingtonpost.com/education/2024/01/02/student-absenteeism-schools-parents-prosecuted/. See also the scholarship of Robert Balfanz, Johns Hopkins School of Education.

[24] Malika Saada Saar, Rebecca Epstein, Lindsay Rosenthal, and Yasmin Vafa, "The Sexual Abuse to Prison Pipeline: The Girls Story," Georgetown Law Center on Poverty and Inequality, 2023, https://genderjusticeandopportunity.georgetown.edu/wp-content/uploads/2020/06/The-Sexual-Abuse-To-Prison-Pipeline-The-Girls%E2%80%99-Story.pdf.

[25] Hannah Levintova, "Thousands of Girls Are Locked Up for Talking Back or Staying Out Late," *Mother Jones*, September/October 2016, www.motherjones.com/politics/2016/09/girls-juvenile-justice-status-offenses/. Levintova explains that gendered discrepancies were present in the earliest laws about juvenile justice in the US. For example, the first juvenile court, established in 1899, included "frequent attendance at saloons and pool halls" and "the use of indecent language" as actionable offenses. In the 1930s, young girls could be prosecuted in

addicts have been prosecuted instead of given the help they need to address their substance abuse.[26] Asylum seekers also experience confinement when they are placed in detention centers as they await their hearing date. 67 percent of detainees held in Immigration and Customs Enforcement (ICE) detention centers have no criminal record.[27]

In jails, detention centers, and prisons, women experience dehumanizing and violent conditions. In 2023, the California Department of Corrections and Rehabilitation logged more than eight hundred complaints of staff sexual abuse, but most advocates believe this to be a significant undercount.[28] Women report widespread sexual abuse as an ordinary aspect of confinement. Human rights abuses also include family separation policies,[29] coerced sterilizations of immigrant women,[30] the shackling of pregnant and laboring women,[31] and the withholding of sanitary napkins from menstruating women.[32] These violations of

---

juvenile court for being "in danger of becoming morally depraved." See also the analysis in this volume by Suzanne Mulligan regarding the Magdalene Laundries in Ireland.

[26] Michelle Goodwin, *Policing the Womb: Invisible Women and the Criminalization of Motherhood* (New York: Cambridge University Press, 2020).

[27] TRAC Immigration, "ICE Detainees," January 13, 2024, trac.syr.edu/immigration/detention stats/pop_agen_table.html.

[28] Sam Levin, "The Women Trapped in Prison with Abusive Guards," *The Guardian*, October 29, 2023, www.theguardian.com/us-news/2023/oct/29/womens-prison-guards-sexual-abuse. See also Bryan Stevenson, *Just Mercy: A Story of Justice and Redemption* (New York: OneWorld, 2015).

[29] Over four thousand children were separated from their parents during the Trump Administration. See Caitlin Dickerson, "We Need to Take Away Children," *The Atlantic*, August 7, 2022, www.theatlantic.com/magazine/archive/2022/09/trump-administration-family-separation-policy-immigration/670604/.

[30] Institute for the Elimination of Poverty and Genocide, "Testimony of Whistleblower Dawn Wooten," September 14, 2020, projectsouth.org/wp-content/uploads/2020/09/OIG-ICDC-Complaint-1.pdf.

[31] Equal Justice Initiative, "Shackling of Pregnant Women in Jails and Prisons Continues," January 29, 2020, eji.org/news/shackling-of-pregnant-women-in-jails-and-prisons-continues/.

[32] Gabrielle A. Perry, "In Prison, Having Your Period Can Put Your Life In Danger," *The Washington Post*, March 25, 2022, www.washingtonpost.com/opinions/2022/03/25/prison-period-danger-health-risks-sexual-abuse/.

maternal rights, consent, bodily integrity, and human dignity persist because of the ways that incarcerated women experience disempowerment *as women* within the criminal justice system.

Incarceration does not just impact the person who is sent to jail or prison. Incarceration reverberates into the lives of their loved ones.[33] Children whose parents are incarcerated experience disruptions in their everyday lives, including transitions to living with grandparents, friends, or in foster care, which sometimes necessitates a transition to a new school environment, social stigma, and elevated levels of anxiety, loneliness, anger, and depression.[34] Some states ban voting rights or food assistance for formerly incarcerated individuals.[35] When mothers are prevented from accessing food assistance programs, their children suffer.[36]

Reproductive justice is a social justice framework that seeks to raise awareness about the unjust social conditions that pregnant and parenting women experience. The human rights abuses that women and girls experience in jails, prisons, detention centers, and juvenile justice facilities undermine reproductive justice. If we are to respond adequately to the systemic failures of the US criminal justice system, we must do so with keen awareness of the ways that racism and misogyny continue to operate within the carceral system. The United States Conference of Catholic Bishops has offered their own version of a "distinctively Catholic" approach to crime and punishment within the US, affirming the human

---

[33] Brian Elderbroom, Laura Bennett, Shanna Gong, Felicity Rose, and Zoë Towns, "Every Second: The Impact of the Incarceration Crisis on America's Families," *Fwd.us*, everysecond.fwd.us/downloads/everysecond.fwd.us.pdf.

[34] Emily Widra, "New Data: People with Incarcerated Loved Ones Have Shorter Life Expectancies and Poorer Health," *Prison Policy Initiative*, July 12, 2021, www.prisonpolicy.org/blog/2021/07/12/family-incarceration/.

[35] Christopher Uggen, Ryan Larson, Sarah Shannon and Robert Stewart, "Locked Out 2022: Estimates of People Denied Voting Rights," *The Sentencing Project*, October 25, 2022, www.sentencingproject.org/reports/locked-out-2022-estimates-of-people-denied-voting-rights/.

[36] Equal Justice Initiative, "Alabama in Minority of States that Ban Food Stamps for People Convicted of Drug Offenses," *Equal Justice Initiative*, December 27, 2013, eji.org/news/alabama-bans-food-stamps-for-people-with-drug-convictions/.

dignity of incarcerated persons and demanding the just treatment of immigrants.[37] Unfortunately, the bishops' so called "pro-life" agenda has focused entirely on the criminalization of abortion and not squarely enough on actual programs of support for women and children, including those who face incarceration. Catholic leaders have much to learn from a reproductive justice framework that attends to the intersectional realities of women's and girls' lives in the US today.

Mary Lilian Akhere Ehidiamhen (Nigeria)

Women and girls in Nigeria face reproductive injustice in many ways. They face sexual violence, an overburdened healthcare system that cannot provide for their health care needs, employment discrimination and workplace harassment, female genital cutting,[38] and child marriage.[39] Unfortunately, even though the purpose of the law is to protect the vulnerable and create safe communities, Nigerian laws often fail to protect Nigerian women.[40] In Northeast Nigeria, the Boko Haram conflict is particularly devastating for women and girls.[41]

---

[37] United States Conference of Catholic Bishops, *Responsibility, Rehabilitation, and Restoration: A Catholic Perspective on Crime and Criminal Justice* (Washington, DC: USCCB, 2000).

[38] Virginia Braun, "Female Genital Cutting around the Globe: A Matter of Reproductive Justice," in *Reproductive Justice: A Global Concern*, ed. Joan C. Chrisler (Santa Barbara, CA: Praeger, 2012), 29–55, 30–31.

[39] By some estimates, twelve percent of girls in Nigeria are married before the age of fifteen, and thirty percent are married before the age of eighteen. See Girls Not Brides, "Nigeria," www.girlsnotbrides.org/learning-resources/child-marriage-atlas/regions-and-countries/nigeria/. See also Odunola D. Oladejo, "A Reproductive Justice Approach to Understanding Yoruba Women's Experiences with Early Marriage and Bride Price in Nigeria" (Oregon: Unpublished Master Thesis, Oregon State University, 2020), 24.

[40] Sylvia Tamale, "Exploring the Contours of African Sexualities: Religion, Law and Power," *African Human Rights Law Journal* 4, no. 1 (2014): 150–177, 158.

[41] Center for Reproductive Rights, "The Center Releases New Report on Sexual and Reproductive Rights in Nigerian Conflict Zones," reproductiverights.org/the-center-releases-new-report-on-sexual-and-reproductive-rights-in-nigerian-conflict-zones/.

I found what Stephanie Ann Puen describes as the injustice Filipino women face in marriage and the family very similar to the situation of women in Nigeria. She asserts that "husbands often force wives to have sex in marriage, claiming there is no such thing as rape in marriage as marriage entitles the man to sex." Further, Puen explains that when a woman becomes pregnant and has children, the man is not really expected to care for them, and often, the woman is left to care for their children. The double standards that Puen points out regarding a man's cultural acceptance of multiple sexual partners and a woman's loss of social status if she has more than one partner is also true in my country. Nigeria is a society that is still very patriarchal, and women have less access to resources, which makes childcare very difficult. In the Philippines as well as in Nigeria, patriarchal cultural norms diminish women's freedom and moral agency. In such a context, the framework of reproductive justice is an important corrective to patriarchy. We can also clearly see the need for Relationship Sex Education (RSE) in a Nigerian context, so women can understand their inherent dignity and can practice voicing their needs to their partners. As Puen and Emily Reimer-Barry have already highlighted, reproductive justice is not restricted only to abortion but includes a comprehensive Relationship Sex Education (RSE). RSE could be of great support to women and men. As a Nigerian residing in the UK, I have the opportunity of delivering RSE curriculum to secondary school students, especially young girls. The aim is for students to understand the importance of communication—especially what healthy intimacy and relationship entail—and so develop a healthy agency rooted in interdependence. However, in Nigeria, RSE is not yet present in the secondary school curriculum. In my experience, I see RSE as an interesting pathway that could support women and girls. Including it in the secondary school curriculum would be an effective strategy for promoting reproductive justice because it can help young women to understand their inherent dignity. Given the many cultural messages that undermine girls' dignity today, such a step would be welcome.

Emily Reimer-Barry (USA)

As I reflect on my colleagues' contributions, I am struck by the shared concerns expressed by Stephanie Puen, Mary Lilian Akhere Ehidiamhen, and Mary Doyle Roche regarding age-appropriate sex education. While my context differs in some respects (I teach undergraduate students at a Catholic university in southern California), I see how my students struggle to make sense of the cultural scripts of college life as they are also asking themselves important questions about their faith, values, identity, and choices. Jennifer S. Hirsch and Shamus Khan, in their book *Sexual Citizens: Sex, Power, and Assault on Campus*, suggest that educators seek out more opportunities to help young people think about their "sexual projects" (the reasons why someone seeks a particular sexual encounter) and how they cultivate "sexual citizenship" (which acknowledges not only one's own but also one's partner's right to sexual self-determination). Hirsch and Khan explain that we have "allowed social conditions to persist in which many young people come of age without a language to talk about their sexual desires, overcome with shame, unaccustomed to considering how their relative social power may silence a peer, highly attentive to their personal wants but deaf to those of others, or socialized to feel unable to tell someone 'no' or to give a clear an unambiguous 'yes.'"[42] This confusion that young people experience is rooted in cultural taboos and structures of injustice, but those too can change for the better, if we have the willpower to contribute to that change. Like Mary Lilian Akhere Ehidiamhen's approach, Hirsch and Khan explain that "schools should consider sex education as a critical part of their educational mission."[43]

One of the data points that will be different in the US context in contrast to the Philippines and Nigeria is the reality of delayed marriage as a trend that seems to have staying power. In the US, on average, men first

---

[42] Jennifer S. Hirsch and Shamus Khan, *Sexual Citizens: Sex, Power, and Assault on Campus* (New York: Norton, 2020), 255.
[43] Hirsch and Khan, *Sexual Citizens*, 266.

marry when they are thirty years old and women when they are twenty-five.[44] On the whole, many of my students are very comfortable admitting that they are not ready for marriage, but they are ready to explore sexual encounters. Faith communities rarely offer honest and compassionate spaces for students to discern and explore these lived experiences. I'm persuaded that Hirsch and Khan are right in that we need to be able to create spaces in which undergraduate students can consider the personal and ethical ramifications of sexual encounters and do so in a context of growth and learning.[45] I find Mary Lilian's description of Relationship Sex Education a wonderful starting point for communities of faith to meet the needs of young people.

As an educator, I am sometimes on the front lines of responding to student disclosures of sexual assault, but even more often, I accompany students as they are thinking through their personal values and considering the kinds of sexual practices that reflect their values. This is holy work and yet can be confusing, given the many mixed messages that our students receive from culture, church, home, and friend groups.

This roundtable discussion of wide-ranging issues and threats to women's flourishing opens up spaces for scholars and students to reflect on the social conditions that undermine the dignity of women and children around the world. We do not have tidy solutions, nor would such solutions be possible. Instead, this discussion can challenge each of us—from wherever we locate ourselves—to reflect on the realities of injustice around us and to commit to working in solidarity to address those realities.

Stephanie Ann Puen, PhD, is a faculty member in the Department of Theology at Ateneo de Manila University. She has taught courses in economics and business ethics, Catholic social thought, gender and sexual

---

[44] Hirsch and Khan, Sexual Citizens, xvii.
[45] See also Karen Peterson-Iyer, *Reenvisioning Sexual Ethics*, 161–169.

ethics, and theology and popular culture at both the Ateneo de Manila University and Fordham University in New York. Dr. Puen has published on these topics for both scholarly and popular publications.

Karen Peterson-Iyer, PhD, is Associate Professor of theological and social ethics in the Department of Religious Studies at Santa Clara University. Her previous publications include "Human Trafficking, Coercion, and Moral Agency in Agricultural Labor," in *Theological Studies* (June 2022), *Reenvisioning Sexual Ethics: A Feminist Christian Account* (Georgetown University Press, 2022), and *Designer Children: Reconciling Genetic Technology, Feminism, and Christian Faith* (Pilgrim Press, 2004).

Mary M. Doyle Roche, PhD, teaches Christian ethics and Catholic moral theology at the College of the Holy Cross in Worcester, MA, USA. Her teaching and research interests include healthcare ethics and ethical issues impacting children and young people.

Emily Reimer-Barry, PhD, is professor in the Department of Theology and Religious Studies at the University of San Diego, where she teaches undergraduate courses in Catholic theological ethics. She is the author of two books: *Reproductive Justice and the Catholic Church: Advancing Pragmatic Solidarity with Pregnant Women* (Sheed & Ward, 2024) and *Catholic Theology of Marriage in the Era of HIV and AIDS: Marriage for Life* (Lexington, 2015).

Mary Lilian Akhere Ehidiamhen, PhD, is a theological ethicist specializing in peace ethics. Her research focuses on how Marshall Rosenberg's nonviolent communication can contribute to Catholic social teaching on peace. Her academic orientation involves paying attention to the experiences of people from their frame of reference (context) and its relationship to their belief system. This is realized through focusing on people's needs and bringing them into dialogue with academics in an interdisciplinary manner.

9. On the Role of the Catholic Church: A Theo-Ethical Roundtable

Simeiqi He (China/USA), Eric Marcelo O. Genilo, SJ (Philippines), Kathryn Lilla Cox (USA), Virginia Saldanha (India), and Julie Clague (UK)

Note from the Co-Editors: In this second roundtable discussion, we posed the questions: "What should be the role of the Catholic Church in advancing justice with regard to reproduction? In your context, is the Catholic Church a resource or a roadblock?"

Simeiqi He (China/USA)

In *C'est La Confiance*, Pope Francis called our attention to the insights of St. Therese of the Child Jesus and the Holy Face. Exalting Therese's exclamation that divine justice is clothed in love as one of her loftiest insights and major contributions to the entire People of God (no. 27), Pope Francis breathed life into the meaning of justice. In this way, he opened new possibilities for the discussion of reproduction. Understanding justice—with divine justice as its highest form—as love, our question now becomes "what should be the role of the Catholic Church in advancing love with regard to reproduction?"

To answer this question, we must first consider the nature of such advance. The Church's capacity to advance love lies in its being as a lover, who is first the beloved. It implies a deeper reality where the Church is advanced by the divine Lover, whose life unfolds indefinitely into life infinitesimal. Such understanding of the Lover's advance expands the meaning of reproduction beyond the narrow definition of giving birth to children for the purpose of preserving the human race toward a much broader horizon to denote the reproductivity of divine love as the living force of the world. Thus, human reproductivity manifests itself in love's doubling and multiplication. It is an expression of the pure act that is divine love. In *Finite and Eternal Being: An Attempt to Ascend to the Meaning of Being*, St. Edith Stein points out that the birthing of children from their parents is not different from the creation of Eve from Adam, both are the result of Christ's self-giving.[1] That is, divine life is immanent in human reproduction as a process of creative transformation of the world. No longer an isolated phenomenon, human reproduction manifests the fecundity of divine creativity and the reproductivity of social life, cultural heritage, the natural world, and the entire undivided universe. It expresses the infinite mysteries of the divine mind and implies absolute freedom fulfilled only in love.

In this sense, the path has been laid out before the Catholic Church if it is to advance justice regarding reproduction. It can only be achieved if the Church is continuously advanced and transformed by the love of God in the process of unceasing conversion in union with its Lover. Pierre Teilhard de Chardin wrote in 1921 that "the Church is still a child. Christ, by whom she lives, is immeasurably greater than she imagines."[2] I believe that, over a century later, these words still ring true today. The Chinese Catholic Church is acutely aware of its need to grow and develop. Despite its impoverished state, many throughout history, especially women, have found consolation, strength, and mercy in its divine Lover. Nonetheless, the maturity and future of the Chinese Church and its capacity to address the question of reproduction depends upon its ability to draw from the depth of its ancient wisdom and to serve as an outpouring source of life for all living beings. The Chinese Catholic jurist John C.H. Wu, who was deeply influenced by Therese, pointed out that the simplest way of understanding the little way of spiritual childhood is to realize that it is reminiscent of the Confucian teaching of filial piety and the Taoist insight

---

[1] Edith Stein, *Finite and Eternal Being: An Attempt to Ascend to the Meaning of Being*, trans. Kurt F. Reinhardt (Washington, DC: ICS Publications, 2002), 513.

[2] Pierre Teilhard de Chardin, *The Heart of Matter*, trans. René Hague (San Diego: A Harvest Book, 1921), 118.

concerning the mystical significance of the little, the feminine, and the new-born;[3] both are inseparable from the process of reproduction. Deep down in the cultural memories of the Chinese Church, there exists an integral meaning of reproduction, where filial piety, femininity, and natality coincide to express the living life that is at once divine, human, and cosmic. Such insight, if allowed to be expressed, might just be the greatest contribution of the Chinese Church to the universal Church and the global community.

Eric Marcelo O. Genilo, SJ (Philippines)

The Church in the Philippines should play a more pastoral role with regard to reproduction. Unfortunately, the Church prefers to use its social and political influence to impose Catholic norms of reproduction on a multi-religious Filipino population. In the Philippine context, the Church has been more of a roadblock to rather than a resource for reproductive justice. The Church's leadership should stop doing the following:

1. *Reinforcing the image of the Philippines as a Catholic nation where Catholic norms must be legislated.* While the Philippines is 85 percent Catholic by baptism, a large majority of its population are either nominal or nonpracticing Catholics. There are also significant numbers of Protestants, Muslims, and those who hold indigenous faith traditions. When it comes to reproductive health issues, the Church uses only a Catholic lens to address society and ignores the rights of non-Catholics and dissenting Catholics to decide on reproductive issues that gravely affect them and their families.[4]

---

[3] John C.H. Wu, *Chinese Humanism and Christian Spirituality* (Kettering, OH: Angelico Press, 2017), 97.
[4] Jose Mario C. Francisco, "People of God, People of the Nation Official Catholic Discourse on Nation and Nationalism," *Philippine Studies: Historical & Ethnographic Viewpoints* 62, no. 3/4 (2014): www.jstor.org/stable/24672316.

2. *Conflating abortion and contraception as if they are the same moral issue.* The pro-life voices that the Church leadership supports are those which identify the evils of abortion with that of contraception. They cause confusion in the faithful with regard to Church teachings on these two issues. One example is the statement from a pastoral letter of the Philippine bishops' conference. It argues against contraception by pointing out that "these artificial means are fatal to human life, either preventing it from fruition or actually destroying it."[5]

3. *Engaging in partisan politics on reproductive issues.* The local church leadership has a long history of organizing a Catholic vote against politicians who do not pass the Church's standards of morality, including those who campaign for better access to contraceptives for poor families. The Church had launched a negative campaign against politicians who supported the passing of a reproductive health law that addressed many issues related to reproductive health, such as HIV prevention, domestic violence, infant and maternal mortality, and sex education in public schools.[6]

4. *Demonizing sex education.* The Church has a deep suspicion against sex education. It has consistently objected to sex education in public schools, fearing that information about sex will automatically lead to promiscuity. The bishops prefer that sex education be done at home by parents, which rarely happens because of cultural taboos in families regarding conversations about sex.

The Church has been so used to wielding immense power and influence on Philippine social life and politics that it finds it easier to simply impose universal norms regarding reproduction rather than make pastoral adjustments to address the extraordinary situations faced by many poor and vulnerable persons. Unless the Church's leadership listens to persons

---

[5] Catholic Bishops' Conference of the Philippines, "Choosing Life, Rejecting the RH Bill," *CBCP Online*, January 30, 2011, cbcponline.net/choosing-life-rejecting-the-rh-billa-pastoral-letter-of-the-catholic-bishops-conference-of-the-philippines/.

[6] Eric Marcelo O. Genilo, SJ "The Catholic Church and The Reproductive Health Bill Debate: The Philippine Experience," *The Heythrop Journal* 5, no. 6 (2014): 1044–1055.

in difficult marital and family situations with attention, compassion, and goodwill and responds to their plight with both justice and mercy, there will always be a disconnection between the hierarchy and the laity and between what the Church preaches and what it actually practices.

Kathryn Lilla Cox (USA)

When thinking about the role of the Catholic Church in advancing justice regarding reproduction, it is helpful to distinguish between the various facets of the Church. While the Pope, bishops, and priests have varying degrees of leadership and teaching responsibilities, they are a small portion of the Catholic Church. As Vatican II taught, the Church is made up of the whole people of God, who have a responsibility to "bring forth fruit and charity for the life of the world" (*Optatum Totius*, no. 16) and accompany all people in "the joys and the hopes, the griefs and anxieties" (*Gaudium et Spes*, no. 1) while working for more just societies.

Speaking as a theologian, I have been involved in reproductive justice discussions for several years with my colleagues. We are participating in advancing reproductive justice with our attention to the issues in this volume. We use our research skills to identify resources that assist in highlighting love as a key component to reproductive justice and call our leadership to change harmful patterns of societal interaction and teaching. We advocate for institutional reform. We have one role in advancing reproductive justice.

Given the call in *Gaudium et Spes* to engage the world, there are various ways the laity can play a role in advancing reproductive justice. For example, those in the healthcare fields could speak out against laws and policies that make it harder for people to receive needed reproductive healthcare, whether it is pre- and post-natal care, contraceptives, disease screenings, or health insurance to assist in covering costs. When voting for politicians, Catholics could consider the politicians' stances on reproductive questions in a holistic manner and vote accordingly, instead of narrowly focusing on one issue. We can talk with our priests, deacons, and other homilists when we hear homilies that reinforce and sanction reproductive injustices from the pulpit. We can also challenge them to support reproductive justice when it is appropriate to the scripture readings.

In the United States of America where I reside, the Church is both a resource and a roadblock. The United States Conference of Bishops, with their voting guide and other materials that focus on abortion as the pre-eminent life issue, truncates their own approach to reproductive justice. They could do more for reproductive justice by advocating more vociferously for economic and healthcare policies that support people who have already been born. They need to recognize that pregnancy is a health condition and that supporting public policy which does not put pregnant people in life-threatening situations is both pro-life and just. Individual bishops and priests are a roadblock when they politicize the Eucharist around reproductive concerns. There are Catholic politicians who advocate and vote for laws and public policies supporting reproductive justice, and as such, they are a resource. Likewise, there are Catholics in organizations, such as Catholics for Choice, that advocate for reproductive justice in several areas. For example, Network, a Catholic lobbyist organization, works to encourage just federal policies, including healthcare reform. In these instances, the Catholic Church is a resource for reproductive justice.

Virginia Saldanha (India)

With its growing population, India is the world's most populous nation with 1.486 billion people.[7] As a multi-religious country, Hindus constitute

---

[7] Esha Roy and Anuradha Mascarenhas, "India's population 142.8 crore in 2023, crosses China's: UN population report," *The Indian Express: Journalism of Courage*, indianexpress.com/article/india/india-population-up-un-sowp-report-life-expectancy-fertility-rate-8564123/.

the majority of India's population, while Christians are a minority, with less than 3 percent of the population and Catholics forming only 1.5 percent of the population.[8] Though today the Hindu right is trying its best to foist Hindu culture and values on people of other faiths, the law of the country prevails in the area of reproductive rights. Due to a powerful women's movement, the Catholic Church's impact on laws affecting reproductive rights is absent.

Abortion is legal in India. However, given the cultural bias against girl children in India, abortion is strictly controlled in order that sex selective abortions can be prevented. While no Catholic hospital will provide abortion services to anyone, Catholics have the option to go to any other hospitals to obtain an abortion. Abortion, or medical termination of pregnancy as it is known in India, is used frequently to prevent unwanted births, while sex selective abortions are punishable under law.

Regardless, when a young woman decides to go ahead with a pregnancy out of wedlock and keep the baby, the Catholic Church needs to support such women. The Church should charge men to take responsibility when they make a girl/woman pregnant. It can do much in changing the mindset of boys and men towards women and ending the double standards of morality it has for men and women. Currently, the Church's pro-life agenda targets only women, not men. Men should be taught to respect women. Rape should be condemned and spoken about in homilies. The incidences of priests' sexual assault against religious sisters should be reduced. Marital rape should be condemned, and mutuality in marriage should be promoted.

The Catholic Church in India is encouraged by the powerful Catholic conservatives in the West to promote their pro-life agenda. A lot of money and resources have been poured into this effort. Some bishops and clergy take every opportunity to denounce abortion in their homilies, while insisting that life begins at the time of conception. This can guilt trip women who are struggling with alcoholic husbands. Often times, these

---

[8] "Statistics," *Catholics India*, catholicsindia.in/statistics/

men come home drunk and force their wives to have sex with them without caring if their wives get pregnant or if they can even afford another child. Women in this case usually terminate the pregnancy by traditional means, such as eating an unripe papaya, or going to a hospital (which is hardly an option). Their decision to pursue abortion is either a result of poverty or because there will be no one to care for the home and the children. Regarding cases in which priests have sex with and impregnate religious sisters and afterwards suggest the sister to have an abortion, we should clearly point out the hypocrisy while also attending to women's suffering in a context of unequal power and secrecy.

Only when women gain full equality with men in the Catholic Church will insensitive anti-woman policies of the Catholic Church be challenged. Presently, women who think critically act according to their conscience. However, a large majority of women who think that the priests are in the place of God suffer tremendous guilt and trauma in their sexual/reproductive lives.

Julie Clague (UK)

In *Justitia in Mundo*, the 1971 Synod of Bishops stated that "Action on behalf of justice and participation in the transformation of the world fully appear to us as a constitutive dimension of the preaching of the Gospel." (no. 6) In other words, Christians are called to put right all injustices, including the breath-taking inequalities, life-threatening social and economic conditions, and harmful cultural norms and practices that make reproduction and childbearing unsafe. Catholics, therefore, join with all people of good will in tackling the scandalous abuses of power and privilege and the unequal access to resources that increase the vulnerability of women and children and impose an intolerably disproportionate health burden on those in low- and middle-income countries.

Throughout history, in its pastoral care and charitable activities, in its advocacy and witness, in its hospitals and shelters, the Catholic Church has been a powerful resource in support of family wellbeing, including maternal and child health. However, the Catholic Church must also attend to the corrective dimension of justice by acknowledging the times when its own understandings and practices of reproductive justice have fallen short and missed the mark.

In the British Isles, there are shameful cases concerning the incarceration of unmarried mothers in Magdalen Laundries, the covert sale of adopted children to US couples, the deportation of orphans to Australia as cheap labor, and the cruel and demeaning treatment and sexual exploitation of vulnerable women and children by Catholics in positions of trust. On the wane are stigmatizing attitudes towards "illegitimate" children, out-of-wedlock pregnancies, and infertile couples, though casual gossip, deceptions, denials, secrecy, and cover-ups concerning pregnancy, paternity, miscarriage, abortion, and adoption remain commonplace. By undertaking a personal, communal, and institutional examination of conscience, Catholics are asked to identify current and historical failures to promote justice with respect to matters of reproduction, including harmful teachings, cultures, habits and organizational structures, as well as individual failings.

Flawed thinking and deficient theologies, which foster damaging attitudes and behaviors, have not been universally eradicated. Non-negotiable norms, such as the inherent dignity of women and the equality of the sexes, are proclaimed but not always put into practice. Presenting procreation as a sacred duty and considering large families as praiseworthy place a heavy burden on women's health and wellbeing. Willing submission and personal sacrifice have been held up as feminine ideals, while the euphemistic language of marital debt and conjugal right has functioned as an ecclesiastical trump-card for husbands to compel their wives, based on the axiomatic principle that justice renders what is due. The paradigmatic patriarchal family, with its *pater familias*, takes its cue as domestic (little) church from its big ecclesiastical brother.

With regards to sex and reproduction, the Catholic Church has tended to operate from an ethic of sin and judgement rather than one of love and justice. Within a framework of self-critical honesty and restorative justice, we Catholics should strive to change the discourse. We must carry out an audit of what needs to be corrected and determine how best to repair the damage. We should admit our errors, pray for forgiveness, and make space for God's healing Spirit.

Kathryn Lilla Cox (USA)

In reading our collective responses to the questions posed to this group, the universality of shame, harm, double standards, the need to re-think various aspects of magisterial teaching and approaches stood out. The particular descriptions of cultural manifestations of reproductive injustice are heart-rending. Yet, my colleagues provided hope as well. Simeiqi He's intercultural approach shows how the Catholic Church can learn from the Chinese Church's wisdom. Eric Genilo's outline for change needed by the Philippine's bishops could serve as a roadmap for other bishops' conferences. He highlights the need for the bishops to adopt a listening stance regarding reproductive justice. They need to learn from their flocks. Virginia Saldanha provides another needed roadmap for reproductive justice. It is a map that does away with double standards for women and men, a map that has no place for rape or other types of sexual violence, and a map that requires us to remember and educate each other that priests are not God. Sadly, Saldanha names the reality that despite proclaiming the equal dignity of women as *imago Dei*, on the ground practices continue to denigrate and treat women as less than equal. Julie Clague raises fundamental moral themes regarding the need to reform moral norms, do away with shaming techniques, and own and repent for reproductive injustices perpetrated by the Church in various ways. She eloquently reminds us that we need to draw upon the Holy Spirit for the work of transformation. Thank you!

Simeiqi He, PhD (China/USA), is a Chinese Catholic theological ethicist and social worker.

Eric Marcelo O. Genilo, SJ, STD (Philippines), is professor of moral theology at the Loyola School of Theology at Ateneo de Manila University and a formator of diocesan seminarians at San Jose Seminary in Quezon City, Philippines.

Kathryn Lilla Cox, PhD (USA), is a research associate in the Department of Theology and Religious Studies at the University of San Diego.

Virginia Saldanha (India) is a feminist theologian, activist, and independent scholar with extensive experience in grassroots organizing.

Julie Clague, MTh (UK), is lecturer in Catholic theology at the University of Glasgow and Director of the Joint Learning Initiative on Faith and Local Communities.

Part 3

Seeking Reproductive Justice
in the
Context
of a
Broken World

10. Considerations for a Comprehensive Sex Education Grounded in Catholic Social Thought for Reproductive Justice in the Philippines

Stephanie Ann Puen

In 2012, the Responsible Parenthood and Reproductive Health Act of 2012, known as the Reproductive Health (RH) Law was passed, improving access to reproductive healthcare for women, requiring comprehensive reproductive health education (CRHE) in schools across the Philippines, while also granting universal and free access to contraceptives. The RH Law "recognizes the right of Filipinos to decide freely and responsibly on their desired number and spacing of children, within the context of responsible parenthood and informed choice, and to access needed reproductive health care information and services."[1] However, the importance of reproductive healthcare is not a common value or perception in the country, nor is family planning, especially for poorer families. Children are perceived as retirement plans and future workers who will contribute to family income and take care of the parents out of *utang na loob* (debt of gratitude). Thus, while poorer families may not necessarily want more children *per se*, having more children is seen as another chance for the family to succeed, especially for poorer families with less economic means. Aside from the cultural perceptions mentioned, this law was met with fierce opposition from the Catholic Church together with those who held on to the more conservative culture in the country. Though there were some Catholic voices who supported the RH Law,

---

[1] Office of the President, *Executive Order No. 12: Attaining and Sustaining "Zero Unmet Need for Modern Family Planning" Through the Strict Implementation of the Responsible Parenthood and Reproductive Health Act, Providing Funds Therefor, and for Other Purposes*, www.officialgazette.gov.ph/downloads/2017/01jan/20170109-EO-12-RRD.pdf.

such as those from the Ateneo de Manila University that argued that a Catholic can support the then-RH bill, most of the Catholic voices lobbied against it, citing freedom of religion, as well as opposing the universal access to contraceptives in health centers in the country.[2]

Contraception and reproductive health continue to be seen as sensitive topics in a country where 78.8 percent report themselves as Roman Catholic.[3] After the RH Law was signed in 2012, it was challenged in court by Catholic groups, citing that it was unconstitutional, which led to a temporary halting of the RH Law from taking effect. Prior to the signing in 2012, the Catholic Bishops' Conference of the Philippines (CBCP) released various statements rejecting the RH Law. In 2009, the CBCP reiterated the immorality of certain reproductive procedures such as abortion, ligation, and vasectomy, and critiqued the then RH bill on having "mandatory reproductive health education from Grade V to Fourth Year High School without consideration of their sensitivity and moral innocence," arguing that "the moral law and the Constitution recognize the right of parents to be the primary educators of their children."[4] In 2010, the CBCP released another statement, stating that "the Church is not against sex education. But for reasons of morality and religious faith, we strongly object to the proposed sex education program. The program is devoid of any substantive moral and religious value

---

[2] Erika M. Sales, "People, President, and the Pulpit: The Politics of the Reproductive Health Bill of the Philippines" (MA Thesis, The Hague, Netherlands: International Institute of Social Studies, December 2012), 1–2; Marita Castro Guevara, Raymond B. Aguas, Liane Peña Alampay, Fernando T. Aldaba, Remmon E. Barbaza, Manuel B. Dy, Jr., Elizabeth Uy Eviota, Roberto O. Guevara, Anne Marie A. Karaos, Michael J. Liberatore, Liza L. Lim, Cristina Jayme Montiel, Mary Racelis, and Augustin Martin G. Rodriguez, "Catholics Can Support the RH Bill in Good Conscience: Position Paper on the Reproductive Health Bill by Individual Faculty of the Ateneo de Manila University," October 15, 2008, aer.ph/pdf/papers/RH_Bill_Ateneo_Faculty.pdf.
[3] Philippine Statistics Authority, "Religious Affiliation in the Philippines (2020 Census of Population and Housing)," February 22, 2023, psa.gov.ph/content/religious-affiliation-philippines-2020-census-population-and-housing.
[4] Arnel Lagdameo, "Reiterating CBCP Position on Family," *CBCP Online*, September 16, 2009, cbcponline.net/reiterating-cbcp-position-on-family/.

formation."⁵ In 2011, the CBCP released another statement, focusing on being pro-life and the use of Natural Family Planning (NFP) as the primary method for reproductive health and regulation, critiquing the arguments that the RH Law advocates used.⁶

In April 2014, the Supreme Court upheld the RH Law in response to the challenges in court, though it did strike down certain provisions: "Health care providers will be able to deny reproductive health services to patients based on their personal or religious beliefs in non-emergency situations. Spousal consent for women in non-life-threatening circumstances will be required to access reproductive health care. Parental consent will also be required for minors seeking medical attention who have been pregnant or had a miscarriage."⁷ The Catholic bishops had succeeded in limiting the scope of the RH law.

While the stipulations on CRHE are still in the law, and the Department of Education (DepEd) has rolled out a curriculum guide in line with the RH Law, advocates for CRHE critiqued the efforts as still being based on conservative values that imply that sex is evil and shameful, which hamper the very objectives of the initiative. There is still a fear that any form of sex education will increase sexual relations.⁸ Some teachers also prefer to stick to an "abstinence only" approach, while still believing that

---

⁵ Nereo Odchimar, "Securing Our Moral Heritage: Towards a Moral Society," *CBCP Online*, July 24, 2010, cbcponline.net/securing-our-moral-heritage-towards-a-moral-society/.

⁶ The CBCP document disagreed that the RH Law would help reproductive health, lessen the spread of sexually transmitted diseases, including HIV/AIDS, and lessen abortion rates and overpopulation and poverty, while also empowering women and helping them be more responsible and take ownership of their bodies. Nereo Odchimar, "Choosing Life, Rejecting the RH Bill," *CBCP Online*, January 30, 2011, cbcponline.net/choosing-life-rejecting-the-rh-billa-pastoral-letter-of-the-catholic-bishops-conference-of-the-philippines/.

⁷ Justin Goldberg, "Philippine Supreme Court Upholds Historic Reproductive Health Law," *Center for Reproductive Rights*, April 8, 2014, reproductiverights.org/philippine-supreme-court-upholds-historic-reproductive-health-law/.

⁸ Julienne Joven, "Do We Actually Have Sex Ed in Philippine Schools?," *CNN*, November 5, 2021, www.cnnphilippines.com/life/culture/Education/2021/11/5/sex-education-philippine-schools.html.

sexuality education should not be taught, thinking that sex education itself is a sin as bad as committing sex.[9] Such an approach, however, does not take into account the harm of the "abstinence only" approach and its impact on the health of the couple, especially in adolescents who are learning this approach in school as the only approach for reproductive health and management.[10]

Access to reproductive health education, care, and services is crucial as part of the country's response to poverty, as well as helping the youth's well-being by decreasing incidence of teen pregnancies and sexually transmitted diseases. While the CBCP disagreed with the data in their statements, access to reproductive health education correlates with lessening the transmission of sexually transmitted diseases and better reproductive health, not just in terms of risk reduction but also helping young people develop and mature into well-adjusted adults with a healthy sexuality and healthy relationships.[11] Economists from the University of the Philippines argued that a government funded family planning program "has been a critical component to sound economic policy and poverty reduction."[12] They continued:

---

[9] Victoria La Bella, "Incorporating Sexuality Education in the Public School System: Perceptions from the Philippines" (M.Sc. Thesis, Amsterdam, Netherlands, Universiteit van Amsterdam, 2014), 44–45.

[10] John S. Santelli, Stephanie A. Grilo, Laura D. Lindberg, Ilene S. Speizer, Amy Schalet, Jennifer Heitel, Leslie M. Kantor, Terry McGovern, Mary A. Ott, Maureen E. Lyon, Jennifer Rogers, Craig Heck, and Amanda J. Mason-Jones, "Abstinence Only Until Marriage Policies and Programs: An Updated Position Paper of the Society for Adolescent Health and Medicine," *Journal of Adolescent Health* 61, no. 3 (2017): 400–403, doi.org/10.1016/j.jadohealth.2017.06.001.

[11] American Academy of Pediatrics, "The Importance of Access to Comprehensive Sex Education," August 11, 2022, www.aap.org/en/patient-care/adolescent-sexual-health/equitable-access-to-sexual-and-reproductive-health-care-for-all-youth/the-importance-of-access-to-comprehensive-sex-education/.

[12] UP School of Economics Faculty, "Population, Poverty, Politics and RH Bill," *INQUIRER.net*, July 28, 2012, opinion.inquirer.net/33539/population-poverty-politics-and-rh-bill.

> At the micro level, large family size is closely associated with poverty incidence, as consistently borne out by household survey data over time. In short, poor families are heavily burdened when they end up with more children than they want (or can afford). Official data from the Family Income and Expenditures Survey (FIES) since 1985 have unambiguously shown that poverty incidence is lower for families with fewer children but rises consistently with the number of children . . . . Moreover, larger families make smaller investment in human capital per child—investment that is crucial to breaking the vicious chain of intergenerational poverty."[13]

The need for CRHE is something that the Catholic Church should help meet rather than oppose. CRHE is in line with the Catholic Church's teaching on integral human development, for women and families' flourishing not just economically but also their fulfillment spiritually, emotionally, psychologically, and culturally. CRHE helps preserve the human dignity of people by protecting their human right to an education, which helps people discern more clearly their vocation regarding family formation. CRHE helps people understand how best to care for their families and themselves in community with other families. Even Pope Francis explains that "respect for those rights 'is the preliminary condition for a country's social and economic development. When the dignity of the human person is respected, and his or her rights recognized and guaranteed, creativity and interdependence thrive, and the creativity of the human personality is released through actions that further the common good" (*Fratelli Tutti*, no. 22). The Second Vatican Council in *Gravissimum Educationis* also emphasizes the importance of "positive and prudent sexual education" (no. 1). "The Catholic Church has documents stressing the importance of autonomy and the right to education, requesting that information be accurate according to the most recent pedagogical, psychological, and didactic sciences, and calling us to uphold

---

[13] UP School of Economics Faculty, "Population, Poverty, Politics and RH Bill."

social responsibility, participating in the development of humanity."[14] Francis continues this call for holistic sexual education in *Amoris Laetitia*, advocating for sexual education that is appropriate to the age of the child and that young people "should be helped to recognize and seek out positive influences, while shunning the things that cripple their capacity for love" (no. 281).

To contribute to the work towards poverty eradication and the flourishing of women and families, this work thus examines how to teach a comprehensive reproductive health education from a Catholic perspective. I argue for the importance of a CRHE in line with Catholic social thought and outline some considerations in teaching a comprehensive reproductive health education grounded in Catholic social thought: 1) The importance of connecting sexual ethics with Catholic social thought; 2) The need to critique and address the way women and family are understood in Philippine culture and how it is taught in Catholic religious education; and 3) The value of teaching moral decision-making and discernment in CRHE, grounded in Catholic social thought.

A Comprehensive Reproductive Health Education in the Philippines

I argue for three considerations that should be reflected in the way the CRHE is crafted and taught, in order that the CRHE be aligned with the kind of integral human development that is taught in the Catholic Church. First, it is important that sexual ethics be connected more closely to Catholic social thought rather than be separated in moral theology and Catholic theological ethics. Second, there is a need to critique and address the understanding of women and family in the Philippines. Lastly, in

---

[14] Mark Levand and Karen Ross, "Sexuality Education as a Moral Good: Catholic Support for Accurate, Holistic Sexuality Information," *Theology and Sexuality* 27, no. 2–3 (2021): 2, doi.org/10.1080/13558358.2021.1872827.

teaching CRHE from a Catholic perspective, there is also a need to teach moral decision-making and discernment.

The Importance of Connecting Sexual Ethics and Catholic Social Thought

First, sexual ethics needs to be connected more closely to Catholic social thought. Sexual ethics has often been considered a taboo subject in the Philippines. There is a lot of *hiya* (shame) or awkwardness when it comes to discussing sex and other sexually related topics such as masturbation, pleasure, or what it means to engage in penetrative or non-penetrative sexual activity with someone. This *hiya* stems from the persisting notion that sex is taboo. Further, some mistakenly claim that a sex-positive approach (or even a willingness to talk about sex) is another form of lust that enables promiscuity. In the conservative culture of the Philippines, to talk about sex is sinful and wrong. Because sex and sexual ethics are often not discussed in class or in the home, misconceptions abound. Misinformation leaves space for abuse to happen, especially regarding lack of consent and unjust power relations. This has led to many unplanned pregnancies and abusive relationships and marriages. Some of those unplanned pregnancies end in unsafe abortions, as abortions are illegal in the Philippines. Meanwhile, domestic violence is commonplace.[15]

Aside from the awkwardness and shame in discussions pertaining to sex, the way it is taught is often in absolutes, without much nuance in terms of context and circumstances, due to the teaching that sins against the sixth and ninth commandment (i.e., sexual sins) have no parvity of matter,

---

[15] United Nations Population Fund, "Country Programme Document for Philippines," September 4, 2018, 2–4, www.unfpa.org/sites/default/files/portal-document/DPFPACPDPH L8_en.pdf; Maria Paz N. Marquez, Elma P. Laguna, Maria Midea M. Kabamalan, Grace T. Cruz, "Estimating the Impact of the COVID-19 Pandemic on Key Sexual and Reproductive Health Outcomes in the Philippines," *University of the Philippines Population Institute*, October 15, 2020, www.uppi.upd.edu.ph/sites/default/files/pdf/UPPI-Impact-of-COVID-19-on-SRH.pdf.

meaning that all sexual sins are grave matter, and never just venial.[16] Sex is often seen as sinful and objectively bad, with no gray areas, but this classification of sexual sins as being all grave matter and the implications of saying such continues to be challenged, most recently by San Diego based Cardinal Robert McElroy.[17] While the Catholic Church has done much in terms of nuancing and navigating the complexities of poverty, economics, and war in official church doctrine in Catholic social thought, there is much less of that in the area of sexual ethics. Much of what is still taught in Christian Living Education (CLE) or Christian Values classes is that abortion and contraception are always wrong, wrapped up in the language of intrinsic evil. While sex can be unitive in CLE, sex is still primarily about procreation. Reproductive health thus becomes reduced to having children, without much discussion on the pleasurable and unitive aspects of sex or even what happens in the period after having the baby, especially for women. Other opportunities to talk about reproductive health education, such as marriage preparation seminars (often called the pre-Cana seminar) for those about to get married in the Catholic Church, focus on natural family planning as the primary way of dealing with sex and reproductive health, while vilifying or rejecting abortion and other forms of contraception with not much nuance or discussion in these topics. This binary way of thinking finds its way into the labels of "pro-life" and "pro-choice" with often no room to nuance arguments that do not fall neatly into these categories. Such labels are often too reductive and unhelpful, and the extreme or polarizing ideas attached to these labels often discourage dialogue.[18]

To respond to this often absolute binary way of thinking, concepts from Catholic social thought help give more nuance to the issues in sexual

---

[16] James F. Keenan, "Raising Expectations on Sin," *Theological Studies* 77, no. 1 (2016): 165–180, doi.org/10.1177/0040563915620466.

[17] Mike Lewis, "Reflections on the McElroy Proposal," *Where Peter Is*, March 10, 2023, wherepeteris.com/reflections-on-the-mcelroy-proposal/.

[18] Tricia C. Bruce, *How Americans Understand Abortion: A Comprehensive Interview Study of Abortion Attitude in the US* (Notre Dame, IN: McGrath Institute for Church Life, 2020), 4.

ethics and reproductive health, using the language of human dignity, justice, and the common good. Leo XIII, in *Rerum Novarum*, explains that consent may be coerced; such papal analysis is helpful in getting students to think about what consent is and what it really means to give one's consent not just in terms of their work but also in a relationship.[19] Discussion of integral human development in Paul VI's *Populorom Progressio*, no. 14, or human dignity, rights and duties, and the common good in John XXIII's *Mater et Magistra*, nos. 11–34, 55–62, serve as foundations for the vision or goals of the human person, which include the roles of one's sexuality and sexual relationships in this vision.

Theologians have also developed helpful categories that connect sexual ethics more closely to Catholic social thought. Margaret Farley's work on just love is now considered a classic text in this regard. Farley helps develop an understanding of love and sex framed by justice, bringing out the aspects of relationships that should be considered when thinking about what it means to be in a romantic relationship with a person, especially in helping young adults understand what it means to engage in just sex and just relationships with others. Farley lists particular characteristics that mark just sex and a just relationship, such as the presence of free consent, mutuality, equality, commitment, fruitfulness, and social justice, serving as reflection matter for young adults in connection with the kinds of

---

[19] Discussing consent in terms of work and the economy, Leo XIII discusses in no. 45 that state and society should "Let the working man and the employer make free agreements, and in particular let them agree freely as to the wages; nevertheless, there underlies a dictate of natural justice more imperious and ancient than any bargain between man and man, namely, that wages ought not to be insufficient to support a frugal and well-behaved wage-earner. If through necessity or fear of a worse evil the workman accept harder conditions because an employer or contractor will afford him no better, he is made the victim of force and injustice" (*Rerum Novarum*, no. 45). This paragraph highlights that consent is not simply about two people giving their assent to a particular set of terms but also the circumstances in how that assent was given, so as to be able to say that true consent was given.

relationships they have, both sexual and non-sexual, and how these characteristics are manifested in their concrete realities.[20]

Another example from the US context is that of Mark Levand and Karen Ross, who also emphasize guiding principles for holistic Catholic sexuality education, namely anthropological justice, respecting individual moral autonomy, and social justice. First, anthropological justice entails a just view of how we as human beings exist and relate to others and with God, which includes the sacredness of our physical bodies.[21] Second, individual moral autonomy ought to be respected, which includes "giving people the information they need to be informed when they make sexual decisions or being confronted with sexual problems in their lives."[22] Lastly, sexual ethics should be understood as an issue of social justice and not just individual private moral issues. Issues of sexuality and reproductive health are not just private decisions. They are also embedded within particular structures that can be oppressive and that are connected to other social justice issues.[23] These three principles are helpful because they link sexual ethics and reproductive health to foundational concepts in Catholic social thought. Doing so helps educators move beyond the false understanding that sex is simply private or that talk of sex is shameful and to be shunned. Issues related to sexual ethics and reproductive health are part of what it means to be human, and they are also issues of justice and the common good.

These examples are rich resources that can be further applied and enculturated in the Filipino context, given the *hiya* that often accompanies discourse on sex. It is important to make clear distinctions between sex and sin. It is also important for educators to discuss sex without shame. Doing so encourages students to be more open about discussing sex, sexual ethics,

---

[20] For more on these characteristics and the framework for just sex that Farley uses, see Margaret A. Farley, *Just Love: A Framework for Christian Sexual Ethics* (New York: Continuum, 2006), 207–244.
[21] Levand and Ross, "Sexuality Education as a Moral Good," 9–11.
[22] Levand and Ross, "Sexuality Education as a Moral Good," 11–12.
[23] Levand and Ross, "Sexuality Education as a Moral Good," 12–13.

and their reproductive health, taking a more active and responsible role in understanding their body and their sexuality in their life. The principles of Catholic social thought encourage thoughtful analysis of complex topics, rather than an absolutist rejection of any form of CRHE whatsoever.

The Need to Critique and Address the Understanding of Women and Family in the Philippines

The underlying assumptions of the role of women and the concept of family in the Philippines also need to be articulated and reframed. CRHE is based on an understanding of gender equality, noting a difference in the two sexes but also rejecting an essentialist understanding of sex and gender, where particular gender roles are ascribed to certain genders. Likewise CRHE also rejects gender bias. Thus, implementing CRHE in schools requires more work towards gender equality and sensitivity when gender bias occurs, which entails "academically rigorous explorations of women's experiences (family life across diverse communities, gender and society, reproductive health trends) in light of the mission of Catholic [educational institutions]."[24]

The role of women, for example, is still heavily tied to child rearing and child bearing. This has an effect on CRHE because male students who hold on to this understanding of the role of women may passively accept their lack of understanding about women's reproductive health. Men can absolve themselves of responsibility in ensuring the well-being of women and potential children. The Department of Education in the Philippines has been critiqued several times due to gender bias appearing in the textbooks being used for students as young as those in first grade.[25] In these

---

[24] M. T. Davila, "Catholic Higher Education and Student Formation in a Post-Roe World: A Proposal for Women's Personhood and Reproductive Autonomy," *Journal of Moral Theology* 12, no. 1 (2023): 120, doi.org/10.55476/001c.66246.

[25] For examples of gender bias in the learning material of students in Philippine education, see John Rey B. Java and Cristabel Rose F. Parcon, "Gendered Illustrations in Philippine Textbooks," *Asia Pacific Higher Education Research Journal* 3, no. 1 (2016): 34–51; Christian Deiparine, "'Archaic':

illustrations and activities in the textbooks, women continue to be seen as emotional babysitters and caregivers, while men are seen as strong and smart breadwinners. Without addressing these fundamental assumptions of gender, CRHE will continue to perpetuate said assumptions, as well as the unjust consequences that said assumptions bring with them.

Theologians have much to offer in this work of challenging the understanding of women in the Catholic Church and in society. Theologian Emily Reimer-Barry reminds the Catholic Church and society to actively listen to women's voices and avoid disinterest and apathy. She advocates for reproductive justice as a framework for understanding women's voices and stories. She explains that "conceptualizing the inherent value of maternal life *and* prenatal life, the moral agency of the pregnant person, and the structural injustices that prevent pregnant people from choosing to parent even when they express ambivalence or sorrow about a decision to terminate a pregnancy . . . is not [all about abortion]."[26] Scholars of Reproductive Justice acknowledge that reproduction is not just a private, biological endeavor. Rather, "nations, political parties, religious and ethnic groups, and other entities claim a stake in reproduction—who should have sex, who should give birth, who should be born, and who should not. These claims turn an intensely private human activity into a matter of public concern, sometimes a public obsession...[that is] deeply politicized."[27]

Theologian Rachel Joyce Marie Sanchez also shows how women's wisdom is a crucial part of a just ecclesial and social framework through a

---

DepEd Official Says Materials with Gender Stereotypes Should Not Be Taught to Students," *Philstar.com*, October 21, 2020, www.philstar.com/headlines/2020/10/21/2051257/archaic-deped-official-says-materials-gender-stereotypes-should-not-be-taught-students.

[26] Emily Reimer-Barry, "Wisdom from a Reproductive Justice Framework," *Journal of Moral Theology* 12, no. 1 (2023): 133, doi.org/10.55476/001c.66249.

[27] Loretta Ross and Rickie Solinger, *Reproductive Justice: An Introduction* (Oakland, CA: University of California Press, 2017), 168.

power-with-others structure.[28] In CRHE, reproductive justice is vital in ensuring that women are not just reduced to their procreative potential. A power-with-others framework such as the one Sanchez argues for is helpful in ensuring that women are not ignored in situations where they are heavily affected and that their voices are taken seriously regarding issues and policies that affect them.

One of the key challenges in teaching CRHE is the lack of male interest. Men do have an important role in reproductive justice. However, "Men often do not feel that this is an important topic to learn about because it is more about the woman and her body since she is the one who ultimately gives birth to the child."[29] While this appears to be a positive development because it acknowledges the woman's autonomy and voice in terms of reproduction, it can prove detrimental to the woman's health if she has a male partner who is not sensitive to or conscious of her reproductive health. Men may, consciously or unconsciously, work against women's reproductive health and gender equality due to lack of knowledge or care. The value of CRHE for men, as well as the role of men in CRHE, is thus an important part of crafting an effective CRHE. CRHE is not just about the reproductive health of women devoid of context, but rather CRHE is about reproductive health of people in connection to their relationships with their partners and families.[30] If done appropriately, a CRHE that engages men in healthy and respectful ways will foster a healthier relationship discernment. When all sexually active persons are educated and well-informed, this has positive effects for the family's health overall and is just for all involved.[31]

---

[28] Rachel Joyce Marie O. Sanchez, "Where Is Women's Wisdom in the Life of the Church?: A Feminist Perspective on the International Theological Commission's 'Sensus Fidei in the Life of the Church,'" *Journal of Feminist Studies in Religion* 32, no. 2 (2016): 27–43.

[29] La Bella, "Incorporating Sexuality Education in the Public School System," 53.

[30] See Hoon Choi, "Fatherhood, Reproductive Justice, and Strategic Invisibility of Men," 122–147, in this volume.

[31] "Policymakers and practitioners reported that greater men's involvement would result in a range of benefits for maternal and child health, primarily through greater access to services and

Assumptions about the family in the Philippines are intimately tied to the reproductive health policies and initiatives in the country, given that the family is seen as inviolable and the basic social institution. However, while it is good that the family is seen as deserving of care, the understanding of particular gender roles within family life is still restrictive. The concept of "mother" in the Philippines reflects the assumption that she stays at home to take care of the children, while the "father" is the one who is the breadwinner of the family. A man who stays at home to take care of children may be seen as "weak" or "less of a man," especially if it is the woman who is making the money. Women who also prioritize their careers are seen as too "bossy" and are met with disapproval if they focus on careers instead of starting or raising a family. They are often met with questions of when they will "get married, settle down, and start a family" or "have children." Family is also still seen as traditionally a mother, father, children, and extended family, such as aunts and uncles, grandparents, cousins, and nieces and nephews. The reception of LGBTQ+ persons in relation to family is also not yet fully welcome.

In a developing country such as the Philippines where many still live below the poverty line, there is also a sense of judgement made on women who have children as single mothers. They were not "responsible" because their parenthood does not fit the standard of what a traditional family

---

interventions for women and children. . . . There was wide agreement that increasing the engagement of men in MCH is important and would yield considerable health and other benefits for families. Many participants emphasized men's cultural role in decision-making regarding access [to healthcare]. They highlighted the many potential benefits of giving men information to inform their decision-making about family health matters. . . . Participants in this study also reported beliefs that including men in MCH services may have benefits for men's own health. In many settings, men have very little contact with the formal health system, particularly for preventative services, and prefer to seek curative services from a traditional healer or pharmacy. For men, as for women, pregnancy and early childhood provides an opportunity to link parents to the health system. Jessica Davis, Joseph Vyankandondera, Stanley Luchters, David Simon, and Wendy Holmes, "Male Involvement in Reproductive, Maternal and Child Health: A Qualitative Study of Policymaker and Practitioner Perspectives in the Pacific," *Reproductive Health* 13, no. 1 (2016): 81, doi.org/10.1186/s12978-016-0184-2.

looks like. This is even the case when a young woman does not desire single parenthood but experiences abandonment by the father of her child.[32] Many families also have someone, either one parent or both, or one of the children, who works abroad as an overseas Filipino worker (OFW), and so many families have either just one parent at home functioning almost as a single parent, while the other is away to earn money for the family, or have even both parents earning money, while the child or children stay with relatives such as aunts or uncles, or grandparents. Because of the structures of poverty that many Filipinos find themselves trapped in, the poor are also accused of being irresponsible and hypersexual, having too many children that they can't afford to feed, and thus are accused of reproductive injustice and in need of reproductive health and values education.[33] For the poor, the children are seen as an extra pair of hands to work for the family and a possible ticket out of poverty; for others, it is seen as the reason why the poor remain poor, becoming an easy way to blame the poor for their situation and further stigmatize their condition. Ascribing agency to poor families without attention to the social conditions in which they make decisions also serves to exonerate more powerful others (including policy-makers) who are in a position to help. While the parents in the family are seen as the primary educators of children, as mentioned by the CBCP in their statements, in practice, parents often leave the education of their children to their schools, due to this setup of having to work and earn money for the family, coupled with the *hiya* of having to discuss topics related to sex and reproduction.

We must, then, connect the concept of family and the concept of integral human development, both categories within Catholic social thought that are underdeveloped in Catholic sexual ethics. Theologian Herman Bavinck makes the case for the importance of family as essential

---

[32] See Kathryn Lilla Cox, "Reproductive Injustice as Social Sin: Mapping Sin Discourse into Debates about Fertility Decisions," in this volume.

[33] See Karen Peterson-Iyer, "Reproductive Justice and Agricultural Labor Migrants," 257–289, in this volume.

to integral human development, where a person is first formed and nurtured—"a person's becoming [integrally] human occurs within the home; here the foundation is laid for the forming of the future [person]...in the Kingdom of God."[34] Integral human development challenges the narrow definitions and gender roles by changing the questions and priorities of the conversation, becoming more inclusive of the LGBTQ+ and single parents. Rather than focusing on the configuration of the family unit or particular gender roles, the question shifts to how members of the family help each other towards their flourishing, given the age-appropriate rights and responsibilities of each person in the family unit. As reproductive justice is concerned with the human right and duty to care for children in an appropriately safe environment, access to key resources and support are also needed to help families become spaces of integral human development.

Integral human development also challenges the preconceived notion that the poor are just irresponsible in matters of the family, reproductive health, or sexual ethics. Together with reproductive justice, integral human development also takes into account the context that families find themselves in and how said context interacts with the families and their decisions. Understanding the different structures at work, how these interact with families, and how they balance different goods and values at stake confronts our assumptions of how people discern, what is in their consciences, and why and how certain people decided in a particular way. It helps us understand how to respond appropriately, in ways that genuinely help people, especially women, towards reproductive justice and reproductive health.

---

[34] Eduardo Echeverria, "Bavinck on the Family and Integral Human Development," *Journal of Markets and Morality* 16, no. 1 (2013): 219, 224–225.

The Value of Teaching Moral Decision-Making and Discernment in Comprehensive Reproductive Health Education

Lastly, in teaching CRHE, it important to remember that the pedagogy and morality to be used are not simply a transmission of knowledge or doctrine but rather journeying with the students in helping them exercise their freedom in ways that promote flourishing and the common good through discernment. Discernment here offers a framework or paradigm for people to make decisions before God, where the possible options are different but potentially good, by looking at one's desires, thoughts, and movements and tendencies within the self.[35] "Education includes encouraging the responsible use of freedom to face issues with good sense and intelligence. It involves forming persons who readily understand that their own lives, and the life of the community, are in their hands" (*Amoris Laetitia*, no. 262). Having concepts and the language from Catholic social thought, as well as a better understanding of the role of women and the family helps people have a more robust foundation for their moral decision-making when it comes to sexual ethics in CRHE, cognizant of the fact that Catholic schools have a hand in forming consciences but do not and should not replace consciences (*Amoris Laetitia*, no. 37). The bishops have a duty to assist in conscience formation, but they overstep their legitimate authority when they seek to dictate to the consciences of the faithful.

The teachers tasked to teach CRHE or anything related to sex and sexual ethics fear that they are ill-equipped to teach such matters and fear that they will say the wrong thing.[36] Shifting the understanding from teaching doctrine to helping students discern and understand themselves,

---

[35] This definition leans heavily on the concept of discernment in Ignatian spirituality but is still open to other spiritualities. For a short and accessible discussion on Ignatian discernment, see Reynaldo Belfort Pierrilus, "Jesuit 101: Finding Our Way Through Ignatian Discernment," *The Jesuit Post*, November 5, 2021, thejesuitpost.org/2021/11/jesuit-101-finding-our-way-through-ignatian-discernment/.

[36] La Bella, "Incorporating Sexuality Education in the Public School System," 51.

including their bodies, allows them to mature and develop their freedom responsibly, rather than teaching them to simply obey what other people say. Developing the students' discernment practices also helps students understand that church teachings continue to develop over time, and they are complex. Church teachings must be discerned and applied in particular circumstances. Such an understanding can liberate teachers from fearing they will lead students astray since moral decision-making of the person is not solely based on what teachers teach but also on the active discernment and conscientious decision-making of the person making the decision in context.

Respecting individual moral autonomy, as highlighted by Levand and Ross, is important in helping people discern their particular situations when it comes to reproductive health. In using their reason and will, people are exercising their freedom, hopefully following their conscience in making decisions for the good of themselves and others. Helping empower people to make decisions that are just and moral and helping people articulate their desires, concerns, and values, these are key in assisting them to discern and make good moral decisions. In exercising such moral autonomy, people also learn what it means to be accountable and to engage in responsible behavior, especially in the realm of sexual relations. However, respecting individual autonomy can be difficult in a more communitarian culture such as that in the Philippines, where most make decisions not just for themselves but in consideration of friends, family, or local community.

Given the Filipino context that is more collectivist, I would also propose highlighting the importance of the communal aspect of this discernment process along with one's moral autonomy. The communal discernment process is "a process undertaken by a community as a community for the purpose of judging what God is calling that community to do."[37] Especially

---

[37] Communal discernment in Ignatian spirituality highlights both the individual's decision-making, values, and concerns. See Jules J. Toner, "A Method for Communal Discernment of God's Will," *Studies in the Spirituality of Jesuits* 3, no. 4 (1971): 124–125.

when conflicting ideas arise in a conflict-averse culture such as that in the Philippines, communal discernment gives a framework that communities can use to handle differing thoughts or help a person take seriously the concerns of others appropriately in moral decision-making, including in sexual ethics and reproductive health-related issues that can be highly contentious. Communal discernment gives a space for articulation, discussion, and deliberation of the discernment processes happening in a community, avoiding the assumption that all consciences will come to the same conclusion given the moral concerns and doctrines at work. Highlighting this communal aspect also resists the temptation of reducing discernment and moral decision-making to individualistic relativism that may be obscured by thinking that "God told me to do something," while at the same time ensuring that the voice of the decision-maker does not get lost among the voices of everyone else.

The reproductive justice framework puts value on the agency of the person discerning. But more than just choosing what to do with one's body, Christian discernment also emphasizes the process and the disposition of the decision-maker—what kind of person am I becoming? Thus, a CRHE that values the decision-making and discernment of a person is not only about the action to be done but also the inclination of the person towards the good. CRHE is formative, helping the person not just make good decisions regarding their reproductive health and its implications but also helping people understand what it means to be human. A Christian approach takes seriously the call to see sexual formation and decision-making in alignment with integral human development outlined in Catholic social thought.

Conclusion

CRHE is not against the teachings of the Catholic Church. This paper highlighted the need for age-appropriate understanding of reproductive health, sex, and sexual ethics. Catholic institutions should reject harmful taboos and instead seek to contribute to a sex education rooted in holistic flourishing and moral development. Catholic schools have a role to play in helping people understand themselves as they grow, and this is not an attack on the person's moral innocence nor is it an encouragement to simply have sex with no sense of the implications therein. Rather, it is about supporting people so that they mature appropriately, with the right information that does not only discuss the physical dimension of reproductive health and sexuality but also the spiritual and ethical aspects of these complex issues. Thus, instead of seeking exemptions or not implementing this aspect of the RH Law in Catholic schools, this work seeks to start a conversation on how Catholic schools might implement CRHE in their own institutions, grounded in Catholic social thought, and towards integral human development.

Stephanie Ann Puen, PhD, is a faculty member in the Department of Theology at Ateneo de Manila University. She has taught courses in economics and business ethics, Catholic social thought, gender and sexual ethics, and theology and popular culture at both the Ateneo de Manila University and Fordham University in New York. Dr. Puen has published on these topics for both scholarly and popular publications.

11. Reproductive Justice and Agricultural Labor Migrants

Karen Peterson-Iyer

According to the United Nations, international migrants in 2019 comprised approximately 3.5 percent (272 million) of the world's total population.[1] While much of this migration is voluntary, it is also a result of the forcible effects of poverty, conflict, sexual and gender-based violence, and deep global economic disparities. Especially for those migrants in the US who live and work on the lower rungs of the socioeconomic ladder, the "American Dream" remains largely elusive. Vast numbers of them struggle not only with the physical challenges of hunger, poverty, and poor access to health care but also with the mental and emotional traumas of displacement, workplace exploitation, harassment and assault, and the psychological impact of a largely unwelcoming US immigration system.

Close to half of all migrants today are women—many of whom are of childbearing age. These women confront most, if not all, of the same challenges as their male counterparts, but they also face distinctive struggles that derive from their status *as women* in a culture that many would characterize as both anti-woman and anti-child.[2] In other words,

---

[1] United Nations Department of Economic and Social Affairs, "International Migrant Stock 2019: Ten Key Messages," September 2019, www.un.org/en/development/desa/population/migration/publications/migrationreport/docs/MigrationStock2019_TenKeyFindings.pdf.

[2] In the United States today, women experience large wealth and income gaps relative to men. They also very frequently encounter household dynamics that result in a gendered division of labor and ultimately disadvantage them with respect to material power. For a helpful discussion of these realities, see Mariko Lin Chang, "The Women's Wealth Gap: What Is It and Why Do We Care?" in *Shortchanged: Why Women Have Less Wealth and What Can Be Done about It* (Oxford Academic online edition, 2012), doi.org/10.1093/acprof:oso/9780195367690.003.0001. In a similar vein, in 2019 approximately one in seven US children were

women of reproductive age are vulnerable in particular ways, not just individually but also on a *structural* level. It is therefore impossible to accurately consider these women's concrete realities without also considering the complicated social forces surrounding reproduction itself. Migrant women's struggles are not simply a matter of individual reproductive choices or even access to reproductive health care. Rather, these struggles involve communal and intersecting questions of gender, race, class, and, importantly, immigration status. Ultimately, reproductive health and well-being are deeply intertwined with these social realities.

Yet, in the US today, conversations about reproductive health rapidly devolve into culture wars that typically characterize the public conversation about abortion. Over the past fifty-plus years, both "pro-life" and "pro-choice" approaches have largely failed to appreciate women's social realities—especially those of socioeconomically struggling and BIPOC (Black, Indigenous, People of Color) women. On the one hand, pro-choice arguments tend to frame abortion in terms of privacy, individual choice, and legal access to abortion, while downplaying the broader societal factors that have led to the decision for an abortion in the first place. On the other hand, pro-life arguments too often frame the question as a matter of the "sanctity of life," effectively disregarding the agency of the pregnant person and even the concrete well-being of born children (and women). As Loretta J. Ross, reproductive justice scholar/activist and co-founder of Sister Song, contends, "In abortion debates of privacy, women's rights, fetuses, and the law, the isolation of abortion from other social justice issues like violence against women fails to incorporate the intersecting issues that actually determine how a

---

categorized as poor and seventy-one percent of these were children of color. These children disproportionately underperform on standard educational metrics and generally experience worse access to healthcare than their non-poor counterparts. Further, juvenile incarceration, escalating levels of gun violence, and domestic abuse can impact children from any economic or racial background, but poor, non-white, and disabled children suffer at disproportionately high rates. See Children's Defense Fund, "Resources: Fact Sheets and Issue Briefs," www.childrensdefense.org/policy/resources/fact-sheets-and-issue-briefs/.

pregnant woman makes the decision to have a baby.... Perhaps the pro-choice/pro-life binary has outlived its shelf life in the past forty years, becoming obsolete.... Abortion presented as a choice became a co-opted neoliberal frame that denied government responsibility for providing healthcare."[3] In the end, it seems that neither approach—"pro-choice" nor "pro-life"—sufficiently addresses the complexity of abortion, and thus our society has remained deeply divided on this most contentious of social issues. And women and children have suffered for it.

Reproductive justice, on the other hand, with its central focus on social analysis, is a far more well-suited concept with which to approach the challenges faced by these very same women and children, including (for the purposes of this essay) poor migrant women. Their struggles ultimately have as much to do with housing, childcare, working conditions, domestic violence, and immigration status as they do directly with abortion. To be sure, it is not that the latter is of little or no significance to impoverished migrant women. But to understand the reproductive struggles of these women purely in terms of individual freedom of choice or even simply *access* to reproductive health care is, in fact, to *mis*-understand their struggles in crucial ways.

What is the role of Catholic teaching in navigating the reproductive struggles of impoverished migrant women? At first glance, the concept of reproductive justice may seem to be a poor fit with the teachings and more specific reproductive stances of the Catholic Church, for whom abortion tends to be the flagship contemporary social issue. Yet, digging a bit deeper reveals a more complicated picture. In fact, Catholic thought, particularly in its more liberationist iterations, contains robust resources for examining suffering within the context of structural injustice. Catholic social teaching (CST) offers various analytical themes—human dignity, the

---

[3] Loretta J. Ross, "Conceptualizing Reproductive Justice Theory: A Manifesto for Activism," in *Radical Reproductive Justice: Foundations, Theory, Practice, Critique*, ed. Loretta J. Ross, Lynn Roberts, Erika Derkas, Whitney Peoples, and Pamela Bridgewater Toure (New York: Feminist Press, 2017), 172 and 178–179.

common good, labor justice, the centrality of the family, hospitality to the immigrant "stranger"—that dovetail well with many of the elements and overall tenor of a reproductive justice approach. In these ways, contemporary Catholic thought can serve to redirect our focus not simply to struggling individual migrant women but also to the *social* and *structural* forces that contribute to or even create those struggles.[4]

In this essay, I examine these matters with special attention to women laboring in the agricultural context, especially farmworker women who are immigrants to the US from across its southern border.[5] My focus here is particularly (though not exclusively) on women working in California's Central Valley—one of the largest farming areas within the United States. Farmworker women here are almost exclusively non-white, and a significant portion of them hail from indigenous communities south of the US-Mexico border. This latter group often speaks neither English nor Spanish fluently; such language and cultural barriers may be added to a long list of other challenges.[6] Moreover, for those who have immigrated without papers across this heavily militarized border, the dangers of farm work have been accompanied by the substantial dangers of migration itself

---

[4] Several other essays in this volume, including those by Julie Clague, Kate Ward, and Kathryn Lilla Cox, point toward various dimensions of these social and structural forces.

[5] As always, language is imperfect here, particularly in the usage of the term "farmworker." Anyone who works on a farm is technically a "farmworker." Yet, as others have correctly pointed out, the term most often refers not to farm owners, managers, administrative assistants, and crop managers but rather to those who labor in the fields to hand harvest fruit and vegetables. Moreover, in the US today the term frequently is used to indicate laborers who have immigrated from Latin America or (at a minimum) are of Latino ethnicity. I therefore employ the term mindfully, with the recognition of the racial, ethnic, and class-based associations it ordinarily conveys. On this theme, see Seth M. Holmes, *Fresh Fruit, Broken Bodies: Migrant Farmworkers in the United States* (Berkeley: University of California Press, 2013), 186–187.

[6] Seth M. Holmes describes a predictable hierarchy of both power and struggle within US agriculture, in which "the more Mexican and the more 'indigenous' one is perceived to be, the more psychologically stressful, physically strenuous, and dangerous one's job. Thus where a migrant body falls on the dual ethnic-labor hierarchy shapes how much and what kind of suffering must be endured." Holmes, *Fresh Fruit, Broken Bodies*, 95; see also 180–181.

and, in some cases, maltreatment in US detention centers if they are unlucky enough to be apprehended in transit. Thus, examining reproductive justice in the concrete context of these women's lives entails attention not just to difficult agricultural labor realities but also to a broken and dangerous US immigration system which squarely intersects with those realities.

While women farmworkers are not always immigrants nor even migrants and while even those who *are* migrants represent only a subsection of migrant workers more generally, it is reasonable to conclude that immigrant women farmworkers are among the most vulnerable of all migrants, socially and economically speaking. It is my contention that the concepts of reproductive justice, with its strong commitment to center vulnerable populations, and a Catholic-styled "preferential option for the marginalized" are both well-suited analytics with which to understand their situation. My central argument is as follows: to the degree that the Catholic Church, in its articulation of the above social themes, can redirect itself from a single-minded focus on abortion *per se* to the more holistic lens provided by reproductive justice, it will more effectively be able to address the challenges faced by these migrant women; and it will thus better be able to carry out its aims of love, justice, and the liberation of the oppressed within an unjust world.

Framing the Problem: Demographics

The contours of migration, especially international migration, form the backdrop for women migrants' situation within agriculture. Before the disruptions to immigration caused by COVID-19, immigration worldwide had been dramatically on the rise for several decades.[7] Globally,

---

[7] United Nations Department of Economic and Social Affairs, Population Division 2020, "International Migration 2020 Highlights," UN Doc. ST/ESA/SER.A/452, 1, www.un.org/development/desa/pd/sites/www.un.org.development.desa.pd/files/undesa_pd_2020_international_migration_highlights.pdf.

the US is home to more international migrants than any other country, and roughly half of these are girls and women.[8] An estimated 86 percent of agricultural workers in the US are foreign born, and 45 percent of all US agricultural workers are undocumented.[9] Most foreign-born undocumented agricultural workers in the US come from Mexico and Central America and speak a language other than English at home. Approximately 37 percent of undocumented agricultural workers are female.[10]

Migration, including agricultural migration, is not driven simply by the individual needs (and wills) of migrants; economic and geopolitical systems have a massive impact on migration, creating and sustaining it in important ways.[11] For example, neoliberal economic policies over the past half century, including those encapsulated by NAFTA (the North American Free Trade Agreement) and CAFTA (the Central American Free Trade Agreement), have resulted in economic crises south of the US border that have necessitated migration northward. Further, US immigration processes have historically been racialized in complicated ways, where immigration policies have often functioned to create "desirable" and "undesirable" categories of immigrants, with the latter ordinarily hailing from largely non-white countries of origin.[12] Black and

---

[8] Migration Policy Institute, "Frequently Requested Statistics on Immigrants and Immigration in the United States," March 14, 2023, www.migrationpolicy.org/article/frequently-requested-statistics-immigrants-and-immigration-united-states-2024.

[9] Raquel Rosenbloom, "A Profile of Undocumented Agricultural Workers in the United States," Center for Migration Studies, August 30, 2022, cmsny.org/agricultural-workers-rosenbloom-083022/.

[10] Rosenbloom, "A Profile of Undocumented Agricultural Workers."

[11] Saskia Sassen, "The Making of Migrations," in *Living With(out) Borders: Catholic Theological Ethics on the Migrations of Peoples*, ed. Agnes M. Brazal and Mary Teresa Davila (Maryknoll, NY: Orbis Books, 2016), 11–22; see also Holmes, *Fresh Fruit, Broken Bodies*, 17.

[12] Sassen, "The Making of Migrations." See also Gwyneth Lonergan, writing in the U.K. context, "Reproductive Justice and Migrant Women in Great Britain," *Women: A Cultural Review* 23, no. 1 (2012): 26–45. Ex-president Donald Trump's 2018 heinous reference to African countries as "shithole" sources of immigrants merely laid bare the racist patterns of immigration policy that have prevailed for decades or even centuries. See Josh Dawsey, "Trump Derides Protection for Immigrants from 'Shithole' Countries," *Washington Post*,

Brown immigrants are far more likely to lack documentation and thus more frequently live in fear of deportation—working in the legal shadows once they have arrived in the US.

Globally speaking, women have come to make up an increasing proportion of all immigrants—a phenomenon recognized as the "feminization of immigration."[13] Among these women, a large proportion are of childbearing age. Indeed, of specific relevance to the present essay, in 2020 the *average* age of farmworker women generally was thirty-nine years old—still within a potentially childbearing phase of life.[14] In total, about half of all farmworkers are parents, but at least in California—the state that employs the vast majority of farmworkers in the US—this figure is far higher for women, standing at 69 percent.[15] Nearly all (95 percent) of these women live with their children.[16]

January 12, 2018, www.washingtonpost.com/politics/trump-attacks-protections-for-immigrants-from-shithole-countries-in-oval-office-meeting/2018/01/11/bfc0725c-f711-11e7-91af-31ac729add94_story.html.

[13] Lígia Moreira Almeida, José Caldas, Diogo Ayres-de-Campos, Dora Salcedo-Barrientos, and Sónia Dias, "Maternal Healthcare in Migrants: A Systematic Review," *Maternal Child Health Journal* 17 (2013): 1346–1354. This pattern of feminization has not been as obvious in the US; see, for instance, United Nations Department of Economic and Social Affairs, Population Division 2020, "International Migration 2020 Highlights," 27 fig. 16, www.un.org/development/desa/pd/sites/www.un.org.development.desa.pd/files/undesa_pd_2020_international_migration_highlights.pdf.

[14] US Department of Labor, "Findings from the National Agricultural Workers Survey (NAWS) 2019–2020: A Demographic and Employment Profile of United States Farmworkers," Research Report No. 16, JBS International, January 2022, www.dol.gov/sites/dolgov/files/ETA/naws/pdfs/NAWS%20Research%20Report%2016.pdf.

[15] US Department of Labor, "Findings from the National Agricultural Workers Survey"; and Aguirre International, "The California Farm Labor Force Overview and Trends from the National Agricultural Workers Survey," www.alrb.ca.gov/wp-content/uploads/sites/196/2018/05/CalifFarmLaborForceNAWS.pdf, 21.

[16] Charlene Galarneau, "Farm Labor, Reproductive Justice: Migrant Women Farmworkers in the US," *Health and Human Rights* 15, no. 1 (2013): 144–160, 146, www.hhrjournal.org/wp-content/uploads/sites/2469/2013/08/Galarneau-FINAL.pdf, citing Aguirre International, "The California Farm Labor Force Overview," 21.

These and other demographic forces combine to create particularly challenging socioeconomic and cultural situations for women migrants in the agricultural world. Thus, when we examine the difficulties faced by these women, it is imperative to adopt an intersectional approach. Such a method demands that we ask not simply what violations exist against individual migrant women but also what intersecting *structural* forces operate to threaten justice for these same workers. As theologian Jeremy Cruz claimed in the wake of the 2022 *Dobbs v. Jackson Women's Health Organization* decision, we must analyze "the complex and evolving intersections of social conditions that diminish and destroy life in uniquely gendered, classed, and racially disparate ways."[17] Further, beyond gender, race, and class *per se* is the category of immigration, since residency status itself—and what some have termed the "crimmigration" of migrant populations—functions as a major determinant of precarity in the US workplace.[18] The existence of such structural forces of violence means that any proposed interventions will need to adopt a lens that is both broad and nuanced, one that is truly intersectional.

Reproductive Justice as a New Lens

Reproductive justice, with its explicitly intersectional nature, is well-suited to such an analysis. Reproductive justice is usually articulated in terms of three general goals, framed as human rights: the right to have a child, the right not to have a child, and the right to raise children in safe and healthy environments.[19] In doing so, it shifts the locus of conversation away from

---

[17] Jeremy V. Cruz, "Avoiding Ethical and Social Conflict about Access to Abortion Care," Catholic Theological Ethics in the World Church, Forum Blog, July 1, 2022, catholicethics.com/forum/access-to-abortion-care/.

[18] Salina Abji and Lindsay Larios, "Migrant Justice as Reproductive Justice: Birthright Citizenship and the Politics of Immigration Detention for Pregnant Women in Canada," *Citizenship Studies* 25, no. 2 (2021): 253–272, doi.org/10.1080/13621025.2020.1859186.

[19] Loretta J. Ross and Rickie Solinger, *Reproductive Justice: An Introduction* (Oakland: University of California Press, 2017), 9.

a narrow emphasis on the individual choice to access abortion, instead highlighting the broader context of childbearing/childrearing and an interpretation of justice that is laser-focused on the concrete realities of society's most vulnerable populations. Advocates of reproductive justice maintain that women cannot make meaningful choices about whether or not to have children if they lack the resources and supports necessary to raise children *well*. They therefore insist on examining the material contexts in which women have, or do not have, children.[20] The emphasis thus expands beyond individual vulnerabilities to structural ones, for instance, the effects on marginalized communities of white supremacy, settler colonialism, global capitalism, patriarchy, and heterosexism.

To be sure, the right *not* to have a child is ordinarily interpreted to include the right to access safe (and legal) abortion. Moreover, women with greater financial resources are far more likely to be able to circumvent legal restrictions on abortion for unwanted pregnancies than are working class and impoverished women. Thus, the burden of restricted access to abortion falls disproportionately on those women and girls who are already most vulnerable. Sometimes this restricted access takes place in ways directly targeting immigrants. For example, the US government has repeatedly taken steps to prevent undocumented minors from accessing abortion. In 2017, under the Trump administration, the Office of Refugee and Resettlement instituted a blanket ban on abortion access for minors in its custody—even in the case of rape.[21] This is a troubling reality on its own, but it is even more problematic when considered alongside the high incidence of sexual violence that takes place within immigration detention

---

[20] Lonergan, "Reproductive Justice and Migrant Women," 28, citing Dorothy Roberts, "Punishing Drug Addicts Who Have Babies: Women of Color, Equality and the Right of Privacy," in *Abortion Wars: A Half Century of Struggle, 1950–2000*, ed. Rickie Solinger (Berkeley, California and London: University of California Press, 1998).

[21] Ariella J. Messing, Rachel E. Fabi, and Joanne D. Rosen, "Reproductive Injustice at the US Border," *American Journal of Public Health* 110, no. 3 (2020): 339–344, 341.

centers.[22] In this context, abortion bans have been used in an especially unjust fashion, as a tool of immigration enforcement to punish and deter future migrants, as well as to reinscribe the deep sexual injustices that already characterize women immigrants' reality.

However, we must be quick to remember that the concept of reproductive justice goes far beyond abortion access. The right *not* to have a child encompasses comprehensive sex education and access to contraception. The right *to* have a child includes the ability to initiate and continue pregnancy safely, accessing necessary maternal and fetal health resources, including prenatal care. The right to parent in safe and healthy environments mandates adequate maternal and infant postnatal care; but it also requires practices and policies that oppose family separation and the mistreatment of children and families, as well as the housing, education, and safe working conditions that protect and benefit women and children. As Leandra Hinojosa Hernández and Sarah De Los Santos Upton summarize, "reproductive violence does not manifest solely in restrictions to abortion; rather, from a Reproductive Justice perspective, reproductive *injustice* at the Mexico-US border manifests through child abuse, maternal abuse, family separation, the restriction of necessary medical practices, and violence against *all* women and families."[23] This more holistic approach demands that we move the conversation beyond an analysis of abortion itself and think more systemically about why women might be driven to seek out abortions in the first place.

---

[22] Human Rights Watch, "Detained and at Risk: Sexual Abuse and Harassment in United States Immigration Detention," August 25, 2010, www.hrw.org/report/2010/08/25/detained-and-risk/sexual-abuse-and-harassment-united-states-immigration-detention. See also Human Rights Watch, "US Records Show Physical, Sexual Abuse at Border," October 21, 2021, www.hrw.org/news/2021/10/21/us-records-show-physical-sexual-abuse-border.

[23] Leandra Hinojosa Hernández and Sarah De Los Santos Upton, "Migrant Gender Violence, Reproductive Health, and the Intersections of Reproductive Justice and Health Communication," in *Communicating Intimate Health*, ed. Angela Cooke-Jackson and Valerie Rubinsky (London: Rowman & Littlefield, 2021), 201–210, 203.

Reproductive Justice and Migrant Farmworker Women

In a 2013 article published in *Health and Human Rights*, ethicist Charlene Galarneau relates firsthand the story of Luz, a teenager working in the Colorado fields who procured an abortion for an unexpected pregnancy. Galarneau describes:

> Summer 1978 in rural Colorado: Luz was 14 years old, working in the melon fields, and pregnant. . . . Family poverty meant that Luz had little choice about working in low wage and relatively dangerous fieldwork without health insurance during summer months and some school weeks. She did not learn about sexuality, reproduction, or contraception in school, from her family, or from the health care provider she occasionally visited. She did not understand how pregnancy occurred until after she was pregnant. An evening migrant education program for teen workers included bilingual (Spanish-English) health screenings and meant that Luz had access to pregnancy testing. Luz and her mother agreed on Luz's decision to end her pregnancy but withheld her pregnancy from Luz's father for fear of his reaction. The unusual presence that summer of a student health worker team with a mandate to expand health care services to migrant farmworkers meant that Luz had reproductive options beyond those typically available. That said, the services that Luz needed cost money and were three hours away by car. She had no money, no car, and no time off from work. This situation imperiled Luz's physical and mental health and constrained her ability to make healthy decisions about her body and her reproduction. . . . Certainly, Luz benefited from reproductive health and rights efforts that had helped make abortion legal and supported the presence of women's reproductive health clinics. That said, these efforts did not enable Luz to prevent her unwanted pregnancy.[24]

---

[24] Galarneau, "Farm Labor, Reproductive Justice."

It is unclear in this account whether Luz was an immigrant to the US. However, born domestically or abroad, her story resonates with those of countless other young farmworker women who face poverty, lack of health care, and a lack of meaningful and empowering information about pregnancy and childbirth. A minor herself, Luz is still very much subject to the support (or lack thereof) of her own mother and father. It is misguided to imagine that the sole relevant concern for Luz is her personal choice to have an abortion or even whether she has access to abortion services.

To begin with, the family poverty in which Luz is enmeshed is the norm for farmworkers.[25] In 2020, the mean personal income of US farmworkers was between $20,000 and $24,999, and 8 percent of workers earned less than $10,000 per year. Migrant and undocumented farmworkers were far more likely to have family incomes below the federal poverty level than "settled" or authorized workers.[26] While exact breakdowns by gender are difficult to find, women are at an additional disadvantage, as they are in most sectors of society. Farmworker wages are often paid in piecemeal fashion, benefiting those of greater physical strength—ordinarily men. In another first-person account, Lucrecia, an immigrant from Oaxaca who spent her entire life picking strawberries, describes how picking expectations have shifted over the course of her own life: "The regular box rate was $1.25, the little box was $1 and the two-pound box was $1.50. If I was able to fill 40 boxes, it was a good day. The younger faster men can pick 70 or 80 boxes a day. . . . The foremen now choose workers who can pick 100 to 130 boxes per day."[27] To complicate the financial picture further, women who have immigrated illegally to the US across its

---

[25] Kate Ward, in her essay in the present volume, "Never Just a Choice: Three Theoretical Approaches to Economic Constraints on Family Formation," 55–89, discusses the ways that economic constraints undermine reproductive flourishing more broadly.

[26] US Department of Labor, "Findings from the National Agricultural Workers Survey," 41, 43.

[27] Farmworker Justice, "Stories from the Field," www.farmworkerjustice.org/stories-from-the-field/.

southern border are more likely to have debts incurred from using the services of a "coyote"—a paid smuggler to usher them across the US-Mexico border. This of course results in additional financial burden, not to mention a high level of personal and physical vulnerability.

Directly connected to women's elevated poverty is an egregious absence of access to adequate health care, including reproductive health care. Generally speaking, farmworkers in the US are sicker than other groups. As physician and medical anthropologist Seth M. Holmes highlights, "these health disparities fall along citizenship, ethnicity, and class lines."[28] Like most farmworkers, Luz lacks health insurance as well as the financial and logistical means to obtain regular health care. In fact, the 1999 California Agricultural Worker Health Survey found that farmworkers and their families had the worst access to health care in the entire state.[29] For undocumented farmworkers, even the adoption in 2010 of the Affordable Care Act (ACA) did little to improve access since the ACA explicitly excludes undocumented persons from its coverage. Notoriously high barriers to Medicaid—including the need to reregister when migrants move around from place to place—and the increasingly common closure of community and low-cost health clinics such as Planned Parenthood translate into dramatically reduced access to reproductive health care, including prenatal health care, for migrant women. Further, the 1976 passage of the Hyde Amendment ensured that while abortion services may have remained legal nationwide until 2022, in most cases only those with private health insurance or the ability to pay out of pocket were actually able to access them. Beyond restricted abortion access, the lack of access to health insurance more generally has meant that migrant farmworker women experience lower access to prenatal care, higher rates of maternal

---

[28] Holmes, *Fresh Fruit, Broken Bodies*, 99.

[29] Margaret Reeves, Terra Murphy, and Teresa Calvo Morales, *Farmworker Women and Pesticides in California's Central Valley*, joint report by Pesticide Action Network North America, United Farmworkers of America AFL-CIO, and Organización en California de Líderes Campesinas (San Francisco: Pesticide Action Network, 2003).

mortality, stillbirth and early neonatal death, and increased incidence of postpartum depression.[30] These health challenges do not end at birth but rather potentially result in developmental challenges for born children—and thus long-term struggles for farmworker families.

It is not only the lack of health insurance that leads to poor access to reproductive health care, however. Gendered access to education and other practical hurdles often disempower girls and women from a young age, with reproductive consequences. Indeed, as Holmes describes for some Mexican indigenous communities, "Due to the assumed role dichotomy . . . between the private, domestic sphere for women and the public sphere for men, women have fewer opportunities for education."[31] As in the case of Luz, low education levels, a lack of information, and poor English (or sometimes even Spanish) skills can deeply compromise migrant farmworker women's ability to access supports for their reproductive health or even to understand the science behind pregnancy itself. Among Latino/a people more generally, Spanish-dominant and immigrant workers (particularly undocumented ones) have a higher health risk profile than English-dominant, domestic-born workers.[32] Further, a lack of cultural competency among health care workers can manifest as misunderstanding of, and intolerance for, indigenous practices in medicine, which may negatively impact both overall and reproductive

---

[30] Hinojosa Hernández and De Los Santos Upton, "Migrant Gender Violence," citing Lily Daniel, "Reproductive Rights Endangered at the Mexico-United States Border," *Urban Legend News*, May 4, 2019, www.urbanlegendnews.org/features/2019/05/04/reproductive-rights-endangered-at-the-mexico-united-states-border/, and citing Daniel Gonzales, "28 Women May Have Miscarried in ICE Custody over the Past 2 Years," *AZ Central*, February 27, 2019, www.azcentral.com/story/news/politics/immigration/2019/02/27/28-women-may-have-miscarried-ice-custody-over-past-2-years/2996486002/; Almeida, Caldas, Ayres-de-Campos, Salcedo-Barrientos, and Dias, "Maternal Healthcare in Migrants," 1346.

[31] Holmes, *Fresh Fruit, Broken Bodies*, 86.

[32] Almeida, Caldas, Ayres-de-Campos, Salcedo-Barrientos, and Dias, "Maternal Healthcare in Migrants"; Patricia Zavella, "Contesting Structural Vulnerability Through Reproductive Justice Activism with Latina Immigrants in California," *North American Dialogue* 19, no. 1 (2016): 36–45.

health.³³ Cultural taboos and shame about sex and the body can also contribute to misinformation among young women such as Luz, leaving them ill-prepared to avoid unwanted pregnancy.³⁴ Finally, a simple lack of transportation and the inability to take time off of work to get to health care facilities means that many migrant farmworker women like Luz find it close to impossible to physically access health care, even when that care is technically available to them.

This compromised access to reproductive health care directly translates into material precarity for these women. Ideological opposition to contraception and abortion aside, the inability to have a predictable measure of control over one's fertility—and the resulting higher rates of unintended pregnancy—further deepens inequality. As psychologists Nancy Felipe Russo and Julia R. Steinberg argue, "the interconnections between women's ability to control reproduction and their ability to take advantage of educational and employment opportunities means that reproductive rights provide a basis to attain the related rights of health, equality, and nondiscrimination, among others. . . . The interconnecting web of reproductive rights with other human rights means that disparities in reproductive justice can undermine efforts to achieve social and economic equality for women, particularly for poor women."³⁵

Beyond inadequate access to reproductive health care, what other components of well-being does a reproductive justice lens direct us to examine? This more holistic and interconnected approach asks us to consider the impact of housing and working conditions on the

---

[33] For a fuller discussion of the role of cultural competency in health care, see the materials on Santa Clara University's Markkula Center for Applied Ethics website: Karen Peterson-Iyer, "Culturally Competent Care in US Clinical Health Care Settings," www.scu.edu/ethics/focus-areas/bioethics/resources/culturally-competent-care/, and more specific to Latino communities, "Culturally Competent Care for Latino Patients," www.scu.edu/ethics/focus-areas/bioethics/resources/culturally-competent-care/culturally-competent-care-for-latino-patients/.

[34] Zavella, "Contesting Structural Vulnerability."

[35] Nancy Felipe Russo and Julia R. Steinberg, "Contraception and Abortion: Critical Tools for Achieving Reproductive Justice," in *Reproductive Justice: A Global Concern*, ed. Joan C. Chrisler (Santa Barbara, CA: Praeger, 2012), 145–171, 145.

reproductive decision making of farmworker women. Farmworker housing in the US is notorious for its poor quality. Many farms house their workers in overcrowded, dilapidated, unsanitary, and otherwise substandard employer-owned housing, often located far from town centers and community services.[36] Lucrecia (referenced above) describes the high degree of overcrowding she personally experienced: "If you want to get ahead here, you have to live in cramped quarters. Here, the rich even have rooms for their pets, but we have no room for ourselves. When we first moved here, there were about twenty people living in this house. Now that my kids have moved on, there are ten now. We needed to share the cost of rent as much as we could."[37] Indeed, in June 2018, the California Institute for Rural Studies concluded that for the Pajaro and Salinas valley alone, a full 45,560 units of farmworker housing would be needed in order to alleviate "critical overcrowding in farmworker households."[38] For migrant families, the burden is particularly heavy for women, who frequently are in charge of the repeated set-ups of new short-term households as migrants must move around to access work opportunities.[39]

Conditions at the workplace itself do not fare much better. The overall poor working conditions in most fields—the backbreaking nature of the work, poor field sanitation, and inadequate safety measures—are widely known. Lesser discussed, however, are the particular burdens that these conditions place upon women. The prolonged standing, bending, dehydration, and general exertion of farm work can entail serious outcomes for pregnant women—including premature labor, miscarriage,

---

[36] See Peterson-Iyer, "Human Trafficking, Coercion, and Moral Agency in Agricultural Labor," *Theological Studies* 83, no. 2 (2022): 245–270, 248.

[37] Farmworker Justice, "Stories from the Field."

[38] California Institute for Rural Studies, *Farmworker Housing Study and Action Plan for Salinas Valley and Pajaro Valley*, June 2018, www.cityofsalinas.org/sites/default/files/departments_files/community_development_files/farmworker_housing_study.saslinas-pajaro.june_15-2018.complete.pdf, ii.

[39] Galarneau, "Farm Labor, Reproductive Justice," 149.

or neonatal death.[40] Further, a lack of easy access to toilets—a frequent complaint in farm work—has a disproportionate impact upon women and especially pregnant women, who are subject to more frequent urinary tract and kidney infections.[41] In a similar vein, the piecemeal nature of the work disincentivizes all workers from walking long distances to use toilet facilities, but this places a heavy burden on women relative to men because of cultural taboos surrounding public urination.[42] Physical challenges such as these, dangerous for any laborer, are particularly disastrous for pregnant women.

Adjacent to these physical dangers are the notorious sexual harassment and abuse that women farm laborers face on a routine basis. Intimate partner violence—sometimes fueled by substance abuse—and the health problems that stem from it are alarmingly high in farmworker communities.[43] In the workplace of the fields, the problem is endemic. Between 80 and 90 percent of women working in California's Central

---

[40] Galarneau, "Farm Labor, Reproductive Justice"; Farmworker Justice Fund, *Farmworker Women Speak Out* (Washington, DC: Farmworker Justice Fund, 1994).

[41] Galarneau, "Farm Labor, Reproductive Justice"; Farmworker Justice Fund, *Farmworker Women Speak Out*; and Julia L. Perilla, Astrid H. Wilson, and Judith L. Wold, "Listening to Migrant Voices: Focus Groups on Health Issues in South Georgia," *Journal of Community Health Nursing* 15, no. 4 (1998): 251–263.

[42] Rosalind P. Petchesky, "Human Rights, Reproductive Health and Economic Justice: Why They Are Indivisible," *Reproductive Health Matters* 8, no. 15 (2000): 12–17.

[43] Lisa R. Fortuna, Carmen Rosa Noroña, Michelle V. Porche, Cathi Tillman, Pratima A. Patil, Ye Wang, Sheri Lapatin Markle, and Margarita Alegría, "Trauma, Immigration, and Sexual Health among Latina Women: Implications for Maternal-Child Well-Being and Reproductive Justice," *Infant Mental Health Journal* 40, no. 5 (2019): 640–658, doi.org/10.1002/imhj.21805; Jonathan B. Wilson, Damon L. Rappleyea, Jennifer L. Hodgson, Tana L. Hall, and Mark B. White, "Intimate Partner Violence Screening Among Migrant/Seasonal Farmworker Women and Healthcare: A Policy Brief," *Journal of Community Health* 39 (2014): 372–377, doi.org/10.1007/s10900-013-9772-z; and Nikki R. Van Hightower, Joe Gorton, and Casey Lee DeMoss, "Predictive Models of Domestic Violence and Fear of Intimate Partners Among Migrant and Seasonal Farm Worker Women," *Journal of Family Violence* 15, no. 2 (2000): doi.org/10.1023/A:1007538810858. See also Keiko A. Budech, "Missing Voices, Hidden Fields: The Gendered Struggles of Female Farmworkers," *Pitzer Senior Theses*, paper 54, scholarship.claremont.edu/pitzer_theses/54.

Valley have reported experiencing sexual harassment, compared with 50 percent in the US workforce more generally.[44] Lucrecia notes her own observations in this regard:

> As a woman working in the fields, if you didn't have a good foreman, you were treated badly. . . . I've also heard complaints by other farmworker women of being sexually harassed. Sometimes women don't want to speak up. There are a lot who have lived through it, but are afraid to say something for fear that they'll be reported to immigration officials. When I was young, I had a foreman who always sought out women to be alone with. He told me he liked me, but I told him I knew he had a wife and mistress. He told me that if I let him do what he wanted to me, I would still have a job. If not, I needed to look for another job.[45]

Sexual harassment and abuse are perpetrated by foremen, supervisors, owners, and even other laborers. Their consequences extend far beyond the fear that they engender; injury, sexually transmitted infections, unplanned pregnancy, substance use, mental health deterioration, and PTSD all potentially result from these forms of abuse.[46] The reality of sexual violence therefore reaches far beyond the immediate harm it perpetrates; it deeply impacts the reproductive lives of farmworker women over time. Thus, to fail to consider it would be to miss an important aspect of what reproductive justice demands altogether.

---

[44] Kristin Heyer, "Familismo Across the Americas: En Route to a Liberating Christian Family Ethic," in *Living With(out) Borders: Catholic Theological Ethics on the Migrations of Peoples*, ed. Agnes M. Brazal and Mary Teresa Davila (Maryknoll, NY: Orbis Books, 2016), 121–131, citing Irma Morales Waugh, "Examining the Sexual Harassment Experiences of Mexican Immigrant Farmworking Women," *Violence Against Women* 16, no. 3 (March 2010): 237–61; Galarneau, "Farm Labor, Reproductive Justice"; see also *Frontline*, season 2013, episode 11, "Rape in the Fields," produced by Andrés Cediel and Lowell Bergman, June 25, 2013.

[45] Farmworker Justice, "Stories from the Field."

[46] Human Rights Watch, *Cultivating Fear: The Vulnerability of Immigrant Farmworkers in the US to Sexual Violence and Sexual Harassment* (Human Rights Watch, 2012), www.hrw.org/report/2012/05/15/cultivating-fear/vulnerability-immigrant-farmworkers-us-sexual-violence-and, esp. 41–46.

Again, most if not all of these struggles are deepened for undocumented immigrants. Even the process of immigration itself is fraught with unique dangers for women. Punitive deportation policies in the US have tended to force migrants to use increasingly isolated routes to enter the US, and rape has become so prevalent along those routes that many women straightforwardly consider it the price one pays for crossing the border.[47] For women who do manage to cross the border but are subsequently detained, further mistreatment awaits. US border detention facilities have been accused of providing inadequate prenatal care to pregnant women and exposing them to elevated miscarriage risks, refusing detained women their necessary gynecological care, forcibly sterilizing detained women, and even shackling pregnant women while giving birth. If true, these all represent examples of state failure to provide the conditions of reproductive justice to these immigrant women.[48] Indeed, some immigration scholars have concluded that the specific mistreatment of pregnant women and families with children is a targeted strategy by the US immigration system to punish and deter future migrants.[49]

Even those undocumented women who are not detained at the border routinely endure a high degree of exploitation once working. The fear of deportation or simply of not having a job the next season haunts many

---

[47] To give but one example, some estimate that 80–90 percent of migrant women have suffered sexual violence in the process of crossing. See Guadalupe Correa-Cabrera and Michelle Keck, "A Dangerous Journey to the US and a 'New Deal' for Migrant Women and Girls," *Brown Journal of World Affairs* 28, no. 2 (2022), bjwa.brown.edu/28-2/a-dangerous-journey-to-the-u-s-and-a-new-deal-for-migrant-women-and-girls/, 4.

[48] Brittany R. Leach, "At the Borders of the Body Politic: Fetal Citizens, Pregnant Migrants, and Reproductive Injustices in Immigration Detention," *American Political Science Review* 116, no. 1 (2022): 116–130, 116, citing American Civil Liberties Union, "Joint Complaint on ICE Detention and Treatment of Pregnant Women," September 26, 2017, www.womensrefugeecommission.org/research-resources/joint-complaint-ice-detention-treatment-of-pregnant-women/, and citing Southern Poverty Law Center, "Trapped, with No End in Sight: A Detained Mother's Struggle to Get Home," February 8, 2019, www.splcenter.org/attention-on-detention/trapped-no-end-sight-detained-mother%E2%80%99s-struggle-get-home.

[49] Messing, Fabi, and Rosen, "Reproductive Injustice."

undocumented farmworker women (and men) and keeps them from reporting mistreatment. The situation is particularly bad for those who migrate from place to place. According to Brinton M. Lykes, many protections ordinarily available to women and girls who live in stable environments—protections such as social services, supportive family structures, and various cultural supports—are not available to migrants.[50]

Of course, reproductive justice in the fullest sense entails not just access to reproductive health care and the remediation of poverty, poor housing, and dangerous treatment and working conditions for women of reproductive age. The third prong of reproductive justice—the right to raise children in a safe and healthy environment—widens our gaze even further to the health and safety conditions of farmworkers' children. In the above example, Luz, who is still a child herself, is certainly not well-equipped to raise a child of her own. As Galarneau notes, childcare is "virtually never an employment benefit of agricultural work, and thus farmworker children either work in the fields, 'play' around the fields while their parents work, or are cared for at home by grandmothers, aunts, or siblings."[51] Thus care for any children Luz may bear would likely fall to her older female relatives, who themselves are likely to be ill-equipped to provide full-time childcare in this way. Even once children are themselves older, the financial burdens are likely to continue. Lucrecia, for instance, describes the added expense she incurred by the need to ensure that her older children were able to attend school.

> I brought my oldest daughter and son with me, and the three of us worked [in the strawberry fields]. They would get out of school in June

---

[50] Brinton M. Lykes, "No Easy Road to Freedom: Engendering and Enculturating Forced Migration," in *Driven from Home: Protecting the Rights of Forced Migrants* (Washington, DC: Georgetown University Press, 2010). See also Hightower, Gorton, and Dem "Predictive Models of Domestic Violence." See also Hightower, Gorton, and DeMoss, "Predictive Models of Domestic Violence and Fear of Intimate Partners Among Migrant and Seasonal Farm Worker Women."

[51] Galarneau, "Farm Labor, Reproductive Justice," 148.

and worked July and August with me to earn money for their school clothes. They went back to school the 15th of September, so they worked with me 40 days. I would bring them back to start school, which is why I couldn't just leave my other apartment. I'd pay $775 rent for my children to stay near their school and then $600 for myself in another town where I was working. I never had any money left after that, but I had to do it.[52]

To complicate matters further, high exposure to pesticides poses an enormous health risk for both farm laborers and their children. Pesticides are responsible not only for high cancer rates and other diseases but also for birth defects, infertility, menstrual dysfunction, and spontaneous abortion.[53] It is likely that women farmworkers have even greater pesticide exposure than men since they are exposed both in the fields and in the home, via cleaning products as well as residual pesticides that settle in indoor spaces. Children are not free from this even in the school setting. Beginning in 1999, a series of lawsuits were raised against the US Environmental Protection Agency, calling for larger buffer zones and tighter restrictions to protect schoolchildren from the harmful effects of pesticide use in farmworker communities throughout California.[54] Together, harmful conditions such as these (lack of affordable childcare, lack of access to decent schools, and disproportionate exposure to dangerous pesticides) directly threaten the health and safety of farmworker women and children and thus directly threaten reproductive justice.

---

[52] Farmworker Justice, "Stories from the Field."
[53] Reeves, Murphy, and Morales, *Farmworker Women and Pesticides*.
[54] Sara Rubin, "Latino Families Sue EPA, Seeking Environmental Justice for Exposure to Pesticides," *Monterey County Weekly*, September 19, 2013, www.montereycountyweekly.com/news/local_news/latino-families-sue-epa-seeking-environmental-justice-for-exposure-to-pesticides/article_5a8692bc-209d-11e3-8231-001a4bcf6878.html; and Talia Buford, "In California, an Unsatisfying Settlement on Pesticide-Spraying," *The Center for Public Integrity*, August 11, 2015, publicintegrity.org/environment/pollution/environmental-justice-denied/in-california-an-unsatisfying-settlement-on-pesticide-spraying/.

Once again, the health and safety burden is even greater on immigrant children who cross the United States' southern border without documentation. Since the early 2010s, most migrants apprehended at this border are families or unaccompanied minors, primarily from Central America.[55] The burden on these families and minors shot up during the years of the Trump administration, when new policies of family separation at the border resulted in thousands of children being separated from their parents and detained for prolonged periods of time in unsafe, prison-like conditions.[56] Accounts proliferated of nursing babies being taken from their mothers and migrant children being transferred to foster care—often never to be reunited with their families.[57] While this horrendous situation was certainly not limited to farmworker communities, the high percentage of farmworkers who are themselves undocumented immigrants means that it is impossible to separate the health and safety of farmworker families from heinous border practices such as these.

Catholic Social Teaching and Justice for Farmworkers

What does Catholic ethics have to contribute to this conversation? Traditionally, Catholic ethics—particularly as it has been engaged in by

---

[55] Correa-Cabrera and Keck, "A Dangerous Journey."

[56] Messing, Fabi, and Rosen, "Reproductive Injustice."

[57] Hinojosa Hernández and De Los Santos Upton, "Migrant Gender Violence," 203, citing Tom Barnes, "US Officials Took Baby Daughter from Mother While She Breastfed in Immigration Detention Centre, Says Attorney," *Independent*, June 14, 2018; see also Leandra Hinojosa Hernández and Sarah De Los Santos Upton, "Critical Health Communication Methods at the US-Mexico Border: Violence Against Migrant Women and the Role of Health Activism," *Frontiers in Communication* 4, no. 34 (2019): 3, citing Dara Lind, "Hundreds of Families Are Still Being Separated at the Border," *Vox*, February 21, 2019, www.vox.com/2019/2/21/18234767/parents-separated-children-families-border-trump-jails; and Leandra Hinojosa Hernández, "Feminist Approaches to Border Studies and Gender Violence: Family Separation as Reproductive Injustice," *Women's Studies in Communication* 42, no. 2 (2019): 130–134, 132, citing Dara Lind, "Trump's DHS Is Using an Extremely Dubious Statistic to Justify Splitting Up Families at the Border," *Vox*, May 8, 2018, www.vox.com/policy-and-politics/2018/5/8/17327512/sessions-illegal-immigration-border-asylum-families.

the Roman Catholic magisterium—has placed a disproportionate emphasis on opposing abortion as *the* defining feature of reproductive ethics. Yet the struggles of farmworker women bring into sharp relief just how impoverished such an approach is. To return to the case of Luz, a narrow focus on the ethics of abortion causes us to miss the root causes and central features of her reproductive struggle: her lack of knowledge and information about pregnancy itself, the grinding poverty that deprived her of both quality education and health insurance, the logistical hurdles that stood between her and adequate health care, a culture that led others to assume free access to her sexualized body, and the challenges to mental health that likely kept her from strong sexual decision making. In addition, if Luz herself is an undocumented immigrant, the fear of deportation would compound all of these problems and place Luz in an even more precarious position vis-à-vis her own and her family's well-being. To ponder abortion and emphasize only the innocent fetus inside of Luz, in isolation from this broader context, is to miss essential components of her concrete reality.

In fact, on many social matters, including those most directly pertinent to agricultural labor, Catholic teaching has a long history of avoiding this sort of narrowly-focused thinking. The history of Catholic labor ethics reveals a framework that digs much deeper than the immediate struggles of poverty and labor rights violations that characterize farm labor; rather, CST at its best frames work itself as an enactment of human dignity and an opportunity to participate meaningfully in the common good.[58] The insistence on a living wage and access to a dignified livelihood are absolutely central to the Catholic understanding and are framed as matters of *justice*, not charity. Thus, the focus here is not simplistically on the struggling individual but also on the systemic and structural issues that pave the way toward those struggles in the first place. Moreover, Catholic thought generally rejects an abstract economic approach to labor ethics,

---

[58] For further discussion of these themes, see Peterson-Iyer, "Human Trafficking, Coercion, and Moral Agency," 260–265.

one that isolates markets from their political and social context; rather, it insists "that economic processes be evaluated in connection to their embodied, material bases and consequences."[59]

This dialectical focus serves as a holistic expression of solidarity. As Catholic ethicist Christine Firer Hinze describes, solidarity "bespeaks individuals' and communities' duties to take appropriate responsibility for the micro- and macro-relations and interdependencies that enmesh them."[60] Alertness to the dynamics of power relations and group identities thus necessarily contributes to Catholic social policy regarding labor. For example, a historical survey of Catholic thought reveals strong support for labor unions and worker cooperatives as tools for everyday workers struggling against systemic injustice. Indeed, the framing of labor ethics as partially a matter of addressing *social structures of sin* spotlights the injustices faced by those who work and live on society's lower economic rungs. Although that power analysis arguably could and should be deepened and made more robust—particularly when it comes to the category of gender—its very existence within Catholic labor ethics indicates a structural sensibility that is, by contrast, lacking when it comes to *re*productive (vs. productive) labor.

In a similar way, Catholic teaching regarding immigration commonly takes a structural, and often markedly radical, posture. In the US, the bishops' 2003 *Strangers No Longer* describes in detail the plight of immigrants to the US from across the US-Mexico border. This document stresses not simply the struggles of individuals but rather the social structures and laws that are largely responsible for those struggles and which might ultimately be used to address them. Here, the church takes a human rights orientation towards migrants while simultaneously highlighting the root causes of migration; it also promotes the rights of refugees and asylum seekers to be reunited with their families, to a

---

[59] Christine Firer Hinze, *Glass Ceilings and Dirt Floors: Women, Work, and the Global Economy* (New York: Paulist Press, 2015), 39.

[60] Christine Firer Hinze, *Radical Sufficiency: Work, Livelihood, and a US Catholic Economic Ethic* (Washington, DC: Georgetown University Press, 2021), 65.

dignified occupation, and to a just, living wage (nos. 31, 34, 35, and 42). Connecting immigration today to the liberation of the Israelites by God in the Hebrew Bible, the bishops insist that the ensuing command to "befriend the alien" be interpreted not merely as a "personal exhortation" but rather as itself structured into Israel's legal system—even as it should be structured into the US legal system, today (no. 25).

Finally, and of great importance to the topic of reproductive justice, the Catholic tradition emphasizes the centrality of family life as a basic human good and as absolutely critical to human identity. Indeed, as Catholic ethicist Kristin Heyer argues, families "comprise our most intimate relationships such that protracted separation threatens our human subjectivity."[61] In other words, human identity itself is intimately bound up with our familial relationships, and a threat to those relationships is inseparable from a threat to the integrity of the human person. Perhaps this is part of the reason that the heinous "zero tolerance" immigration policies of 2018, resulting in the forcible separation of parents from their children and the brutal caging of large numbers of those children at the US-Mexico border, engendered such widespread anger across the US.[62] Sadly, mistreatment of children at the border is not new; the US bishops criticized analogous (though less widespread) mistreatment fifteen years earlier as "shameful," insisting, "Because of their heightened vulnerability, unaccompanied minors require special consideration and care" (*Strangers No Longer*, no. 82).

Yet, at the same time, Catholic understandings of family and reproduction have tended to incorporate unhelpful and essentialist characterizations of gender complementarity and reductive portrayals of motherhood as women's feminine "genius." A focus on self-gift as women's "special" and natural contribution vis-à-vis parenthood

---

[61] Heyer, "Familismo," 124.
[62] Nomaan Merchant, "Hundreds of children wait in Border Patrol Facility in Texas," June 18, 2018, apnews.com/article/mcallen-texas-border-patrols-ap-top-news-us-news-9794de32d39d4c6f89fbefaea3780769.

reinforces a sanitized version of motherhood, one that effectively bypasses the material precarity of real, live farmworker women—mothers or not.[63] As Heyer points out, such problematic views function to legitimize unjust domestic caregiving arrangements and obscure the real yet unpaid work that women perform domestically.[64] Indeed, Hinze argues at length that the social critique embedded within Catholic labor ethics does not extend far enough in its analysis of gender and gender's relation to caring labor. Women—farmworkers or not—are responsible for a disproportionately high proportion of the caring work (both paid and unpaid) of modern life. And that work of care tends to be poorly remunerated and carry lower social status, thereby increasing women's economic vulnerability.[65]

Such gendered short-sightedness, combined with the related, narrowly conceived opposition to abortion as the moral *sine qua non* of reproductive ethics, leads Catholic reflection about the reproductive struggles of women—including migrant farmworker women—to fall woefully short. What is needed instead is the more expansive and probing focus on root causes and systemic injustices which more often characterizes other aspects of Catholic ethics. Here is where Catholic thought would do well to take a page out of the reproductive justice playbook. Rather than narrowing in on abortion *per se*, Catholic ethics must widen its reproductive lens to incorporate the components of reproductive justice described above: sexuality education, health care access, safe housing, and freedom from poverty, gendered violence, and the fear created by unjust immigration policies. Indeed, these categories fit well with the more holistic approach that characterizes much of Catholic thought on labor and immigration ethics. If the elaboration of human dignity in the context of the common good is to include the holistic reproductive well-being of migrant farmworker women such as Luz, it must in solidarity call for pathways to live a safe and empowered life in

---

[63] See, for example, John Paul II, *Mulieris Dignitatem* ("On the Dignity and Vocation of Women on the Occasion of the Marian Year").

[64] Heyer, "Familismo," 125.

[65] Hinze, *Glass Ceilings and Dirt Floors*, esp. 97–101.

which women do not find themselves facing unwanted pregnancies in the first place. In the final part of this essay, I offer some preliminary suggestions for concrete policies that such an approach might entail.

Joining the Issues: Suggestions for Change

Speaking from the Brazilian context, Catholic sister Ivone Gebara has argued against an approach to reproductive choice that focuses only on the moral principles embedded in narrow analysis of abortion itself. Gebara maintains that such an analysis has a very different meaning for poor women than rich women. She poses, "Moral principles are important, but what does any principle mean when today, at this moment, you are pregnant and you have nothing to nourish your three or four children already birthed? What does a moral principle mean when a woman is coerced by her partner to have an abortion, to choose between him and the as-yet-unformed child? What does it mean to honor a principle when you face the threat of the loss of your job because you are pregnant?"[66] Gebara's incisive questions direct us away from a constricted individualistic posture, to attend more fully to the concrete reality of women's lives—particularly those women laboring on the lowest rungs of the socioeconomic ladder. In our own US context, there can be no doubt that this includes migrant farmworker women. Attending to these women's concrete reality means attending to the matter of abortion *always and only* within a broader set of proposals promoting social structures that support their well-being and that of their children after birth. Along these same lines, theologian Thia Cooper insists that long before arriving at the matter of abortion, "we need first to move toward making sure our structures choose life, that they prioritize the lives of those already with us."[67]

---

[66] Ivone Gebara, "The Abortion Debate in Brazil: A Report from an Ecofeminist Philosopher Under Siege," *Journal of Feminist Studies in Religion* 11, no. 2 (1995): 129–135, 132.

[67] Thia Cooper, "Race, Class, and Abortion: How Liberation Theology Enhances the Demand for Reproductive Justice," *Feminist Theology* 24, no. 3 (2016): 226–244, 240.

Let us again reflect briefly on the cases of Luz and Lucrecia. The lens of reproductive justice allows us to see that inferior access to reproductive health care extends the issue far beyond the question of abortion. Poverty, lack of safe housing and workplace conditions, the inaccessibility of quality education, the difficulty of accessing safe and affordable care for their children, and the precarity associated with immigration status all detract in substantial ways from their reproductive well-being. These all constitute *major*—not secondary—considerations that directly impact these women's flourishing. To seek policies that meaningfully address these struggles is to attend to justice in a far more complete and holistic way than is accomplished by ensuring, or banning, the choice to abort a pregnancy.

What might be some of the concrete steps that society could take—and that churches could actively support—to promote justice for these women? We must begin by ensuring and extending adequate reproductive health services, holistically understood. For most proponents of reproductive justice, this will include safe, affordable, accessible abortion and contraception. But, even for those who, like some Catholic believers, reject such measures for ideological or religious reasons, there is so much more to be done. Women must have easy access to preventive health services such as pap smears, mammograms, and comprehensive sex education that includes STI prevention; pregnant women must receive adequate prenatal care; and new mothers must receive sufficient breastfeeding and perinatal support. The use of *promotores*—community health workers who themselves hail from the communities that they support—is an effective way to make headway on such changes.[68] But these changes also require an infusion of public funds if they are to be widely implemented and made truly accessible to women like Luz and

---

[68] Gloria Sayavedra, Ron Strochlic, and Bertha Sarmina García, "'If We Don't Speak, Our Voices Won't Be Heard': Organizing Farmworkers through Poder Popular," National Center for Farmworker Health, October 2008, lib.ncfh.org/?plugin=ecomm&content=item&sku=7865. See also the gender-specific farmworker organizing work of Lideres Campesinas, www.liderescampesinas.org/.

Lucrecia. Further, health insurance itself must be not just *available* but also *portable* across county and state lines, if it is to meaningfully help farmworkers who are migrant.[69] This is particularly true for undocumented workers who are currently blocked from the benefits of portability in part by their exclusion from the Affordable Care Act.

The environments in which these women work and live and raise children must also be made much, much safer. Reproductive justice requires that affordable housing specifically include workers and their families in rural areas. If owners themselves provide housing for their workers, such housing must be held to high standards of safety and livability, particularly where children are present.[70] At the workplace, better field sanitation (including more and closer toilet facilities) and readily available information (in their native languages) about how to protect oneself and one's family from excessive pesticide exposure are central aspects of reproductive justice. Society must insist that these measures are taken by growers and vigorously enforced by regulators.

In a similar vein, growers and crew members who harass or assault women farmworkers must be aggressively punished with deterrence as the goal; reproductive justice demands that we ensure women are safe to leave their homes and work without fear of such violence.[71] Federal inspections to this end must be given funding and genuine "teeth" in order to serve as a more reliable tool of justice.[72] On the flip side, empowerment initiatives—with leadership drawn from within farmworker communities

---

[69] Farmworker Justice, "Stories from the Field."

[70] In January of 2023, a spree of deadly shootings took place on two farm sites in Half Moon Bay, California; subsequent investigation of the shootings revealed deplorable housing conditions for farmworkers there and across much of California. See José Vadi, "Half Moon Bay Shooting Rehashes California's Historic Resistance to Humanely Housing Farmworkers," *Cal Matters*, February 13, 2023, calmatters.org/housing/2023/02/half-moon-bay-farm-housing/.

[71] Leandra Hinojosa Hernández and Sarah De Los Santos Upton, "Insiders/Outsiders, Reproductive (In)justice, and the US-Mexico Border," *Health Communication* 35, no. 8 (2020): 1046–1050.

[72] Farmworker Justice Fund, *Farmworker Women Speak Out*.

themselves—should be funded, developed, and promoted, in order to educate women about their legal rights and options in the face of sexual harassment and other forms of violence. Such initiatives must also effectively take on the enormous issue of domestic violence that disproportionately characterizes the home lives of farmworker women and children.

Poverty, of course, exacerbates all the above conditions. Poverty is a major cause of suffering, direct and indirect, for migrant farmworkers. As political scientist Rosalind Petchesky argues, poverty creates enormous barriers to reproductive and sexual rights; it will be unachievable to try to protect such rights without also a strong campaign for economic justice and an end to poverty.[73] Along these lines, the achievement of reproductive justice relies upon support for grassroots organizing and unionization, particularly when the latter serves to move farmworkers closer to goals such as fair compensation, including a living wage. Catholic social teaching already includes strong support for labor justice, tightening the connection to reproductive justice. It is not difficult to see how the poverty into which Luz and Lucrecia were born contributed to the struggles they have experienced to provide for their families and to raise their children in safe and healthy environments.

A major part of such anti-poverty intervention, viewed through the lens of reproductive justice, is to provide for the care of children. This means high quality, affordable childcare as well as the promotion of *shared* caregiving duties. It is egregious that the care of children has been almost universally omitted from the employment equation for farmworker families. As long as women—individually or as a group—are understood to be the main (and often sole) providers of domestic caregiving, they will remain at a massive economic disadvantage. Thus, instead of raising up motherhood as women's defining role (and feminine "genius"), thereby burdening women with disproportionate caregiving duties and inviting economic struggle, Catholic teaching should stress the importance of

---

[73] Petchesky, "Human Rights."

mutuality in parenting. In this way, they could advance the goal of safer and more stable home environments for children and the genuine economic empowerment of women.

In addition, the deeply broken US immigration "system" intersects in real and painful ways with the reproductive lives of many or even most farmworker women. Heinous family separation policies at the border and the mistreatment of pregnant and breastfeeding migrant women are just the tip of an immoral iceberg, one whose effects will be felt far into the future. As Leandra Hinojosa Hernández poignantly writes, "US government-sanctioned separation of asylum-seeking migrant families at the US-Mexico border is reproductive injustice in its most extreme forms: It cages families; it traumatizes children and exposes them to mental and physical risks; and it erodes the central family unit in efforts to defend and protect the 'sovereignty' of the United States."[74] Again, while not *all* migrant farmworker women are immigrants to the United States, many are. For these women, the challenges described above are compounded by living under the conditions of profoundly flawed immigration policies and practices.

Hence, immigration reform, including meaningful pathways to citizenship, are an indispensable part of the conditions of reproductive justice. Stable pathways to citizenship for undocumented workers would help alleviate the fear of deportation that causes them to accept mistreatment and forgo pursuing their rights. In particular, immigration policy needs to be altered in order to regularize the status of unaccompanied children as well as migrant women and girls, especially those who have been victims of crime, abuse, and exploitation.[75] Indeed, the US Conference of Catholic Bishops themselves call for US immigration policy to be reformed to help families to stay intact and parents to stay with their children and to protect immigrating children themselves who currently live under a state of extreme precarity (*Strangers*

---

[74] Hernández, "Feminist Approaches to Border Studies," 132.
[75] Correa-Cabrera and Keck, "A Dangerous Journey."

No Longer, nos. 66–67). Even more fundamentally, justice calls for a change in US geopolitical and economic policies, with an aim towards a more just and equitable international economy and an eye toward identifying the ways that globalization has contributed to political and economic unrest—and the subsequent need to emigrate in the first place.

Finally, the wide lens of reproductive justice asks us to critically examine the xenophobia and negative representation of immigrants, BIPOC persons, and LGBTQ+ communities that characterizes so much of US culture today. The construction of the US identity as primarily white and "native-born" directly translates into the injustices against migrants of color, who make up the vast majority of farmworkers in the US today.[76] Additionally, LGBTQ+ migrants, especially trans* migrants, experience extremely high levels of precarity and violence, including both in their countries of origin and once they arrive in the US—often by US immigration agents themselves.[77] In this context, cultural shift work done on both individual and organizational levels must be a part of any integrated strategy for change that seeks reproductive justice as its goal.[78]

Conclusion

Examining and seeking to alter the root causes of unjust immigration practices and policies, poverty, poor housing and workplace conditions, and inadequate childcare provision and education may seem to be a long way away from strictly reproductive concerns. But the lens of reproductive justice shows that it is not. These considerations are absolutely essential to a truly effective strategy for women's well-being, one that includes and promotes the genuine flourishing of migrant women farmworkers.

---

[76] Gwyneth Lonergan describes an analogous situation in Great Britain; see Lonergan, "Reproductive Justice and Migrant Women."

[77] Leandra Hinojosa Hernández and Sarah De Los Santos Upton, "Transgender Migrant Rights, Reproductive Justice, and the Mexico-US Border in the Time of COVID-19," *QED: A Journal in GLBTQ Worldmaking* 7, no. 3 (2020): 142–150, esp. 146–147, doi.org/10.14321/qed.7.3.0142.

[78] Zavella, "Contesting Structural Vulnerability."

Moreover, these more holistic concerns are *already* present within Catholic social teaching. Rather than its persistent and narrowly-focused proscription of abortion, Catholic ethics would do better to incorporate the structural themes of reproductive justice into its overall framing of ethical reproduction. Not only would such a move deepen and nuance the Catholic conversations and teachings surrounding abortion, it would also strengthen the connections between these teachings and aspects of the tradition which genuinely promote a "preferential option" for marginalized persons and groups—here, migrant women farmworkers. In this way, the incorporation of reproductive justice into Catholic teaching furthers its aim of *genuine human flourishing* in a world that too often seems bent on denying it.

Karen Peterson-Iyer, PhD, is associate professor of theological and social ethics in the Department of Religious Studies at Santa Clara University. Her previous publications include "Human Trafficking, Coercion, and Moral Agency in Agricultural Labor," in *Theological Studies* (June 2022); *Reenvisioning Sexual Ethics: A Feminist Christian Account* (Georgetown University Press, 2022); and *Designer Children: Reconciling Genetic Technology, Feminism, and Christian Faith* (Pilgrim Press, 2004).

12. Rachel Is Weeping for Her Children: Theological Reflections on Intersectional Reproductive Justice and Maternal Health

Mary M. Doyle Roche

This chapter moves through the methodological steps of Catholic social teaching: seeing, judging, and acting. Beginning with "the signs of the times" and the experiences of Black women, I will lay out the stark realities of maternal and infant mortality and morbidity in the United States and extend this to the many threats to young Black lives. Social analysis of the statistics on maternal mortality and morbidity points, unsurprisingly, to the economy of slavery and enduring white male supremacy as root causes of death and near-death for pregnant Black women and their children. Theological reflection that employs themes including the dignity of the person, solidarity with the vulnerable, participation in the common good, and the principle of subsidiarity, all through an antiracist and antimisogynist lens, yields a framework for reproductive justice that better captures lived experiences of reproductive oppression and points toward the kinds of practices and policies that actually support women and children. The 2022 U.S. Supreme Court Decision in *Dobbs v. Jackson Women's Health Organization* has not only eroded reproductive rights regarding safe abortion access but also compromised women's access to quality obstetrical care.[1] Resistance to this reproductive injustice is gaining strength at the grassroots level in ways that include but are not limited to

---

[1] Supreme Court of the United States, Dobbs, State Health Officer of the Mississippi Department of Public Health, et al. v. Jackson Women's Health Organization, et al, www.supremecourt.gov/opinions/21pdf/19-1392_6j37.pdf. The Guttmacher Institute conducts research and policy analysis on the impact of abortion bans on women of color, www.guttmacher.org/2023/01/inequity-us-abortion-rights-and-access-end-roe-deepening-existing-divides.

securing access to safe abortions and contraception. Here, I raise up women-led initiatives aimed at enhancing women's reproductive health, ensuring safe pregnancy, labor, and delivery, and promoting infant and child flourishing.

Maternal and Infant Mortality and Morbidity in the United States

In 2017, the staff of *ProPublica* published a series of articles on maternal mortality and morbidity in the United States, which has one of the highest rates of maternal death among wealthier countries. "Lost Mothers" tells the stories of women who died tragically of pregnancy and childbirth related causes.[2] Women of many racial, ethnic, religious, educational, geographical, and economic backgrounds die each year in the United States during pregnancy, childbirth, and the postpartum period. While strides have been made globally to improve maternal mortality, the trend in the US is moving in the other direction.[3] The challenges are particularly acute in rural communities with little or no access to obstetrical care, a situation made worse by the closure of maternity wards in already underserved areas.[4] Many healthcare practitioners and ethicists have

---

[2] Nina Martins, Emma Cillekens, and Alessandra Freitas, "Lost Mothers" *ProPublica*, July 17, 2017, www.propublica.org/article/lost-mothers-maternal-health-died-childbirth-pregnancy. The World Health Organization defines these mortality rates as "the annual number of female deaths from any cause related to or aggravated by pregnancy or its management (excluding accidental or incidental causes) during pregnancy and childbirth or within 42 days of termination of pregnancy, irrespective of the duration and site of the pregnancy." www.who.int/data/gho/indicator-metadata-registry/imr-details/4622.

[3] Jovanni R. Spinner, Sheila Carrette, and Joylene John-Sowah, "The Maternal Mortality Crisis in the Black Community," in *Black Women and Public Health: Strategies to Name, Locate, and Change Systems of Power*, ed. Stephanie Y. Evans, Sarita K. Davis, Leslie R. Hinkson, and Deanna J. Wathington (Albany, NY: SUNY Press, 2022), 67.

[4] Spinner, Carrette, and John-Sowah, "The Maternal Mortality Crisis in the Black Community," 71; Alisa Valentin and Christy M. Gamble, "Rural Black Maternal Health in

highlighted women's increased vulnerability after the 2022 U.S. Supreme Court decision in *Dobbs v. Jackson Women's Health Organization*, as state legislators enact laws that can have chilling effects on the care of women in crisis.[5] Though all pregnant, birthing, and postpartum persons are affected because childbearing itself comes with risks that are often unacknowledged, disparities, particularly along lines of race and ethnicity, are glaring.

One piece in the *ProPublica* series, "Nothing Protects Black Women from Dying in Pregnancy and Childbirth," explores the impact of race on health outcomes for women of color and accounts for differences in income and educational level.[6] Highly educated and affluent women of color, even those who are physicians themselves, continue to be disproportionately represented in mortality and morbidity statistics.[7] The devastating numbers are attributed in part to unconscious bias (and perhaps some conscious bias) on the part of healthcare professionals who then dismiss the experiences and early warning signs reported by Black patients generally and Black women in particular. According to the Centers for Disease Control and Prevention (CDC), "Black women are three times more likely to die of a pregnancy-related cause than white women," noting that bias, underlying medical conditions, structural racism, and other social determinants of health play roles in the phenomenon.[8]

---

the Age of Digital Deserts," in Evans, Davis, Hinkson, and Wathington, *Black Women and Public Health*, 143–144.

[5] For example, "Dialogue After *Dobbs*, Toward Reasoned Dialogue and Constructive Conversation on Abortion" *Journal of Moral Theology*, 12, no. 1 (2022): 89–144, jmt.scholasticahq.com/article/66268.

[6] Nina Martin and Renee Montagne, "Nothing Prevents Black Women from Dying in Childbirth" *ProPublica*, December 7, 2017, www.propublica.org/article/nothing-protects-black-women-from-dying-in-pregnancy-and-childbirth.

[7] Stephanie Y. Evans, Sarita K. Davis, Leslie R. Hinkson, and Deanna J. Wathington, "Introduction: Race, Gender, and Public Health: Social Justice and Wellness Work" in Evans, Davis, Hinkson, and Wathington, *Black Women and Public Health*, 11.

[8] Centers for Disease Control and Prevention, "Working Together to Reduce Black Maternal Mortality," www.cdc.gov/healthequity/features/maternal-mortality/index.html.

Theological Reflections on Reproductive Justice and Maternal Health

The peril extends to Black infants. According to a 2018 *New York Times Magazine* article, "Why America's Black Mothers and Babies are in a Life-or-Death Crisis," penned by journalist Linda Villarosa,

> Black infants in America are now more than twice as likely to die as white infants—11.3 per 1,000 black babies, compared with 4.9 per 1,000 white babies, according to the most recent government data—a racial disparity that is actually wider than in 1850, 15 years before the end of slavery, when most black women were considered chattel. In one year, that racial gap adds up to more than 4,000 lost black babies. Education and income offer little protection. In fact, a black woman with an advanced degree is more likely to lose her baby than a white woman with less than an eighth-grade education.[9]

High blood pressure, cardiovascular disease, pre-eclampsia, and eclampsia all play significant roles in maternal mortality. Infant mortality rates are impacted by the number of infants with low birthweight. The statistics are staggering, and they may represent only a fraction of the problem because, as Villarosa notes, it has been more than ten years since official federal data were updated and "Only about half of the states and few cities maintain maternal-mortality review boards."[10]

Social Analysis and a Public Health Lens

Morbidity and mortality for Black mothers and children in the United States is rooted in the history and ongoing impact of white supremacy. Villarosa has further developed her analysis and placed it in the context of racialized healthcare injustice more broadly in *Under the Skin: The Hidden Toll of Racism on American Lives and the Health of Our Nation*.

---

[9] Linda Villarosa, "Why America's Black Mothers and Babies are in a Life-or-Death Crisis," *New York Times Magazine*, April 11, 2018, www.nytimes.com/2018/04/11/magazine/black-mothers-babies-death-maternal-mortality.html.

[10] Villarosa, "Why America's Black Mothers and Babies are in a Life-or-Death Crisis."

Villarosa's work builds upon the earlier groundbreaking research of Dorothy Roberts in her 1997 *Killing the Black Body: Race, Reproduction, and the Meaning of Liberty*, where Roberts notes, "For slave women, procreation had little to do with liberty. To the contrary, Black women's childbearing in bondage was largely a product of oppression rather than an expression of self-definition and personhood."[11] The practice of slavery, particularly after the trading of enslaved people between nations became illegal (in theory) in 1808, incentivized the control of the reproductive lives of enslaved persons in order to maximize economic gain for owners of enslaved people. Strategies employed by owners of enslaved people included forcing tensions between productivity in work and the needs of young children, "shattering the bonds" of mothers and children at the auction block, and child-stealing. In this context, Roberts frames contraceptive practice, abortion, and infanticide as forms of resistance to enslavement.[12]

Yet Roberts highlights that movements for reproductive liberty have also themselves been racist from the start. White supremacy under slavery sought control over Black women's reproductive capacity to maximize profits. White supremacy under Jim Crow sought control over Black women's bodies as part of a program of eugenics. In both cases, the reproductive lives of Black women were regulated in order to achieve the social and economic goals of white people.[13] So, as Angela Davis claims, controlling pregnancy and childbirth becomes a *right* for those with racial and economic privilege and a *duty* for those without those advantages.[14]

Killing the Black Body presumes the right to abortion guaranteed in the 1973 Supreme Court decision in *Roe v. Wade* (overturned in 2022 in the *Dobbs* decision) but critiques the women's movement for its narrow focus on abortion rights as matters of personal choice. For Roberts, taking

---

[11] Dorothy Roberts, *Killing the Black Body: Race, Reproduction, and the Meaning of Liberty* (New York: Random House, 1997), 23.
[12] Roberts, *Killing the Black Body*, 33–45.
[13] Roberts, *Killing the Black Body*, 56.
[14] Roberts, *Killing the Black Body*, 58.

seriously Black's women's experiences of pregnancy, childbirth, and mothering yields a more comprehensive view of reproductive justice than the view that dominates white feminisms, namely liberty as merely immunity from interference and coercion that is protected by a Constitutional right to privacy. Again, Roberts frames the issue quite clearly,

> Black women, on the other hand, especially those who are poor, must deal with a whole range of forces that impair their choices. Their reproductive freedom, for example, is limited not only by the denial of access to safe abortions, but also by the lack of resources necessary for a healthy pregnancy and parenting relationship. Their choices are limited not only by direct government interference in their decisions, but also by the government's failure to facilitate them.[15]

In the 1990s, research teams from Boston University and Georgetown University undertook the Black Women's Health Study in response to the recognition that research up to that point had been conducted primarily with White women patients. Not long into the study, it became clear to the team that what needed to be studied was not so much *race* but the *impact of racism*. They adapted a tool used to measure impacts of "everyday race-related insults" on healthcare disparities and sought to include impacts of institutionalized racism and the toll structural racism takes on women's bodies. They arrived at the conclusion that "for black women in America, an inescapable atmosphere of societal and systemic racism can create a kind of toxic physiological stress, resulting in conditions—including hypertension and pre-eclampsia—that lead directly to higher rates of infant and maternal death. And that societal racism is further expressed in a pervasive, longstanding racial bias in health care—including the dismissal of legitimate concerns and symptoms—that

---

[15] Roberts, *Killing the Black Body*, 300.

can help explain poor birth outcomes even in the case of black women with the most advantages."[16]

The Black Women's Health Study confirmed and nuanced additional research conducted by Arlene Geronimus of the University of Michigan School of Public Health beginning in the late 1980s. Geronimus had begun developing the theory of *weathering*, in which "high-effort coping from fighting against racism leads to chronic stress that can trigger premature aging and poor health outcomes."[17] As an adjective, *weathered* signifies the effects of harsh conditions over time. As a verb, *weathering* suggests courage and endurance in the face of such conditions. When applied to the context of maternal and child health, Villarosa notes "something about being a Black woman in America is bad for her body and her baby"[18] and, according to Sarah Rubin and Joselyn Hines, the act of mothering itself becomes a radical practice of resistance.[19]

Theological Reflection

A voice was heard in Ramah, sobbing and loud lamentation; Rachel weeping for her children, and she would not be consoled, since they were no more. (Matthew 2:18)

Christian ethicist Kelly Brown Douglas recalls the image of Rachel in her epilogue to *Stand Your Ground: Black Bodies and the Justice of God*, "A

---

[16] Villarosa, "Why America's Black Mothers and Babies are in Life-or-Death Crisis." See also Linda Villarosa, *Under the Skin: The Hidden Toll of Racism on American Lives and the Health of Nation* (New York: Random House, 2022), 74–80.

[17] Villarosa, *Under the Skin*, 80.

[18] Villarosa, *Under the Skin*, 80.

[19] Sarah Rubin and Joselyn Hines, "As Long as I Got Breath in my Body: Risk and Resistance in Black Maternal Embodiment," *Culture, Medicine, & Psychiatry* 47, no. 12 (2023): 495–518. The authors note (505–506), "For many moms in our study, pregnancy and the postpartum period contained revelatory moments of embodied knowledge where they feel gratified and virtuous centering their children. For others, centering children is a shift in perspective regarding their community and environment" and "everywhere she looks she sees the way her surroundings endanger her children."

Mother's Weeping for Justice."[20] Written in direct response to the murder of Trayvon Martin and the acquittal of his killer, *Stand Your Ground* is a forceful critique of American exceptionalism that costs the lives of a litany of Black people who are subjected to violence from neighbors, strangers, and law enforcement. Douglas unites the biblical image of Rachel with the mothers of Black people who have been murdered. We might do the same for Black mothers and their children harmed by and lost to reproductive injustice.

Rachel is a key figure in the Genesis narrative. Like many female figures in the Bible, her story is closely tied to her reproductive status (Genesis 29; 30:22–24). Barren for many years while her sister delivered sons to Jacob, she eventually gives birth to Joseph, who is later sold into slavery by his brothers, but who would eventually rise to power and influence in Egypt in a time of famine. Rachel leverages the taboo around menstruation to escape detection by Laban, transforming pollution into power (Genesis 31:35). She later dies in childbirth while delivering Benjamin (Genesis 35:16–20).[21]

As a matriarch of the people of Israel, Rachel is later recalled by the prophet Jeremiah during a time of exile and great desolation, "In Ramah is heard the sound of sobbing, bitter weeping! Rachel mourns for her children, she refuses to be consoled for her children—they are no more! Cease your cries of weeping, hold back your tears! There is compensation for your labor—oracle of the LORD— they shall return from the enemy's land. There is hope for your future—oracle of the LORD— your children shall return to their own territory" (Jeremiah 31:15–17) A mother in distress and grief over her children is a powerful metaphor for the wrenching experience of exile and the power of God's love and promises for the people of Israel. Childbirth, a sign of divine favor, is also a "symbol

---

[20] Kelly Brown Douglas, *Stand Your Ground: Black Bodies and the Justice of God* (New York: Oribis, 2015).

[21] Susan Niditch, "Genesis," in *The Women's Bible Commentary*, ed. Carol A. Newsom and Sharon H. Ringe (Louisville: KY: Westminster/John Knox, 1992), 15, 21.

of death" and "approaching calamity."[22] In the infancy narrative found in Matthew's gospel, the image of Rachel is employed again during the account of the slaughter of the innocents, the vicious powerplay on the part of Herod, "standing his ground of power," to shore up his control and ego (Matthew 2:18).[23] The abject horror is at once palpable and unimaginable. Each voice raised in the chorus of lamentation is radically unique but together they point to systematic violence and structural sin. Douglas reflects, "Into the midst of a mother's deepest pain and suffering God is present in the world bringing hope."[24] Compensation for the labor of childbearing and childrearing, a hope-filled future for Black mothers and infants, and children returned home from exile offer a powerful vision of reproductive justice.

Dignity, Solidarity, and a Preferential Option for the Vulnerable through the Lens of Black Mamas Matter

Unfortunately, the pro-life movement in many Christian communities, including the Catholic Church, has neglected the richness, complexity, and ambiguity of the biblical imagery of Rachel's lament in favor of an "all lives matter" approach to the ethics of reproduction and as a direct response to the Movement for Black Lives. This approach, while claiming to hold the moral high ground of a commitment to intrinsic human dignity, is, in practice, a stumbling block for intersectional reproductive justice as it undermines the lived dignity of Black bodies. The Black Lives Matter movement, sparked by a creative social media hashtag in response to the murder of Trayvon Martin, was founded by three human rights activists, Alicia Garza, Patrisse Khan-Cullors, and Ayo Tometi. Black Lives Matter also served as an important corrective to the predominantly white

---

[22] Kathleen M. O'Connor, "Jeremiah," in Newsom and Ringe, *The Women's Bible Commentary*, 173.
[23] Kelly Brown Douglas, *Stand Your Ground*, 228.
[24] Kelly Brown Douglas, *Stand Your Ground*, 228.

and affluent feminist movement embodied in the first Women's March after the 2016 United States presidential election.[25] As I have already noted, movements for reproductive justice have often excluded the experiences of women of color and prioritized the kinds of justice claims made by relatively affluent white women. Scholars including Dorothy Roberts and Brittney Cooper have noted that the history of civil rights for women is marred by the frequent betrayal of Black women as white women accepted compromises that leverage their racial privilege. White racial solidarity has been stronger than gender solidarity; economic solidarity among the affluent and those who aspire to that status has been stronger than gender solidarity.[26]

Black Lives Matter corrects the de facto devaluing of Black persons and communities. The compelling hashtag, the work of experienced and courageous Black women, was then coopted and misused to advocate for "blue" lives, lives of police officers and law enforcement professionals. The cooptation went further as majority culture white Christians hedged their bets by claiming that "all lives matter." Black Lives Matter has never called into question the intrinsic dignity of human persons as persons. Rather it has claimed personhood, echoing proclamations made throughout the history of civil rights in the United States: I am a Man. I am Somebody. Ain't I a Woman?[27] To say that "all lives matter" in a racist context

---

[25] Alicia Garza, *The Purpose of Power: How We Come Together When We Fall Apart* (New York: One World, 2020); Patrisse Khan-Cullors and asha bandele, *When They Call You a Terrorist: A Black Lives Matter Memoir* (St. Martin's Press, 2018).

[26] Roberts, *Killing the Black Body*; Brittney Cooper, *Eloquent Rage: A Black Woman Discovers Her Super Power* (New York: St. Martin's Press, 2018). For a theological analysis of human solidarity at the intersections of race and gender, see M. Shawn Copeland, *Enfleshing Freedom: Body, Race, and Being* (Minneapolis, MN: Fortress Press, 2023), 36, 67, 93–105.

[27] Claiming personhood for Black Lives has a rich historical tradition. "I am a Man" was a rallying cry used by civil rights activists during the Memphis Sanitation Strike of 1968. The National Museum of Civil Rights at the Lorraine Hotel, www.civilrightsmuseum.org/i-am-a-man. "I am Somebody" was proclaimed by black female hospital workers in Charleston, South Carolina in 1969 and featured in a documentary of the same name by Madeline Anderson, www.civilrightsmuseum.org/washing-society-i-am-somebody. Activist for racial and gender

advances the fiction of reverse racism. As author and activist Ijeoma Oluo notes, "Racism is any prejudice against someone because of their race, *when those views are reinforced by systems of power*."[28] The systems, structures, laws, etc., are set up in ways that assume the dignity of some persons, white men in particular, but place a burden of proof of humanity on persons of color, women and children, and queer persons. To say "all lives matter" is at best disingenuous and, at worst, white-supremacist. It is a way for churches to claim some vision of good-people-on-both-sides neutral ground, sidestepping real claims for racial justice that might impinge upon the comfort of white people and communities. To say that all lives matter may be technically true in an abstract, existential way, but it is hardly true in lived experience. In lived experience, claims that all lives matter increase the vulnerability, indeed the disposability, of Black bodies, female bodies, pregnant bodies, and queer bodies. It avoids the difficult but necessary task of taking the side of those whose vulnerability is most urgent.

To *matter* is to be important, to have weight, substance, intrinsic value, influence. It suggests subjectivity and agency. Things that matter must be taken into account.[29] Saying that all lives matter is essentially a way to say that no lives matter as much or more than affluent cis-gendered white men. Claiming the sanctity of all life might say something about who God is and what might matter to God, but it hardly describes the concrete decisions and actions of people with power and privilege, those who decide, in practical terms, what matters, who matters, to whom, why, and for what purpose. This is not a solidaristic assertion about the dignity of all persons but is rather a tool of white supremacy used to distort a fundamental claim

---

justice Sojourner Truth delivered a speech later titled, "Ain't I a Woman," to the Women's Rights Convention in Akron, Ohio on March 29, 1851.

[28] Ijeoma Oluo, *So You Want to Talk About Race?* (New York: Hachette, 2019), 27. Emphasis mine.

[29] jennifer s. leath, Nontando Hadebe, Nicole Symmonds, and Anna Kasafi Perkins, "Black Feminism, Womanism, and Intersectionality Discourse," *Journal of Moral Theology* 12, Special Issue 1 (2023): 157–175, doi.org/10.55476/001c.75199.

of Christian anthropology. As Cole Arthur Riley reflects in *This Here Flesh: Spirituality, Liberation, and the Stories that Make Us*, "Injustice has survived by cowering behind the guises of morality and ethics. The whole charade is diabolical. True justice has little concern for good and bad, and is much more interested in protecting and affirming dignity with tangible actions and repair."[30]

To say "Black Lives Matter," or "Black Mamas' Lives Matter," actually comes closer to conveying Christian theological and anthropological commitments. To say that Black mothers and their children matter is to capture the heart of reproductive justice and a preferential option for the poor and vulnerable.

White supremacy, Christian white nationalism, and misogyny are particularly virulent in the United States with devastating consequences for the sexual and reproductive participation of BIPOC and LGBTQIA+ persons in the common good. The Catholic Church has been and continues to be complicit in perpetuating the unjust social conditions that undermine the dignity of particular persons and the common good of society and the people of God. The Catholic Church's reproductive politics have had consequences that belie its claims to value the intrinsic dignity and sanctity of all human life. We can no longer ignore the link between the programs of white supremacy and misogyny in the U.S. and campaigns to end the legal rights to abortion, to limit access to birth control, to end the right to marriage for same-sex couples, and to exclude transgender, non-binary and non-conforming persons from religious, educational, and healthcare spaces. The practical effect of measures taken by the Church to severely restrict reproductive healthcare access for women and girls and gender affirming medicine and mental healthcare and to expand the "right" to discriminate against LGBTQIA+ persons in employment has not decreased the number of crisis pregnancies and abortions. It has not improved the maternal and infant mortality rates

---

[30] Cole Arthur Riley, *This Here Flesh: Spirituality, Liberation, and the Stories that Make Us* (New York: Convergent, 2023), 123.

among Black women and children. It has not advanced the health, well-being, and the fundamental and inviolable dignity of women and girls. It has not shored up the resources that all parents and families, especially vulnerable families, need to promote their children's flourishing. Rather, these measures have bolstered support for political candidates who advocate for disenfranchising BIPOC voters through voter suppression, easing access to guns and military weapons, criminalizing Black and trans bodies, undermining accountability for sexual assault and the murder of Black and trans bodies, eroding vital resources for equitable public education, erasing the histories of racism, settler colonialism, and accounts of BIPOC achievement, legitimizing anti-immigrant hate, denying healthcare to poor people, and dismantling protections for the natural environment.[31]

Sexual intimacy, reproduction and parenting, and gender presentation and performance are all forms of social participation, all ways in which people both build the common good of society and receive its benefits. Like access to education and meaningful work, reproductive justice as participation in the common good requires conditions and institutions that are characterized by intersectional justice, which is justice that recognizes multiple forms and historic patterns of oppression that overlap and reinforce each other like racism, gender inequity, fear of queer bodies, and poverty. Sexual intimacy, reproduction, parenting, and gender presentation are human goods, but they must not be romanticized or idealized; they require the arduous work of informed personal and communal conscience. An "all lives matter" approach favors a vision of the human in the abstract (which is white, cis-gendered male, heterosexual), denies history, invalidates lived experiences, and thwarts genuine solidarity across difference. It is an attempt to give moral credence to claims of color blindness, gender blindness, status blindness. It prefers a disingenuous

---

[31] This passage is based on an essay that appeared in the North American Forum of *The First*, a monthly newsletter for Catholic Theological Ethics in the World Church. Mary M. Doyle Roche, "Parents' Rights, Politics, and Justice for Young People," April 1, 2022, https://catholicethics.com/forum/justice-for-young-people/.

equality to the pursuit of equity across difference. Differences do matter. People often attempt to convey commitment to intrinsic dignity on the interpersonal level with phrases like "it doesn't matter to me that you are [fill in the blank: BIPOC, LGBTQIA+, a girl]." In the pursuit of equity, differences in identity and experience do matter if we are to get intersectional reproductive justice right. It matters that my neighbor, colleague, friend, or family member has a racial or gender identity different from mine. These elements of their stories matter to me and should matter to church leaders. What brings them joy or sorrow matters. What endangers their lives matters. What brings a measure of safety and security matters. If intersectional identities don't matter then nothing compels us to closely examine the impact of laws and policies that on their face treat people equally but in fact simply shore up injustice based on race, gender, and class.

Characteristics of Reproductive Justice for Catholic Ethics

Informed by biblical narratives and themes in Catholic social teaching, including the dignity of the person, the common good, and solidarity with the vulnerable, reproductive justice is a comprehensive ethic that lifts up and prioritizes the experiences of Black women and girls. It is interested in healthy bodies, minds, and spirits, meaning not only the absence of disease and mere survival but also the flourishing of women in every aspect of their sexual and reproductive lives. Reproductive justice is comprehensive in the sense that reproduction includes conceiving, gestating, birthing, and raising another generation. Reproductive justice includes respect both for autonomy in making reproductive choices and for the relationality that is required throughout life, perhaps most especially in raising infants, children, and young people.

Reproductive justice considers reproduction to be a deeply personal experience but not one that has only the condition of privacy to guide it.

Reproductive justice's commitment to the dignity of the person is grounded in both autonomy and interdependence in the context of the common good. So, reproductive justice also envisions sexual activity, gender expression, reproduction, and parenting as matters of *participatory* justice. Sexual activity, gender expression, reproduction, and parenting are contributions to the common good of society. This is not to say that reproduction is meant only to serve the interests of the collective or the interests and the advantage of the affluent in the guise of what is common. The common good entails social conditions that allow people to flourish. The common good is stronger when Black women can make choices to have children, not have children, give birth in conditions they choose with access to the best prenatal medical care, and raise children in healthy environments without fear.

Intersectional approaches to reproductive justice also recognize the common good as both a set of social *conditions* and a set of social *constructions*. The social construction of human experience is inevitable as communities shape language, tell stories, create meaning, and organize social life. We are always in a process of constructing, deconstructing, and reconstructing experience. Experiences of gender, pregnancy, childbirth, motherhood, and maternal distress are socially constructed. Black and white bodies are socially constructed. The key question is whether or not the stories Christians tell and pass on about gender, pregnancy, childbirth, motherhood, and maternal distress are capacious enough to reflect the reality of the most vulnerable women and girls. Do they make space for the lament of Black women and girls? Cole Arthur Riley provides much needed nuance to lament as an intergenerational phenomenon in reflecting on Jeremiah 9:20, "Hear, O women… teach your daughters a dirge, and each to her neighbor lament." She writes, "I shouldn't need to recite a litany of wounds and injustices and decay in order to justify my sadness. In lament, our task is never to convince someone of the brokenness of this world; it is to convince them of the world's worth in the first place."[32]

Reproductive justice is guided by subsidiarity in that it abides by the dignity of individual, personal conscience, prioritizes local and grassroots wisdom about health needs and priorities, and still maintains a role for multiple institutions, including the government, in advancing rights as both immunities from undue interference and positive claims for concrete support. As Roberts claimed in *Killing the Black Body*, "The abstract freedom to choose is of meager value without meaningful options from which to choose and the ability to effectuate one's choice."[33] There are a number of initiatives lead by Black women that operate at the local, national, and international levels. They provide concrete services for women and infants, conduct critical research into the causes of and potential interventions for maternal and infant morbidity and mortality, advocate for public policy change, and strive for cultural transformation around women's health.

From Rachel Weeping to SisterSong: Witnesses to Reproductive Justice

What does reproductive justice look like? Where have we glimpsed just responses to unjust circumstances, conditions, constructions? This essay has focused on the shameful rates of maternal and infant morbidity and mortality for Black woman and children in the United States, and to these grave injustices, we might add a school to prison pipeline for Black boys, parental separation due to the mass incarceration of Black people, and the murder of Black bodies by law enforcement and other white "stand your ground" proponents. Working for intersectional reproductive justice can take the form of lending support and solidarity to the innovative work of Black women.

---

[32] Cole Arthur Riley, *This Here Flesh*, 98, 104–105.
[33] Roberts, *Killing the Black Body*, 309.

For example, SisterSong Women of Color Reproductive Justice Collective is a multiethnic collaborative, based in the southern US, that focuses on organizing for reproductive justice. Claiming reproductive justice as a human right, SisterSong emphasizes that reproductive rights are about access more than choice and widens the scope beyond abortion rights. They write, "Abortion access is critical, and women of color and other marginalized women also often have difficulty accessing: contraception, comprehensive sex education, STI prevention and care, alternative birth options, adequate prenatal and pregnancy care, domestic violence assistance, adequate wages to support our families, safe homes, and so much more."[34] Founded in 1997, SisterSong offers training in organizing for reproductive justice and recognizing the many intersecting oppressions that impact women's reproductive and maternal health. They build and sustain partnerships between many anti-racist grassroots organizations and raise funds to support birthing people of color.

The Black Mamas Matter Alliance (BMMA) similarly addresses policy change, culture shift, and innovative research programs that inform political policy and health practice. BMMA advocates for women's empowerment, "We intentionally center Black women's leadership. Black women have the knowledge, expertise, and skills to generate and implement solutions that will improve maternal health, rights, and justice, but sometimes lack the platforms necessary to support and amplify their work."[35] BMMA highlights "culturally-congruent practices" including Black midwifery and comprehensive doula services.

The Mother Lab (Maternal Outcomes for Translational Health Equity Research) at Tufts University School of Medicine Center for Black Maternal Health and Reproductive Justice supports research in maternal health from a public health perspective. Led by Dr. Ndidiamaka Amutah-Onukagha, the Mother Lab sponsors an annual Black Maternal Health

---

[34] SisterSong, www.sistersong.net/reproductive-justice.
[35] Black Mamas Matter Alliance, blackmamasmatter.org/.

Conference and fundraising initiatives to provide concrete support to birthing people, their infants, and families.[36]

One model of prenatal care being offered in the spirit of intersectional reproductive justice is the Centering Pregnancy Model®.[37] Featured in an article by Kiera Butler, "Pregnant While Black," the centering model uses group prenatal care appointments that build community and solidarity among women, leverage that space to deliver information and education more efficiently, and provide even more one-on-one time with a healthcare professional than is usually the case in traditional models of care.[38] Women's agency over their care is respected and encouraged as they record health data and help set the agenda for discussion. The approach leads to better outcomes for women and infants and mitigates racial disparities, and may be especially useful in areas that are under-resourced in terms of personnel but not practical knowledge and wisdom.[39] This confirms the wisdom of Dr. Prabhjot Singh, the director of the Arnhold Institute for Global Health at the Icahn School of Medicine at Mount Sinai, who studies community health worker models and how they can be used in the United States: "When you have an organized community-based team that connects technical clinical issues with a deep, embedded set of relationships, you can make real breakthroughs."[40]

Conclusion

In the gospels, women matter. They matter when they have been spurned and ostracized. They matter when they are making claims for their children, including their daughters. Those who are constructed as impure

---

[36] Motherlab, motherlab.org/.

[37] Information on the Centering Pregnancy® model can be found at centeringhealthcare.org/what-we-do/centering-pregnancy.

[38] Kiera Butler, "Pregnant While Black," *Mother Jones*, July/August, 2018, 13–15.

[39] The Centering Healthcare Institute in Boston links to a bibliography of research on centering care at centeringhealthcare.org/why-centering/research-and-resources.

[40] Villarosa, "Why America's Black Mothers and Babies are in a Life-or-Death Crisis."

and unclean matter. Those with heavy burdens and few resources matter. Those who are grieving matter. Women and girls matter to Jesus. They matter in the reign of God. To be sure, their sexual, marital, medical, and reproductive histories matter to the stories of their lives, to their whole truths, but they are not weaponized by Jesus to exclude, shame, or demean. The reign of God is good news for them and their children, down through the generations.

Any adequate ethic of reproductive justice from a Catholic perspective must take its lead from the experiences and advocacy of women of color. It must begin with a lament, rising like Rachel's weeping over the deaths of Black women and children during pregnancy, childbirth, and the postpartum period. Rather than perpetuate a romanticized construction of pregnancy and motherhood, it must root itself in the experience of struggle even as it strives to alleviate suffering and build the common good for all people.[41] Improving the disgraceful, and deteriorating, statistics on maternal and infant morbidity and mortality for Black people in the United States will take effort at every level of healthcare delivery and research and requires structural changes beyond raising consciousness about inter-personal bias. Rhetoric about the sanctity of all life and the vocation of motherhood is empty without a steadfast claim that the lives of Black mothers and children matter. Rhetoric about choice too is empty when it is leveraged by white, affluent supporters of abortion rights without sufficient attention to the social conditions that allow for real choices that include not having children, having children, and raising children in communities of justice and compassion. Intersectional reproductive justice is rooted in lament but branches out toward the flourishing of Black women and children.

---

[41] See Bryan Massingale, *Racial Justice and the Catholic Church* (Maryknoll, NY: Orbis, 2010), 20–24.

Theological Reflections on Reproductive Justice and Maternal Health

Mary M. Doyle Roche, PhD, teaches Christian ethics and Catholic moral theology at the College of the Holy Cross in Worcester, MA, USA. Her teaching and research interests include healthcare ethics and ethical issues impacting children and young people.

13. Reclaiming Women's Agency for Reproductive Justice in Nigeria Today: Flourishing for Mother and Child in Situations of Constraints

Mary Lilian Akhere Ehidiamhen

The issue of reproductive rights generally—and specifically for Nigerian women—is debated today because of constraints placed by Catholic teachings on reproductive health and public policies influenced by both culture and religion. These constraints have negative impacts on women's agency and on women's right to resist sexual exploitation and gain access to other important rights. Catholic teachings condemn all forms of artificial birth control, such as direct contraception, direct abortion, and direct sterilization. However, the official Church teaching encourages the use of natural means of fertility control. In *Humanae Vitae*, Paul VI prohibits the use of artificial contraceptives because they are said to obstruct the natural reproductive process. Drawing on a particular interpretation of the natural law, Paul VI encourages married couples to only engage in sexual intercourse during the wife's infertile periods if couples seek to control their birth rate.

The teaching of *Humanae Vitae* sparked negative reactions from several leading Catholic theologians when it was first promulgated. According to Joseph Selling, many lay Catholics disagreed with the teaching and refused to put it into practice. Selling attributes the reason for the rejection to "a failure in communication or a lack of adequate understanding in the part of either the laity or the hierarchy."[1] The document generated two tensions that "undermine the credibility of

---

[1] Joseph A. Selling, *Reframing Catholic Theological Ethics* (Oxford: Oxford University Press, 2018), 17–18.

moral theology in general."[2] First, according to Selling, the hierarchy insisted that the teaching forbidding artificial means of birth regulation "must be accepted because it came from the 'highest authority', that could not make a mistake on such an important issue." Controversy over this teaching created "a stalemate that has lasted for nearly fifty years in the Roman Catholic church and has reached a point where one's 'submission' to the teaching has become a test for Catholic orthodoxy applied to anyone who seeks ordination or applies for a position to teach moral theology."[3] Second, the emergence of human immunodeficiency virus (HIV) and acquired immune deficiency syndrome (AIDS) in the early 1980s contributed to the tension because the teaching of *Humanae Vitae* neglects the situation of marital union in which a spouse is HIV-positive and could spread infection to their spouse if they do not use a condom as a prophylactic.[4] The argument of Paul VI in *Humanae Vitae*—that all sexual acts must be open to procreation[5]—thus endangers the lives of people in serodiscordant relationships. Some Catholic women rejected the teaching because it exposes women to perpetual childbearing by promoting that all sexual acts must retain a procreative aim, while prohibiting artificial birth control methods by declaring them inherently wrong.[6] Some American Catholic theologians disagreed with the teaching and wrote that spouses should be allowed to use their conscience to decide to use contraceptives in some situations.[7] A year after *Humanae Vitae* was promulgated, a survey showed that 44 percent of women of childbearing age were using artificial birth control. By the mid 1970s, more than 80

---

[2] Selling, *Reframing Catholic Theological Ethics*, 18.
[3] Selling, *Reframing Catholic Theological Ethics*, 18.
[4] Selling, *Reframing Catholic Theological Ethics*, 12.
[5] Selling, *Reframing Catholic Theological Ethics*, 18.
[6] Harriet Sherwood, "Fifty Years On, and Catholics Are Still in Turmoil Over Contraception," *The Guardian*, July 22, 2018), www.theguardian.com/society/2018/jul/22/humanae-vitae-catholic-birth-control-ban-fifty-years.
[7] Charles Curran, "*Humanae Vitae*: Fifty Years Later," *Theological Studies* 79, no. 3 (2018): 520–542, 520.

percent of Catholics in the US rejected the prohibition of contraceptives.[8] Hence, the hierarchy's insistence on the acceptance of *Humanae Vitae* leaves me to wonder about the place of empathy toward women. How are we to reconcile Catholic teachings on the gift of human reason, Catholic teachings on the inviolability of conscience, and Catholic teachings that forbid contraception, abortion, and sterilization? With Selling, I wonder how the Church can move forward in a way that encourages faithful Catholics to make decisions according to their consciences.[9]

As a woman religious, who is deeply concerned for the health and well-being of women in Nigeria, I am troubled by the way that Catholic teachings on reproductive health have fostered misunderstanding and even distrust between clergy and the laity. *Lumen Gentium* puts forward the teaching that all share a "true equality" in building up the Body of Christ and suggests that, in the Church, there is "no inequality on the basis of race or nationality, social condition, or sex" (no. 32). Despite this teaching, inequality persists. A recent study from the United Nations explains that "the most recent data from 68 countries show that an estimated 44 percent of partnered women are unable to make decisions over health care, sex or contraception. As a result, nearly half of all pregnancies are unintended."[10] Such data invites us to question why so many women around the world are denied the "right to decide freely and responsibly the number and spacing of their children."[11] When Catholic teachings ignore factors that constrain women's agency and needs in relation to their reproductive life and health, women suffer. This is especially true for women in Nigeria. A better way forward would instead empower women to make thoughtful

---

[8] Sherwood, "Fifty Years On."
[9] Selling, *Reframing Catholic Theological Ethics*, 16.
[10] United Nations Population Fund (UNFPA), *State of World Population 2023: 8 Billion Lives, Infinite Possibilities: The Case for Rights and Choices* (New York: UNFPA, 2023), 4, www.unfpa.org/sites/default/files/pub-pdf/SWOP2023-ENGLISH-230329-web.pdf.
[11] UNFPA, *State of World Population 2023*, 4.

decisions about their bodies and lives, thereby enabling women, their families, and societies to flourish.[12]

Consequently, this paper aims at a Catholic feminist examination of the importance of reproductive justice for women in Africa and specifically Nigeria. Additionally, it deconstructs the conditions that constrain women's reproductive autonomy and their ability to stand up for their needs,[13] and explores other complicating factors that undermine reproductive flourishing. The paper further investigates reclaiming women's agency from the perspective of a needs-based approach, which argues that human needs motivate human actions toward flourishing for mother and child.

Reproductive Justice and the Threats to Women's Reproductive Rights and Agency in Africa/Nigeria

In 1994, during the International Conference on Population and Development (ICPD) organized by the United Nations (UN), a group of African American women introduced the term reproductive justice.[14] They coined the term because of the realization that the manner in which wealthy white women in the women's rights movement defined issues concerning women did not represent the worldview, situation and interests of marginalized women and women of color.[15] These scholar-activists "maintained that reproductive safety and dignity depended on having the resources to get good medical care and decent housing, to have a job that paid a living wage, to live without police harassment, to live free

---

[12] UNFPA, *State of World Population 2023*, 28.
[13] Marshall Rosenberg, *Nonviolent Communication: A Language of Life*, 3rd ed. (Encinitas, CA: PuddleDancer Press, 2015), 52–57.
[14] Joan C. Christler, "Introduction: A Global Approach to Reproductive Justice – Psychosocial and Legal Aspects and Implications," *William and Mary Journal of Women and the Law* 20, no. 1 (2003): 1–24, 1.
[15] Loretta J. Ross and Rickie Solinger, *Reproductive Justice: An Introduction* (Oakland: University of California Press, 2017), 55.

of racism in a physically healthy environment," and that these were "fundamental conditions for reproductive dignity and safety."[16] According to Loretta Ross, one of the founders of SisterSong,[17] reproductive justice is "the complete physical, mental, spiritual, political, social and economic well-being of women and girls, based on the full achievement and protection of women's human rights."[18] While reproductive justice advocates defend access to contraception and abortion as morally legitimate, these issues are not the primary focus on the movement.[19] Given that racism and classism continue to impact the lives of women, some people have no access to reproductive health care facilities and services such as abortion and contraceptives, even when such services are legal. Disparities in access result from many complex factors, including immigration status, structural racism, economic resources, gender-based violence, unfavorable work policies, lack of education, and so forth.[20] Reproductive justice scholarship has described the structural factors that prevent people from experiencing reproductive flourishing. Thus, the relationship between reproductive justice and Catholic social justice is the ethical framework that "weaves reproductive rights with social justice."[21]

Women's reproductive rights are endangered in many places around the world. Reproductive rights involve the freedom to make decisions

---

[16] Ross and Solinger, *Reproductive Justice*, 56.

[17] For more information about SisterSong and their reproductive justice advocacy, see their website: www.sistersong.net/about-x2.

[18] Sara P. Diaz, "A Map for Feminist Solidarity: How to Teach about Women of Color and Reproductive Justice in Jesuit WGS Classrooms," *Feminist Teacher* 27, no. 1 (2016): 24–46, 26. See also Loretta J. Ross, "Understanding Reproductive Justice: Transforming the Pro-Choice Movement," *Off Our Backs* 36, no.4 (2006): 14–19.

[19] Nancy Felipe Russo and Julia R. Steinberg, "Contraception and Abortion: Critical Tools for Achieving Reproductive Justice," in *Reproductive Justice: A Global Concern*, ed. Joan C. Chrisler (Santa Barbara, CA: Praeger, 2012), 145–171, 145.

[20] Loretta J. Ross, "Reproductive Equity," Catholics for Choice, 2023, www.catholicsforchoice.org/issues/reproductive-choice/.

[21] Loretta J. Ross, "Reproductive Equity."

about issues regarding a person's reproductive health.²² According to the World Health Organization (WHO) reproductive rights involve "the basic right of all couples and individuals to decide freely and responsibly the number, spacing and timing of their children and to have the information and means to do so, and the right to attain the highest standard of sexual and reproductive health. It also includes their right to make decisions concerning reproduction free of discrimination, coercion and violence, as expressed in human rights documents."²³ However, this definition does not represent the experiences of African women who have limited access to health facilities. I now turn to factors that threaten women's reproductive rights and agency and impede reproductive justice in Nigeria.

Factors that Threaten Women's Reproductive Rights and Impede Reproductive Justice in Nigeria

In the context of Nigeria, there are several factors that threaten women's reproductive rights and agency, thus hindering the realization of reproductive justice. Scholars have claimed that culture and religion are to blame, especially when they promote a patriarchal worldview that perceives women's sexual and reproductive autonomy as a threat to the existing patriarchal system.²⁴ For example, the Association for Women's Rights in Development explains that the effects of Nigeria's patriarchal conservatism are significant for women and girls who face high rates of sexual violence. Further, "Sexual and reproductive healthcare is extremely limited; Nigeria alone contributes more than 10 percent of the global burden of maternal deaths, despite representing only 2.5 percent of the

---

²² Chitu Womehoma Princewill and Anita Riecher-Rössler, "Education and Reproductive Autonomy: The Case of Married Nigerian Women," *Narrative Inquiry in Bioethics* 7, no. 3 (2017): 231–244, 232.

²³ United Nations, "Report of the International Conference on Population and Development," September 13, 1994, www.un.org/development/desa/pd/sites/www.un.org.development.des a.pd/files/a_conf.171_13_rev.1.pdf.

²⁴ Russo and Steinberg, "Contraception and Abortion," 147.

global population, and a 2013 study showed that only 16 percent of Nigerian women of reproductive age (15–49) have access to and use contraceptives."[25] According to data published by the United Nations, more than four out of five Nigerian women lack the freedom to determine their reproductive rights and are not able to prevent unintended pregnancies; some Nigerian women who face unplanned pregnancies resort to unsafe abortion, while others give birth and do their best to raise their children amidst challenging circumstances.[26] Nigerian women experience much discrimination. Too often, because of cultural assumptions, women are believed to exist solely for the benefit of men.[27]

Tragically, religious teachings can contribute to these assumptions, undermining the dignity of women. Religious doctrines about marriage, for example, contribute to the invisibility of married women's suffering, especially when husbands believe they have divinely sanctioned power over their wives, who must submit to them. According to Adeniyi Israel Adekunle, the concept of "marital rape" is "alien in Nigeria."[28] Further, efforts to reform laws on the basis of gender and opportunity equality are often rejected by the National Assembly. All these factors negatively impact women's reproductive health in the country.[29]

---

[25] Olu Timehin Adegbeye, "Nigeria: Not Left Out of the Global Rollback of Sexual and Reproductive Rights," Association for Women's Rights in Development, 2023, www.awid.org/news-and-analysis/nigeria-not-left-out-global-rollback-sexual-and-reproductive-rights.

[26] Adegbeye, "Nigeria: Not Left Out." See also UNFPA, *State of World Population 2023*, 12.

[27] Melissa Browning, *Risky Marriage: HIV and Intimate Relationships in Tanzania* (Lanham, MD: Lexington, 2013), 25–28.

[28] Adeniyi Israel Adekunle, "Marital Rape: An Examination of the Current Position of Law in Nigeria," *This Day*, September 7, 2021, www.thisdaylive.com/index.php/2021/09/07/marital-rape-an-examination-of-the-current-position-of-law-in-nigeria#.

[29] Lilian Akhirome-Omonfuegbe, "A Critical Appraisal of Women's Reproductive Rights in Nigeria," *Journal of Sustainable Development Law and Policy* 10, no. 1 & 2 (2019): 258–280, 277. See also Nkolika Ijeoma Aniekwu, *Reproductive Health Law: A Jurisprudential Analysis of Gender Specific Human Rights for the African Region* (Nigeria: Ambik Press, 2011), 84.

Additionally, bride price,[30] by bestowing reproductive authority to men while decreasing the reproductive autonomy of women, results in domestic violence and continuous patriarchy.[31] In Nigeria, women often bear the blame of infertility and the inability to bear a male child, which negatively impact their marriage and reproductive justice.[32] Consequently, the Nigerian culture approves polygamy for men, while the family and society treat women without a male child with less respect.[33] Patriarchy, which promotes absolute respect for men, hinders women's reproductive autonomy. For instance, in the Ikwerre community in Rivers state, Nigeria, a woman cannot decide about her reproductive health without the husband's consent.[34] Such a decision without the husband could lead to a divorce or physical violence.[35] Thus, the patriarchal system in Nigeria promotes violence against women and constrains their agency in relation to their reproductive health and justice. Unfortunately, patriarchy is legitimized by fixation in cultural practices that are detrimental to the flourishing of women.

---

[30] Bride price refers to the money and items a man pays to marry a woman. The intending husband pays the money and items (as requested by the woman's family) to the intending wife's family and kinsmen. Solomon Ademiluka, "Bride Price and Christian Marriage in Nigeria," *HTS Teologiese Studies/Theological Studies* 77, no. 4 (2021): 1–8, 1. The intention for paying a bride price is to validate the marriage, although it automatically bestows ownership of the woman to the man because the woman's family gives nothing in exchange for having the man. Consequently, some men use it as an opportunity to sexually exploit their wives against their consent, and their wives have no right to refuse sexual intercourse whenever their husbands request it. Refusal of sexual intercourse sometimes results in domestic violence against the woman. See also Browning, *Risky Marriage*, 33.

[31] Odunola D. Oladejo, "A Reproductive Justice Approach to Understanding Yoruba Women's Experiences with Early Marriage and Bride Price in Nigeria," (Oregon: MA Thesis, Oregon State University, 2020), 24.

[32] Oladejo, "A Reproductive Justice Approach," 25–26.

[33] Oladejo, "A Reproductive Justice Approach," 26.

[34] Spousal consent laws are not exclusive to Nigeria. See, for example, the analysis of Stephanie Ann Puen in this volume, "Considerations for a Comprehensive Sex Education Grounded in Catholic Social Thought for Reproductive Justice in the Philippines."

[35] Princewill and Riecher-Rössler, "Education and Reproductive Autonomy," 238.

Another cultural and religious practice that affects women's reproductive rights, autonomy, and justice is Female Genital Cutting (FGC). FGC involves the removal of the clitoris, not for medical reasons but to control female sexuality.[36] FGC can be performed during infancy without the child's consent or as a rite of transition to adulthood which may or may not involve the consent of the person involved. Such a practice is based on religious, cultural, or social reasons.[37] Traditional Female Genital Cutting (TFGC) raises the question of agency as it is mainly based on social pressure which compels compliance.[38] For instance, 27 percent of Nigerian women between age 15 and 49 have experienced FGC despite the existence of policies to prevent it in Nigeria. Unfortunately, because of inadequate awareness, implementation and monitoring, laws and policies tend to be ineffective.[39]

Cultural norms and traditions are major obstacles to implementing reproductive rights in Nigeria.[40] Though section 42 (1) of the Nigerian Constitution promotes freedom from discrimination, discriminatory practices hinder the implementation of that section of the Constitution. Women continue to experience employment discrimination, and men are overrepresented in the public sector. Even when they achieve employment,

---

[36] Mary Nyangweso Wangila, *Female Circumcision: The Interplay of Religion, Culture, and Gender in Kenya* (Maryknoll, NY: Orbis, 2007), 8–9, 45–76.

[37] Virginia Braun, "Female Genital Cutting around the Globe: A Matter of Reproductive Justice," in *Reproductive Justice: A Global Concern*, ed. Joan C. Chrisler (Santa Barbara, CA: Praeger, 2012), 29–55, 30–31.

[38] Braun, "Female Genital Cutting," 32.

[39] Akhirome-Omonfuegbe, "A Critical Appraisal," 276. See also Jane Muthumbi, Joar Svanemyr, Elisa Scolaro, Marleen Temmerman, and Lale Say, "Female Genital Mutilation: A Literature Review of the Current Status of Legislation and Policies in 27 African Countries and Yemen," *African Journal of Reproductive Health* 19, no. 3 (2015): 34. For analysis of a case study within the Catholic moral tradition, see Meghan J. Clark, "Charity, Justice, and Development in Practice: A Case Study of the Daughters of Charity in East Africa," *Journal of Moral Theology* 9, no. 2 (2020): 1–14, 9–14, jmt.scholasticahq.com/article/13334-charity-justice-and-development-in-practice-a-case-study-of-the-daughters-of-charity-in-east-africa.

[40] Isabel Apawo Phiri and Sarojini Nadar, eds., *African Women, Religion, and Health: Essays in Honor of Mercy Amba Ewudziwa Oduyoye* (Maryknoll, NY: Orbis, 2006), 4–9.

women receive less pay for their services and experience inequality compared to their male counterparts. Therefore, many Nigerian women have less access to resources and constitute the majority of impoverished Nigerians, which affects their reproductive health and decision-making.[41] Religion and culture each play a critical role in enforcing laws concerning reproductive rights because of their influence in public policies. For instance, abortion is criminalized in Nigeria unless the abortion was performed to save the life of the mother. However, critics argue that abortion restrictions result in a greater number of illegal and unsafe abortions, which endanger the lives and reproductive health of women.[42] Annually, out of fifty thousand maternal deaths, twenty thousand occur because of complications from unsafe abortions.[43] Laws against abortion and contraceptives can also lead low-income women to unintended pregnancies and childbirth; some women, out of extreme desperation, even "resort to dumping their babies in dustbins, in pit toilets, and in canals," according to a report by the Center for Reproductive Rights.[44] Laws against abortion are not particular to Nigeria. Generally, in Africa, the restrictive law regarding abortion makes it impossible for women to have access to safe abortions. 97 percent of the abortion performed in Africa are unsafe.[45] Sub-Saharan Africa accounts for 57 percent of the estimated 358,000 of the global yearly maternal deaths.[46] Therefore, in

---

[41] Akhirome-Omonfuegbe, "A Critical Appraisal of Women's Reproductive Rights in Nigeria," 276.

[42] Egondu Grace Ikeatu, "Violations of Women's Reproductive Rights in Nigeria," *Nnamdi Azikiwe University Journal of International Law and Jurisprudence* 11, no. 2 (2020): 157–174, 170–171.

[43] Center for Reproductive Rights, "Women's Reproductive Rights in Nigeria: A Shadow Report," reproductiverights.org/wp-content/uploads/2018/08/Nigeria-CEDAW-1998.pdf. See also Chiweshe Malvern and Catriona Macleod, "Cultural De-colonization versus Liberal Approaches to Abortion in Africa: The Politics of Representation and Voice," *African Journal of Reproductive Health* 22, no. 2 (2018): 49–59, 49–50.

[44] Center for Reproductive Rights, "Women's Reproductive Rights in Nigeria."

[45] Malvern and Macleod, "Cultural De-colonization," 52.

[46] Princewill and Riecher-Rössler, "Education and Reproductive Autonomy," 231.

Africa and specifically Nigeria, laws and policies influenced by cultural and religious norms constrain women's agency in issues concerning their reproductive health leading to reproductive injustice, maternal death, and lack of flourishing for mother and child.

Another problem militating against women's reproductive rights in Nigeria is the inability to match realities with laws and policies. There are laws that promote access to information on reproductive health and family planning. However, during sessions or classes, "issues of birth spacing and limiting the number of one's children" are hardly addressed.[47] In addition, Nigerian law does not consider spousal rape (which could result in unintended pregnancy and undermines birth spacing) as a crime because it is legitimized with the idea that a married woman is expected to be open to sexual intercourse with the husband whenever he asks for it.[48] Besides, in Nigeria, a female victim of rape hardly gets justice because she must provide evidence to validate her case.[49] Consequently, the victim gets frustrated while the perpetrator gets acquitted. Victims of rape often do not report their rape experiences to avoid stigmatization. This is an addition to rape exposing women to unintended pregnancies and sexually transmitted diseases.[50]

Generally, the purpose of law is to protect the vulnerable and to promote integral human flourishing. But because of the influence of religion and culture in Nigeria, the law does not serve this noble purpose.[51] When the law fails to protect Nigerian women, this threatens both reproductive justice and human flourishing. According to Sylvia Tamale, law, religion, and culture in Africa are used to dehumanize those whose

---

[47] Center for Reproductive Rights, "Women's Reproductive Rights in Nigeria."
[48] Ikeatu, "Violations of Women's Reproductive Rights in Nigeria," 161.
[49] See also "Religio-Cultural Underpinnings of Gender and Reproductive Injustice and Their Impact on Women's Agency in India" in this edited volume by Virginia Saldhanha, who examines similar legal barriers for survivors of sexual violence in India.
[50] Ikeatu, "Violations of Women's Reproductive Rights in Nigeria," 161.
[51] Teresia Mbari Hinga, *African, Christian, Feminist: The Enduring Search for What Matters* (Maryknoll, NY: Orbis, 2017), 3–10, 176–178.

sexuality do not conform to the norm, including homosexuals, prostitutes, single mothers, rape survivors, widows, and persons living with HIV.[52] Conservative Christians and Muslims in Africa focus on sexuality as the highest moral concern while neglecting the pressing moral issues such as corruption and embezzlement of public funds that require immediate attention.[53] Consequently, women's agency to determine their reproductive rights is often restrained through religion, culture, and law.[54] Affirming Tamale's position on the need to focus less on sexuality and focus more on bigger moral problems that need attention, Pope Francis during his journey from the Central African Republic was asked about his position concerning the need to use condoms to prevent HIV since Africa is being devastated by the disease. In response, Francis explained that the question is too narrow. Francis said there are bigger problems that need attention, such as "malnutrition, exploitation, slave labor, the lack of drinking water: these are the problems." He continued, "Let's not worry about using this or that bandage for a small wound. The big wound is social injustice, environmental injustice, the injustice I mentioned with exploitation and malnutrition."[55] Pope Francis further used the analysis of healing on the sabbath—"Tell us, Master, is it permissible to heal on the sabbath"—to drive his message home (I shall return to this later).[56] Hence, Tamale and

---

[52] Sylvia Tamale, "Exploring the Contours of African Sexualities: Religion, Law and Power," *African Human Rights Law Journal* vol. 14, no. 1 (2014): 150–177, 158. See also Nontando Hadebe, "Can Anything Good Come from Nazareth? Come and See!: An Invitation to Dialogue between Queer Theories and African Theologies," *Concilium* 5 (2019): 81–90.

[53] Tamale, "Exploring the Contours," 158. Jesuit theologian and Nigerian scholar Agbonkhianmeghe E. Orobator describes "the big five" as governance, integrity of creation, genetically modified organisms, resource extraction, and domestic justice. See Agbonkhianmeghe E. Orobator, "Ethics Brewed in an African Pot," *Journal of the Society of Christian Ethics* 31, no. 1 (2011): 3–16, www.jstor.org/stable/23562639.

[54] Tamale, "Exploring the Contours of African Sexualities: Religion, Law and Power," 168.

[55] Pope Francis, "In-flight Press Conference of His Holiness Pope Francis from the Central African Republic to Rome," November 30, 2015, www.vatican.va/content/francesco/en/speeches/2015/november/documents/papa-francesco_20151130_repubblica-centrafricana-conferenza-stampa.html.

[56] Pope Francis, "In-flight Press Conference."

Pope Francis remind Africans that less energy should be placed on using laws, religion and cultural norms that diminish reproductive health and women's agency. Instead, laws should be used to protect the vulnerable and promote reproductive justice, while also paying attention to other bigger moral issues that promote social injustice.

Another significant challenge results from cultural pluralism and the reality of diverse experiences across the continent of Africa—a continent home to fifty-four countries, over three thousand ethnic groups, and over two thousand living languages.[57] African countries have diverse cultures, so researchers must avoid speaking for others in such a way that they homogenize African culture. Such homogenization negatively affects conversations about reproductive justice in Africa. Such conversations are influenced not only by voices within but also well-funded groups that offer external pressures to conform—whether they be foreign aid mandates, non-governmental organizations, churches, or multi-national corporations. We see this conflict regarding abortion in particular in Obianuju Ekeocha's assertion that abortion is "unAfrican," based on her tribal perspective which generalizes the prohibition of abortion for all Africans.[58] According to Ekeocha, an African pro-life leader, the efforts of Europeans and North Americans to promote legalization of abortion in Africa is not for liberation but neocolonialism. She further argues that "most of the African communities actually believe by their traditions and their cultural standards that abortion is a direct attack on human life."[59] In response, Mette Gjerskove, a Danish Socialist Member of Parliament,

---

[57] Statista Research Department, "Number of Living Languages in Africa, 2022," July 18, 2023, www.statista.com/statistics/1280625/number-of-living-languages-in-africa-by-country/#:~:text=Number%20of%20languages%20spoken%20in%20Africa%202022%2C%20by%20country&text=As%20of%202022%2C%20there%20were,with%20over%20200%20living%20languages.

[58] Malvern and Macleod, "Cultural De-colonization versus Liberal Approaches to Abortion in Africa," 55.

[59] Obianuju Ekeocha, "African Woman Schools UN Delegate on Why Pushing Abortion is 'Neo-Colonialism'," *Life Site News*, April 5, 2016, www.lifesitenews.com/news/watch-african-woman-schools-un-official-on-why-pushing-abortion-is-neo-colo/.

argues that in her discussions with several African women, she discovered that different women want different things. She further argues that "my lesson learned ... being from a colonizing society ... is to allow people to make their choices," and "to freely decide over their own bodies, their own sexuality, how many babies they want, if they want contraception, if they want abortion ... The way to avoid a new colonization is to let people make their own choices."[60] Both Ekeocha and Gjerskov tend to speak for the whole of Africa from their own perspectives. Ekeocha's homogenization of African culture undermines the voices of other women, while Gjerskov pays attention to reclaiming women's agency and their freedom to choose for themselves as rational beings capable of making informed decisions, even as some claim this is an unAfrican perspective. A way forward must recognize the importance of centering African women, allowing women to speak for themselves and make choices, even as they do so in contexts influenced by many complex factors that are beyond their control.[61]

Furthermore, inadequate education, lack of economic resources, and conflict affect reproductive rights and justice in Africa/Nigeria. Religious bodies sometimes capitalize on the ignorance of the people and, without sufficient scientific proof, suggest to their members not to use contraceptives despite the increase in sexually transmitted diseases. Such assertions are usually based on the assumption that contraceptives (condoms) are insufficient in preventing sexually transmitted diseases. Some Catholic bishops continue to encourage countries that have a large number of persons affected by HIV/AIDS to avoid using condoms because they mistakenly argue that condoms do not prevent HIV transmission, while neglecting the scientific proof by World Health Organization (WHO) that condoms, when used correctly for every sexual

---

[60] Ekeocha, "African Woman Schools UN Delegate."
[61] For an analysis of the economic constraints that impact women's decisions to form a family, see Kate Ward, "Never Just a Choice: Three Theoretical Approaches to Economic Constraints on Family Formation," in this volume.

act, reliably prevent the spread of HIV.[62] A scientific study conducted by WHO and the US National Institutes of Health shows that "intact condoms . . . are essentially impermeable to particles the size of STD pathogens including the smallest sexually transmitted virus . . . condoms provide a highly effective barrier to transmission of particles or similar size to those of the smallest STD viruses."[63] This reveals the tension between religious assumptions and scientific discoveries.

Conflict also undermines reproductive justice. In Northeast Nigeria, the Boko Haram conflict impacts negatively on the sexual and reproductive health and rights of women. The Boko Haram conflict exposes women to different kinds of gender-based violence, such as sex trafficking, rape, and forced marriage, leading to sexually transmitted diseases, unwanted pregnancy and maternal deaths.[64] Hence, poverty, ignorance, and conflict prevent women from enjoying reproductive justice.

Reclaiming Women's Agency: The Needs-Based Theory

Given these extensive threats to reproductive justice in Nigeria, how can women reclaim their agency, and what should be the role of the Catholic Church in advancing reproductive justice? A woman's ability to identify her needs is essential for reproductive justice and the flourishing of mother and child. A needs-based approach does not begin with norms that are promulgated by a person in authority. Rather, a needs-based approach focuses on the person in her vulnerability and gives careful attention to how she recognizes, names, and describes her needs. A needs-based approach involves healthy intimate relationships, respect for one's partner,

---

[62] Steve Bradshaw, "Vatican: Condoms Don't Stop AIDS," *The Guardian*, October 9, 2003, www.theguardian.com/world/2003/oct/09/aids.
[63] Bradshaw, "Vatican: Condoms Don't Stop AIDS."
[64] Center for Reproductive Rights, "The Center Releases New Report on Sexual and Reproductive Rights in Nigerian Conflict Zones," reproductiverights.org/the-center-releases-new-report-on-sexual-and-reproductive-rights-in-nigerian-conflict-zones/.

the importance of self-care, providing a safe environment for childbirth, care, and development. Individual needs and social needs must be analyzed separately. For example, successful childbirth requires "a material environment adequate to basic pre-and post-natal health needs," while "the societal need for biological reproduction will often conflict with other individual needs—particularly those of women."[65] However, the ability of a woman to identify and stay connected to her needs gives her the agency to make choices based on these needs and the strategies to satisfy the needs at any given time.

Marshall Rosenberg's needs-based theory offers a helpful framework for reclaiming women's agency. According to Rosenberg, we live in a world where people are easily criticized for expressing their needs. Women are the highest victims of such criticisms. "For centuries, the image of the loving woman has been associated with sacrifice and the denial of one's own needs to take care of others. Because women are socialized to view the caretaking of others as their highest duty, they often learn to ignore their own needs."[66] Women who have internalized such beliefs reveal their needs in a manner that reinforces the belief that their needs do not matter. For fear of expressing her needs, even when a woman is tired and needs rest, she feels afraid to express it by enumerating all the tasks she performed during the day. The listeners, instead of understanding her needs, would rather resist it because the woman expressed herself in a manner that undervalues her needs.[67] Citing an example of his mother, Rosenberg posits that during a workshop he attended with her, he observed his mother's reaction during a discussion with other women on "how frightening it was to be expressing their needs."[68] His mother felt very disgusted and sad when she realized that, for thirty-six years, she was angry

---

[65] Len Doyal and Ian Gough, "A Theory of Human Needs," *Critical Social Policy* 4, no. 10 (1984): 6–38, 19.
[66] Rosenberg, *Nonviolent Communication*, 55.
[67] Rosenberg, *Nonviolent Communication*, 56.
[68] Rosenberg, *Nonviolent Communication*, 56.

with her husband for not satisfying her needs and she "never once clearly told him what she needed."[69] Many women find it difficult to identify and express their needs. Instead, "They hint around and go through all kinds of convolutions, but never would they ask directly for what they needed."[70] Thus, Rosenberg's mother, like other women, was unable to identify and clearly express her needs because of cultural conditioning, lack of awareness that she is motivated by needs, and the lack of language to clearly pinpoint her needs and express them to her husband and others.

Needs are important for wellbeing because they motivate human actions,[71] and their satisfaction requires agency. Agency "refers to the experience of choice and volition in one's behavior and to the personal authentic endorsement of one's activities and action."[72] This implies a person's capacity to make choices of actions and take responsibility for the actions. Therefore, human actions are important for understanding and identifying needs. People need the mental capacity, autonomy, and freedom to choose the actions to satisfy their needs.[73] Additionally, connecting with feelings enables people to identify their needs. Feelings are messengers that alert people that their needs are met or unmet and they use emotional words to express it to others.[74] Survival and autonomy are basic needs necessary for human flourishing. They provide opportunities for realizing other goals.[75] Edward Deci and Richard Ryan affirm that there is a relationship between need and goal because satisfying a need leads to

---

[69] Rosenberg, *Nonviolent Communication*, 56.

[70] Rosenberg, *Nonviolent Communication*, 56.

[71] Marina Milyavskaya and Richard Koestner, "Psychological Needs, Motivation, and Well-Being: A Test of Self-Determination Theory Across Multiple Domains," *Personality and Individual Differences* 50, no. 3 (2011): 387–391, 387.

[72] Milyavskaya and Koestner, "Psychological Needs," 387.

[73] Doyal and Gough, "A Theory of Human Needs," 15.

[74] Marshall B. Rosenberg, *A Model for Nonviolent Communication* (Philadelphia, PA: New Society Publisher, 2003), 18–20.

[75] Doyal and Gough, "A Theory of Human Needs," 15.

achieving a goal.[76] For them, needs refer to "innate psychological nutriments that are essential for ongoing psychological growth, integrity, and well-being."[77] They identify needs for autonomy, relatedness, and competence as examples.[78] These needs are necessary for healthy development and if unmet, might lead to negative impacts. In addition, "A need is a construct that stands for a force that organizes perception, apperception, intellection, conation and action in such a way to transform in a certain direction an existing, unsatisfying situation."[79] Thus, need is what motivates a human action. People identify their needs through connecting with their feelings and perform actions that would support them in meeting the needs. Lack of agency in satisfying needs has negative impacts on human beings, especially women.

Reclaiming women's agency will require undoing women's cultural conditioning that enslaves them to that image of the loving woman that has been associated with sacrificing and denying her own needs to take care of others.[80] Women are socialized to view the caretaking of others as their priority, and they often learn to ignore their own needs.[81] They also find it difficult to clearly express their needs to others. Consequently, women continue to forget that they need to first acknowledge their need for self-care in order to care for others.[82] However, contemporary society continues to expect women to care for others, satisfy their husbands' sexual needs, and remain open to procreation before caring for themselves. Such expectations from women undermine reproductive justice. For instance, in Nigeria, a woman is expected to care for her husband by

---

[76] Edward L. Deci and Richard M. Ryan, "The 'What' and 'Why' of Goal Pursuits: Human Needs and the Self-Determination of Behavior," *Psychological Inquiry* 11, no. 4 (2000): 227–268, 228.
[77] Deci and Ryan, "The 'What' and 'Why,'" 228–229.
[78] Deci and Ryan, "The 'What' and 'Why,'" 228–229.
[79] Deci and Ryan, "The 'What' and 'Why,'" 228–229.
[80] Browning, *Risky Marriage*, 119–150.
[81] Rosenberg, *Nonviolent Communication: A Language of Life*, 55.
[82] Matthew Linn, Sheila Fabricant, Dennis Linn, *Healing of the Eight Stages of Life* (Mahwah, NJ: Paulist Press, 1988), 186.

preparing food for him, washing his clothes, and making herself available for sexual intercourse whenever her husband requests for it, or the husband can rape her if she refuses. This suggests that the woman has no right over her body, and it impacts negatively on her agency and reproductive rights. Imagine a woman whose husband asks her for sex every day without contraceptives because he thinks they are obeying the Church's law. Or consider the situation of a woman whose husband began sleeping with other women outside their marital union. She felt unsafe to sleep with her husband without a condom because she was no longer sure that the husband was HIV-negative. What would be the fate of that woman? Here the Church laws have left her stranded to bear the consequences of being a fertile woman, a faithful wife, and a woman who cannot assert control over her own reproductive health.[83]

A needs-based approach offers women the opportunity to reclaim their agency through the awareness that need is what motivates human actions and they should be courageous to express their needs. Rosenberg's mother only realized that living from the energy of one's needs is very empowering after having lived with her husband for thirty-six years. Many women are not aware of the role connecting and expressing needs play in their life because they have been socialized (including in Catholic spaces) not to care about their own needs but to always prioritize the needs of others. In addition, even when some women are aware of their needs, they lack the language to express them because of fear of being judged. Consequently, needs-consciousness and the ability to communicate needs are essential for women to reclaim their agency. Need awareness is a process that involves a person's constant self-connection to reflect on a previous or an ongoing experience. Through reflecting on the experience, the person can identify the feelings that emanate from the experience because feelings assist in identifying the needs that are present in the experience. Pleasant feelings reveal met needs, while unpleasant feelings reveal unmet needs. Once the person can identify the needs, the person then communicates it by using

---

[83] Browning, *Risky Marriage*, 39–97, 135–188.

clear, positive, and action language to ask for support in satisfying the needs.[84] This involves dialogue about needs and taking responsibility for one's needs. In a situation whereby a husband asks the wife for sex and the wife is not disposed, how can she respond using the needs-based approach? A creative way of responding might be to connect with how she feels about the request to enable her to identify her needs at that moment which might be the need for rest, safety, understanding, support, and so forth. Having identified the needs, she could express them to the husband using a compassionate language that invites dialogue. Needs-consciousness can support couples to use dialogue in resolving issues concerning reproductive rights and health, and other marital issues. The ability of women to develop the needs-consciousness will enable them to reclaim their agency to take responsibility for their needs and to make thoughtful decisions about their reproductive capacity. It involves considering the circumstances surrounding them because individuals living in relationship with others do not take decisions in isolation as they consider the needs of other associates such as their spouse, the extended family, the state, and economic resources.[85] Achieving this will require socialization of women and their spouses in nonviolent communication which is a needs-based and dialogue approach.

A Role for the Catholic Church in Nigeria

The Catholic Church's role in advancing reproductive justice in Nigeria must take a multi-sectoral approach in order to address the complex issues discussed in this essay, including poverty, gender-based violence, and neocolonialism. An approach is needed that is rooted in justice and nonviolence. Africa could take inspiration from a needs-based and dialogue approach. The latter shares deep affinity with the teaching of the

---

[84] Rosenberg, *Nonviolent Communication*, 6–7.
[85] Catherine Powell, "Up from Marriage: Freedom, Solitude, and Individual Autonomy in the Shadow of Marriage Equality," *Fordham Law Review* 84, no. 1 (2015): 69–78, 74.

Catholic Church and is rooted in equal dignity of the spouses which ensues from human dignity, voice, and bodily integrity (which are also values in a reproductive justice framework) with the aim to promote agency, responsibility, dialogue, and mutual recognition. The Church should contribute by playing a role of accompaniment while focusing on questions such as: What are each person's needs? How can we support spouses in using their conscience in their marital relationships? Such an approach moves away from the top-down Church teaching framework. It involves the Church listening to people's needs and together exploring with them sustainable strategies to meet their needs without making decisions for them. It also involves the Church's ability to use conflict mediation skills to support spouses' marital issues. Consequently, conflict mediation strategies for dealing with marital conflict are needed. What does a needs-based approach say when one partner declares a need and the other partner declares a competing need? How is the negotiation to unfold? If both partners are equal, then how are competing needs negotiated? Rosenberg's conflict mediation approach provides excellent strategies for dealing with marital conflicts because of its focus on empathy and equality in satisfying disputants' needs.[86] Thus, the Church can take inspiration from Rosenberg's mediation approach and be a role model in dialogue (synodality), which points towards the possibility of negotiating needs without violence.

This is a broader way of being Church. Pope Francis affirms: "He who accompanies does not substitute the Lord, does not do the work in the place of the person accompanied, but walks alongside him or her, encouraging them to interpret what is stirring in their heart, the quintessential place where the Lord speaks."[87] Effective accompaniment finds its root in spiritual kinship, because we are sisters and brothers, members of the same community journeying together. Accompaniment

---

[86] Rosenberg, *Nonviolent Communication*, 161–177.
[87] Pope Francis, "General Audience," January 4, 2023, www.vatican.va/content/francesco/en/audiences/2023/documents/20230104-udienza-generale.html.

without inclusive kinship might lead to excessive dependency and infantilization,[88] as seen in the past whereby a small group of clergy makes decisions for married couples without involving them. The church needs to empower her members with the "art of accompaniment" which teaches to step into the space of the other with caution. "The pace of this accompaniment must be steady and reassuring, reflecting our closeness and our compassionate gaze which also heals, liberates and encourages growth in the Christian life" (*Evangelii Gaudium*, no. 169). Thus, the role of the church is to accompany married couples in their marital journey and allow them to discover sustainable strategies that can support them in meeting their reproductive needs depending on their circumstances.

Furthermore, the equality of women, together with their rights to self-determination and bodily integrity, is very important for the flourishing of mother and child. Consequently, a woman needs the agency to be able to decide whether she is ready to yield to her husband's sexual demands at a particular time. Such a decision should be explored together by spouses on the bases of understanding, equality, and respecting each other's needs. The decision whether to use contraceptives or not should be left for the spouses, especially the woman. Leaving spouses with only the option of natural family planning can lead to unintentional pregnancy and resulting harm for married women. Some women do not understand their monthly cycle, and they are not able to know when they are fertile or not. Some cannot demand periodic abstinence from their partners even as they have good reasons to avoid pregnancy.[89] A focus on social justice and reproduction would enrich Nigerians positively.

The needs of women and the needs of society need not be opposed. The entire society benefits when women experience safety in intimate relationships and when their health is protected in pregnancy, childbirth, and the recovery period. The church's teaching on family formation

---

[88] Francis, "General Audience."
[89] Susan Rakoczy, "A Gendered Critique of The Catholic Church's Teaching on Marriage and Family: 1965–2016," *Scriptura* 115, no. 1 (2016): 1–19, 17.

should thus be developed with a focus on accompaniment, discernment, and inclusive kinship. The Catholic Church should promote a kind of flourishing which enables women to take responsibility for their reproductive rights and health in collaboration with their spouses. It requires empowering couples through accompaniment and education on needs-consciousness and how to communicate their needs to one another in nonviolent ways that promote dialogue. Protecting existing life is as important as protecting the unborn.

Conclusion

Factors such as culture and religion, societal laws and policies, politics of representation, lack of economic resources, conflict, inadequate education, and more continue to hinder reproductive justice in Nigeria. This paper has examined the importance of reclaiming women's agency for reproductive justice to enable the flourishing of mother and child in Nigeria. It explored the Catholic framework which prohibits spouses from using artificial contraceptives and abortion for women. While these teachings aim to protect life, they do not demonstrate respect for women's needs in complex cases. We need a framework that promotes women's agency. Reproductive justice offers Nigerian women the opportunity to gain access to reproductive rights and health.

The paper further explored a needs-based approach to support reclaiming women's agency and boost their ability to take responsibilities for their needs, express them to others and satisfy the needs with adequate and sustainable strategies. The needs-based approach will also support spouses and the Catholic church in advancing reproductive justice in Nigeria. It offers spouses the awareness that their actions are motivated by their needs. Needs-consciousness will enable women and their spouses to take responsibility for their actions in alignment with the Catholic value of responsible parenthood. Further, spouses should be encouraged in mutual discernment rooted in mutual respect. A needs-based approach offers spouses the opportunity to use dialogue in resolving reproductive conflicts. Within this framework, the Catholic Church's role is to accompany spouses in issues concerning reproductive health. It involves including and allowing spouses to use their conscience in decision making, instead of making laws for them. Training spouses in nonviolent communication will support them in applying the need-based approach in their everyday life.

Mary Lilian Akhere Ehidiamhen, PhD, is from Nigeria and is a member of the Congregation of Sisters for Christian Community (SFCC). She is a certified trainer of Nonviolent Communication with the Center for Nonviolent Communication (CNVC), based in Austin, Texas, USA. She specializes in theological ethics with a specific interest in peace ethics, having studied at the Faculty of Theology and Religious Studies, KU Leuven, Belgium. Dr. Ehidiamhen's research focuses on how Nonviolent Communication (NVC) can enhance Catholic social teaching on peace. Her academic approach emphasizes understanding people's experiences from their own perspectives and examining the relationship between these experiences and their belief systems. She achieves this by addressing individuals' needs and facilitating dialogue between them and academics in an interdisciplinary manner. She completed a Postgraduate Certificate in Religious Education at St. Mary's University, Twickenham, London, and is currently teaching at St. Ignatius College in Enfield, London.

14. Risking Women's Lives, Denying Women's Experiences: CDF Statements on Sterilization in Catholic Hospitals

Eric Marcelo O. Genilo, SJ

John Paul II's 1988 Apostolic Letter on the Dignity and Vocation of Women, *Mulieris Dignitatem* (MD) honors and praises the vocation of motherhood. "Through conceiving and giving birth to a child, a woman 'discovers herself through a sincere gift of self'" (no. 18). The document relates the motherhood of every woman with the motherhood of Mary and her participation in bringing the Son of God into the world. "Each and every time that motherhood is repeated in human history, it is always related to the Covenant which God established with the human race through the motherhood of the Mother of God" (no. 19). The letter only briefly mentions the difficulties that women undergo in childbearing. It makes reference to the transition from pain to joy of a mother giving birth described in the Gospel of John: "When a woman is in travail she has sorrow, because her hour has come; but when she is delivered of the child, she no longer remembers the anguish, for joy that a child is born into the world" (Jn 16: 21). The pain of childbirth is associated with the effects of original sin and is imagined as a mother's sharing in the Paschal Mystery, exemplified by Mary's sorrow at the foot of the cross.

On a spiritual level, comparing human motherhood with the motherhood of Mary can be a source of consolation and inspiration for some. On a practical level, however, such a comparison can be too idealized as it glosses over the risks and dangers that pregnant and would-be mothers face. The scriptural narrative of Mary's miraculous conception and birth of Jesus is far removed from the experiences of women who have to deal with absent, abusive, or irresponsible partners, difficulties with family planning, marital rape, domestic violence, life-threatening pregnancies, cesarean births, miscarriages, and so forth. While the apostolic letter recognizes the "feminine genius," it gives little attention to the experiences of women who are often denied agency on matters of sexuality and reproduction. This disregard for women's experiences can lead to misguided and misinformed pastoral approaches that expose women and their children to grave harm.

This chapter explores one area of church teaching where women's contexts are disregarded. In the first three sections, I discuss three documents of the Congregation for the Doctrine of the Faith (CDF, later known as the Dicastery for the Doctrine of the Faith) on sterilization in Catholic hospitals. Spanning forty-three years, these documents neglected significant realities that affect the capacity of women to safeguard themselves, their children, and their marriages. In the fourth and final section of the essay, I retrieve a solidly probable opinion developed before Vatican II by moral theologians John Ford and Gerald Kelly, who used casuistry, moral principles, and pastoral approaches that are attentive to women who face the possibility of dangerous pregnancies. I argue that their probable opinion can be instructive for pastors and laity as they discern how to apply the church's teaching on sterilization. I conclude the essay by explaining how such a retrieval advances justice for women today.

The 1975 CDF Responses to Questions Concerning Sterilization in Catholic Hospitals

The encyclical *Humanae Vitae*, promulgated by Paul VI in 1968, reaffirmed the teaching of Pius XI in *Casti Connubii* (1930) prohibiting direct sterilization as a means of birth regulation. "Equally to be condemned, as the magisterium of the Church has affirmed on many occasions, is direct sterilization, whether of the man or of the woman, whether permanent or temporary" (*Humanae Vitae*, no. 14). Applying this prohibition to the context of Catholic hospitals, the bishops of the United States included in the 1971 edition of the *Ethical and Religious*

Directives (ERD) for Catholic Health Care Facilities the following directives:

> 18. Sterilization, whether permanent or temporary, for men or for women, may not be used as a means of contraception.
>
> 20. Procedures that induce sterility, whether permanent or temporary, are permitted when (a) they are immediately directed to the cure, diminution, or prevention of a serious pathological condition and (b) a simpler treatment is not reasonably available. Hence, for example, oophorectomy or irradiating of the ovaries may be allowed in treating carcinoma of the breast and metastasis therefrom and orchidectomy is permitted in the treatment of carcinoma of the prostate.[1]

In the mid-1970s, the uneven application of Directive 20 in Catholic hospitals become a concern of the US bishops' conference. Some bishops have allowed different interpretations of the directive and there were dissenting opinions from theologians. To prevent confusion and misunderstanding of the teaching of the Church, the National Conference of Catholic Bishops (NCCB, later to become the USCCB) sought clarification from the Vatican. Four questions were submitted to the CDF with the last question expressing the primary concern of the NCCB: "Can we accept the general prohibition of direct sterilization in Catholic hospitals and still make a number of exceptions in particular cases to solve pastoral problems?"[2]

The CDF addressed the questions of the NCCB in its 1975 document "Responses to Questions Concerning Sterilization in Catholic Hospitals." On the question of the liceity of contraceptive sterilization as

---

[1] Catholic Physicians' Guild, "Ethical and Religious Directives for Catholic Health Facilities," *The Linacre Quarterly* 39, no. 1 (1972): 9–12, 11.

[2] Eugene F. Diamond, "Sterilization in Catholic Hospitals," *The Linacre Quarterly* 55, no. 1 (1988): 57–66, 58, doi.org/10.1080/00243639.1988.11877938.

a means to cure, lessen, or prevent a pathological condition, the CDF gave a direct answer:

> 1. Any sterilization which of itself, that is, of its own nature and condition, has the sole immediate effect of rendering the generative faculty incapable of procreation, is to be considered direct sterilization, as the term is understood in the declarations of the pontifical Magisterium, especially of Pius XII. Therefore, notwithstanding any subjectively right intention of those whose actions are prompted by the care or prevention of physical or mental illness which is foreseen or feared as a result of pregnancy, such sterilization remains absolutely forbidden according to the doctrine of the Church. And indeed the sterilization of the faculty itself is forbidden for an even graver reason than the sterilization of individual acts, since it induces a state of sterility in the person which is almost always irreversible.
>
> Neither can any mandate of public authority, which would seek to impose direct sterilization as necessary for the common good, be invoked, for such sterilization damages the dignity and inviolability of the human person. Likewise, neither can one invoke the principle of totality in this case, in virtue of which principal interference with organs is justified for the greater good of the person; sterility intended in itself is not oriented to the integral good of the person as rightly pursued "the proper order of goods being preserved" inasmuch as it damages the ethical good of the person, which is the highest good, since it deliberately deprives foreseen and freely chosen sexual activity of an essential element. Thus article 20 of the medical-ethics code promulgated by the conference in 1971 faithfully reflects the doctrine which is to be held, and its observance should be urged.[3]

The document affirms the prohibition in Directive 20 of the ERD against medical procedures that are directly intended to sterilize a person

---

[3] Sacred Congregation for the Doctrine of the Faith, *Responses to Questions Concerning Sterilization in Catholic Hospitals*, www.vatican.va/roman_curia/congregations/cfaith/documents/rc_con_cfaith_doc_19750313_quaecumque-sterilizatio_en.html.

temporarily or permanently to address a current or anticipated medical pathology. The CDF rejects the use of the principle of totality to justify sterilizing medical procedures for the sake of maintaining or protecting the overall physical and psychological health of a person. The document also prohibits the public's use of private theologians' dissenting opinions to contradict the magisterium's teaching.

The CDF document does not prohibit medical treatments that are directly intended to cure an existing pathology but have unintended contraceptive or sterilizing side effects. *Humanae Vitae* already permits such treatments: "The Church does not consider at all illicit the use of those therapeutic means necessary to cure bodily diseases, even if a foreseeable impediment to procreation should result there from—provided such impediment is not directly intended for any motive whatsoever" (*Humanae Vitae*, no. 15). For example, the treatment or removal of a cancerous uterus is allowed even if such a procedure has the unintended but foreseen result of impairing the patient's reproductive capacity. This is a recognized application of the principle of double effect. What the CDF had in mind in its prohibition are sterilizing procedures on healthy or currently non-threatening reproductive organs intended to prevent a future threat to the life, health, or well-being of the person due to pregnancy. For example, a tubal ligation to avoid future pregnancies that can worsen an existing heart or kidney condition is considered an illicit direct sterilization.

In a letter to all US bishops, the NCCB-USCCB president Cardinal Joseph Bernardin confirmed the magisterium's teaching on sterilization and the validity of Directive 20: "I am writing to give assurance that the 1971 guideline stands as written and that direct sterilization is not to be considered as justified by the common good, the principle of totality, the existence of contrary opinion, or any other argument. This means that Catholic hospitals, as a matter of institutional policy, may not authorize sterilization procedures for reasons other than those contained in the guidelines."[4]

For married women whose life or health may be at risk in case of pregnancy, the pastoral advice that the Church gives them is to either abstain entirely from sexual relations or to use natural family planning. The Church presents sexual intercourse in marriage as a freely chosen act by consenting spouses who value each other's good and the good of their family and community. Spouses are expected to cooperate in living out marital chastity, especially in practicing natural family planning. Real situations on the ground contradict such an idealized expectation of the marriage life of couples. Pope Francis, in *Amoris Laetitia* (AL), urged for a realistic consideration of the situation of families and the challenges they face. He gave examples of the challenges women face in their marital relationships:

> The word of God constantly testifies to that somber dimension already present at the beginning, when, through sin, the relationship of love and purity between man and woman turns into domination: "Your desire shall be for your husband, and he shall rule over you" (Genesis 3:16). (no. 19)

> I think particularly of the shameful ill-treatment to which women are sometimes subjected, domestic violence and various forms of enslavement which, rather than a show of masculine power, are craven acts of cowardice. The verbal, physical, and sexual violence that women endure in some marriages contradicts the very nature of the conjugal union. (no. 54)

The presumption that married women can easily convince their husbands to practice natural family planning or to abstain from sex entirely to avoid life-threatening pregnancies is not only unrealistic but is also ignorant of the situation of women who are denied the ability to negotiate sexual

---

[4] Diamond, "Sterilization in Catholic Hospitals," 59.

relations with their spouses. The CDF document ignores the cultural and religious traditions and attitudes of many societies where women are not treated as equal to men in marriage and are obliged to provide sexual satisfaction for their husbands. Sexual violence against women by their partners or spouses is a grave problem in both developed and developing countries.

For example, the National Family Health Survey 5 conducted in India for the period 2019–2021 reveals that "29% of ever-married women had experienced some form of physical or sexual violence from their husbands."[5] and "of the 4,169 women who are (or used to be) married and have experienced sexual violence, 82% said that the perpetrator was their husbands. Of them, a large majority (84%) said that their husbands physically forced them to have sexual intercourse even when they did not want to.[6] The Center for Disease Control in the United States estimates that one in five women have had contact with sexual violence by an intimate partner, based on the 2015 National Intimate Partner and Sexual Violence Survey.[7] According to a UN Women 2020 campaign against gender–based violence, marital rape is not a crime in 34 countries.[8]

While the Church endorses natural family planning (NFP) as an effective and safe way for married couples to plan their families, its adoption and usage depend on the spouses' concrete situation and willingness to practice NFP consistently. Physical and sexual violence in

---

[5] Padma-Bhate Deosthali, Sangeeta Rege, and Sanjida Arora, "Women's Experiences of Marital Rape and Sexual Violence within Marriage in India: Evidence from Service Records," *Sex Reproduction Health Matters* 29, no. 2 (2022): doi.org/10.1080/26410397.2022.2048455.

[6] Parvati Bethu, "Marital Rape: Most Married Women are Sexually Abused by their Husbands, Says NFHS Data," *The Hindu Business Line*, May 16, 2022, www.thehindubusinessline.com/data-stories/data-focus/marital-rape-most-married-women-are-sexually-abused-by-their-husbands-says-nfhs-data/article65409875.ece.

[7] Center for Disease Control and Prevention, *National Intimate Partner and Sexual Violence Survey: 2015 Data Brief-Updated Release*, November 2018, stacks.cdc.gov>cdc_60893_DS1.

[8] UN Women, *Ad Campaign: A Spotlight on Legal Gaps to End Violence against Women*, www.unwomen.org/en/digital-library/multimedia/2020/11/campaign-laws-endviolence.

marriage is a serious obstacle to NFP.[9] Married couples where one or both partners have physical, emotional, or psychological challenges that impair discipline and regularity in activities will find it difficult to use the modern NFP methods that require constant monitoring of signs of ovulation and consistent observance of abstinence during fertile periods. Circumstances that limit the sexual relations of couples only to prescribed times (e.g., conjugal visits in prisons, scheduled home visits of spouses working abroad, etc.) can also be obstacles to applying NFP. While modern methods of NFP are actively promoted by the Church, knowledge and usage of these methods can vary from country to country. In the Philippines, Catholics comprise around 85 percent of the population, but less than 1 percent of Filipino women use NFP.[10] It is estimated that approximately 1 percent of women in the United States use NFP, while globally, NFP usage is around 3.6 percent. Some women cannot identify their ovulation time using body temperature or cervical mucus monitoring due to irregular periods, abnormal uterine or cervical bleeding, temperature fluctuations from systemic illnesses, and cervical or vaginal infections. These women would be prevented from using various NFP methods effectively.[11]

While the 1975 CDF document seeks to provide clear guidance and prevent confusion regarding the meaning of direct and indirect sterilization in treating medical conditions, it focuses primarily on the reproductive organs and physical aspects of sterilization. The document disregards the concrete experiences of women and the multitude of social, marital, and biological factors that present difficulties in applying the teaching on sterilization without causing harm to the woman's health, her

---

[9] Susan Rakoczy, "A Gendered Critique of the Catholic Church's Teaching on Marriage and the Family: 1965–2016," *Scriptura* 115, no. 1 (2016): 1–19.

[10] Philippines Statistics Authority, *2017 National Demographic and Health Survey*, psa.gov.ph/sites/default/files/PHILIPPINE%20NATIONAL%20DEMOGRAPHIC%20 AND%20HEALTH%20SURVEY%202017_new.pdf.

[11] Sharon Sung and Aaron Abromivitz, *Natural Family Planning*, www.ncbi.nlm.nih.gov/books/NBK546661/.

marriage, and the children to be born. The document presumes to address committed and highly motivated couples who can easily practice sexual abstinence to avoid a potentially dangerous pregnancy. Unfortunately, many couples cannot fit into this idealized image. The document fails to provide a humane and person-oriented response to real situations of women and married couples.

The 1993 CDF Responses to Questions Proposed Concerning "Uterine Isolation" and Related Matters

As early as the 1950s, Catholic ethicists have considered the case of a woman with a uterus scarred by repeated caesarian deliveries to the point of potentially failing in a subsequent pregnancy, with an accompanying risk to the lives of the mother and fetus. Can a hysterectomy remove the damaged uterus before another pregnancy occurs? As an alternative to a hysterectomy, can the damaged uterus be "isolated" through a less invasive tubal ligation during a caesarian delivery, wherein a woman's fallopian tubes are cut, tied, or blocked to prevent fertilization permanently? The Vatican had not yet made a declaration before 1993 on whether the removal of such a damaged uterus or uterine isolation would be licit medical interventions to prevent future harm.

The moral theologian Gerald Kelly used probabilism to address this specific case of sterilization. In moral theology, probabilism is applied to situations where there is doubt regarding the applicability of a law to a particular moral case. A law that is affected by doubt, either of its application or existence, cannot oblige a person's conscience.[12] A moral opinion of a theologian can rise to the level of a solidly probable opinion that the public can follow if it is held by a significant number of reputable theologians (extrinsic probability) and has an internal logic (intrinsic probability) that makes sense to moral experts. A probable opinion on a

---

[12] Eric Marcelo Genilo, SJ, *John Cuthbert Ford, SJ: Moral Theologian at the End of the Manualist Era* (Washington, DC: Georgetown University Press: 2007), 41.

moral case can guide pastoral practice if the magisterium has yet to give a definite response to the case and if the magisterium has not forbidden the application of the probable opinion.

Kelly proposed a "probable opinion" that a hysterectomy of a damaged uterus is an indirect sterilization and is thus licit.[13] In the influential moral manual *Contemporary Moral Theology: Marriage Questions*, Kelly and his fellow moralist John Ford argued that it was licit to allow the removal of a damaged uterus that was at risk of failing in a succeeding pregnancy.[14] Their opinion was deemed solidly probable to guide pastoral practice until the magisterium could make a definitive judgment on the matter. The reputations of Ford and Kelly gave their probable opinion sufficient credibility and weight that the 1971 Ethical and Religious Directives for Catholic Health Facilities made room for the possibility of a hysterectomy in an extraordinary medical situation:[15]

> 22. Hysterectomy is permitted when it is sincerely judged to be necessary to remove some serious uterine pathological condition. In these cases, the pathological condition of each patient must be considered individually, and care must be taken that a hysterectomy is not performed merely as a contraceptive measure or as a routine procedure after any definite number of Cesarean sections."[16]

Regarding uterine isolation, ethicists held that there is a moral difference between isolating a damaged uterus through tubal ligation and removing the same uterus through a hysterectomy. While both procedures can render a patient permanently sterilized, the former is considered an illicit direct sterilization while the latter can be justified in some instances as an

---

[13] Diamond, "Sterilization in Catholic Hospitals," 57.

[14] John Ford and Gerald Kelly, *Contemporary Moral Theology: Marriage Questions* (Westminster, MD: Newman Press, 1963) 328–337.

[15] Thomas O'Donnell, "'Uterine Isolation' Unacceptable in Catholic Teaching," *The Linacre Quarterly* 61, no. 3 (1994): 58–59.

[16] Catholic Physicians' Guild, "Ethical and Religious Directives for Catholic Health Facilities," 11.

indirect sterilization using the principle of double effect. The term "uterine isolation" might also be misused to justify other contraceptive acts, such as using a diaphragm or a cervical cap to prevent problematic pregnancies. For these reasons, uterine isolation was not included in Directive 22 as a permissible medical response to treating a uterus with a severe pathological condition.[17]

Persistent questions surrounding the scarred uterus case and uterine isolation led the CDF to issue the instruction *Responses to Questions Proposed Concerning "Uterine Isolation" and Related Matters* in 1993. The CDF made a distinction between the case of a damaged uterus, which poses an immediate threat to the life of a mother after delivery, and a weakened uterus that does not present an immediate danger to the life of a woman while she is not pregnant but can pose grave harm to her and her unborn child if she becomes pregnant. The CDF allowed the removal of the uterus in the former case but did not in the latter case. In the latter case, the CDF argued that removing the weak uterus did not have a proper therapeutic character but aimed to prevent future pregnancies and was, therefore, a direct sterilization. Such a procedure is not to be allowed in Catholic hospitals. The CDF also prohibited tubal ligation or "uterine isolation" to substitute for a hysterectomy of a uterus with a serious pathological condition.

> Q. 1. When the uterus becomes so seriously injured (e.g., during delivery or a Caesarian section) so as to render medically indicated even its total removal (*hysterectomy*) in order to counter an immediate serious threat to the life or health of the mother, is it licit to perform such a procedure notwithstanding the permanent sterility which will result for the woman?
> R. Affirmative.
> Q. 2. When the uterus (e.g., as a result of previous Caesarian sections) is in a state such that while not constituting in itself a present risk to the life or health of the woman, nevertheless is foreseeably incapable of carrying

---

[17] Diamond, "Sterilization in Catholic Hospitals," 62–64.

a future pregnancy to term without danger to the mother, danger which in some cases could be serious, is it licit to remove the uterus (hysterectomy) in order to prevent a possible future danger deriving from conception?
R. Negative.
Q. 3. In the same situation as in no. 2, is it licit to substitute tubal ligation, also called "uterine isolation," for the hysterectomy, since the same end would be attained of averting the risks of a possible pregnancy by means of a procedure which is much simpler for the doctor and less serious for the woman, and since in addition, in some cases, the ensuing sterility might be reversible?
R. Negative.[18]

The CDF's prohibition on sterilizations to prevent future dangerous pregnancies lacks an adequate consideration of the experience of women who face the risk of life-threatening pregnancies and miscarriages. The CDF refers to the marital acts that can lead to risky pregnancies as "sexual acts freely chosen" implying that affected couples should either avoid intercourse permanently or use NFP regularly. It appears that the CDF is blaming at-risk pregnant women for irresponsibly putting themselves in danger if they chose to have sex. As mentioned in the previous section, some women are in situations where they are not free to refuse sexual intercourse with their partners, and NFP is not possible for some couples due to their marital, physical, psychological, and social conditions. What should an at-risk married woman do if her husband lacks the capacity or desire for sexual abstinence, whether permanently or in the context of NFP? Does she refuse sex with her spouse and risk straining their marriage or provoking domestic violence? Does she wait until she gets pregnant, knowing she will likely lose her child and endanger her life before she can have the medical intervention the CDF allows? In effect, the CDF is asking

---

[18] Congregation for the Doctrine of the Faith, *Responses to Questions Proposed Concerning "Uterine Isolation" and Related Matters,* www.vatican.va/ roman_curia/congregations/cfaith/documents/rc_con_cfaith_doc_31071994_uterine-isolation_en.html.

at-risk women to place themselves in harm's way to preserve their reproductive organs until the last moment of functionality. For the CDF, real and present danger of death during pregnancy seems to be the only reason to remove a weakened or damaged uterus. Simply saying that there is no danger to the at-risk woman as long as she does not get pregnant is gravely insensitive to the experience of many women who cannot prevent their partners from forcing them to have sex.

The 1993 CDF response was integrated into the *2007 Ethical and Religious Directives for Catholic Health Facilities* of the US bishops' conference and is currently expressed in Directive 53:

> 53. Direct sterilization of either men or women, whether permanent or temporary, is prohibited in a Catholic healthcare institution. Procedures that induce sterility are permitted when their direct effect is the cure or alleviation of a present, and serious pathology and a simpler treatment is not available.[19]

Doctors working in Catholic hospitals in the United States face a difficult choice: whether to proceed with a medically-indicated sterilization for a woman whose health or life may be endangered in a future pregnancy and risk administrative sanctions from their Catholic facility (e.g., the loss of admitting privileges) or avoid violating the directives of their institution by having the patient transfer to a non-Catholic health facility to have the sterilizing procedure they need.

Transferring a patient can lead to delayed treatment that would be detrimental to the patient's health. A woman's health insurance may only apply to her local Catholic hospital and not to another hospital, resulting in onerous additional costs for her procedure. With the mergers of Catholic facilities with other medical institutions, a woman might find out too late about her hospital's religious directives when it is no longer

---

[19] United States Conference of Catholic Bishops (USCCB), *Ethical and Religious Directives for Catholic Health Facilities Sixth Edition*, www.usccb.org/resources/ethical-and-religious-directives-catholic-healthcare-services.

medically advisable for her to be moved to a non-Catholic hospital.[20] The situation can be further complicated if the Catholic facility is the only hospital serving a remote area and the nearest non-Catholic health facility is not easily accessible. "Women who are on Medicaid or live in rural areas often have only one hospital they can go to—one-third of Catholic hospitals are rural community hospitals."[21] A 2020 US study identified fifty-two Catholic short-term acute care hospitals designated as their region's "sole community hospital" (located at least thirty-five miles from the nearest similar hospital).[22]

Many doctors believe that the Church's directive that prevents women from receiving medically-indicated sterilizations from Catholic facilities goes against the best interest of patients and "poses a 'risk of harm' to women by violating the accepted standard of care, especially for women who are already getting a C-section and would need an unnecessary second surgery."[23] There was a case where a patient sued a Catholic facility for denying medically-indicated sterilization that resulted in distress, delayed treatment, additional expenses, and new surgical risks because of the need to transfer to a non-Catholic facility for their procedure.[24]

A 2012 study of obstetrician-gynecologists working in religiously affiliated health facilities showed that those working in Catholic

---

[20] Julia Kaye, Brigitte Amiri, Louise Melling, and Jennifer Daven, "Healthcare Denied: Patients and Physicians Speak Out About Catholic Hospitals and the Threat to Women's Health and Lives," American Civil Liberties Union, www.aclu.org/report/report-health-care-denied?redirect=report/health-care-denied.

[21] Patricia Miller, "'A Risk of Harm': Catholic Hospital's Ban on Tube Tying," *The Atlantic*, January 2, 2015, www.theatlantic.com/health/archive/2015/01/a-risk-of-harm-catholic-hospitals-ban-on-tube-tying/383903/.

[22] Tess Solomon, Lois Uttley, Patty Hasbrouck, and Yoolim Jung, "Bigger and Bigger: The Growth of Catholic Health Systems," Community Catalyst 2020, www.communitycatalyst.org/resources/publications/document/2020-Cath-Hosp-Report-2020-31.pdf.

[23] Miller, "A Risk of Harm."

[24] Carrie Baker, "Catholic Hospital Denies Woman a Medically Necessary Sterilization, Putting Her Health and Well-Being at Risk: 'It's Wrong and It's Dangerous,'" *Ms. Magazine*, August 10, 2021, msmagazine.com/2021/08/10/catholic-hospital-woman-sterilization-health-care/.

institutions are most likely (52 percent) to report a conflict with their institution's religion-based policies on patient care.[25] The potentially harmful effect of strict implementation of Directive 53 on the life and health of at-risk women has led to inconsistencies in its application in Catholic facilities. A study in 2013 revealed wide diversity in the interpretation of Directive 53 in Catholic hospitals in seven US states. Out of 176 hospitals surveyed, "eighty-five or 48 percent of these hospitals provided a total of 20,073 direct sterilizations in violation of the ERDs."[26] A less strict interpretation of the directive was applied either by the Catholic facilities or by the bishops in whose jurisdiction the facilities were located.

The dangerous situations created by Directive 53 for at-risk women in the United States, where one out of six hospital beds is in a Catholic health facility, are a direct result of the 1993 CDF response that inadequately considered the experiences of women and the medical complications they face related to pregnancy. The CDF has placed women's lives and their unborn children in harm's way by simply focusing on precisely determining what constitutes direct or indirect sterilization without considering the human consequences of what is allowed or prohibited. The constant and unrelenting focus on preserving a woman's reproductive capacity even at the risk of her health shows a fragmented, disembodied, and inadequate view of women that does not respect their totality as integral persons deserving the best medical care available for themselves and their family. The CDF's moral stance on the plight of women who face the possibility of life-threatening pregnancies turns a blind eye to the realities of sexual violence and coercion in marriage and the social justice implications of limiting the healthcare options of persons dependent on Catholic medical institutions in their locality.

---

[25] Debra Stulberg, Annie Dude, Irma Dahlquist, et al., "Obstetrician-gynecologists, religious institutions, and conflicts regarding patient-care policies," *American Journal of Obstetrics Gynecology* 207, no. 73 (2012): 1–5, doi.org/10.1016/j.ajog.2012.04.023.

[26] Sarah Hapenney, "Divergent practices among catholic hospitals in provision of direct sterilization," *Linacre Quarterly* 80, no. 1 (2013): 32.

The 2018 CDF Response to a Question on the Liceity of a Hysterectomy in Certain Cases

Twenty-five years after the publication of the 1993 CDF response, the magisterium deemed it necessary to return to the case of hysterectomy for women with a damaged uterus. The 2018 CDF response clarifies that it does not negate nor invalidate the teaching of the 1993 response. Instead, it aims to complete the previous document by addressing a case where a hysterectomy can be allowed.

> Question: When the uterus is found to be irreversibly in such a state that it is no longer suitable for procreation and medical experts have reached the certainty that an eventual pregnancy will bring about a spontaneous abortion before the fetus is able to arrive at a viable state, is it licit to remove it (hysterectomy)?
>
> Response: Yes, because it does not regard sterilization.[27]

The CDF argues that the above case differs from the cases addressed by the 1993 response. While the 1993 document dealt with cases where a damaged uterus can fail during pregnancy, the 2018 document described a case where medical experts have judged with certainty that a damaged uterus can no longer bring a pregnancy to term. In this case, the uterus can no longer fulfill its natural procreative function.[28] The removal of this non-functional uterus will not be sterilization, according to the CDF, because

---

[27] Congregation for the Doctrine of the Faith, "Response to a Question on the Liceity of a Hysterectomy in Certain Cases," press.vatican.va/content/salastampa/it/bollettino/pubblico/2019/01/03/0005/00014.html#en.

[28] The CDF approach to the damaged uterus case in both its 1993 and 2018 statements reflects a physicalist approach to sexual ethics that sees the human body as a blueprint of God's purpose for every human faculty, disregarding the importance of other dimensions of the human person for moral discernment. For a critique of this physicalist approach to the human person, see Charles Curran, "Catholic Social and Sexual Teaching: A Methodological Comparison," *Theology Today* 4, no. 4 (1988): 437–438.

there is no longer any procreative function to impede. "Removing a reproductive organ incapable of bringing a pregnancy to term should not therefore be qualified as direct sterilization, which is and remains intrinsically illicit as an end and as a means."

While the 2018 response intended to address a hysterectomy case not covered by the 1993 response, it provoked dissenting opinions claiming that this new document contradicts the 1993 response and the Church's teaching on sterilization.[29] The 2018 response states that "the objective of the procreative process is to bring a baby into the world, but here the birth of a living fetus is not biologically possible. Therefore, we are not dealing with a defective, or risky, functioning of the reproductive organs, but we are faced here with a situation in which the natural end of bringing a living child into the world is not attainable." Some object to this description of procreation as bringing a child into the world (live birth), pointing out that the magisterium has always treated the moment of fertilization as the moment of procreation and the start of human life. The National Catholic Bioethics Center (NCBC) raised the following concerns:

> While the response affirms that removing a uterus that is incapable of carrying a child to viability is not *per se* a direct sterilization, it does not offer a comprehensive rationale and explanation—including a full and specific medical scenario—under which performing such a hysterectomy would, in practice, be morally legitimate. . . . A matter of concern to some theologians, however, is how this response might be cited in the future, with its definition of procreation focused on live birth and its seeming opening of the door to a "pastoral" permission for women who can conceive children without being able to carry them to viability to procure hysterectomies to avoid further miscarriages.[30]

---

[29] Joshua Schulz and William Hamant, "Non-Sterilizing Hysterectomies: A Catholic Critique of the CDF," *Linacre Quarterly* 87, no. 2 (2020): 182–195.

[30] National Catholic Bioethics Center, "Commentary on the CDF Responsum of 10 December 2018," February 19, 2019, www.ncbcenter.org/resources-and-statements-cms/commentary-on-the-cdf-responsum-of-december-10-2018.

In the debate over the orthodoxy of the 2018 CDF response, the voices of women facing difficult choices regarding their reproductive health remain unheard. The language of the CDF and its critics show a narrow focus on children and childbearing while disregarding the women who have to face the effects and dangers of risky pregnancies. For example, the 2018 CDF response states, "the malice of sterilization consists in the refusal of children: it is an act against the *bonum prolis*." Such a description of the wrongness of sterilization seems to imply that those who seek sterilization do not want children, disregarding the fact that certain pregnancy situations carry severe risks to the health and life of both mother and child. Not all women who seek sterilization refuse to raise children; some desire children but cannot undergo pregnancy without risking harm to themselves and their unborn child.

In interpreting the CDF document, the National Catholic Bioethics Center declares that "any dangers to the health or life of the woman expected to arise as a result of future pregnancy, and any dangers to a potentially conceived child, should play no role in establishing a therapeutic rationale or 'proportionate reason' for performing a hysterectomy in the non-pregnant state."[31] To say that anticipated dangers to the mother or unborn child from a future risky pregnancy should not play any role in one's discernment over whether or not to have a sterilizing procedure goes against common sense, self-preservation, and Christian charity. Protecting human life and avoiding injury of both mother and child will always weigh more significantly in the decision-making of doctors, patients, and the patient's family than the strict adherence to church rules.

In the debate over the proper interpretation and application of the 2018 response to cases of hysterectomy, the final sentence in the document is barely accorded attention: "It is the decision of the spouses, in dialogue with doctors and their spiritual guide, to choose the path to follow, applying the general criteria of the gradualness of medical intervention to

---

[31] National Catholic Bioethics Center, "Commentary on the CDF Responsum."

their case and to their circumstances." This is a critical sentence highlighting the agency of those directly affected by risky pregnancies. Even if removing a defective uterus to prevent future harm is an illicit direct sterilization by church definition, a woman and her family's decision to proceed with this medical intervention to protect life and health should be respected and protected under the principle of the primacy of conscience.

A Way Forward: Retrieving the Probable Opinion of John Ford and Gerald Kelly

Before the 1993 CDF response, removing a damaged uterus to prevent a future risky pregnancy was justified by the solidly probable opinion of moral theologians John Ford and Gerald Kelly. John Ford and Gerald Kelly claimed that they had been consulted about the case of the scarred uterus at least a hundred times in twenty years.[32] Ford had previously held that the pre-emptive removal of a uterus scarred and weakened by repeated caesarian deliveries was direct sterilization. Still, he changed his position after studying medical data on maternal mortality. A study by Cornelius O'Connor, a medical doctor, showed that mothers who undergo an operation to remove their weakened uterus immediately after a cesarean operation have a 1 percent mortality rate compared to 2 percent mortality for mothers who, after a cesarean operation, do not have their weakened uterus removed.[33] This means there is a greater danger of death for a woman who retains a weakened uterus after a caesarian operation because of the possibility of a future pregnancy that can rupture the uterus. A woman who has her weakened uterus removed during her caesarian

---

[32] Ford and Kelly, *Marriage Questions*, 328.

[33] See, for example, Cornelius O'Connor, "The Problem of the Repeat Caesarean Section: A Preliminary Study," *American Journal of Obstetrics and Gynecology* 53, no. 6 (1947): 914–926. Ford does not provide a footnote reference to O'Connor's study. This article by O'Connor was published after Ford's article in *Theological Studies* that references O'Connor.

operation could face other life-threatening complications from her surgical procedure. Still, the danger of uterine rupture in a future pregnancy would no longer threaten her. For Ford, this 1 percent difference in mortality was sufficient reason to justify the removal of the weakened uterus both medically and theologically:[34]

> Is the difference between 2% mortality and 1% mortality a serious matter? If one were to look at the question from the opposite side, one might say: the conservative technique is 98% safe and the radical procedure is 99% safe. This very slight increase in safety is not enough to justify the sterilization. But to a surgeon the difference between 1% and 2% mortality is a very important, in fact, a decisive difference. "Twice as good a chance to survive" is a very big thing to a patient, and that is exactly what is represented by the difference between 1% and 2% mortality. Theologians recognize that a 1% danger of death is a very real danger and teach that persons who are undergoing an operation involving that amount of danger, or even less, are to be given the sacraments as persons who are truly in danger of death. Such persons are entitled to all the privileges which canon law allows *in periculo mortis*. Now, it seems to me that a danger of death twice as great as that is objectively a very important and serious matter, constituting a sufficient reason for permitting sterilization.[35]

Ford and Kelly, in their moral manual *Marriage Questions*, used the principle of double effect to justify cesarean hysterectomy, saying that it was licit to intend the good effect of preserving the health of the patient by removing a presently pathological uterus while at the same time not directly intending the resulting sterilization. To prove this point, Ford used a technique called "supposition."

---

[34] John C. Ford, "Notes on Moral Theology," *Theological Studies* 5, no. 4 (1944): 495–538, 514–517, doi.org/10.1177/004056394400500405.
[35] Ford, "Notes on Moral Theology," 515.

> The supposition here would be that a woman has a double uterus (a condition that occasionally exists), one damaged, and one healthy. Granted the supposition, the removal of the damaged uterus would eliminate the source of danger without at the same time inducing sterility. This indicates very strongly that the damaged uterus is a separate cause of danger and that it may be made the precise object of surgical intervention even in the normal case without at the same time any direct intent of sterilization.[36]

Ford acknowledged that applying the principle of double effect was "notoriously slippery and open to dispute" in complicated cases such as the scarred uterus case. However, he believed there was less danger of abusing such a principle if its results coincided with common sense. Ford asked the rhetorical question: "Is it in accord with common sense to tell a woman who has had many cesareans: 'You have worn out this uterus in the service of motherhood. Nevertheless, you must keep it; and if you wish to protect yourself against the danger inherent in using it, you must abstain from marital intercourse'?"[37]

Ford's rhetorical question addressed the objection of some moralists that a present danger to the patient was needed to justify mutilation of an organ, such as the scarred uterus. Ford challenged such a view by quoting Pius XII's words on applying the principle of totality. Pius XII said that the principle of totality can be used to justify mutilations to preserve life, to repair damage, and to avoid damage.[38] Even if an existing danger was required, Ford asserted that the weakened uterus presented such a danger in the circumstances of normal married life. Ford and Kelly defined danger as "in a set of circumstances from which one can foresee with certainty or probability a future impending evil."[39] They considered the normal married

---

[36] John C. Ford and Gerald Kelly, "Notes on Moral Theology," *Theological Studies* 15, no. 1 (1954): 52–102, 70, doi.org/10.1177/004056395401500103.

[37] Ford and Kelly, "Notes on Moral Theology," 71.

[38] Ford and Kelly, *Marriage Questions*, 335.

[39] Ford and Kelly, *Marriage Questions*, 335.

life of a woman with such a damaged uterus and believed that such a woman was in danger of conceiving again. Ford and Kelly rendered this decisive judgment: "To say that she can avoid this danger by imposing perpetual abstinence on herself and her husband is to require a degree of heroism to which our moral principles do not oblige her."[40]

Ford and Kelly were able to propose their probable opinion because they viewed the circumstances of the case from the perspective of the woman who is forced to deal with the tension between the demands of her marital life and the potential dangers of her medical condition. By acknowledging the experience of these women and their right to avoid grave risks to themselves and their future children, Ford and Kelly fashioned a moral opinion that is attentive to the human condition of married women. This person-centric stance is more consistent with medical standards of care, Christian charity, and common sense than the impersonal moral calculation of the three CDF responses that focused only on reproductive organs and their functionality. This same person-centric stance presently influences some Catholic facilities to provide sterilization services in violation of the ERD so that the care of at-risk women will not be compromised. Unlike the CDF responses that focused on preserving women's childbearing capacity regardless of possible future harm, Ford and Kelly viewed women as integral human beings dealing with complex personal, marital, familial, and social relationships and responsibilities.

Conclusion

The 1975, 1993, and 2018 CDF documents on sterilization have created an unjust situation for women at risk of a future dangerous pregnancy. These documents limited the access of women to life-saving sterilizations in Catholic hospitals. Rather than listen to the experiences of women and

---

[40] Ford and Kelly, *Marriage Questions*, 335–336.

address the challenges they face with pastoral solicitude, the CDF documents placed on these women the burden of avoiding risky pregnancies even when they do not always have the agency to negotiate sexual relations in their marriage. The standard pastoral advice to abstain from marital intercourse or practice natural family planning is inapplicable in marriages where sexual coercion and domestic violence are present. While women may not always have the power to negotiate marital activity, they should have the capacity to protect themselves from harm that stems from their difficult marital and personal situations.

The physicalist focus of the magisterium on a woman's reproductive system prevents serious consideration of the social, cultural, religious, and personal factors that constrain marital sexual activity from being a free and loving act. The CDF documents contradict the personalist framework of Catholic social teaching that calls for adequate consideration of all dimensions of a person aimed at integral human development. John Paul II declares that "the Church's sole purpose has been care and responsibility for the human person, who has been entrusted to her by Christ himself" (*Centesimus Annus*, no. 53). Benedict XVI asserts that "authentic human development concerns the whole of the person in every single dimension" (*Caritas in Veritate*, no. 11). If the Church's teachings on sterilization are to be consistent with Catholic social teachings, it must adopt a personalist approach that considers the personhood of women in all dimensions and circumstances. To ignore the threats that women face in sexual relations and childbirth is to ignore the lived reality of many women and prevent them from receiving the care and protection that is due to them as human beings created in God's image.

The theologians Ford and Kelly have shown that a person-oriented approach is possible when analyzing the case of the scarred uterus. Using the resources of the moral manuals of their time, Ford and Kelly were able to argue that the removal of a severely weakened uterus in danger of failure in a future pregnancy is an indirect sterilization that can be licitly performed.

Still unrestricted by CDF directives, Ford and Kelly were able to navigate the church's norms on sterilization while paying serious attention to the challenges of marital life experienced by women. A retrieval and revival of their moral arguments and personalist approach can contribute to correcting the physicalism of the CDF statements and provide a more integral and humane solution to a dire situation many women face. The moral tradition has much to offer from its treasury of wisdom that can help the Church re-orient itself away from past moral statements that are unhelpful to vulnerable persons who deserve care, respect, attention, and fullness of life as God's children.

Eric Marcelo O. Genilo, SJ, STD, is professor of moral theology at the Loyola School of Theology at Ateneo de Manila University and a formator of diocesan seminarians at San Jose Seminary in Quezon City, Philippines. He earned his licentiate and doctoral degrees at Weston Jesuit School of Theology (Cambridge, Massachusetts). His research specializations include the development of moral doctrine, fundamental moral theology, and bioethics. He is the author of *John Cuthbert Ford: Moral Theologian at the End of the Manualist Era* (Georgetown University Press, 2007).

15. Catholic Health Care and Reproductive Justice: Whose Conscience Has Priority When Conscience Claims Collide?

Emily Reimer-Barry

Do Catholic hospitals in the US facilitate or inhibit reproductive justice for pregnant patients?[1] It is a complex question that requires an examination of the Catholic health care system and its policies, the place of Catholic health care in the framework of all US health care, competing claims about social justice, and competing claims of conscience. Catholic teachings on conscience are clear and straightforward: a person is obliged to form and follow their conscience. But our communities are ill-equipped to navigate the confusion and conflict that emerges when conscience claims compete or when one's conscience obliges an action that violates a duty one holds as part of one's employment responsibility. Navigating professional roles and responsibilities is also part of how one lives out one's moral values. Theologians in the Catholic tradition have expanded our understanding of conscience by careful attention to the formation of the agent and the process of discernment.[2] These developments are important as we consider how Catholic health care institutions can better foster reproductive justice for patients who seek care in alignment with their own conscientious discernment. Given this volume's focus on reproductive justice, I limit my focus in this chapter to conscientious discernment regarding reproductive health. But conscience claims are not limited to cases of reproductive health care in medicine. Properly understood,

---

[1] Special thanks to virtual table members who provided valuable feedback and corrections during the workshop for this essay. I am also grateful for the research support of the Steber Professorship, University of San Diego.

[2] See Kathryn Lilla Cox, "Reproductive Injustice as Social Sin: Mapping Sin Discourse into Debates about Fertility Decisions," 90–121, in this volume.

conscience claims should impact many more aspects of patient care. While these debates are relevant to a broad range of moral questions encountered in medicine today—issues such as care for uninsured patients, rationing of resources, the public health crisis of gun violence, pharmaceutical interventions in adolescent mental health, gender-affirming care for transgender persons, prescribing of PrEP therapy for HIV prevention among sexually active patients, and dispensing of opioid medications during an ongoing opioid epidemic—I cannot do justice to the multi-dimensional questions these issues pose.[3] If my focus on communal discernment and the prioritizing of patient needs is compelling for cases involving reproductive health care, it is worth probing whether it would also be applicable in other kinds of medical discernments.

In *Amoris Laetitia*, Pope Francis explained that pastors are called to "form consciences," not to "replace them" (no. 37). Francis has also asserted the right of Catholic health care professionals to conscientious objection, including the right to refuse to perform abortions at the request of pregnant patients.[4] What happens when a patient's conscience is in conflict with the provider's conscience? How are these competing claims to be negotiated? Is not a conscientious refusal on the part of a health care provider a "replacement" of the patient's own conscientious conclusion?[5]

---

[3] Nor will I be able to attend to competing religious liberty claims, such as when a Jewish physician seeks to provide care to a Hindu patient in a Catholic hospital.

[4] Francis, "Address of His Holiness Pope Francis to the Participants in the Congress Promoted by the Italian Society of Hospital Pharmacy and Pharmaceutical Services of Health Authorities," October 14, 2021, www.vatican.va/content/francesco/en/speeches/2021/october/documents/20211014-farmaceutica-ospedaliera.html.

[5] The physician's role as gatekeeper is one that I cannot analyze in full within the scope of this argument. It is relevant not only in cases of reproductive health, which is the focus of this paper, but also cases in which the physician refuses care in other situations such as refusing to provide breast enlargement surgery for teenagers, refusals to dispense opioid drugs, refusal to prescribe non-standard pharmaceuticals such as Ivermectin to treat Covid-19, or turning away of indigent patients or patients on Medicare/Medicaid. Francis admits that it is a "very delicate issue, which requires both great competence and great rectitude." Francis, "Address of His Holiness Pope Francis to the Participants in the Congress Promoted by the Italian Society of Hospital Pharmacy

This essay examines the ways in which competing conscience claims have been negotiated and some of the ongoing problems with the current situation. I argue that the United States Conference of Catholic Bishops unfairly restricts reproductive health care on the basis of their interpretations of Catholic doctrine, including Church teachings on conscience and religious liberty. Competing goods in Catholic health care are commonplace, and current strategies for resolving these issues exacerbate reproductive injustice for patients. Drawing on the work of philosopher Carolyn McLeod, this essay forwards the argument that when genuine conflict is present, the patient seeking a medicine or intervention consistent with the standard of care should have their needs prioritized; in such cases, attention must also be given to the moral injury and lack of integration experienced by some health care providers.

Catholic Health Care in the US

Catholic health care systems in the United States profess a deep and abiding commitment to justice. In Catholic teachings, "Society ensures social justice by providing the conditions that allow associations and individuals to obtain their due" (*Catechism*, no. 1943). The *Ethical and Religious Directives for Catholic Health Care Services* is in its sixth edition and governs the delivery of care in institutionally based Catholic health care services.[6] The *Ethical and Religious Directives for Catholic Health Care Services* explain that foundational commitments include promotion of human dignity, care for the poor and uninsured, and contribution to the common good.[7] The Catholic Health Association explains that "Catholic health care carries out the healing ministry of Jesus in a complex

---

and Pharmaceutical Services of Health Authorities," October 14, 2021, www.vatican.va/content/francesco/en/speeches/2021/october/documents/20211014-farmaceutica-ospedaliera.html.

[6] United States Conference of Catholic Bishops (USCCB), *Ethical and Religious Directives for Catholic Health Care Services*, 2018, 4. www.usccb.org/about/doctrine/ethical-and-religious-directives/upload/ethical-religious-directives-catholic-health-service-sixth-edition-2016-06.pdf.

[7] USCCB, *Ethical and Religious Directives for Catholic Health Care Services*, 8.

Catholic Health Care and Reproductive Justice: Whose Conscience Has Priority?

environment—a fragmented health care system, millions of Americans uninsured or underinsured, enormous competition, challenges in reimbursement, proliferating technologies, and numerous biomedical and scientific advances."[8] In alignment with the principles of Catholic social teachings, Catholic hospitals are mission-driven institutions that seek to create more healthy and just communities through the provision of medical care and the administration of rehabilitation and nursing home facilities.[9]

In the United States, Catholic health systems control 16.6 percent (one in six) of the hospital beds in the country and, in some states, more than twenty percent of the hospital beds.[10] According to the Catholic Health Association, every day more than one in seven patients are cared for in a Catholic hospital. 498,580 full-time employees and 208,283 part-time workers are employed in Catholic hospitals.[11] In forty-six regions, the only regional hospital is a Catholic hospital. At a time when rural hospitals are closing at unprecedented levels, many pregnant people find themselves in

---

[8] Catholic Health Association of the United States, "Ethics Overview," 2023, www.chausa.org/ethics/overview.

[9] This is not to say that Catholic institutions always live up to their mission. My thanks to Kate Ward for pointing this out in our virtual table workshop. In practice Catholic health care administrators must make difficult decisions about how to prioritize care. A recent example of failures to live up to their stated mission can be found in the report of the National Nurses United, which demonstrated that Ascension Health, one of the largest Catholic health care providers in the US, was accelerating a trend of closing labor and delivery units. See Aleja Hertzler-McCain, "Catholic Bishops Silent as Ascension Hospital System Shrinks Maternity Care," *Religion News Service*, April 8, 2024, religionnews.com/2024/04/08/catholic-bishops-silent-as-ascension-hospital-system-shrinks-maternity-care/.

[10] Emily Reimer-Barry, *Reproductive Justice and the Catholic Church* (Lanham, MD: Sheed & Ward, 2024), 62–65. See also Hayley Penan and Amy Chen, "The Ethical & Religious Directives: What the 2018 Update Means for Catholic Hospital Mergers," National Health Law Program, January 2, 2019, 2.

[11] Catholic Health Association of the United States, "U.S. Catholic Health Care," 2024, www.chausa.org/about/about/facts-statistics.

"health care deserts."[12] The hospital system in the US is still facing challenges with staffing and workplace burnout in the wake of the Covid-19 pandemic.[13]

Catholic hospitals must conform to the *Ethical and Religious Directives for Catholic Health Care Services* promulgated by the United States Conference of Catholic Bishops.[14] In alignment with authoritative

---

[12] More than 150 rural hospitals closed between 2005 and 2019, and another 19 shut down in 2020. See Dennis Thompson, "Hundreds of Hospitals Could Close Across Rural America," *U.S. News and World Report,* January 16, 2023, www.usnews.com/news/health-news/articles/2023-01-16/hundreds-of-hospitals-could-close-across-rural-america#:~:text=More%20than%20150%20rural%20hospitals,received%20while%20the%20pandemic%20raged. More than 600 rural hospitals—nearly 30 percent of rural hospitals nationwide—are at risk of closing in the near future, according to the Center for Healthcare Quality and Payment Reform. See Marcus Robertson, "631 Hospitals at Risk of Closure, State by State," Becker's Healthcare Report, January 3, 2023, www.beckershospitalreview.com/finance/631-hospitals-at-risk-of-closure-state-by-state.html?utm_medium=email&utm_content=newsletter. The Catholic Health Association argues that Catholic health systems have kept rural hospitals open and care available for those who would not otherwise have it. See CHA, "Rural Health Care Policy Brief," 2024, www.chausa.org/advocacy/policy-briefs/rural-health-care. Some journalists argue, however, that the footprint of Catholic health care places women's comprehensive health care decisions in jeopardy. Regarding a hospital acquisition in New Mexico, see Nina Martin, "Blue State Barriers and the Messy Map of Abortion Access," *Reveal,* March 9, 2024, revealnews.org/podcast/blue-state-barriers-and-the-messy-map-of-abortion-access/?fbclid=IwAR1HDlPxeWZ5yiSyK0lZVG5TmtFg4HmVZiAUkSe5WvXkMjwfLauS5wxDvFc.

[13] Hailey Mensik, "Staffing Overtakes Financial Challenges as Top Concern," *Health Care Dive,* February 7, 2022, www.healthcaredive.com/news/staffing-shortages-top-concern-for-hospital-CEOs-COVID/618402/. According to US News and World Report, 46 percent of health care workers reported experiencing burnout in 2022, up from 32 percent in 2018. See Brianna Navarre, "How Hospitals and Health Systems are Battling Burnout in Health Care," *US News and World Report,* November 16, 2023, www.usnews.com/news/live-events/articles/2023-11-16/how-hospitals-and-health-systems-are-battling-burnout-in-health-care#:~:text=By%20Brianna%20Navarre-,Nov.,2023%2C%20at%2011%3A37%20a.m.&text=Burnout%20reportedly%20costs%20the%20U.S.,up%20from%2032%25%20in%202018.

[14] United States Conference of Catholic Bishops, *Ethical and Religious Directives for Catholic Health Care Services,* no. 4, www.usccb.org/about/doctrine/ethical-and-religious-directives/upload/ethical-religious-directives-catholic-health-service-sixth-edition-2016-06.pdf.

magisterial teachings, these directives forbid direct contraception, direct sterilization, direct abortion, and some infertility treatments including in vitro fertilization. They can also limit the treatment options patients have to prevent pregnancy as a result of sexual assault.[15] In cases of complex pregnancy complications for pregnant people with wanted pregnancies, the *Ethical and Religious Directives* explain that a way forward is always sought that achieves good outcomes for both mother and prenate. The bishops write: "The Church's defense of life encompasses the unborn and the care of women and their children during and after pregnancy."[16] However, journalists and scholars have documented accounts of pregnant people being turned away from care by Catholic hospitals even when facing serious complications, causing unnecessary delays in their care.[17] This is all the more troubling given that it is actually quite common for a woman's only health care choice to be a Catholic hospital. For some patients, conscientious refusals lead to life-or-death scenarios.[18]

---

[15] United States Conference of Catholic Bishops, *Ethical and Religious Directives for Catholic Health Care Services*, directive 36.

[16] United States Conference of Catholic Bishops, *Ethical and Religious Directives for Catholic Health Care Services*, no. 16. The document cites Pope John Paul II, "Address of October 29, 1983, to the 35th General Assembly of the World Medical Association," *Acta Apostolicae Sedis* 76 (1984): 390.

[17] Judy Stone, "Healthcare Denied at 550 Hospitals Because of Catholic Doctrine," *Forbes*, May 7, 2016, www.forbes.com/sites/judystone/2016/05/07/health-care-denied-at-550-hospitals-because-of-catholic-doctrine/?sh=7f125c5c5ad9. See also Michael Hiltsiz, "Here's another case of a Catholic hospital interfering with patient care," *Los Angeles Times*, January 11, 2016, www.latimes.com/business/hiltzik/la-fi-mh-catholic-hospital-interfering-with-medical-care-20160108-column.html; Claudia Buck and Sammy Caiola, "Transgender patient sues Dignity Health for discrimination over hysterectomy denial," *Sacramento Bee*, April 20, 2017. See Nelson's analysis of *Means vs. USCCB*, a case argued by the ACLU, in Lawrence J. Nelson, "Disputes over Previability Pregnancy Termination," in *Conscience & Catholic Health Care: From Clinical Contexts to Government Mandates*, ed. David E. DeCosse and Thomas A. Nairn, OFM (Maryknoll, NY: Orbis, 2017), 131.

[18] Dr. Savita Halappanavar died from sepsis after her request for an abortion was denied in Galway, Ireland. See "Woman Dies After Abortion Request Refused at Galway Hospital," BBC News, November 14, 2012, www.bbc.com/news/uk-northern-ireland-20321741. The death of Valentina Milluzzo was also a result of infection after miscarriage in Italy. See BBC

Catholic bishops do not train in medical school as part of their path to the priesthood and the episcopacy. But they have an enormous platform in shaping public opinion about health care policies. Canon law gives the local ordinary significant authority over his diocese, and when his diocese includes a Catholic hospital, it is the local ordinary who has the final word about the scope of care in that hospital.[19] Collectively, bishops also hire lawyers and lobbyists to shape public policies[20] and speak in the public square about moral and medical issues, including via social media. Recent examples include leaders such as Cardinal Burke and Archbishop Cordileone refusing publicly to be vaccinated for Covid-19.[21] Bishop Strickland of Tyler, Texas, also refused to be vaccinated[22] and even discouraged parents from having their children vaccinated for Covid-19, in contradiction to recommendations from the Centers for Disease Control and Prevention, Pope Francis, the Pontifical Academy of Life,

---

News, "Italy Abortion Row as Woman Dies After Hospital Miscarriage," October 20, 2016, www.bbc.com/news/world-europe-37713211. Regarding a life-or-death discernment in a Catholic hospital in the US, see M. Therese Lysaught, "Moral Analysis of Procedure at Phoenix Hospital," *Origins* 40, no. 33 (2011): 537–549; Bishop Thomas J. Olmsted determined that the procedure constituted a direct abortion. National Catholic Bioethics Center, "Commentary on the Phoenix Hospital Situation," *Origins* 40, no. 33 (2011): 549–551. McBride's excommunication was later lifted, and she was reinstated in her position. See Union of Catholic Asian News, "Excommunication Lifted," www.ucanews.com/news/excommunication-lifted-on-nun-who-approved-an-abortion/38039#.

[19] For a critique, see Todd A. Salzman and Michael G. Lawler, *Pope Francis and the Transformation of Health Care Ethics* (Washington, DC: Georgetown University Press, 2021), 158–160.

[20] For more, see the USCCB Government Relations website www.usccb.org/offices/government-relations.

[21] Brian Fraga, "Archbishop Cordileone Reveals He's Not Vaccinated for COVID-19, Drawing Sharp Criticism," *National Catholic Reporter*, December 3, 2021, www.ncronline.org/news/coronavirus/archbishop-cordileone-reveals-hes-not-vaccinated-covid-19-drawing-sharp-criticism.

[22] "Bishop of Tyler" on social media: twitter.com/Bishopoftyler/status/1384115228409884678?s=20&t=TC6ErLsuJOd1usN8euu3bQ. In 2023, Pope Francis relieved Bishop Strickland of the pastoral governance of Tyler, Texas. See Nicole Winfield, "Pope Francis Removes a Leading US Conservative Critic," *AP News*, November 11, 2023, apnews.com/article/pope-tyler-bishop-strickland-removed-0f9f0be7d5938b36d6e7ead8c33e5150.

and other bishops.²³ One of the curious aspects of the *Ethical and Religious Directives* is the way that they assume that bishops have competency to adjudicate difficult medical cases and that they alone speak for the Catholic Church.

Conscience Claims in Conflict?

As noted in the introduction to this volume, reproductive justice is a holistic framework that seeks to transform unjust social structures so that people can flourish in healthy sexual relationships and so that parents have all they need to care for their children. The human rights framework of reproductive justice advocates for the right to have a child, the right to not have a child, and the right to parent children in safe and healthy conditions.²⁴ Forward Together (formerly Asian Communities for Reproductive Justice), while not using the term "conscience," nevertheless explains how a reproductive justice framework centers the moral decision of the woman: "Reproductive Justice is achieved when women, girls, and individuals have the social, economic, and political power and resources to make healthy decisions about our bodies, sexuality and reproduction for ourselves, our families and our communities."²⁵ This focus on the "healthy decisions" of the woman demonstrates an implicit understanding of conscience by advocating that women should be able to make health care decisions for themselves.

Unsurprisingly, tensions arise between this vision of women's decision-making and restrictions imposed by the policies of Catholic hospitals. The

---

²³ Jack Jenkins, "Firebrand Texas Bishop Strickland Tests Limits of Conservative Catholic Dissent," *National Catholic Reporter*, February 1, 2022, www.ncronline.org/news/people/firebrand-texas-bishop-strickland-tests-limits-conservative-catholic-dissent.
²⁴ Loretta J. Ross and Rickie Solinger, *Reproductive Justice: An Introduction* (Oakland: University of California Press, 2017), 9.
²⁵ Forward Together, *A New Vision for Reproductive Justice*, 2005, forwardtogether.org/tools/a-new-vision/. See also INCITE! Women of Color Against Violence, *Color of Violence: The INCITE! Anthology* (Durham, NC: Duke University Press, 2006).

claim that women should be able to make the decision to procure a tubal ligation (sterilization) or an abortion is not supported by the *Ethical and Religious Directives*. In official magisterial teachings, abortion is not considered legitimate health care; abortion is described as unjustified killing of the innocent (*Dignitas Infinita*, no. 47).[26] Catholic leaders advocate for laws that protect unborn life and refuse to acknowledge how these laws can sometimes lead to the coercion of pregnant patients.[27] It is worth noting that there is not universal consensus among Catholics that prohibiting legal abortion is the right course of action to promote social justice.[28]

Can we bridge these tensions between the defense of women's agency in reproductive justice and the defense of unborn life in Catholic hospital policies? Not easily. Certainly, there are important opportunities for coalitions that work on shared issues of concern, of which there are many. But Catholic hospitals need to continue to reflect on how policies in place today can foster reproductive injustice instead of reproductive justice. The bishops draw upon Church teachings regarding the sanctity of life and religious freedom to justify the policies in place, but patients and employees are beginning to raise more questions about whether it is appropriate for religious leaders to wield their power in this way, by constraining the medical choices for patients in Catholic facilities and for employees of Catholic institutions (regardless of the employees' religious commitments).[29]

---

[26] See also Brian M. Kane, "Ethics-What is Abortion?" *Health Progress: Journal of the Catholic Health Association of the United States*, Winter 2023, www.chausa.org/publications/health-progress/article/winter-2023/ethics---what-is-abortion.

[27] Kathleen Bonnette explains: "Laws prohibiting abortion may violate a woman's bodily integrity and, thus, be seen as intrinsically evil." She demonstrates that, on both "sides" of the abortion debate, Catholics can have principled stances in which they seek to resist an intrinsic evil. See Kathleen Bonnette, "Holding the Tensions: Female Bodily Integrity as an Intrinsic Good," *Journal of Moral Theology* 12, no. 1 (2023): 113–117, 114. doi.org/10.55476/001c.66245.

[28] For example, Catholics for Choice is a non-profit advocacy group of pro-choice Catholics. Their website can be found at www.catholicsforchoice.org/.

[29] Salzman and Lawler, *Pope Francis and the Transformation of Health Care Ethics*, 192.

Reproductive Injustice: Remembering Victims of Forced Sterilizations and Testimonies of Dangerous Pregnancies

Black feminist scholar of law and sociology Dorothy Roberts recounts in chilling details the ways that racism influenced policies related to sterilization and incarceration; for example, Black men were sterilized while incarcerated in Indiana as part of the state's attempt "to render every male sterile" during their incarceration in 1902. Over the course of ten years, Dr. Harry C. Sharp performed 456 vasectomies on inmates in Indiana.[30] During the civil rights movement, Fannie Lou Hamer raised awareness about operations known as "Mississippi appendectomies"—sterilizations performed on Black women without their knowledge or consent, sometimes postpartum and sometimes when they sought care for another medical issue such as uterine tumors.[31] White physicians justified their actions on the basis of their "obligations to society." As one physician said, "The welfare mess cries out for solutions, one of which is fertility control."[32] In one case in 1973, the Southern Poverty Law Center found than "an estimated 100,000 to 150,000 poor women had been sterilized annually under federally funded programs. Half of the patients were Black."[33] While White middle-class women increasingly sought sterilization as part of their own reproductive decision-making, Black, Puerto Rican, and Indigenous women were being pressured to accept sterilization if they gave birth to children outside of wedlock. Roberts comments: "It is amazing how effective governments—especially our own—are at making sterilization and contraceptives available to women of color, despite their inability to reach these women with prenatal care, drug

---

[30] Dorothy Roberts, *Killing the Black Body: Race, Reproduction, and the Meaning of Liberty* (New York: Vintage, 2017), 66.
[31] Roberts, *Killing the Black Body*, 90.
[32] Roberts, *Killing the Black Body*, 92.
[33] Roberts, *Killing the Black Body*, 93.

treatment, and other health services."[34] Harriet A. Washington's carefully documented book *Medical Apartheid: The Dark History of Medical Experimentation on Black Americans from Colonial Times to the Present* uncovers not just sterilization abuses but patterns of White physicians engaging in unjust and nonconsensual medical experimentation on Black patients, as well as the ways in which policies about diseases that disproportionately impact communities of color (tuberculosis, HIV) have gone from being "protective to punitive."[35]

On the one hand, in light of the history of forced sterilizations against women of color in US history, Catholic hospitals' rejection of contraception and sterilization may seem to create safe spaces for female patients to seek care, knowing that patients will not be pressured to violate Catholic teachings. In this case, structural policies at Catholic hospitals may be said to promote patient freedom for those whose values align with the *Ethical and Religious Directives*. This view is incomplete. First, it shows institutional respect only for the consciences that align with the hospital policies, restricting patient care for others. Secondly, it exudes a paternalism—"Father knows best"—attitude that actually undercuts the patient's important discernment process.[36] Additionally, Catholic hospitals are not free from the racism and paternalism that shaped the attitudes and behaviors of the physicians who engaged in such egregious coercion against patients in the last century.[37] While important initiatives to address systemic racism in Catholic health care are underway,[38] scholars

---

[34] Roberts, *Killing the Black Body*, 94–95.
[35] Harriet A. Washington, *Medical Apartheid: The Dark History of Medical Experimentation on Black Americans from Colonial Times to the Present* (New York: Anchor, 2006), 332.
[36] See Eric Marcelo O. Genilo, SJ, "Risking Women's Lives, Denying Women's Experiences: CEF Statements on Sterilization in Catholic Hospitals," in this volume.
[37] Lauren Freeman and Health Stewart, "Microaggressions in Clinical Medicine," *Kennedy Institute of Ethics Journal* 28, no. 4 (2018): 411–449. See also Michael Jaycox, "Black Lives Matter and Catholic Whiteness: A Tale of Two Performances," *Horizons* 44, no. 2 (2017): 306–341, doi.org/10.1017/hor.2017.121.
[38] Kathy Curran and Dennis Gonzales, "Health Equity—Catholic Health Care Systems Confront Racism through 'We are Called,'" *Health Progress*, Spring 2022,

note that Catholic hospitals function in a society in which many institutions are governed by the internal codes of Whiteness.[39] In addition, the sexism of the Catholic tradition has shaped the way that Catholic hospitals—even those run by orders of women religious—have been forced to yield to the demands of bishops. It is appropriate for readers today to react with horror and shame at the testimonies of women's forced sterilizations. Coerced sterilizations are clear violations of the norms of justice and patient autonomy and have no place in health care today, Catholic or otherwise. But what about those cases in which patients seek sterilization, in conscience? Could Catholic rejection of their requests also be considered a violation of reproductive justice?

In the tumultuous years after the Second Vatican Council, women religious in the US discerned in community how best to update their own understandings of their roles in society and in Church, and some communities changed their habits of dress, living arrangements, and primary ministries as a result of these discernments.[40] An important area of concern that women religious faced was whether and how they could "participate in the evolution of Church teaching."[41] Sixty-seven hospitals in the US at that time were run by the Sisters of Mercy, in fifty-seven dioceses, in thirty-one states, with more than twenty-eight thousand beds

---

www.chausa.org/publications/health-progress/article/spring-2022/health-equity---catholic-health-care-systems-confront-racism-through-we-are-called.

[39] Traci C. West, *Disruptive Christian Ethics: When Racism and Women's Lives Matter* (Louisville: Westminster John Knox, 2006), 112–140

[40] Anne E. Patrick, SNJM, "Framework for Love: Toward a Renewed Understanding of Christian Vocation," in *A Just and True Love: Feminism at the Frontiers of Theological Ethics: Essays in Honor of Margaret A. Farley*, ed. Maura A. Ryan and Brian F. Linnane, SJ (Notre Dame: University of Notre Dame Press, 2007), 303–337; Sandra M. Schneiders, IHM, *Buying the Field: Catholic Religious Life in Mission to the World* (New York: Paulist, 2013), 647.

[41] Christine Schenk, CSJ, *To Speak the Truth in Love: A Biography of Theresa Kane, RSM* (Maryknoll, NY: Orbis, 2019), 109. On Catholic health care systems run by the Ursuline sisters see Cory D. Mitchell and M. Therese Lysaught, "Equally Strange Fruit: Catholic Health Care and the Appropriation of Racial Segregation," *Journal of Moral Theology* 8, no. 1 (2019): 36–62.

in acute, long-term, and psychiatric facilities, and the sisters in leadership sought to align the hospital policies with best practices in medicine.[42] When the Sisters of Mercy conducted a thorough investigation into the morality of tubal ligation in the late 1970's, they explained: "We believe that tubal ligation, in certain circumstances is an appropriate procedure and a necessary component of holistic health care and that failure to provide this service in these circumstances may cause harm to persons."[43] Particular cases under discussion included the following:

> Mrs. A—28 years old with four children; suffers from thrombophlebitis, which has been complicated by a pulmonary embolism
> Mrs. B—39 years old with eight living children; has had two spontaneous miscarriages; suffers from rheumatic heart disease with mitral stenosis. Further pregnancies would accelerate her medical condition.
> Mrs. F—42 years old, with three children; suffered for many years with severe bronchiectasis [permanent inflammation of bronchial tubes] with increasing difficulty each succeeding pregnancy; continual progression of pulmonary illness.[44]

Women religious, with experience in hospital administration, explained that tubal ligation was a pastoral issue insofar as it was a "medical problem, an ethical issue, and a women's question."[45] In 1983, after many attempts to dialogue with members of the Vatican and with bishops in the US, the sisters were forced to comply with Vatican directives and were forbidden from allowing tubal ligations in any hospital owned or operated by the

---

[42] Schenk, *To Speak the Truth in Love*, 142.
[43] "Statement of the General Administrative Team Relative to Hospital Policy on Tubal Ligation: A Response to the Recommendations of the Church/Institute Committee," Mercy Heritage Center Archives, Belmont, NC. Cited by Schenk, *To Speak the Truth in Love*, 147.
[44] Schenk, *To Speak the Truth in Love*, 145.
[45] Schenk, *To Speak the Truth in Love*, 144.

Sisters of Mercy of the Union.[46] Sister of Mercy Theresa Kane explained in 1984 that "a serious obstacle to women serving in all ministries within the Church is the structural prohibition of ordination."[47] In her own experiences of leadership among the Sisters of Mercy, including their administration of Catholic hospitals, Sister Theresa found that the exclusion of women from ordination "in practical terms prohibits women from functioning as fully participating members in decision-making roles." In effect, the institutional conscience of the Vatican was imposed on the Sisters of Mercy, with direct impact on the provision of care for patients, and in some cases in violation of the patient's own conscience. These experiences are also experiences of reproductive coercion and reproductive injustice.[48]

Moral Conscience in Church Teaching

When analyzing issues of competing goods in patient care at Catholic hospitals, an important framework in the Catholic moral tradition is the teaching that one is obliged to follow one's conscience.[49] According to the Second Vatican Council: "Conscience is the most intimate center and sanctuary of a person, in which he or she is alone with God, whose voice

---

[46] Schenk, *To Speak the Truth in Love*, 203. Margaret A. Farley, RSM, offered an analysis of the tubal ligation crisis to colleagues in 1982. Farley, "Power and Powerlessness: A Case in Point," *Proceedings of the Catholic Theological Society of America* 37 (1982): 116–117. Farley explained that the Mercy sisters' "desire to draw concerned persons into dialogue on the issue [of tubal ligations]" led to an "ultimatum" from the Vatican. See also Anne E. Patrick, *Liberating Conscience* (New York: Continuum, 1996), 41–48.

[47] Theresa Kane, RSM, "Pastoral on Women," 1984, in Schenk, *To Speak the Truth in Love*, 207.

[48] See also Eric Marcelo O. Genilo, SJ, "Risking Women's Lives, Denying Women's Experiences: CDF Statements on Sterilization in Catholic Hospitals," 334–357.

[49] See John Paul II, *Veritatis Splendor*, no. 60.

echoes within them. In a marvelous manner conscience makes known that law which is fulfilled by love of God and of neighbor."⁵⁰

Religious liberty claims broaden this feature of Catholic doctrine, insisting not only that one is obliged to follow one's conscience but that the state must respect the right of religious people to practice their faith. Catholic bishops have interpreted this to mean that Catholic hospitals should be able to practice medicine in conformity to magisterial teachings, without the state's interference. According to John Paul II, religious liberty is "the right to live in the truth of one's faith and in conformity with one's transcendent dignity as a person" (*Centesimus Annus*, no. 47).⁵¹ Drawing on *Dignitatis Humanae*, the *Catechism of the Catholic Church* claims that "nobody may be forced to act against his [sic] convictions, nor is anyone to be restrained from acting in accordance with his [sic] conscience in religious matters in private or in public, alone or in association with others, within due limits" (no. 2106).⁵² The United States Conference of Catholic Bishops has invoked religious liberty in a number of key debates that some characterize as "culture war" issues: their opposition to same sex marriage,⁵³ opposition to the passage of the Equal Rights Amendment,⁵⁴ and opposition to legal abortion.⁵⁵

---

⁵⁰ See *Gaudium et Spes*, 16. In the same section, the Council fathers explain that an erroneous conscience does not lose its dignity, despite a caution that conscience can grow "sightless as a result of habitual sin."

⁵¹ John Paul II described religious liberty as the "source and synthesis" of human rights.

⁵² Quoting *Dignitatis Humanae*, no. 2. As noted previously, Pope Francis has also spoken in support of the rights of medical personnel to invoke their conscience to refuse to provide particular therapies and to refuse participation in particular procedures including abortion.

⁵³ USCCB, "Marriage and Religious Liberty," www.usccb.org/issues-and-action/marriage-and-family/marriage/promotion-and-defense-of-marriage/upload/Handout-Religious-liberty-FAQs-2.pdf.

⁵⁴ USCCB, "The Equal Rights Amendment, with Robert Vega," 2023, www.usccb.org/resources/equal-rights-amendment-robert-vega.

⁵⁵ USCCB Secretariat of Pro-Life Activities, "Conscience Protection on Abortion: No Threat to Life," 2018, www.usccb.org/issues-and-action/religious-liberty/conscience-protection/upload/Federal-Conscience-Protection-on-Abortion-No-Threat-to-Life-CTformats.pdf.

Theologians on Conscience

Catholic theologians have analyzed and developed Church teachings on conscience in order to integrate relevant scholarship on human cognition, social sin, and spirituality. Feminist scholars in particular have demonstrated the impoverished understanding of conscience that presents conscience as a decision that must conform to authoritative teachings of the magisterium.[56] There are three dimensions of conscience: capacity, process, and judgment.[57] Conscience is the capacity of a moral agent to know the good. In this sense, conscience attends to value and is able to recognize competing values in a given situation when relevant. Conscience is also a moral science, a process of discovering specific goods and naming actions as right or wrong. Conscience can also be described in a third way as a judgment for action in particular circumstances. Feminist theologian Kathryn Lilla Cox explains that conscience is multi-dimensional, pulling together "our cognitive, affective, bodily, and spiritual dimensions."[58] This way of thinking about conscience as multi-dimensional and integrative is deeply connected to scriptural accounts of the human agent responding to God's invitation to love, as well as the practices of Christians throughout Christian tradition, including the wisdom of religious communities asking how God's will is disclosed in the everyday realities of one's life. "Following one's conscience," Cox explains, "requires focus on what God is bringing forth, where new life is arising, what is being cleansed or washed away—in short, discerning and responding to where God is acting in our lives."[59] Cox expands on this analysis in her contribution for this volume, in which

---

[56] Anne. E. Patrick describes this position as "ecclesiastical fundamentalism" in Patrick, *Liberating Conscience*, 31. See also Elizabeth Sweeny Block, "Conscience," in *T&T Clark Handbook of Christian Ethics*, ed. Tobias Winwright (London: Bloomsbury, 2020).

[57] Timothy O'Connell, *Principles for a Catholic Morality, Revised Edition* (New York: HarperOne, 1990), 109–113.

[58] Kathryn Lilla Cox, *Water Shaping Stone: Faith, Relationships, and Conscience Formation* (Collegeville: Liturgical, 2015), x, 80–81.

[59] Cox, *Water Shaping Stone*, x.

she explains that sin prevents us from discerning the good.[60] Conscience, in other words, is not a perfect cognitive instrument but is shaped also by one's social location and experiences of both finitude and sinfulness.[61]

Another aspect worthy of attention is the development of a person's moral conscience throughout their lifetime. Moralists in the Catholic tradition have noted that in childhood and adolescence, the moral conscience is in an early stage of development. A growth ethic values the increasing capacity of the moral agent over time, seeing that the teenager, young adult, and more mature adult develop over time in their capacity to understand and apply the good in particular situations. In early stages of moral development, following the commands of a moral authority can be good and healthy, but over time, a moral agent should come to the awareness themselves of what their own conscience commands. Moral maturity means the ability to make decisions for oneself, attuned to wisdom from relevant authorities and to the complexity of the task at hand. This is not a simplistic process but rather an awareness of the need to discern, within particular contexts, the right course of action. Moral theologian and Spiritan priest Rev. Richard M. Gula has explained that if we only do something because an authority figure tells us to do it, we are not making a mature decision.[62] We misunderstand conscience if we think it requires Catholics simply to "obey the Church" instead of making informed decisions as a result of their own prayerful discernment.

Gula explains that moral conscience is "me coming to a decision." The moral conscience is how we determine how to live out our deeply-held values in our own particular life circumstances. As the moral agent discerns, she may ask herself reflective and open-ended questions such as: "What kind of person am I becoming? What would a good person do in

---

[60] Kathryn Lilla Cox, "Reproductive Justice as Social Sin: Mapping Sin Discourse into Debates about Fertility Decisions."

[61] See also Elisabeth Vasko, *Beyond Apathy: Theology for Bystanders* (Minneapolis: Fortress, 2015), 54; and James F. Keenan, SJ, "Conscience" in *The Moral Life: Eight Lectures* (Washington, DC: Georgetown University Press, 2024), 55–74, 58.

[62] Richard M. Gula, *Reason Informed by Faith* (Mahwah, NJ: Paulist, 1989), 124.

this situation? Which course of action is the most loving act?" These questions are related to the moral agent's self-discovery and attention to virtue over time, with the everyday constraints that are an inevitable aspect of human finitude.[63]

Moral agents also must look at the big picture, the pattern of our lives.[64] Individual actions are interpreted within the larger pattern or direction of our lives. We reflect on our values, what is at stake in the decision, we bring this discernment to prayer, and we ask others for help. But at the end of the day, it must be our own decision. Jesuit theologian James Bretzke describes the "spiral" of conscience formation as: formation, information gathering, discernment, decision, action, reflection, reconsideration, and potential reform.[65] Bretzke's spiral is a reminder that conscience formation is not a strictly linear process. It involves ever deepening, growth in authenticity over time. Decisions impact each other over the course of a lifetime.[66]

Church Teaching and Conscience Formation

Conscience is formed in community. Cox argues: "For better or worse, human beings help shape each other."[67] Increasingly, Catholic theologians are concerned with how sexism, ableism, transphobia, colonialism, White supremacy, ethnocentrism, and economic inequality malform Christian consciences and prevent human agents from recognizing the good.[68] Cox

---

[63] Cristina L. H. Traina, *Finitude, Feminism, and Flourishing: On Being Mortal, Like Everyone Else* (Mahwah, NJ: Paulist, 2024).
[64] See Patrick, *Liberating Conscience*, 190–191.
[65] James T. Bretzke, SJ, *A Morally Complex World: Engaging Contemporary Moral Theology* (Minneapolis: Liturgical, 2004), 138–144.
[66] See also Anthony Marinelli, *Conscience and Catholic Faith: Love and Fidelity* (New York: Paulist, 1991), 29.
[67] Cox, *Water Shaping Stone*, 86.
[68] See also Elizabeth Sweeny Block, "Why Is This Magazine Called Conscience?" *Conscience* 44, no. 2 (2023): 16–20.

elaborates: "Communities of influence include family, friends, coworkers, and our ethnic communities. Specific religious influences include Scripture, the triune God, Church, and religious communities. Laws, media, role models, expert authorities, and culture are other sources that shape and form moral agents."[69] *Conscience formation* is the process by which a moral agent's conscience is formed; this process does not merely impose an external authority requiring obedience.[70] Cox explains that ecclesial participation shapes the moral agent's conscience in key ways. The Church is the "shaper of moral character" in various ways through liturgy, prayer, and community organizing.[71] The Church is also the "bearer of the moral tradition," not only in the sense of authoritative Church teachings but also in the context of school systems, catechetical programs, monastic communities, and other facets of Christian moral formation. The Church is also a "community of moral deliberation," modeling what it means to discern the presence of God in our everyday lives and shaping an ecclesial response to structural injustices through legislative lobbying efforts and mass media.[72] All of these are important to keep in mind because they serve as reminders that the Church forms believers not only through magisterial teaching but also through communal practices and faith formation over the course of one's life. Anne E. Patrick explains that "the Church does not supply the perfect answer to all our moral questions, but it gives us a community where faithful moral reasoning can go on, always with attention to the values Jesus cherished and with confidence in his continued presence in our midst."[73]

Within any discernment, it is important to understand not only what the Church teaches, but why. But Church teachings do not "dictate" to

---

[69] Cox, *Water Shaping Stone*, 86.
[70] Lisa Fullam, "Abortion in the Catholic Conscience," *Conscience*, August 8, 2023, www.catholicsforchoice.org/resource-library/abortion-in-the-catholic-conscience/.
[71] Cox, *Water Shaping Stone*, 88.
[72] Cox, *Water Shaping Stone*, 88–89.
[73] Patrick, *Liberating Conscience*, 38.

conscience. Rather, Church teachings are supposed to guide and inform.[74] In *Amoris Laetitia*, Francis emphasized the importance of discernment within the specifics of each situation and admitted the importance of "differentiated pastoral care according to various social and cultural contexts" (no. 248). A key aspect of conscience is that it is subjective, contextual, and self-directing. *My* conscience directs *my* behavior. My conscience does not *impose* behavior on other moral agents, who must make *their own* discernment in conscience about their behavior. But this is precisely the challenge moral agents experience today in health care settings. Our human community is based on multi-dimensional cooperation. Can we move forward in such a way that my conscience is also concerned with and attentive to the conscience of another? If my professional role requires responsibility for the care of another, how should my conscience direct my behavior in a way that respects that person's own conscience claim?

The United States Conference of Catholic Bishops has forwarded legal arguments in the past decade asserting a novel approach to conscience in the tradition. I distinguish within these arguments between the conscience of the institution; the conscience of the medical provider (nurse/doctor); and the conscience of the patient. I am concerned that the bishops' approach is problematic because it departs from the traditional teaching mandating respect for another's conscience and seeks instead an approach that demands coercion and conformity.

Conscience of the Institution

When the bishops of the Catholic Church submit *amici curiae* to attempt to persuade the Supreme Court, they claim to speak for the collective members of the Catholic Church and draw upon Church teachings in

---

[74] Marinelli, *Conscience and Catholic Faith*, 65–81.

doing so.⁷⁵ A recent case provides an example. The bishops' lawyers explain that a New York regulation requiring employee healthcare plans to cover abortion violates the religious autonomy of the Catholic Church. "Dragooning religious organizations into becoming complicit in abortion is no mere health-and-safety regulation: it is an intolerable invasion of religious autonomy."⁷⁶ The bishops claim that as an institution the Catholic Church should not be forced to require their employee healthcare plans to cover abortion. This is an institutional conscience claim, advocating for a novel understanding of a collective conscience that is not found in authoritative Catholic teachings on conscience.

The USCCB's amicus brief in the *Obergefell v. Hodges* case (2015) is an example of the legal reasoning employed by the bishops when they seek to conflate Church teaching, moral law, and civil law. There, they write:

> If this Court were to declare Church teaching to be mere bigotry, then the conflict between constitutional rights to act on such religious beliefs—i.e., the rights to free exercise, speech, and association—versus a newly created constitutional right of two people of the same sex to civil marriage will never cease.⁷⁷

The bishops' lawyers thus argue that they have the right—in conscience— to discriminate on the basis of sexual orientation. They go on: "Religiously-affiliated nonprofit organizations have had to cease providing adoption and foster care services for vulnerable children because of the

---

⁷⁵ For a list of these amici, see "Amicus Briefs," www.usccb.org/offices/general-counsel/amicus-briefs. The bishops write about their role in forming consciences in USCCB, *Forming Consciences for Faithful Citizenship (2023)*, www.usccb.org/issues-and-action/faithful-citizenship/upload/forming-consciences-for-faithful-citizenship.pdf.

⁷⁶ USCCB, Amicus Brief, *Roman Catholic Diocese of Albany v. New York State Department of Financial Services* (2021), 3, www.usccb.org/resources/20-1501acTheChurchOfJesusChrist OfLatter-DaySaints.pdf.

⁷⁷ USCCB, Amicus Brief, *Obergefell v. Hodges* (2015), 24, www.usccb.org/sites/default/files/about/general-counsel/amicus-briefs/upload/Obergefell-v-Hodges.pdf.

redefinition of marriage."⁷⁸ The amicus cites *Roe*, claiming that the 1973 decision "led to decades of litigation in which the claimed abortion right is pitted against other constitutional rights (e.g., paternal rights, parental rights involving minors, and conscience rights)." They predict a similar outcome—"a panoply of Church-state litigation for decades to come"—if the Court were to endorse legal same sex marriage.⁷⁹

In claiming that the institutional Church has a conscience, the USCCB's legal team does not rely on evidence gathered from surveys of Catholics, nor do they provide any sociological data that would indicate a majority of Catholics support the USCCB's interpretation. Instead, they argue that as bishops they speak for the Church in the public square. They write: "The Catholic Church's teaching on marriage is deeply embedded in its understanding of God and the human person," ignoring available evidence of same sex marriages among Catholics and of overwhelming Catholic lay support for such civil rights in the LGBTQIA+ community. In the Fulton case, the bishops' lawyers explained that "providing foster care represents a core religious exercise for Catholics."⁸⁰ The bishops sought legal protection for refusing to place foster children with same-sex couples. Similarly, with regard to abortion regulations, they cite Church teachings on the dignity of unborn life and the immorality of abortion, not evidence that a majority of Catholics in the US oppose legal access to abortion (such data does not exist).⁸¹

---

[78] USCCB, Amicus Brief, *Obergefell v. Hodges* (2015), 24. They cite Catholic Charities of Boston. Another recent case involved Catholic Social Services of Philadelphia. See USCCB, Amicus Brief, *Fulton v. Philadelphia* (2020), www.usccb.org/about/general-counsel/amicus-briefs/upload/2020-06%20Ful_v_CoPA_SupCrt_AmicusBrf_FINAL.pdf.
[79] USCCB, Amicus Brief, *Obergefell* (2015), 23.
[80] USCCB, Amicus brief, *Fulton* (2020), 27. www.usccb.org/about/general-counsel/amicus-briefs/upload/2020-06%20Ful_v_CoPA_SupCrt_AmicusBrf_FINAL.pdf.
[81] USCCB, Amicus Brief, *Dobbs v. Jackson Women's Health* (2021), www.usccb.org/about/general-counsel/amicus-briefs/upload/Dobbs.final_.pdf. Gregory A. Smith, "Like Americans Overall, Catholics Vary in Their Abortion Views," Pew Research Center, May 23, 2022, www.pewresearch.org/short-reads/2022/05/23/like-americans-overall-catholics-vary-in-their-abortion-views-with-regular-mass-attenders-most-opposed/.

The USCCB consists of 274 men, most of whom are white, and all of whom are beyond middle age. They are hardly representative of the lived experiences and political convictions of the US Catholic Church, which in fact contains diverse racial, linguistic, cultural, and ethnic communities, as well as viewpoint diversity.[82] Moreover, the institutional Church is a powerful social entity. This fact becomes more relevant when we consider what is at stake when consciences conflict in Catholic hospitals.

Conscience of the Medical Provider

Health care professionals—whether they are physicians, physician assistants, nurses, pharmacists, or other professionals dispensing medical care—also make important conscience claims. Health care professionals are in professional roles with professional duties. They also work within particular health care systems that impose institutional policies and other kinds of constraints, including the rules imposed by insurance companies, the limitations of equipment and diagnostic capabilities, and the everyday challenges of team-based provision of care. Medical providers receive training that empowers them within the professional setting to diagnose a patient and determine an appropriate course of action based on the specifics of the case. The medical provider has power, including power over the patient, but this power is not absolute; it is relational and contingent. A medical provider's power may be limited because of their status within the hierarchy of their particular team; likewise, the medical provider's power may be constrained by their economic dependence on their paycheck to pay their family's bills or fears of possible prosecution, incarceration, and loss of medical license if they fail to uphold medical and legal standards. The worldview (and conscience) of the medical provider is shaped by myriad social forces including their faith, race, class, ethnic group, language, gender, geographical context, and other patterns of

---

[82] See Mary Jo McConahay, *Playing God: American Catholic Bishops and the Far Right* (Brooklyn, NY: Melville House, 2023), ix–xi.

socialization. Medical providers have diverse viewpoints; not all providers agree on specific positions or stances taken by the Catholic hierarchy, nor do they always share the moral perspectives of their patients. Medical providers, whether Catholic or not, who work in Catholic health care institutions, are nevertheless expected to conform to the judgment of the local ordinary in his interpretation of the *Ethical and Religious Directives*. The medical provider could face job loss if they fail to do so. This is the case even though theologians such as Anne E. Patrick have argued that "giving diligent attention to official teaching is expected of Catholics, but this does not mean abdicating their own judgment and responsibility."[83]

Catholic teachings assert that health care providers are called to form and follow their conscience; policies of Catholic hospitals expect that the conscience of the provider will conform to the local ordinary's interpretation of the *Ethical and Religious Directives*. Scholars who study moral injury among health care workers explain that moral injury can occur "when someone engages in, fails to prevent, or witnesses acts that conflict with their values or beliefs."[84] Feelings resulting from morally injurious experiences can include guilt, remorse, shame, distress, withdrawal, and self-blame.[85] Moral injury can result from many different kinds of professional encounters, including cases of conscientious provision of care and conscientious refusal of care. In such cases, the

---

[83] Patrick, *Liberating Conscience*, 39. Lori Freedman explains that physicians have developed practices to serve their patients within Catholic hospitals through what she calls "workarounds," but that this "highly idiosyncratic approach to delivering care almost guarantees unequal access." Lori Freedman, *Bishops and Bodies: Reproductive Care in American Hospitals* (New Brunswick, NJ: Rutgers University Press, 2023), 111.

[84] Patricia Watson, Sonya B. Norman, Shira Maguen, and Jessica Hamblen, "Moral Injury in Health Care Workers," U.S. Department of Veterans Affairs, www.ptsd.va.gov/professional/treat/cooccurring/moral_injury_hcw.asp.

[85] Patricia Watson, Sonya B. Norman, Shira Maguen, and Jessica Hamblen, "Moral Injury in Health Care Workers," U.S. Department of Veterans Affairs, www.ptsd.va.gov/professional/treat/cooccurring/moral_injury_hcw.asp. See also Marcus Mescher, "Toward a Taxonomy of Moral Injury: Confronting the Harm Caused by Clergy Sexual Abuse," *Journal of the Society of Christian Ethics* 23, no. 2 (2023): 75–91.

physician, nurse, or pharmacist may feel that their beliefs and moral compass have been disrupted, and they might feel a sense of powerlessness or helplessness. Whether the action involved dispensing of (or refusal of) medications, participating in (or refusing) a procedure such as a dilation and curettage, tubal ligation, or a vasectomy, the health care provider may feel profound spiritual anguish and alienation.

Conscience of the Patient

The patient, too, is expected to form and follow their conscience. The patient's conscience, like the provider's, is formed within specific contexts and shaped by their identities and positionality. The patient's responsibilities within health care systems are typically explained in the context of honestly providing their correct and complete medical history; asking questions if they do not understand a treatment plan; treating others with respect; paying for their care; and following the policies of the institution where they seek care.[86]

Of particular importance in our moral analysis here is the fact that the patient is, in comparison to the institution and the provider, the most vulnerable. The patient has sought care for a particular medical issue and is in need of assistance. In some extreme cases, the patient's own life is at risk.[87] Patients experience limitations in their choices about medical care as

---

[86] Examples abound across health care institutions, but one example of "Patient Responsibilities" can be found here: UNC Health, "Patient Rights and Responsibilities," www.nashunchealthcare.org/patients-visitors/patient-rights-and-responsibilities/#:~:text=Patients%20are%20responsible%20for%20keeping,they%20refuse%20the%20planned%20treatment.

[87] A patient in Oklahoma was asked to "wait in her car" until her situation became so life-threatening that the hospital could treat her molar pregnancy without fear of violating the abortion ban currently in place there. Selena Simmons-Duffin, "In Oklahoma, A Woman Was Told To Wait until She's 'Crashing' for Abortion Care," April 25, 2023, www.npr.org/sections/health-shots/2023/04/25/1171851775/oklahoma-woman-abortion-ban-study-shows-confusion-at-hospitals. See also Christian De Vos, "No One Could Say," April 25, 2023, phr.org/our-work/resources/oklahoma-abortion-rights/; Michele Heisler, Tamya Cox-

well. The patient may freely choose to seek care in a Catholic hospital, but it may also be the case that the patient seeks care at the Catholic hospital out of duress. They are there because that is where the ambulance was routed, or that is the only hospital in the region, or that is the only hospital covered by an employer's insurance.

When patients experience breach of trust by symbolic actors with an institution, this betrayal can wound their relationship with ecclesial institutions and lead to spiritual distress.[88] Similarly, when a patient seeks reproductive health care and that health care is denied because of the institution's or health care provider's conscience claim, the patient can experience shame, confusion, a limited sense of moral agency, and self-doubt as to the veracity of their own conscience's claim. A patient might feel powerlessness or helplessness because the person they trusted to provide unbiased care cannot fulfill their request.

Conscientious Refusals and the Practice of Medicine

In *Conscience and Reproductive Health Care*, philosopher Carolyn McLeod explains the impact of legal conscientious refusals by health care providers on patients and, more broadly, on the field of medicine. McLeod's argument is not focused primarily on Catholic hospital systems. Instead, most of her examples are drawn from public sector hospitals where providers have legal discretion regarding whether and how to treat patients, resulting in the widespread use of conscience to deny patients' requests for contraception and abortion. McLeod's argument is relevant for Catholic hospitals as well in that she recognizes the moral complexity of reproductive health care decisions and articulates norms that seek to resolve the claims of the major stakeholders. McLeod recognizes the reality of conflicts between patients and providers and seeks to develop an

---

Touré, and Risa Kaufman, "US Abortion Bans Violate Patients' Right to Information and to Health," *The Lancet* 401, no. 10387 (2023): doi.org/10.1016/S0140-6736(23)00808-5.

[88] Mescher, "Toward a Taxonomy," 88–91.

argument that avoids the erosion of trust in the health care profession that can happen when providers remain unwilling to provide medical care that is part of the standard of care.[89]

McLeod argues that "conscientious objectors in health care have a moral obligation to prioritize the health care interests of their patients and the public over their own conscience, and that regulations on conscientious refusals should reflect this fact."[90] A key claim in McLeod's argument is that health care providers have a *fiduciary* responsibility; as gatekeepers to health care, they have great responsibility.[91] Fiduciaries, according to McLeod, possess power that is discretionary, in the form of authority rather than mere influence or control, and over the significant practical interests of the beneficiary.[92] Beneficiaries (in this case, the patients) are vulnerable to the abuse or misuse of fiduciary power; the primary fiduciary duty, says McLeod, is one of fidelity to one's beneficiary.[93] Physicians regularly respect patient autonomy but can and should simultaneously make discretionary judgments about how to present factual diagnostic data to the patient, about how to present the patient's options clearly and fairly so that the patient can make an

---

[89] Defining standard of care is perhaps the most contested claim in this essay. Philosopher Carolyn McLeod differs from the USCCB on this important point. The USCCB does not consider elective abortion to be part of the standard of care. McLeod, on the other hand, argues that if a procedure or medication is "legally required or permitted and deemed by the objector's health professional association to be central to good health care," then it should be called part of the "standard services." Thus, McLeod empowers medical licensing bodies and similar professional organizations in determining what counts as "standard." Carolyn McLeod, *Conscience in Reproductive Health Care: Prioritizing Patient Interests* (Oxford, UK: Oxford University Press, 2020), 3-5.

[90] McLeod, *Conscience in Reproductive Health Care*, 1. McLeod believes the "interests of patients in receiving standard services should be prioritized over the conscience of health care professionals," 178.

[91] McLeod, *Conscience in Reproductive Health Care*, 8.

[92] McLeod, *Conscience in Reproductive Health Care*, 121–122.

[93] McLeod, *Conscience in Reproductive Health Care*, 122–123.

informed decision, and about how to carry out the patient's informed decision.[94]

McLeod notes that in the field of obstetrics and gynecology, contraception, sterilization, and abortion are among those services that are considered part of the standard of care; when patients request these services and are refused care (either because of the hospital's policies or the provider's conscience claim), the patient is not merely inconvenienced but *harmed*.[95] McLeod notes that patients who ask for an abortion are usually in a vulnerable position; they have already decided that they need this procedure in order to safeguard other values, which may include their physical and/or mental health, their education, the wellbeing of dependents they already care for, or financial security.[96] According to McLeod, providers who refuse care harm patients by threatening the patient's moral identity, sense of security, and reproductive autonomy.[97]

In the wake of the *Dobbs v. Jackson Women's Health Organization* ruling by the Supreme Court of the United States—a ruling celebrated by US bishops and by leaders of the pro-life movement—fourteen states have enacted a total abortion ban and twenty-seven states have abortion bans based on gestational duration.[98] Conscientious refusals are increasingly impacting patient care not only in Catholic hospitals but in secular ones as well. Dr. Leah Torres, an OB-GYN at the West Alabama Women's Center in Tuscaloosa, Alabama, recently recounted a case in which a thirteen-year-old survivor of sexual assault sought an abortion, but a local hospital

---

[94] McLeod, *Conscience in Reproductive Health Care*, 131.
[95] McLeod, *Conscience in Reproductive Health Care*, 43–64.
[96] McLeod, *Conscience in Reproductive Health Care*, 74. See also Diana Greene Foster, *The Turnaway Study: Ten Years, a Thousand Women, and the Consequences of Having—or Being Denied—and Abortion* (New York: Scribner, 2020), 21–23.
[97] McLeod, *Conscience in Reproductive Health Care*, 43–64.
[98] Supreme Court of the United States, *Dobbs v. Jackson Women's Health*, 2022, www.supremecourt.gov/opinions/21pdf/19-1392_6j37.pdf. Guttmacher Institute, "State Bans on Abortion," April 12, 2024, www.guttmacher.org/state-policy/explore/state-policies-abortion-bans.

would not accept the patient for a dilation and curettage procedure even though Dr. Torres believed that carrying the pregnancy would cause harm to the thirteen-year-old patient.[99] Dr. Torres sought more information:

> I call the head of the department for an explanation. "We don't have the staff for it," he claims. I press on. "You don't have the staff for a standard D&C?" He clarifies that they don't have enough staff because no one is willing to assist on the procedure. He assures me, however, that he and his staff are "very compassionate," despite the fact that they are now forcing this 13-year-old to be re-traumatized.[100]

Dr. Torres does not share the head of department's conclusion that their staff is "very compassionate." Instead, she sees the harm that results for the thirteen-year-old patient. In this case, as in many others in the post-*Dobbs* context, conscientious refusals can have long and lasting damage for patients. From a reproductive justice stance, the patient has clearly been harmed by gender-based violence and that harm is compounded by the inability of the patient to protect her own health.[101]

A Way Forward: Communal Discernment in Complex Cases

Carolyn McLeod argues that we can *value* conscience without *requiring* that we permit conscientious refusals by physicians in health care

---

[99] Dr. Leah Torres, "Why Alabama? Providing Abortions in a State that Outlawed Them," *Conscience*, March 10, 2023, www.catholicsforchoice.org/resource-library/why-alabama-providing-abortions-in-a-state-that-outlawed-them/. Alabama's abortion law does not permit exceptions in cases of rape but does permit abortion to save the health of the mother.

[100] Torres, "Why Alabama? Providing Abortions in a State that Outlawed Them."

[101] See also the case of Keisha as reported by Loretta J. Ross in "Conceptualizing Reproductive Justice Theory: A Manifesto for Activism," in *Radical Reproductive Justice: Foundations, Theory, Practice, Critique*, ed. Loretta J. Ross, Lynn Roberts, Erika Derkas, Whitney Peoples and Pamela Bridgewater Toure (New York, Feminist Press, 2017), 170–232, 170, 174–175.

settings.[102] *How* we value conscience matters. Conscience should not be used to coerce vulnerable others. Similarly, feminist theologians in the Catholic moral tradition have argued that our understanding of conscience need not focus exclusively on the "judging faculty," but instead should attend to the *process of the discernment* of the moral agent in community. In order to achieve a culture of care that values conscience, we need to adopt both the practice of communal discernment and preferential option for the vulnerable patient who seeks medical care within the spectrum of the standard of care according to professional medical licensing. In the patient-provider relationship, we must attend to power differentials and the probable result of harm to the patient who is denied reproductive care. Catholic health care institutions should respond to patients' needs and must use the process of discernment to name competing goods and negotiate a way forward in specific contexts that seeks to achieve patient needs most equitably.

Communal discernment requires honest accompaniment, listening to all parties, analysis of all possible options, and genuine cooperation. Tensions and conflicts are inevitable and yet can be negotiated respectfully with attention to justice. Justice for the Catholic hierarchy in this case should mean that authoritative Church teachings are clearly communicated to all relevant parties so that they can inform the conscientious deliberations of all actors. But these teachings should not be imposed unilaterally as if they alone have claims to conscience. The Church must move away from ecclesiastical fundamentalism and toward a method of respectful dialogue and communal discernment. The medical provider's claim to conscience is also of value but does not hold absolute power. For a medical provider to obstruct a patient's access to standard care is morally repugnant and unfair. However, it does not follow that the medical provider must in every situation provide care that they find morally objectionable. Referrals are often a valuable solution that minimizes the provider's cooperation and prevents moral injury to the

---

[102] McLeod, *Conscience in Reproductive Health Care*, 41.

provider, while also assisting the patient to access care.[103] In those cases in which the patient cannot be referred elsewhere, the provider can and should provide the medical care that the patient needs. In such cases as providers who provide contraception, sterilization, or abortion, we must also attend to the moral injury endured by the provider who sacrifices their moral integrity in order to further the patient's conscience. When a genuine conflict is present, the patient's interests should be prioritized, not the institution's or the provider's interests. The moral injury that results for the health care provider is a disvalue that the moral community should name and lament. However, this disvalue can be tolerated in order to prioritize the higher good of the patient's medical needs.[104]

Conclusion

Protracted legal battles and the bishops' participation in the culture wars undermine the building up of a cohesive social fabric attentive to the common good of society.[105] Womanist theologians working in the health care arena suggest a response inclusive of consciousness-raising, awareness, and prevention efforts; these too are important in addressing unplanned pregnancy in its social manifestations.[106] Investment in prevention is necessary but not sufficient when we consider how women of color are treated within Catholic hospitals and how in some cases their discernments in conscience are blocked by other more powerful agents. The late Dr. Shawnee Daniels-Sykes advocated for the training of "lay

---

[103] Referrals can also delay care, which can lead to unnecessary anxiety and even suffering for the patient. Referral is not always a just resolution for every party.

[104] On lament in cases of moral tragedy, see Kate Jackson-Meyer, *Tragic Dilemmas in Christian Ethics* (Washington, DC: Georgetown University Press, 2022).

[105] In *Fratelli Tutti*, Francis reminds readers that the goal of politics in the common good.

[106] Elizabeth A. Williams, "Talking God and Talking Cancer: Why Womanist Ethics Matters for Breast Cancer Prevention and Control among Black Women," *The Rising Global Cancer Pandemic: Health, Ethics, and Social Justice* JMT CTEWC Book Series 2 (Eugene, OR: Pickwick, 2002), 82–97, doi.org/10.55476/001c.38700.

health advocates who are attentive, intelligent, rational, and responsible about the emergency in black health."[107] We need a new approach to reproductive health care that privileges communal discernment, the patient's conscience, the medical team's role in accompaniment, and proportionate reason as a valuable tool to weigh values and disvalues in a complex discernment. The role of Catholic bishops in this process includes a fair description of Church teachings for multiple constituencies in order to form consciences. But bishops should not dictate to the consciences of providers and patients. The entire ecclesial community bears responsibility for building up the common good, and one part of that work requires building trust between medical providers and patients, responsive to patients' real needs. To be of service to patients will require some sacrifices of Catholic providers of last resort, for which lament will sometimes be necessary. It is this author's hope that the suffering thus endured by health care providers will lead to shared vulnerabilities and opportunities for solidarity between health care providers and their patients. When providers demonstrate compassion by suffering with their patients, they model what it truly means to practice Christian servant leadership today.

Emily Reimer-Barry, PhD, is associate professor in the Department of Theology and Religious Studies at the University of San Diego, where she teaches undergraduate courses in Catholic theological ethics. She is the author of two books: *Reproductive Justice and the Catholic Church: Advancing Pragmatic Solidarity with Pregnant Women* (Sheed & Ward,

---

[107] Shawnee M. Daniels-Sykes, "Code Black: A Black Catholic Liberation Bioethics," *Journal of the Black Catholic Theological Symposium*, ed. Cyprian Davis, OSB, Kimberly Flint-Hamilton, and Cecilia Moore 3 (2009): 29–61. See also *Catholic Bioethics and Social Justice: The Praxis of US Health Care in a Globalized World*, ed. M. Therese Lysaught and Michael McCarthy (Collegeville: Liturgical, 2018).

"Catholic Health Care and Reproductive Justice: Whose Conscience Has Priority?" 2024) and *Catholic Theology of Marriage in the Era of HIV and AIDS: Marriage for Life* (Lexington, 2015).

16. Religio-Cultural Underpinnings of Gender and Reproductive Injustice and Their Impact on Women's Agency in India

Virginia Saldanha

India is the world's most populous democracy, with a population estimated at 1.4 billion people.[1] India has a diversity of religions and cultures. Religious practice is often a source of comfort and meaning-making and forms one's identity in powerful ways. Discussions of reproductive health care, fertility, and family planning in India are deeply influenced by religious teachings and values. For many religious communities, fertility is described as a sacred blessing, and women are often praised for their role in childbearing. However, a focus on women's duty to bear children can also unfairly limit a woman's value to her contribution to reproduction. In part because of the rise of the women's movement and growing legal protections for women, fertility rates are falling in India, even as they remain higher than fertility rates of women in more affluent countries. Every religious group in the country has seen its fertility rates fall in recent decades, including the majority Hindu population and the Muslim, Christian, Sikh, Buddhist, and Jain minority groups.[2] A holistic view of Indian life will show that declining fertility rates is not itself an indicator of justice for women. Reproductive injustice in India also includes high rates of sexual violence, high rates of infant

---

[1] Laura Silver, Christine Huang, and Laura Clancy, "Key Facts as India Surpasses China as the World's Most Populous Country," Pew Research Center, February 9, 2023, www.pewresearch.org/short-reads/2023/02/09/key-facts-as-india-surpasses-china-as-the-worlds-most-populous-country/.

[2] Silver, Huang, and Clancy, "Key Facts as India Surpasses China as the World's Most Populous Country."

mortality, and the precarity that results from poverty.³ In India, patriarchal attitudes cut across cultures and all areas of social life. While religion helps many women to cope with the drudgery and violence in their lives, patriarchal religious teachings disempower women and undermine their agency. The overarching reality of violence has impacted women's capacity to stand up for their rights and assert themselves as autonomous agents of their own destiny.

As a scholar-activist writing from India, I utilize a Catholic feminist methodology as I reveal how patriarchal religious teachings within Hinduism and Christianity empower men to dominate over women in the family, in the workplace, and in society. Catholic feminist method involves criticism of patriarchy within the tradition, attention to women's experiences, and advocacy for social transformation.⁴ This chapter begins with criticism of religio-cultural socialization, traditions that shape a culture of violence, and analysis of the reality of poverty in India. My experience of working with women for the past thirty years dealing with women's cases of violence and oppression in everyday life informs my writing on women's reality. Then I move to advocacy for social transformation, centering a claim shared by both Catholic teachings and the women's movement: the inherent dignity of women. While religious teachings exacerbate reproductive injustice for Indian women today, religious communities also carry resources for social transformation. I argue that, moving forward, religious communities must work to transform women's reality of pervasive violence that result in the sexual and reproductive injustices experienced by women throughout India.

---

³ According to the Pew Center, infant mortality in India in 2020 was 27 deaths per 1,000 live births, which is higher than the infant mortality rates of neighboring Bangladesh, Nepal, Bhutan, and Sri Lanka, and much higher than China and the U.S. See Silver, Huang, and Clancy, "Key Facts as India Surpasses China as the World's Most Populous Country."

⁴ Cristina L. H. Traina, "Christian Feminist Theological Ethics," *St. Andrews Encyclopaedia of Theology*, www.saet.ac.uk/Christianity/ChristianFeministTheologicalEthics.

Indian Women's Experience of Patriarchy in Religion and Culture

Catholic feminist theologian Anne M. Clifford explains that *patriarchy* refers to "systems of legal, economic, and political relations that legitimate and enforce relations of dominance in a society."[5] In patriarchal societies, the status of women and children is one of inferiority. While men tend to be the gatekeepers of patriarchy, women socialized within this ideology may also in turn normalize and validate patriarchal attitudes about their rightful submission to men. Indian scholar Kochurani Abraham explains that patriarchal attitudes are sustained by culturally inscribed language, socio-religious customs, and practices; further, "In the Indian context, religion is a major factor that still succeeds in legitimizing the gendered boundaries of culture through its precepts."[6] As the majority religion, Hinduism shapes Indian culture in particular ways. Naseera N.M. and Moly Kuruvilla explain the contemporary patriarchal attitudes in India by tracing their roots to the ancient legal text, the *Manusmriti*, which had a significant role in creating the Brahmanic patriarchy, caste system, and heteronormative structures of ancient India, the impact of which is still felt today across the country.[7] They explain that religion is a potent force behind patriarchal social life and structure; further, religious voices in India "propagate male supremacy and male control over women and suppress their sexuality, mobility, and reproductive choices. They characterize women as physically, mentally, emotionally and sexually inferior to men."[8] Wendy Doniger and Brian K. Smith elaborate on the role of *The Manusmriti* in shaping Hinduism:

---

[5] Anne M. Clifford, *Introducing Feminist Theology* (Maryknoll: Orbis, 2002), 18.
[6] Kochurani Abraham, *Persisting Patriarchy: Intersectionalities, Negotiations, Subversions* (Cham, Switzerland: Springer/Palgrave Macmillan, 2019), 168.
[7] Naseera N.M. and Moly Kuruvilla, "The Sexual Politics of *The Manusmriti*: A Critical Analysis with Sexual and Reproductive Health Rights Perspectives," *Journal of International Women's Studies* 23, no. 6 (2022): 1.
[8] Naseera N.M. and Moly Kuruvilla, "The Sexual Politics," 3.

> *The Manusmriti* is a pivotal text of the dominant form of Hinduism as it emerged historically and at least in part in reaction to its religious and ideological predecessors and competitors. More compendiously than any other text, it provides a direct line to the most influential construction of the Hindu religion and Indic society as a whole. No modern study of Hindu family life, psychology, concepts of the body, sex, relationships between humans and animals, attitudes to money and material possessions, politics, law, caste, purification and pollution, rituals, social practice and ideals, and world renunciation and worldly goals, can ignore Manu.[9]

Feminist scholars in India have amplified these concerns by explaining that the laws of Manu took steps to control reproduction by controlling women's access to knowledge and by establishing guidelines for sexuality and family life.[10] *The Manusmriti* is a book similar to the Bible for Christians. In Hinduism, it emphasizes the importance of women's purity, chastity, and submission to male authority. Marriage and motherhood are upheld as natural vocations for women, and marriage customs focus on the husband's control of the family.[11] In Indian society, girls are trained in cooking, proper care of the home, and setting the almirah so that "they can successfully manage their husband's homes."[12] Her childhood is a preparation for service in marriage. According to the *Manusmriti*, "Her father protects her in childhood, her husband protects her in youth, and her sons protect her in old age."[13] In other words, a woman is never fit for independence. The idea women need to be protected by a man is

---

[9] Wendy Doniger and Brian K. Smith, *The Laws of Manu* (New Delhi, India: Penguin Classics, 1991), 5.

[10] Sukumari Bhattacharji, *The Indian Theogony: A Comparative Study of Indian Mythology from the Vedas to the Puranas* (Cambridge: Cambridge University Press, 2007). See also Uma Chakravarti, *Gendering Caste: Through a Feminist Lens* (Calcutta: Stree Press, 2003).

[11] Patrick Olivelle, *Manu's Code of Law: A Critical Edition* (Oxford: Oxford University Press, 2004), 9–12.

[12] Tanya Malik, "Being a Brown Daughter," HerZindagi, www.herzindagi.com/society-culture/brown-daughters-paraya-dhan-patriarchal-mindset-freedom-article-226481.

[13] Olivelle, *Manu's Code of Law*, 3.

embedded into an Indian woman's psyche. Indian women are socialized to be passive and compliant in family and intimate relationships.[14]

Historian Gerda Lerner explains that in a patriarchal society, men and women are described as "essentially different creatures, not only in their biological equipment, but in their needs, capacities, and functions."[15] Lerner explains that religious traditions describe the "social function" of women as naturally subordinate to men and "assigned to them by God."[16]

Christian teachings also participate in this patriarchal framing of women's divinely-ascribed roles. Scholars continue to debate how to best interpret the biblical passages that seem to adopt patriarchal attitudes (such as Exodus 20:17, Deuteronomy 5:21, Deuteronomy 22:28–29, Ephesians 5:22–24, 1 Corinthians 11:7–10, and 1 Timothy 2:12). These scriptures have been weaponized within the tradition when interpreted as the divine sanction for considering women and girls as property, focusing on women's duty to bear children, demanding wifely submission, and socializing women to accept secondary status.[17] A widely-cited example of patriarchal attitudes among Christian theologians comes from the second century apologist Tertullian of Carthage, who described women as "the devil's gateway."[18] Tertullian's interpretation of the fall of Adam and Eve continues to influence theology from a patriarchal perspective and

---

[14] Indira Sharma, Balram Pandit, Abhishek Pathak, and Reet Sharma, "Hinduism, Marriage & Mental Illness," *Indian Journal of Psychiatry* 55, supplement 2 (2013): S243–S249, doi.org/10.4103/0019-5545.105544/. In a recent legal case, the Jharkhand High Court "observed that serving elderly mothers-in-law or grandmothers-in-law is both a cultural practice and an obligation for women in India. The Court also underscored that the wife's insistence to live separately from such in-laws is unreasonable." See Sparsh Upadhyay, "Obligatory for Women to Serve," *Live Law*, January 23, 2024, www.livelaw.in/high-court/jharkhand-high-court/jharkhand-high-court-obligatory-woman-serve-mother-in-law-preserve-indian-culture-demand-live-separately-unreasonable-247457?infinitescroll=1.

[15] Gerda Lerner, *The Creation of Feminist Consciousness: From the Middle Ages to Eighteen-Seventy* (New York: Oxford University Press, 1993), 4.

[16] Lerner, *The Creation of Feminist Consciousness*, 4.

[17] Clifford, *Introducing Feminist Theology*, 46–91.

[18] Serinity Young, ed., *An Anthology of Sacred Texts by and about Women* (Crossroad: New York, 1994), 46.

therefore Church teachings and attitudes towards women. John Chrysostom, a fourth century theologian, explains that "among all savage beasts, none is found so harmful as women."[19] Thomas Aquinas described woman as a "misbegotten male" and naturally subject to man.[20] In contemporary Catholic theology, gender complementarity focuses on gender difference as key to a proper understanding of human anthropology and sexuality.[21] Gender complementarity reinforces patriarchy when Church teachings assign men to roles of power in family life and ecclesial life, such as describing the father as the head of the family and an ordained clergyman (priest or bishop) as one who represents Christ, who acts through him.[22]

Kochurani Abraham documents the real-world impacts of such patriarchal assumptions about men's power. Abraham points to the quantitative data in her research with Catholic women in Kerala which indicates that 62.5 percent of the women acknowledge that they tolerate abusive behaviour for the sake of the children and family peace. Scriptures are quoted to support the subservience of women and endorsing the

---

[19] As cited in Leonila V. Bermisa, "Facing the Reality of Clergy Sexual Misconduct in the Church," in *Body and Sexuality: Theological-Pastoral Perspectives of Women in Asia*, ed. Agnes M. Brazal and Andrea Lizares Si (Manila: Ateneo de Manila University Press, 2007), 221. See also Rosemary Radford Ruether, *Sexism and God-Talk: Toward a Feminist Theology* (Boston: Beacon Press, 1983).

[20] Young, *An Anthology of Sacred Texts*, 68–69. See also Clifford, *Introducing Feminist Theology*, 30.

[21] XVI General Ordinary Assembly of the Synod of Bishops, *A Synodal Church in Mission: Synthesis Report of the First Session* (October 4–29, 2023), 9a, www.synod.va/content/dam/synod/assembly/synthesis/english/2023.10.28-ENG-Synthesis-Report.pdf. See also Congregation for Catholic Education, *Male and Female He Created Them: Towards a Path of Dialogue on the Question of Gender Theory in Education* (Vatican, 2019), 4, www.vatican.va/roman_curia/congregations/ccatheduc/documents/rc_con_ccatheduc_doc_20190202_maschio-e-femmina_en.pdf. See also Mary Ann Case, "The Role of the Popes in the Invention of Complementarity," *Religion and Gender* 6, no. 2 (2016): 156.

[22] Sacred Congregation for the Doctrine of the Faith, *Inter Insigniores*, no. 5, www.vatican.va/roman_curia/congregations/cfaith/documents/rc_con_cfaith_doc_19761015_inter-insigniores_en.html.

headship of men over women.²³ Abraham elaborates on women's strategies for survival and self-care in such relationships, explaining that "women adjust their behaviour" in order to minimize violence. But "in doing so, their ability to insist on monogamy, negotiate safer sex or refuse sex is limited. For most of the women regardless of economic state, patriarchal control was felt very strongly in the area of sexuality and conjugal relations, where the decisions about how to plan the family are also taken mostly by the husbands."²⁴

Catholic traditions of Mariology can also be tools of patriarchal oppression, as when the Mother of Jesus is described as pure, docile, and pious. Catholic women are socialized in a way that makes them compliant victims of violence and abuse. In my own work, I have observed that messages regarding women's natural capacity for love, forgiveness, and humility can be used against women who face abuse, as they are told that they have special capacities to forgive their abusers. Such theologies seem to unjustly tolerate the abuse of women by men. In other cases, women are blamed for the abuse they suffer, drawing on such characterizations of women as seductress or temptress, much like Tertullian's description of Eve. Women who experience abuse can then feel guilt and shame, thinking they caused the abuse themselves.

A further concern within Christian theology is the Christological claim that redemption only comes through suffering. A distorted interpretation of Jesus's suffering and his admonition to "take up your cross" can be unfairly applied to women suffering from abuse, which disempowers vulnerable women and distorts the message of Christ's suffering. Abraham's research confirms this distorted pattern, as when she explains:

> Women tend to believe that the suffering that is intrinsic to their gendered condition is virtuous and divinely ordained. Thus religion serves to mask the basic concerns of gender power equations that

---

[23] Abraham, *Persisting Patriarchy*, 114.
[24] Abraham, *Persisting Patriarchy*, 108–109.

underlie women's exploitation by making them believe that God is at work in their lives and their suffering is redemptive.[25]

A closer look at the suffering that Indian women experience in daily life can help us to see the layered nature of structural violence they face, whether from coerced sex, the structural injustice of the legal system, dowry-related violence, poverty, or clerical abuse. Religious culture inscribed by patriarchy is biased in favor of the male; it has created a society where women face violence from the womb to the tomb. Both Christian and Hindu religious teachings create a culture that exalts the status of a married woman and mother, requires women's submission to men, and praises her silence in the face of violence. We see evidence in survey data from 2018 in which a majority of respondents (86.4 percent) felt it was acceptable to harshly criticize or beat a woman. Other instances where violence was perceived to be acceptable include the following cases: if she left the house without permission (54.4 percent); if she failed to prepare meals for men in the family (41.2 percent); if she disobeyed men in the family (24.3 percent); and if she spent money without asking (26.3 percent).[26] Most Indian women at some time in their lives have experienced some form of physical or psychological violence in their own family, on the street, or at work. According to the crime data for the year 2021, there was a rise of 26 percent of crimes against women in India over a period of six years. With tens of thousands of rape cases reported annually, India has gained the moniker, "the rape capital of the world."[27] Julie George explains that "systemic misogyny, caste and class biases, religious and political interests together protect and reinforce the imputing of power-holders," and that these structural factors lead to a situation in

---

[25] Abraham, *Persisting Patriarchy*, 146.
[26] Manya Rathore, "Attitude Towards Acceptability of Violence against Women in India in 2018, by Social Norms," July 10, 2023, *Statistica*, www.statista.com/statistics/1127335/india-attitude-to-acceptability-of-violence-against-women-by-social-norms/.
[27] Geeta Pandey, BBC News, Delhi, "Rising Crimes against Indian Women in Five Charts," September 13, 2022, www.bbc.com/news/world-asia-india-62830634.

which women who experience sexual violence "are unable to use the justice system successfully."[28] Women's experience in reporting crimes indicates structural injustices within Indian society, especially given that the conviction rate is abysmally low. Julie George explains:

> India has enacted new laws and policies to empower women; yet, its actions often have tended to reinforce patriarchal norms and values and put women's concerns in jeopardy. India still continues to witness incessant episodes of rape, sexual abuse, honor killings, and other such atrocities against women. These incidents reveal the diverse ways in which all the dimensions of a woman's identity, including caste, class, religion, gender, age, sexual orientation, ethnicity, disability, geography, and personal history overlap and determine how a woman experiences womanhood and confronts violence.[29]

Further, married women do not have bodily autonomy in Indian law, which does not recognize marital rape as a criminal offense. The penal code prohibiting rape includes an exception for "sexual acts by a man with his own wife."[30] This gives the man control over his wife's body, meaning he can demand sex. This attitude of male entitlement to women's bodies is too often defended on both religious and cultural grounds. Girls are taught from a young age to accept intrusion of their body-space. Rape myths persist. Commenting on the rape of two young women (one in Delhi in

---

[28] Julie George, SSpS, "Intersectionality at the Heart of Oppression and Violence against Women in Law: Case Studies from India," *Journal of Moral Theology* 12, Special Issue 1 (2023): 108–131, 119.
[29] George, "Intersectionality at the Heart of Oppression," 108–109.
[30] Government of India, Section 375 of the Penal Code, exception 2. "Sexual intercourse or sexual acts by a man with his own wife, the wife not being under fifteen years of age, is not rape." New Delhi: National Informatics Centre: www.indiacode.nic.in/show-data?actid=AC_CEN_5_23_00037_186045_1523266765688&orderno=424. See also Lauren Frayer, "Marital Rape Is Still Legal in India. A Court Decision Could Change That," *National Public Radio*, February 8, 2022, www.npr.org/sections/goatsandsoda/2022/02/08/1047588035/marital-rape-india.

2012 and the other in Mumbai in 2013), a senior female government official remarked: "Rapes take place because of a woman's clothes, her behaviour and her being at inappropriate places."[31] Since women are often blamed for attracting violence, many prefer to remain silent about violence inflicted on them. Some women choose not to disclose their experience of sexual violence because of shame-based discourse. Lawyer Seema Sammridhi explains that "people continue to have such regressive thoughts that a woman who has been raped is 'impure.'"[32] In some cases, rape survivors agree to marry their rapists, since the damage to their reputation (despite their victimization) may prevent them from finding a suitable partner in the wake of their experience of rape; in some cases, this also enables the rapist to avoid jail.[33]

Dowry-related violence also speaks to the toxic culture that undermines women's flourishing in India. Dowry is the tradition of giving money or durable household items to the groom's family by the bride's parents. A girl child is called "*Paraya dhan*" in Hindu families, which means she is a liability. Money spent on her education and well-being is considered a contribution to another family. The dowry given to her when she marries is seen as wealth leaving the family. Dowry has given rise to much greed that has spurned violence done to wives/daughters-in-law resulting in violent death, or driving young wives to take their own lives. Statistics released in 2022 by the National Crime Records Bureau reveal an average of twenty dowry related deaths every day reaching upwards of seven thousand deaths per year, despite the fact that India passed a law in 1961

---

[31] "Indian Official Blames Women for Rapes," *Al Jazeera News*, January 29, 2014, www.aljazeera.com/news/2014/1/29/indian-official-blames-women-for-rapes.

[32] Poorvi Gupte, "How India's Rape Survivors End Up Marrying Their Rapists" *Article 14*, August 25, 2020, www.article-14.com/post/how-india-s-rape-survivors-end-up-marrying-their-rapists.

[33] Agence France Presse in Mumbai, "India's Top Judge Tells Rapist to Marry Victim to Avoid Jail," *The Guardian*, March 4, 2021, www.theguardian.com/world/2021/mar/04/indias-top-judge-tells-accused-rapist-to-marry-victim-to-avoid-jail.

called "The Dowry Prohibition Act" which prohibits giving or taking dowry.[34]

A further threat to the girl-child in India results from pregnancy terminations for reasons of sex selection. One rationale for aborting a female fetus (*female feticide*) is the prospect of having to pay a dowry to the future bridegroom of a daughter.[35] Too often, religious worldviews exacerbate the hardships of parents of girl-children. As Nehaluddin Ahmad explains, "While sons offer security to their families in old age and can perform the rites for the souls of deceased parents and ancestors, daughters are perceived as a social and economic burden."[36] This attitude is reflected in the sex ratio of the Indian population, where the sex ratio in 2024 was 106 males per 100 females, while in 2011 the sex ratio was 943 girls to every 1000 boys.[37] A decline in the 0–15 age group indicates the lack of health care and nutrition received by girl children. In urban areas, the female/male sex ratio (929/1000) compared to rural areas (949/1000) indicates that education and economic status of families increases the risk for elimination of girl children.

---

[34] Ministry of Women and Child Development, Govt. of India, "Dowry Prohibition Act 1961", wcd.nic.in/act/dowry-prohibition-act-1961. Examples of dowry deaths include such devastating stories as: "Three sisters found dead in a well with their children after leaving disturbing messages: Our in-laws are the reason," AFP news, June 8th 2022, www.cbsnews.com/news/3-sisters-found-dead-with-children-dowry-violence-india/. See also Clement Campos, "Doing Christian Ethics in India's World of Cultural Complexity and Social Inequality," in *Catholic Theological Ethics in the World Church*, ed. James Keenan, SJ (New York: Continuum, 2007), 82–91; Shaji George Kochuthara, "Dowry as a Social Structural Sin," in *Feminist Catholic Theological Ethics: Conversations in the World Church*, ed. Linda Hogan and Agbonkhianmeghe Orabator (New York: Orbis, 2014), 108–122.

[35] Manvir Singh, "How Dowries are Fuelling a Femicide Epidemic," *New Yorker*, June 12, 2023, www.newyorker.com/magazine/2023/06/19/how-dowries-are-fuelling-a-femicide-epidemic.

[36] Nehaluddin Ahmad, "Female Feticide in India," *Issues in Law and Medicine* 26, no. 1 (2010): 13–29, pubmed.ncbi.nlm.nih.gov/20879612/.

[37] United Nations, "World Population Prospects 2022," population.un.org/wpp/Download/Standard/Population/. See also "2011 Census in India," *Statistics Times*, statisticstimes.com/demographics/country/india-sex-ratio.php.

A further example of the ways in which patriarchal religious teachings undermine health and safety for Indian women can be found in the examples of violence against women by Catholic clergy. Until recently, such violence has been shrouded in silence. I have previously explained how clericalism reinforces male domination in cases of abuse: "Religious sisters have been impregnated by priests/bishops. The sisters are asked to abort, or if discovered late, sent away to have the baby who is given up for adoption and the sister dismissed. She pays the price, maybe even the child too, but never the clergyman."[38] Patriarchy persists in the structures of the Catholic Church when women who joined religious life to live a life of service are unwittingly tricked into sexual relations by clergy.[39] As Catholic theological ethicist Shaji George Kochuthara explains, the hierarchical structure of Indian society, gender relations based on patriarchy and postcolonial attitudes provide a "fertile ground for abuse."[40] Women who want to continue to live their religious vocation have been compelled to remain silent about their abuse. If they choose to flag the abuse, they are also punished by being marginalized in their congregations for tarnishing the good name of the priesthood. Women's subservient position in the Church makes her a victim either way. Jaisy A. Joseph explains that the

---

[38] Virginia Saldanha, "When Spiritual Power Destroys Life—Sexual Abuse in the Catholic Church," in *Abuse in the Church*, ed. Michelle Becka, Huang Po-Ho and Gianluca Montaldi. *Concilium*, 402 (2023): 125–136, 125.

[39] Lucetta Scaraffia, "Without any Touching: A Serious Wound," *L'Osservatore Romano*, February 1, 2019, www.osservatoreromano.va/en/news/without-any-touching. In a widely publicized case, Bishop Franco Mulakkal was arrested for the rape of a religious sister. See "In a First, Bishop Franco Mulakkal to Go on Trial in Nun Rape Case," *Times of India*, April 10, 2019, timesofindia.indiatimes.com/city/kochi/chargesheet-filed-in-nun-rape-case/article show/68802284.cms. The bishop was subsequently acquitted and submitted his resignation. The bishop was allowed to retire, according to news reports. See "Bishop Franco Mulakkal, Acquitted in Rape Case, Steps Down," *Outlook India*, June 1, 2023, www.outlookindia.com/national/bishop-franco-mulakkal-acquitted-in-rape-case-steps-down-not-disciplinary-action-says-pope-representative-news-291354.

[40] Shaji George Kochuthara, "The Sexual Abuse Scandal and a New Ethical Horizon: A Perspective from India," *Theological Studies* 80, no. 4 (2019): 931–949, doi.org/10.1177/0040563919874517.

"pervasiveness of shame transforms survivors into scapegoats" and undermines justice-seeking work for survivors of sexual abuse by clergy.[41] I have argued elsewhere that the Catholic category of "sin" is used by clerics to cover criminal offenses. Their abuse is then regarded as "a sin to be forgiven," but not as a crime.[42] Such a framing enables them to control the response and limit public disclosure, given canon law's protection of the seal of the confessional.

Finally, both poverty and caste distinctions compound the suffering faced by Indian women in daily life.[43] While experts praise the reduction of extreme poverty in the past ten years, poverty in India remains pervasive and is influenced by a combination of historical, economic, social, and political factors.[44] The rigid caste system practiced in India where upper caste hegemony controls the lives of the lower castes (who form the cheap labor base in India) perpetuates poverty for millions. It is important also to recognize the gendered dimension of caste-based injustice, as low-caste women have reduced access to equal educational opportunities. Many women in poverty take up highly exploitable domestic cleaning work as it is the only work within their skill set. Though the caste system is officially not part of Catholic culture, the attitudes towards those in poverty are similar to the majority in Indian society.[45]

Poverty and caste create social conditions that undermine reproductive justice. Women in poverty face limited access to prenatal care, reduced access to contraceptives, and reduced power in intimate relationships,

---

[41] Jaisy A. Joseph, "Responding to Shame with Solidarity: Sex Abuse Crisis in the Indian Catholic Church," *Asian Horizons* 14, no. 2 (2020): 381–392. See also Daniel J. Fleming, James F. Keenan, and Hans Zollner, eds., *Doing Theology and Theological Ethics in the Face of the Abuse Crisis* (Eugene, OR: Pickwick, 2023).

[42] Saldanha, "When Spiritual Power Destroys Life," 125.

[43] On caste distinctions in Hindu society, see Gail Omvedt, "Caste System and Hinduism," *Economic and Political Weekly*, March 13, 2004, www.epw.in/journal/2004/11/discussion/caste-system-and-hinduism.html.

[44] World Bank, "Country Profile: India," Poverty and Inequality Platform, 2023, pip.worldbank.org/home.

[45] George, "Intersectionality at the Heart of Oppression," 123–124.

especially when she is dependent on her partner for her material wellbeing.[46] India accounts for a shocking 20 percent of all maternal deaths globally.[47] Poor women who lack basic literacy are not aware of their rights or government programs that are available to them to access health facilities to maintain their sexual and reproductive health. The Center for Reproductive Rights explains that a focus on demographic targets within population policy discussions has failed to prioritize a human rights-based framework. India's National Population Policy focuses on state incentives and opens up the possibility of coercion instead of securing reproductive rights and equity for women in Indian society.[48] Women's situation of poverty robs them of their agency. When women are socialized within religious communities to put other people's needs before their own, this can undermine women's reproductive decision-making and health care. Her priority is to feed her family. Her husband's and children's needs are put before her own. She will not even eat if the food is not enough to go around. She has been socialized to think of everyone else's needs before her own. So she does not have the time, energy, or the little money needed to get to a health care facility.

Towards Social Transformation: The Women's Movement in India

The threats to women's flourishing in India are complex and rooted in ideologies of patriarchy as well as concrete systems of legal, political, and religious inequities. If we are to move towards reproductive justice for women in India, we have to think about the role of social movements creating sustainable change in culture, laws, and practices. Such a social

---

[46] Center for Reproductive Rights, "Reproductive Rights in Indian Courts," 2, reproductiverights.org/sites/default/files/documents/Reproductive-Rights-In-Indian-Courts.pdf.

[47] Dumeetha Luthra and Susan Meiselas, "In Silence: Maternal Mortality in India," Human Rights Watch, October 6, 2009, www.hrw.org/video-photos/photo-essay/2009/10/06/silence-maternal-mortality-india.

[48] Center for Reproductive Rights, "Reproductive Rights in Indian Courts."

transformation cannot happen overnight. We need to change not only the ways that we think about gender and power but also the ways we address sexual violence, poverty, health care, and more. The women's movement in India has been at the forefront of such social change activism. Since the 1970's women's groups have focused on issues of sexual violence and domestic violence in particular.[49] All of the laws that have been promulgated to protect women have come into being because of the strong advocacy of women activists. This work must continue and should have the explicit support of the Catholic Church in the years ahead. For this to happen, Catholic leaders need a new way of talking about the inherent dignity of women that supports women's agency. As Catholic scholar Sandra M. Schneiders explains, "If feminism is defined as an intellectual, spiritual, and practical commitment to the full personhood of every human being and right relationships among all creatures, it must be espoused by Christians as a Gospel imperative."[50] She goes on to explain that while the world changes, "the gospel call to prophetic engagement in the transformation of the world into the Reign of God has not changed."[51]

Pope Francis has initiated a renewed urgency in tackling complex social issues and affirming the sacred dignity of all.[52] In *Evangelii Gaudium*, Francis describes an ecclesiology rooted in social action. Francis invites readers to "go forth from our own comfort zone in order to reach all the 'peripheries' in need of the light of the Gospel" (no. 20). Francis described the "inescapable social dimension of the Gospel message" (no. 258). He

---

[49] Sophia Powers, "Contextualizing the Indian Women's Movement, Class, Representation and Collaboration," Tate Research Publication, 2021, www.tate.org.uk/research/in-focus/seven-lives-dream-sheba-chhachhi/contextualising-indian-womens-movement.

[50] Sandra M. Schneiders, *With Oil in Their Lamps: Faith, Feminism, and the Future* (Mahwah, New Jersey: Paulist, 2000), 122.

[51] Schneiders, *With Oil in Their Lamps*, 122.

[52] Throughout his pontificate, Francis has taken on complex issues and sought to inspire and empower the faithful to discern a way forward rooted in the common good. See Conor M. Kelly and Kristin Heyer, eds., *The Moral Vision of Pope Francis: Expanding the US Reception of the First Jesuit Pope* (Washington, DC: Georgetown University Press, 2024).

straightforwardly declared that "the dignity of each human person and the pursuit of the common good are concerns which ought to shape all economic policies" (no. 203). Pope Francis in *Amoris Laetitia* denounces violence to women in families:

> Unacceptable customs still need to be eliminated. I think particularly of the shameful ill-treatment to which women are sometimes subjected, domestic violence and various forms of enslavement which, rather than a show of masculine power, are craven acts of cowardice. The verbal, physical, and sexual violence that women endure in some marriages contradicts the very nature of the conjugal union. (no. 54)

Francis appreciates the women's movement, saying, "We must nonetheless see in the women's movement the working of the Spirit for a clearer recognition of the dignity and rights of women" (no. 54). He also refers to "the reprehensible genital mutilation of women practiced in some cultures and also of their lack of equal access to dignified work and roles of decision-making. History is burdened by the excesses of patriarchal cultures that considered women inferior" (no. 54). Catholic theologians have noted key themes that Francis addresses in his approach to family and gender justice, including accompaniment, personalism, discernment, and gradualism.[53] These are especially important in the Indian context, where the call to advance synodality can empower women to have a seat at the table in new and creative ways. Francis brings hope as he advocates for a listening Church. His penchant for compassion also moves him to understand the reality of people's situation. Francis names as relevant the "concrete complexity of one's limits" (*Amoris Laetitia*, no. 303) and demands attention to dignity and justice within everyday realities.

For too long, Catholics in India have restated patriarchal interpretations of Sacred Scripture, which seemed to give divine support

---

[53] Emily Reimer-Barry, "*Amoris Laetitia* at Five" *Theological Studies* 83, no. 1 (2022): 109–132, 112.

to cultural practices that see women as naturally subservient to men.[54] But feminist biblical hermeneutics has radically reshaped the way that biblical texts are interpreted today and has opened up creative and constructive approaches to reconsidering how Jesus treated women and what it means to follow Jesus in our own context today.[55] Examples abound of liberationist approaches to the gospel narratives, including what Natalia Imperatori-Lee explains as Jesus's interactions with women, including "in friendship with women, in defense of women, as a healer of women, and as a student of women."[56] If we interpret Scripture as a resource for the contemporary women's movement in India, we can find surprising resources within the gospel narratives. In the story of a woman "caught in adultery" (Jn 8:1–11), Jesus said to the men, "He who is without sin can cast the first stone." No one stoned her. Jesus actually pointed to the sins of the men who are complicit in the sin of adultery. Jesus did not condemn her but liberated her and empowered her to live her life anew. Within the story of the woman suffering with the flow of blood (Lk 8:43–48), Jesus's powers heal the woman who touches him. In the Asian context, this healing miracle speaks as well to the power over blood taboos. In Luke 10:38–42, when Martha complains to Jesus that her sister Mary is not helping her in the housework but sitting at his feet listening to him teaching his disciples, Jesus reminds Martha that housework is not the center of a woman's life; like her brothers, she also is entitled to learn from

---

[54] Monica J. Melanchthon, "Toward Mapping Feminist Biblical Interpretations in Asia," in *Feminist Biblical Studies in the Twentieth Century: Scholarship and Movement* (Society of Biblical Literature, 2021): 105–119.

[55] Classic texts in this regard include Elisabeth Schüssler Fiorenza, *In Memory of Her: A Feminist Theological Reconstruction of Christian Origins* (New York: Crossroad, 1983), *Bread Not Stone: The Challenge of Feminist Biblical Interpretation* (Boston: Beacon, 1984), *But She Said: Feminist Practices of Biblical Interpretation* (Boston: Beacon, 1992), Elizabeth Johnson, *She Who Is: The Mystery of God in Feminist Discourse, 25th Anniversary Edition* (New York: Crossroad, 2017), and *Consider Jesus: Waves of Renewal in Christology* (New York: Crossroad, 1992).

[56] Natalia Imperatori-Lee, *Women and the Church: From Devil's Gateway to Discipleship* (Mahwah: Paulist Press, 2024), 141.

the teacher. Imagine how such an interpretation can uphold a more just approach to inclusive and equitable educational opportunities for girls and young women in India today. John 20:11–18 narrates the encounter of Mary Magdalene with the risen Jesus and his command to her to go and tell all his disciples that he has risen. Mary Magdalene has been given the honor of being called "apostle to the apostles," yet women are kept out of leadership in the Church today.

As we have seen, there are considerable resources within the Catholic tradition for advancing prophetic engagement in social transformation. Women in India have begun to engage with religion by resisting patriarchal worldviews and exercising what Abraham calls "spiritual agency."[57] Such an approach is not free of conflict. But we must creatively move through this conflict in order to build a more just world. Evelyn Monteiro points out that "any effort to free women from the shackles of tradition is bound to create division and disturbance in a male-dominated society. Such divisions and turbulence are signs that the reign of God is at hand and that the subjugated and marginalized are also rightful beneficiaries of fullness of life."[58]

Women religious and feminist activists in India are already leading the way in these important projects. Christianity empowers women through education and their many hospitals and healthcare centers in rural areas.[59] Women religious in India work in the rural areas with the poorest of the poor, running healthcare centers to provide mother and child care to women, especially during pregnancy and in the postpartum period. The Catholic Health Association of India (CHAI) is a Network of 3,572 Healthcare and Social Service Institutions across India. By serving twenty-one million (approximately 1.5 percent of India's population) patients

---

[57] Abraham, *Persisting Patriarchy*, 212.

[58] Evelyn Monteiro, SCC, "Re-imaging Woman and Reshaping Her Destiny," in *Body and Sexuality: Theological-Pastoral Perspectives of Women in Asia*, ed. Agnes M. Brazal and Andrea Lizares Si (Manila: Ateneo de Manila University Press, 2007), 149.

[59] Christian Connections for International Health, "Faith-Based Healthcare in India," January 2021, www.ccih.org/faith-based-healthcare-in-india/.

annually across the country, most of them poor, the people of CHAI—sisters and non-religious alike—translate the core values of compassion, affordability and quality care into their daily work. CHAI has 2,345 primary healthcare centers which are based in rural settings.[60] Their work is but one example of the strong, proactive women's movement in India, which provides examples of women's capacities for leadership and social change even in a patriarchal culture and religious climate. While some feminist activists in India have distanced themselves from their religious communities and some even from their families to be able to exercise their agency in freedom, this speaks more to the exclusionary frameworks of patriarchal religious institutions than to the deficiencies of women. In my work, I have had the privilege of witnessing the strength and resilience of women throughout the feminist movement in India, women who affirm the gospel values of mercy and justice as they use their professions as lawyers, social workers, teachers, and doctors to bring freedom and justice to all women, especially women from the lower castes and the poor. The women's movement in India has an important role to play in engaging religious voices in a critical and constructive way, now and in the future.

Virginia Saldanha is a feminist theologian, activist, and independent scholar with extensive experience in grassroots organizing and service. Saldanha has previously served as the executive secretary of the Commission for Women in the Archdiocese of Bombay; on the Commission for Women, Catholic Bishops' Conference of India; and in the Office of Laity, Family and Women's Desk in the Federation of Asian Bishops' Conferences. In these roles, Saldanha worked for the empowerment of women in Church and society and worked as a peer navigator in cases involving violence against women. Saldanha has worked

---

[60] Catholic Health Association of India, "Who We Are," 2023, www.chai-india.org/overview_who-we-are/.

in various leadership capacities in women's organizations, including as founder and secretary of the Indian Women Theologians Forum; as founding member of Indian Christian Women's Movement; as founder of Rainbow Catholics India; as board member of Catholic Women's Council; as board member of Majlis Legal Centre, Mumbai; and as advisory board member of Streevani, Pune, India. Saldanha's contributions to academic discourse include her monograph, *Woman: Image of God* (2005), two edited volumes and two co-edited volumes.

Epilogue: The Dangers of Gender Theory

Emily Reimer-Barry

The thing you need to know about women
the pontiffs explain
    is that women are really good at suffering.

She will be saved through childbearing

Women are so good at giving of themselves
They are brilliant at loving
especially when it hurts
See how she hides her pain
See how she knows her proper place

Holy men in their Roman collars teach about *the need to respect the natural order*
They write the laws
              make the deals
                              uphold the traditions

We cannot separate the masculine and the feminine from God's work of creation

She's the helper

The creation of woman is thus marked from the outset by the principle of help

In giving themselves to others each day women fulfill their deepest vocation

She knows her place

Women must not appropriate to themselves male characteristics contrary to their own feminine originality

Be like Mary, they say.
    She always said yes
        Just say yes

Mary attains a union with God that exceeds all the expectations of the human spirit

Be like Mary
Follow your son as he is tortured by the State
See him die in agony
    dying of starvation
        hanging from a Southern tree
            shot by police
                sent off to fight in somebody else's war
Mary, the men say, was the perfect woman
    obedient
        submissive
            compliant
                helper to man

Mary didn't complain, they say

She kept all these things in her heart

Hold it in
    bury it
        suppress it
                Smile!
Fake it so you can make it

*Almost always in silence, they carry life forward. It is the silence and strength
 of hope.*

Believe us, we mean it

The Church highlights the definite critical issues present in gender theory

*Desiring a personal self-determination
 is to make oneself God*

But what if her strength is not that she suffers but that she sees?
Sees from her suffering
that there is another way

She sees the possibility of repair
    of binding wounds
        of breaking bread
            of bearing life
                of managing her fertility
                    of saying no
                        of saying yes yes yes
                            of telling our stories

What stories they'd hear
if only they cared to listen
to how *gender theory plays a central role.*

Emily Reimer-Barry
April 8, 2024[1]

---

[1] Italicized portions can be found in 1 Timothy 2:15; *Dignitas Infinita*, no. 60; *Amoris Laetitia*, no. 286; "Letter to Women," no. 7; "Letter to Women," no. 12; *Mulieris Dignitatem*, no. 10; *Mulieris Dignitatem*, no. 3; Luke 2:19; *Dignitas Infinita*, no. 46; *Dignitas Infinita*, no. 56; *Dignitas Infinita*, no. 57; *Dignitas Infinita*, no. 56.

www.ingramcontent.com/pod-product-compliance
Lightning Source LLC
Chambersburg PA
CBHW071228290426
44108CB00013B/1329